CUSTODY

CUSTODY

THE SECRET HISTORY OF MOTHERS

LARA FEIGEL

WILLIAM
COLLINS

William Collins
An imprint of HarperCollins*Publishers*
1 London Bridge Street
London SE1 9GF

WilliamCollinsBooks.com

HarperCollins*Publishers*
Macken House, 39/40 Mayor Street Upper,
Dublin 1, DO1 C9W8, Ireland

First published in Great Britain in 2026 by William Collins

1

Copyright © Lara Feigel 2026

Lara Feigel asserts the moral right to be identified as the author of this work
in accordance with the Copyright, Designs and Patents Act 1988

A catalogue record for this book is available from the British Library

ISBN 978-0-00-883681-8 (Hardback)
ISBN 978-0-00-883682-5 (Trade paperback)

Quotations from Sylvia Plath reprinted with permission of Faber; extracts from *A Rose in the Heart*; *Country Girl*; *The Lonely Girl*; *Girls in their Married Bliss* and *Time and Tide* by Edna O'Brien reprinted by permission of Peters Fraser & Dunlop on behalf of the Estate of Edna O'Brien; quotations from Carlo Gébler reprinted with permission of Little Brown; quotations from Britney Spears reprinted with permission of Gallery Books, a division of Simon & Schuster, Inc. from *The Woman In Me* by Britney Spears. Copyright © 2023 by Britney Jean Spears. All Rights reserved; quotations from Alice Walker reprinted with permission of Joy Harris Literary Agency; quotations from Rebecca Walker reprinted with permission of 3 Arts Entertainment

Every effort has been made to credit material used in this book to contact the respective copyright holder for permission. If your material has not been credited, please contact us and we will update in future editions.

All rights reserved. No part of this publication may be reproduced, stored in a retrieval system, or transmitted, in any form or by any means, electronic, mechanical, photocopying, recording or otherwise, without the prior permission of the publishers.

Without limiting the exclusive rights of any author, contributor or the publisher of this publication, any unauthorised use of this publication to train generative artificial intelligence (AI) technologies is expressly prohibited. HarperCollins also exercise their rights under Article 4(3) of the Digital Single Market Directive 2019/790 and expressly reserve this publication from the text and data mining exception.

Set in Adobe Garamond Pro by Palimpsest Book Production Limited, Falkirk, Stirlingshire

Printed and bound in the UK using 100% renewable electricity at CPI Group (UK) Ltd

This book contains FSC™ certified paper and other controlled sources to ensure responsible forest management.

For more information visit: www.harpercollins.co.uk/green

CONTENTS

PROLOGUE — 1

Chapter 1 — 13
Caroline Norton

Chapter 2 — 59
George Sand

Chapter 3 — 127
Elizabeth Packard, with a Guest
Appearance by Britney Spears

Chapter 4 — 187
Frieda Lawrence, and the Women Who
Tramped Unwittingly Alongside Her

Chapter 5 — 239
Edna O'Brien

Chapter 6 — 291
Alice Walker

EPILOGUE	347
ACKNOWLEDGEMENTS	379
LIST OF ILLUSTRATIONS	383
NOTES	387
INDEX	413

PROLOGUE

A woman plunges into the river Indre, fully dressed. To anyone passing by, she must look mad or worse – driven by a death wish. But for her there is the relief of cool water sluicing hot skin, after walking for hours in the thirty-degree heat. She swims in the gently flowing water, weighed down by two layers of ankle-length fabric. In Paris she's becoming notorious for her habit of wearing men's clothes but here, at her ancestral home deep in the Loire valley, she's wearing the voluminous dresses of her times. She gets out and walks on, her clothes drying clammily in the sun, and then swims again, hanging her wet dress on a bush this time and swimming in her petticoat. Once more, she races on, testing her body, pushing it – by the end of the day she'll have walked nine miles. She is exhausting herself with these exertions, turning the loveliness of the summer countryside into a setting as gruelling as it is ecstatic. She is waiting to appear in court, sacrificing her reputation to fight for her children against a husband driven by punitive anger.

She has to keep moving, because to stop would leave her confronting the quieter emptiness of sadness and fear. These children, who she's always taken for granted are hers, could be taken from her. And they know it, as children usually do.

Her seven-year-old daughter at boarding school writes sadly to her mother, experiencing this brief, unwanted separation as the lifetime of division that her father wants for her. She tells her dutifully about the eclipse of the sun she's witnessed, assuring her that she's done all the spelling in her letters herself. Her twelve-year-old son is more involved in her affairs. His friends at school read about the court case in the newspapers; he knows what's said about his mother as a woman who writes and a woman with lovers, and he defends her. 'I have courage for my age,' he assures her, aware that this is a battle and that he is required to take a side. 'If my father loses he will think he is dishonoured, but I don't want you to lose, my poor *vieille*.' He's her protector, but he's also a troubled boy who wishes none of this was happening, and fantasises that one day his parents might reconcile.[1]

This is George Sand, fighting for Maurice and Solange in 1836. It could be Frieda Lawrence fighting for Monty, Elsa and Barby in 1912; or Edna O'Brien struggling to keep hold of Carlo and Sasha in 1964; or Britney Spears trying to retain custody of Sean Preston and Jayden James in 2008. For decade after decade, century after century, women have battled for their children and been found wanting. *Custodire*. To care. To look after. To guard. To restrain. Maternal care is, we are constantly told, the most natural of functions. But it comes at a price when the law is involved. And all too often custody can be more a question of restraint than of care.

Every custody story can tilt into tragedy at any stage. At the heart of every breakup, there are already two irreconcilable points of view. When the courts are involved, they stoke the battles of the relationship into new, ever more vehement conflagrations. There are winners and losers here and the child is the prize.

These cases happen now in blandly carpeted municipal rooms, and with less fanfare than they did in George Sand's day. It was in one of these that I fought for my children in the dull desolation of the winter of the pandemic, and discovered what it means to subject your capacity for love and care to a legal test likely to leave one parent high on the power of a win and the other traumatised by the vilification that so often forms a part of these proceedings.

Your children, I had been told by a friend as I embarked on my divorce, will be ripped in half. She sketched with her hand a line running straight down the middle of her body between the top of the head and the toes. I denied it at the time, but it was turning out that she was right about my son, as she was right about George Sand's children, and Edna O'Brien's. It's an image that's been with us since King Solomon threatened to split a child in half in the ultimate version of 50/50 custody. With this grotesque threat, he purported to identify which of the two women before him was the 'good' mother: the mother capable of such great maternal sacrifice that she was prepared to renounce possession of her child altogether in order that the boy could live.

I had moved to the countryside from London for six months with the children at the beginning of the pandemic. My ex-husband didn't have time to help much with weekday homeschooling or childcare, and I faced being crammed into a small upstairs flat all week with two rambunctious children. So he agreed to the move and I managed hurriedly to rent out my flat and rent a furnished house in Oxfordshire just before the lockdown began, with the children going to their father at weekends. We were in a world of toy parachutes flying in green fields and sandcastles made in the expansive garden; our cat became an outdoor cat and caught her first mouse, and we even gave names to the local donkeys. The new rhythms made sense, and it became clear that our hectic London life hadn't been working well. Our version of 50/50 custody had involved our eight-year-old son moving between us for one or two nights at a time, and I realised how bad all the transitions had been for him. The children were both happier and calmer here, and after a few months, I wondered if it was possible to stay.

My ex-husband opposed the move. He still had more faith than I did in the version of 50/50 custody we'd had in London, while I was beginning to question whether strict parity of time was always the solution most conducive to the children's wellbeing. We ended up in court because he was prepared for me to keep our two-year-old daughter but not our son. I began the case believing that I could make an argument for the life my son had with me, his mother, living in the countryside. I naively thought we could do this without lawyers, representing ourselves and treating the judge like a sort of family friend, seeking advice together. I quickly began to feel that I was being judged not only as a mother but as a woman. I came away from court feeling I had been held to account by standards I had mistakenly believed feminism to have eradicated. Women weren't meant to write books or own property; and if we aren't sufficiently emotional and sufficiently repentant, we can't be the kinds of mothers who put our children first. The experience of being cross-questioned in the witness box remains one of the most difficult of my life to date. For months afterwards, the polished, insinuating voice of the barrister rang out in my head when I woke in the night and entered my dreams, asking questions more luridly accusatory than the ones I'd faced in court. 'You act unilaterally, don't you, over and over again?' 'You don't put your children first, do you?' 'You just do what you want, whenever you want?' I answered back despairingly, coming up with better answers than I'd managed in court, but even in these private nocturnal reveries I failed to have the final word.

In the weeks between hearings, as the weather turned and it became clear we were heading towards another lockdown, I began to read about women in a similar situation. I was desperately in need of distraction from my ex-husband's barrister's speeches, which seemed to run through my head day and night. I found this distraction in the letters of women two centuries earlier who seemed also to be faced by men still driven by the pain and anger of the marriage, and by a legal world unable to resist punishing women who had transgressed the norms of what a respectable wife and mother should be.

Walking across the foggy meadows to the courtroom, I was walking alongside George Sand in the 1830s French countryside, as she raced in her wet clothes along the hot river bank. I was walking alongside the scintillating writer and socialite Caroline Norton in 1830s London, when her philandering husband accused her publicly of adultery with the prime minister, and then asserted his right to their two-, four- and six-year-old children. 'I could hear their little feet running merrily over my head while I sat sobbing below – only the ceiling between us, and I am not able to get at them,' she wrote, after failing to retrieve them.[2]

Norton, like Sand, had attempted to embody a moment of change when Enlightenment possibilities of autonomous human subjects came together with the Romantic cult of personal sentiment and individual self-creation. They were pioneering freer possibilities for the lives of women. But now they were discovering that though they could defy the patriarchy in their homes, the legal system remained stubbornly oppressive. And it was turning out that there was one crucial aspect of human life that that even the most hopeful and progressive visions of modernity had not made enough room for: motherhood. Mothers were not meant also to be writers and desiring women. And the men who relied on women to mother their children turned out to reserve the right to snatch the children away, imposing their will and shoring up patriarchal authority when the women asked too much for themselves. These were the ambivalent, gendered contradictions of modernity that continued to play out in my own times.

I was walking too alongside clever, troubled, determined Elizabeth Packard in 1860s Illinois, when her pastor husband got her incarcerated in a 'mental asylum' for challenging his religious views. She was too articulate, too persuasive: she was undermining his authority and might be a harmful influence on their children.

They fought back, these women. In England, Caroline Norton used her literary flair and her connections in Parliament to initiate the 1839 Custody of Infants Act, which gave married women the right to petition for custody of children under seven. In France, George Sand managed to win her case and even to keep her house. Elizabeth Packard led successful campaigns to change the law in the United States on the rights of married women to both custody and property, and to not be declared insane without a trial. Packard's reforms came at the beginning of a briefly heroic and genuinely emancipatory era of American law, when US lawyers distanced themselves from English common law and led the way internationally in speaking up for the rights of children. But all the children of these women suffered despite their mothers' courage – or because of it. There are dead children in these stories, sick children and traumatised ones. Custody can drive you mad.

I lost my case. My son was to live mainly with his father, and my daughter mainly with me, though they'd be together for weekends and holidays, alternating between us. I could see that I'd moved the children away from their father and hurt and enraged him in the process. I wasn't astonished that my ex-husband won, though I was surprised the court was prepared to separate the siblings. But I was shocked at the arguments that had been successfully used against me. It turned out that I lived in a culture where women might be too wilful, too independently minded, to be seen as good mothers.

As my daughter and I adjusted to being on our own in the grim January lockdown that ensued, I continued to read about women fighting for custody.

By the time that the aristocrat, housewife and intellectual Frieda Weekley eloped with D. H. Lawrence in 1912, a British adulterous mother had been granted custody. But precedents were slow to take hold as norms, and they didn't apply if you were a woman who had been original, and outrageous, and set new patterns for how a woman could live. Frieda Lawrence had no hope of continuing to see her children, and fifty years later, the turbulent, steely chronicler of Irish womanhood, Edna O'Brien, feared that the same would still be true for her, even if the sounds of the swinging sixties could just about be heard from the courtroom. This was, after all, the era in which the Right Honourable Lord Denning, the Justice of Appeal, had just taken two children away from the adulterous mother who had been their primary carer with the pronouncement that 'to be a good mother involves not only looking after the children, but making and keeping a home for them with their father' and that 'in so far as she herself by her conduct broke up that home, she is not a good mother'.[3]

The visionary, radical, embattled writer and activist Alice Walker didn't go to court when she and her civil rights lawyer husband Mel Leventhal split up in 1976. She was Black, she was bisexual – she knew how court cases for mothers like her tended to go, and she understood the bloody mess that ensues when motherhood becomes entangled with the law; when the visceral bodily experience of birthing a child is faced with the coldly linguistic, disembodied world of the courtroom. Instead, they came up with a solution together: one of the oddest custody arrangements of their generation. For the rest of her childhood their daughter Rebecca would alternate between her parents for two-year periods, going between a white suburban Jewish life in New York and a Black hippy life in San Francisco, and feeling like she didn't quite fit in in either world.

Reading about Rebecca clarified for me that the 50/50 custody setup we'd had for our son before I left London hadn't been working. Rebecca's experiences became a kind of extreme test for what it means to give a child two homes and expect them to be equally at home in both. She also felt she was living out the failure of the civil rights movement and what she saw as the failure of feminism to account for the demands of motherhood. And yet *The Color Purple*, which Alice Walker wrote during these tortuous years, is one of the richest accounts of care we have – all the more so because care here, though always bodily and almost always womanly, is a communal matter that goes beyond the vision of the nuclear family that still shapes the court system.

As I read about these women, I found that everywhere I looked in the present, I seemed to encounter custody stories too. Going about my daily life in a bucolic, bustling village in Oxfordshire, it seemed that everyone's lives had been marked by custody. The man who painted my house had sole custody of a daughter from one marriage but no right even for contact with the daughter from his previous marriage. The man who fixed my fence was about to go to court because his wife was offering him only alternate weekends and an evening a week.

'Don't do it,' I said, speaking from experience.

'I would pay £50,000 for medical bills if my daughter was dying,' he said. 'Why wouldn't I pay that to prevent her being taken away from me?'

The law cases never end. I went to see a chiropodist whose ex-husband had become so addicted to going to court that he hired lawyers to contest every possible issue, from holiday arrangements to where exactly their handovers should take place. Meanwhile, a woman working with homeless charities in Oxford told me about a woman who had lost custody of her child because she had no home, only to be refused housing benefit because she did not have custody of the child she needed a house to be able to fight for. I heard about several immigrant mothers married to British men who were losing citizenship at the same time as they lost custody, and who therefore weren't entitled to legal aid, even if the men had been abusive.

Custody flashed across the news cycles. Angelina Jolie and Brad Pitt went back and forth to court, with their oldest son joining his mother in accusing his father of physically and emotionally terrorising his children: 'You have no consideration or empathy toward your four youngest children who tremble in fear when in your presence. You will never understand the damage you have done to my family.' Kanye West turned to social media to complain about Kim Kardashian: 'I WANT TO BRING MY KIDS TO MY HOME TOWN OF CHICAGO TO SEE MY BASKETBALL TEAM PLAY FOR 7 THOUSAND PEOPLE AND KIM IS STOPPING THAT. HOW IS THAT JOINT CUSTODY?' The actor and comedian Jason Sudeikis served legal papers filing for custody to Olivia Wilde while she was on stage talking about her new film. And, as always, there was Britney Spears, the mother who could never be seen as a good enough mother and whose loss of her children had played out in real time before her fans, as Caroline Norton's had centuries earlier for the fans and detractors who read about her case in newspaper reports and souvenir pamphlets and in her own devastating accounts. Norton and Spears became test cases for generations of mothers who used their stories to probe their own notions of how much freedom a mother should be allowed.[4]

My kids. My basketball team. Your children. The possessive pronouns flow through all the court cases I read about. By turns we claim our children for ourselves and offer them up, demanding the other parent should step up and parent. My child. Your child. Our child. It is so absurd, that anyone should own another person. But how can we avoid this feeling, when these children began their lives deep inside our bodies? Legally, we don't own our children as Victorian fathers once did, but responsibility can feel close to ownership, and it is so hard to care for our children without controlling them. One of the most frightening aspects of parenthood is the fact that we are all losing custody all the time, as children get older. The court process accelerates this but also denatures it: 'Care and Control'; 'Parental Responsibility'; 'Child Arrangements'. The law attempts to split custody up into its various components and to do away with the word 'custody' altogether but in doing so it reveals that it is precisely custody, with its dual connotations of care and control, that we still fight over.

I decided to tell the story of six women who had fought for their children and been found wanting, and through their stories to tell the stories of hundreds of other women, men and children whose cases are less well known and well documented, but who were caught in the same tides of historical change. I wanted to do everything I could to bring out the voices of the children involved in these custody cases – children whose voices have often been painfully silent in court. But I wanted to write it as a book centred on mothers because, though plenty of fathers have lost custody cases over the centuries, it is mothers who have consistently been on the receiving end of the most punitive aspects of custody judgments; mothers who have been excessively idealised and then vilified when they fail to live up to the ideals; mothers who have been feared precisely for the fleshy bonds of blood and milk that enmesh them with their babies – to the point that maternal 'enmeshment' has now become a standard part of terminology used by court-appointed psychologists and judges who are frightened that there is something excessive about maternal love. According to Jacqueline Rose in her book *Mothers*, by providing life, mothers offer a Freudian promise of plenitude that can never be fulfilled, and so we make mothers 'the objects of licensed cruelty'.[5]

I wanted to write this as a book of stories because mothers enter courtrooms as storied figures. In custody hearings, the most intimate aspects of our lives as women and mothers are exposed in the public sphere. Stories are told about us, and we respond with stories of our own. Judges weigh these stories against each other and come up with stories called judgments, and then send us out into the world to co-parent a vulnerable child who fears precisely the strife that has just been intensified by the court. Ultimately, this is a book that sees custody as the knot where motherhood, ideology and power get tied together. And because questions about power for women are questions about feminism, it's a book about the tortuously ambivalent relationship between feminism and motherhood.

The idealisation of the good feminist can be as dangerous as the idealisation of the good mother. Every generation of feminists has been troubled by motherhood, and too often, feminists have seen emancipation and care as at odds with each other. They've been unwilling to fight for women as mothers, frightened that celebrating women as care-givers returns us to essentialist, patriarchal ideas about gender. And plenty of mothers have repudiated feminism. It's always been clear that mothers in court are better off downplaying any feminist principles. Perhaps I shouldn't have been surprised that I lost my case. It is very hard to be a feminist fighting in courts where the most immediately appealing arguments are often still based on outmoded and oppressive ideas about women and motherhood. It makes sense that the custody campaigners who did best in the nineteenth century argued on behalf of children rather than mothers. And it makes sense that second-wave feminists found themselves briefly but fatally on the same side as fathers' rights groups in the 1970s and 1980s.

The stories I'm telling are all about biological mothers and fathers. These are women who give birth to their children, and the experience of carrying a baby in the womb and releasing a fragile creature into the world pervades early motherhood, as possession shifts to responsibility. For Caroline Norton and Edna O'Brien, pregnancy and childbirth brought an intense, symbiotic mother-bond; for Alice Walker, it resulted in a more ambivalent rage and disbelief. But all the women who came close to losing custody here asserted a raw cry of ownership. 'It is surely hard that the man can take them from the woman who bore them, & loves them better than all the world,' Caroline Norton lamented. In turn, the fathers' possessiveness may have been all the more desperate because of the belatedness of fatherhood. 'I can do what I please now with you, my boy,' servants reported George Norton telling his son. There are other books to be written about custody cases involving adoption or trans parents. But I suspect that the male–female roles are tenacious here too, shaped by centuries of legal history.[6]

As for the fathers. The fathers who win have been harmed as well by the roles they can feel compelled to adopt in court – by the punitive stance the law can seem to require. And there are loving fathers who suffer too in the courts; good enough fathers who have been unstinting in their care and are painfully missed by the children they have lost. The best film about custody in recent years has been made by a father, Noah Baumbach, who went through a custody case himself. *Marriage Story* knows that custody is at heart a tragedy, albeit one flecked with painful moments of hilarity. Hegel defines tragedy as an irreconcilable conflict between two equally valid concepts of the good, and this is what is going on here. The film knows too that we can feel most married just when we are getting divorced – that the court turns the volatile battles of a marriage into something more like trench warfare, with children caught in the line of fire. It also knows that law and morality are as entwined as ever. And, tellingly, this film written and directed by a father knows that fathers have a blanker canvas than mothers on which to sketch their vision of what a father should be, and that mothers have it harder than fathers in the courts. The mother's barrister warns her how this is going to be and she's right – women have to live up to an impossible ideal:

> People don't accept mothers who drink too much wine, and yell at their child, and call him an asshole. I get it. I do it too. We can accept an imperfect dad. Let's face it, the idea of a good father was only invented like thirty years ago. Before that, fathers were expected to be silent, and absent, and unreliable, and selfish, and we can all say we want them to be different. But on some basic level, we accept them. We love them for their fallibilities, but people absolutely don't accept those same failings in mothers. We don't accept it structurally, and we don't accept it spiritually. Because the basis of our Judeo-Christian whatever is Mary, Mother of Jesus, and she's perfect. She's a virgin who gives birth, unwaveringly supports her child and holds his dead body when he's gone. And the dad isn't there. He didn't even do the fucking. God is in heaven. God is the father, and God didn't show up. So you have to be perfect, and Charlie can be a fuck up, and it doesn't matter. You will always be held to a different, higher standard.

She's right, and so is the father's lawyer, who warns him that this is going to be tragic, whoever wins. 'Getting divorced with a kid is one of the hardest things to do,' he says, 'it's like a death without a body.'[7]

But in fact there is a body – it's a child's body, and it carries the venom of the courtroom within it forever, even if it hasn't been visibly ripped in half.

I

CAROLINE NORTON

Tuesday 29 March 1836. A father bundles three small children into a hackney coach – knobbly knees knocking as they rattle across London. The driver hurries, bumping his way between carriages and buses as the rain sloshes down; this is the wettest March on record. Their mother will visualise this scene over and over again in the weeks that follow, and I find myself visualising it now. It's a scene that will play out for centuries to come: children rushed into a future they haven't chosen, turned into possessions in an adult war.

The boys – six-year-old Fletcher, four-year-old Brinsley and two-year-old William – are driven up the sodden edge of St James's Park where they can see the fat sheep eating grass, up through St James's Square where there are figs at the end of summer, into Marylebone. They know something is wrong. They hardly ever travel alone with their father, and today they were due to go to Dorset with their mother. Fletcher coughs away in the damp coach. His mother always wraps him up when he's ill, but George Norton doesn't know the ins and outs of these bodies as she does. He hasn't lain anxiously listening to Fletcher coughing in the night. Fletcher knows that his mother would want him to have his scarf, but with his father it's best not to complain.

They're deposited in a hotel bedroom and left to their own devices.

Do they play hide and seek in the cupboards and under the bedclothes? Does Fletcher get cross with William because he doesn't know the rules? I see Fletcher and Brinsley sitting in anxious, fidgety silence, and William toddling around, climbing onto chairs, almost knocking over vases that Fletcher rushes to rescue. Soon they are hurried into another cab and rattled up along Duke Street to Manchester Square. Now they're at the house of Miss Vaughan, a querulous relative of George's who has always been open in her dislike of his wife. (Perhaps Fletcher has listened hard enough to the servants' gossip to wonder if there's something suspect about her fondness for his cash-strapped father.) No one tells the boys why they're here. There's no time, anyway, because a Mr Knapp (Miss Vaughan's property agent) bundles them into yet another coach and takes them to another of Miss Vaughan's houses. There's no sign of their father and no word on when they're to see their mother. No one is attempting to make this seem normal.

They may hear their mother when she arrives and shouts and sobs at Mr Knapp, only for him to call the police and send her away. She thinks she hears them running around upstairs. On no account are they to see their mother, Knapp has been told, so eventually she leaves, bewildered, and makes the journey to her brother alone. She's been looking forward to this trip to Dorset with her sons. She's been so exhausted by her husband's temper that she was glad when her brother made it clear that the invitation didn't extend to him. She's been ill all winter, like Fletcher, and hoped they could recover together in Dorset, in a house with servants and luxuries provided by her brother's rich wife. Instead, this: public humiliation and personal despair.

'I wish I had never had my children,' she writes from Dorset to the prime minister, Lord Melbourne, the close friend who many believe to be her lover, '– pain & agony for the first moments of their life – dread & anxiety for their uncertain future – and now all to be a blank.' She fears that her husband wants to use his power over their children to drive her either to act so disgracefully that he can divorce her, or to return to him on painfully restrictive terms. 'I came away without being able even to kiss them & say good bye – if they keep my boys from me I shall go mad.'¹

I. Rupture

'You know he professes the greatest contempt for female intellect'

Caroline Norton thought that she was the powerful one. This was her mistake. She thought that she was an emancipated woman in an ever more emancipated world. She thought that the children were hers because they loved her best. She thought that she was the winning player in the power games with her husband. She was wrong. This was a play that she was directing: snubbing him in front of her influential friends; having the last word in their arguments. But at any moment, he could wrench down the curtain and confront her with the real world in which the power had been his all along.

It had been clear when they married in 1827 that they were badly matched, but Caroline's mother had decided he was their best option. Caroline Sheridan had staked everything on wit because her sisters were staking everything on beauty. She was going to charm men with her cleverness; she would marry as the heir to her playwright-cum-politician grandfather, Richard Sheridan. And so, she swore in public, she gained a reputation as a mimic, she began to write and, in an era when many women used male pseudonyms, she published her poems under her own name. She was a woman in motion, a woman riding fast into the hunt – though never with enough money for a horse of her own. It was a risk, even in their raffish, Whiggish enclave of the aristocracy, to gamble on brilliance. And it turned out that between them, she and her widowed mother were too frightened to see the risk through. They panicked at the crucial moment and accepted George Norton: a man who had fallen in love with Caroline on sight when she was only a schoolgirl, and who was apparently too obtuse to notice that she was a Whig and a wit and an entirely unsuitable wife for a dim-witted Tory on the make.

The only man Caroline had actually loved had been forbidden by his parents to marry her and had died before they'd had the chance to elope. It wasn't a promising start, and the life she wanted – hosting exuberant, erudite dinner parties and writing poetry and producing babies to expand the tender melange of her own family – required a husband, but didn't require that husband to loom all that large within it. Or so she hoped, turning hope into confidence because she was nineteen and, so far, everything had just about worked out. As for her mother: after her bankrupt husband Tom Sheridan died of tuberculosis, she'd been left with sole responsibility for three daughters without dowries and a son without prospects.

And so in July 1827 Caroline found herself waiting for George in the dim vestibule of one of the grandest churches in London, black eyes and hair flashing against the white of her dress, wondering why this man who'd been so impatient to marry her was late for their wedding. Finally he arrived, sweaty and frustrated. He'd come by cabriolet – a one-man mini-carriage – and his horse had bolted and dragged him across London. Caroline had her retort ready. 'Well, Mr Norton, you are come at last, and look handsomer, I declare, than I expected.' It was less a witticism than a brave and somewhat shaky attempt at high-spirited gallantry. She proceeded down the aisle, accompanied by Douglas Kinnaird, a close friend of Lord Byron's, and the raffish friend of her raffish father.[2]

Kinnaird must have known how incompatible a husband he was handing her over to. The Nortons weren't just Tories. They were known as 'Ultra Tories' because of their ardent opposition to the Reform Act. George Norton's father had been a prominent MP and an acclaimed soldier, who could boast he'd been wounded at Waterloo. George Norton shared his father's views but not his promise; he'd been elected as MP to the family seat in Guildford but was unpopular, and at twenty-seven had no other prospects. The families differed politically and in their attitudes towards women. Norton women lived quietly; they didn't write books or make speeches at dinner parties.

Neither Kinnaird nor anyone else tried to stop the match, and Caroline and George were hurled into the sudden, outrageous intimacy of married life. They took a house in Storey's Gate, Westminster, right in the centre of political London and, despite a lack of funds, Caroline began to host parties, becoming one of the most appealing hostesses among the Whig circles she'd grown up in. George finally had in his bed the pretty girl he'd watched walking around the Surrey countryside when she was sixteen, but had little to say to her. He didn't read; he didn't enjoy arguing about politics. It didn't help that the Whigs were gaining steady ground against the Tories, who went through one prime minister after another trying to hold together an uneasy coalition government. George felt lost in this marriage, so he asserted control. He forbade her outings; he refused her access even to the money she made herself; he started arguments about what constituted permissible behaviour for ladies (was her married aunt uncouth in deciding to dance?), and he hit her when she disagreed with him.

Determinedly, though a little shakily, Caroline seemed to be thriving, nonetheless. Her first book – an accomplished, overblown poetry collection called *The Sorrows of Rosalie*, detailing the tragic fall of an unwed mother – sold well in 1829 and was applauded as 'an extraordinary effort by so young a person' in *The Times*. This was the same year as the Nortons had their first son, Fletcher, and the book paid for the expenses of the birth.[3]

Motherhood came more easily to Caroline than it had to Rosalie in her tale. She liked all her babies; a head latched onto the breast, the pricking of the milk, the sleepy sucking. She breastfed for longer than many women of her class. There was a nursemaid and a nursery – she had it repainted a pale stone colour – but she did a lot of the daily caring herself, entertaining and educating the children, tending to them through illnesses and seeking out warm, soft wool for their infant dresses. 'I miss him dreadfully,' she wrote when Fletcher was away for a few days as a toddler, 'and am continually forgetting that he is not in the house.' Fletcher was followed in 1831 by Brinsley – '<u>very</u> dark, with long thick hair & a perfect beauty' – and then in 1833 by William.4

She was a mother, and this anchored her, but she was also a beautiful and unhappily married young woman, hungry for men. She singled out Lord Melbourne, who'd been a friend of her idealised, absent father. Melbourne was handsome, self-confident, lazy and a known womaniser. In 1828, Caroline was twenty and he was forty-nine. His wife, Lady Caroline Lamb, had just died after a volatile marriage (it was she who described her lover Byron as 'mad, bad and dangerous to know'). Melbourne was ready to adore this young adventuress, and there was a tenderness and a thoughtfulness to this friendship that did credit to them both. Reading the letters that she wrote to him daily while apart, I sense her becoming more eloquent and more wise in the glow of his esteem. He didn't ask much from her and he offered a lot. He could take it when, at a party, she grabbed his hat off his head and kicked it high over his shoulder – it's a scene both very appealing and rather difficult to envisage. He brought a kind of stateliness to her impetuousness; he gave her gifts of horses, money – whatever she needed. He was old enough not to be jealous of her time or her children. 'Farewell dear Lord,' she wrote at the end of a letter in 1831 after thanking him for the gift of a horse; 'you asked me rather a conceited question as to how I stood affected to you by absence. My Lord[,] absence makes no difference with me; your letters do because they are the pleasantest I get.' She meant it. These years would have been considerably less happy for her without him.⁵

Perhaps George would have quashed this if he'd felt more confident about his own prospects. But he was voted out in 1830, too unpopular even to hold onto the family seat, and he needed a job. This was the general election that brought the Whigs to power – and Caroline was glad to ask Lord Melbourne, now Home Secretary, to help. Of course she was; the shift in the balance of power in Westminster brought a shift in her marriage, and this was her chance to demonstrate it.

In 1831 Melbourne got George a job as a magistrate. Meanwhile, Caroline published more books and further tested the faultlines of her marriage by becoming a noisy and committed member of the campaign for electoral reform.

She came from a family of reformers. Her father and her grandfather had fought for the rights of the poor and wanted to extend the vote. Now, with her usual mixture of buccaneering showiness and genuine passion, she took this on as her cause. She was full of eloquent conviction and could do a lot of good, campaigning in Whig drawing rooms. She liked being at odds with George and his Ultra Tory cronies, and more affably at odds with Melbourne, who was too old-fashioned to want to widen the franchise. She ran ahead, cajoling him into the future, and as Home Secretary in a government with a narrow majority, he knew that he had to join her. She made it easier for him to move with the times, writing excitedly to him about becoming 'enamoured' of William Godwin's *Caleb Williams*, his 1794 impassioned call for the end of tyrannical governments in the wake of the French Revolution, and about how – she did not yet know how much this would affect her personally – it was one of her 'manias that the English law does not protect the lower orders against the higher'.⁶

In September 1831, Prime Minister Charles Grey finally had his Reform Bill passed in Parliament, only for it to be rejected by the

House of Lords in November, resulting in riots across the country: prisons were attacked, and prisoners freed; a fire was started at Nottingham Castle. In London, there was talk of 3,000 people armed with wooden staves planning to gather in Islington. George Norton enrolled ordinary local inhabitants of Whitechapel as special constables and Melbourne met the organisers and threatened them into calling the protest off. Caroline Norton wrote rather self-importantly to her sister that 'we think we have taken such effectual measures that no great riot will take place', revealing the limits of her enthusiasm for protest and her pleasure in being close to her protector.[7]

Finally, after resigning and threatening to fill the House of Lords with newly created Whig peers, Earl Grey managed to get the bill through in June 1832. The Reform Act reorganised the political system but still only 18 per cent of the adult male population could vote. More protests followed, and in 1834 Caroline marched alongside 30,000 trade union members to submit a petition to Melbourne protesting on behalf of the 'Tolpuddle Martyrs' – six Dorset agricultural workers who had been severely sentenced for taking a secret oath to join a union. 'I pique myself on being the only "lady of fashion" who walked with the famous "Trades Union procession" when cannon were planted on the Admiralty and the government was quaking with fear,' she later wrote. Melbourne came down hard on the protestors but remained favourably disposed to his lady of fashion.[8]

In July 1834 Melbourne briefly became prime minister when Lord Grey resigned. Always more a gentleman of leisure than a civil servant, he didn't want the extra work, but he didn't anyway last long; in November, William IV dismissed Melbourne and called on the Tories to form a government. The Tories were riven with internal divisions and were even less popular than the Whigs with the newly enlarged electorate. They didn't manage to gain a majority in the 1835 general election and Melbourne half-reluctantly became prime minister again. For Caroline, life was getting closer to how she'd hoped it would be. She was taking part in conversations that decided politics; she was happy as a mother, especially when she could get her children away from London. There were trips to be near her mother who had an apartment at Hampton Court, where they were entertained by a deer they named Hugh who ate out of the children's hands. Brinsley wouldn't sit down to breakfast till Hugh had joined the table.

And she was admired – and not just by Melbourne. There was the young politician and writer Benjamin Disraeli, who dubbed her 'Starry Night' (in contrast to her sister Helen's 'Sunny Day') and wrote to ask her for political advice. The painter Benjamin Haydon became besotted by this 'bit of Greek sculpture just breaking into life'. She laughed off his advances but then half-unwillingly half-fell for Edward Trelawny, a war-wounded, twice-divorced hero who had organised the cremation of Percy Shelley and presented Shelley's widow Mary with her husband's heart. Indeed, Trelawny had even built the boat that overturned, leaving the poet's body to be washed ashore.[9]

George Norton's admiration for Caroline turned out to be the most fickle of all. He became more violent, more petulant every year. Surely it humiliated him as much as her when, one morning when she was pregnant with their third son, he demanded she swap breakfast seats so he could have his favourite chair with the view of the garden, and then deliberately scalded her hand with a hot tea-kettle. There are stories every few months of him hitting her, or forcing her to run alongside the carriage after throwing her out of it.

They tried. She nursed him through illnesses; he apologised and promised change. 'You are a good kind hub in the long run, and don't believe me when I say harsh things to you, waking or sleeping,' she wrote in 1834 after a draining period looking after him in France. Nothing changed. He was cruel by temperament, but perhaps he'd have been less cruel with a woman who brought out fewer of his insecurities. Her open friendships with men could seem intended to humiliate him, and it was all the more humiliating that he relied on Melbourne for his job.[10]

Reading their letters, I can feel them pushing each other into extreme, caricatured versions of themselves. This can happen so easily in a marriage: both spouses come to define themselves by their differences. So Caroline became more flirtatious, more witty, more committed to freedoms. And George became more inward, more taciturn, more rigid in his notion of acceptable behaviour. It wasn't just their personalities but of course their visions of the world that were at odds. Caroline's version of Whig society was a leftover from the eighteenth-century pleasure garden: ladies and gentlemen exchanging witticisms and gallantries on a relatively equal social footing, valuing politeness, brilliance and sensibility. Her friends were living out Enlightenment ideals of autonomous self-creation and equality, given new energy by the Romantic cult of sensibility. By contrast, George's army father had given him early training in the values of taciturn manliness, order and control, that increasingly characterised Victorian society.

If the nineteenth century was a famously difficult time to be a woman, then it was a very difficult time to be a man as well. Around this time, the historian Thomas Carlyle would eulogise the burly 'Man of Practice', wrestling with obstacles with 'sheer obstinate toughness of muscle' and 'toughness of heart'. The manly man of this era made decisions on behalf of his family and brought his wife under the harmonious canopy of his stronger will. George was not independent: his wife had found him his job and earned much of their income. He was so indebted to the man he suspected to be her lover that he had named his youngest son after him, and there was a portrait of Melbourne on the drawing-room table. He was failing as a manly man, so he committed to 'manliness' with such confused fervour that it turned into cruelty and bullying. He hadn't been brought up to be generous in love, and he was surrounded by people who saw physical violence as a just about acceptable part of marriage. The 1790 case of *Evans v Evans* was still widely cited, allowing men across the country to get away with abusing their wives with its verdict that: 'Mere austerity of temper, petulance of manners, rudeness of language . . . even occasional sallies of passion . . . do not amount to legal cruelty'. For her part, Caroline doesn't seem to have realised quite how difficult their marriage was for George, who may have had it in him to be a more generous husband with a different wife.[11]

Her writing also unsettled him. She was always writing, when she wasn't socialising or with the children. She hardly slept – looping, curling, scratching sentences into being, late into the night. George relied on her income, but he didn't take her work seriously. In 1830 she had visited factories with him in Manchester and proposed to write something about the children working long, painful days there. George, as she'd later put it, 'laughed at the notion'. 'You know he professes the greatest contempt for female intellect,' she told a correspondent.[12]

Why are some men so suspicious of writing women? Is it simply that they're suspicious of thinking women? Perhaps he, and the many men like him, are right to be suspicious, because writers churn the material of their lives into new patterns, using their work to think through the questions of their lives.

In May 1835 Caroline Norton published paired novellas, *The Wife* and *Woman's Reward*. The latter is the story of a long-suffering, self-sacrificing young woman called Mary and her violent and selfish brother Lionel. Mary, wise and beautiful, though not as clever as her creator, falls in love with William Clavering, a man who shared Lord Melbourne's first name, wit and good looks. Both Lionel and Clavering go into politics, find themselves opposed, and dislike each other so much that Lionel pleads with Mary to give up Clavering for his sake. Mary agrees, and this becomes the tragedy of her life. Her reward is a late love of a kind that Caroline herself perhaps hoped for. Clavering's wife dies and he offers her 'the dregs of a heart, which in its youth was all yours'.[13]

It's a moving, passionate novel that was rightly praised in *The Times* as a highly accomplished book, albeit an 'essentially feminine' one. The reviewer found its portraits of men two-dimensional, but I think much of the novel's power comes from Lionel's familiar combinations of charm, cleverness, violence and ignorance. Mary keeps hoping that Lionel's temper signifies passion, but she comes to see that he's an unfeeling man. This won't have made easy reading for George Norton, if he read it, and nor will the portrait of wisdom and real feeling in the Melbourne-inspired Clavering. Even in Parliament, Clavering never a utters a sentence 'of the truth of which he was not himself thoroughly convinced'. And in late middle-age, his lips thin and compressed and his eyes sad, his brow retains 'all the noble and imperishable beauty of earlier times'.[14]

It's not surprising that Melbourne admired the novel, though he thought she'd made Lionel 'too d-----d a beast' – perhaps he feared Norton's wrath, and feared that he and Caroline would never have the happy ending she had written into being for him with her more demure heroine. Perhaps Caroline feared this too. The novel is revealing in its attitude towards wit. Clavering is witty – it's a big part of his appeal – but the idealised heroine, Mary, is resolutely not. It's Mary's aunt, Mrs Bolton, who was once 'a wit', and who tells Mary ruefully that she's lucky not to be afflicted by wittiness herself. Wit is not a talent to be envied, Mrs Bolton says, 'since it requires merely high spirits, a desire to shine, and a moderate share of intellect in its possessor'. She adds that remorse often followed the triumphs of her stinging reproaches.[15]

With Caroline firing a portrait of a cruel and violent man into the drawing rooms and bedrooms of the nation, it's probably not a coincidence that the early summer of 1835 was a difficult time for the Nortons. George was irascible and Caroline was frightened because she was pregnant again. She took refuge with her sister, Georgia, while her brother Brinsley negotiated for her return, persuading George to promise less violence and more money, though he also threatened to keep the children if she insisted on a separation. She returned to find that nothing had changed, and she attributed the miscarriage that followed in August to 'the agitation and misery to which I had been exposed'. George left his sickly wife to go off shooting in Scotland and left her brother to settle her doctor's bills. There was a period of recuperation, brightened by the deer near her mother's house, and then Caroline retaliated by taking her children to Brighton, where Trelawny had a sailing boat. 'He is the hunchiest man that ever looked like a gentleman – and the growliest, and the least complimentary knight who ever sat among women and the kindest to children,' Caroline wrote to her mother. She was glad of the time with her boys, who she gave 'breakfast with prawns, dinner with bad cookery, & tea with smiles', and glad of the brooding longing of a man with an exceptional talent for it.[16]

She was so unhappy that she continued tussling with the question of whether to leave; but she told Edward Ellice, an elder statesman politician who had become something of a protector during these years, that her mother declared she would be heartbroken if she did, '& for *my* heart, they doubt whether I have one to break'. Next, she took the children to her sister's for a month. 'I am always better anywhere away,' she told Trelawny in December, explaining that the 'weight & the clank' of the chains that incarcerated her at home wore her out. Then she and Fletcher became ill again and she set her hopes on their both recovering at her brother's house in April. But George was angry he wasn't invited.[17]

Perhaps she should have been more careful to avoid humiliating her husband. She seems to have given up on the marriage as a marriage, though. And so she wasn't prepared for how swiftly everything escalated when, the night before she and the children left for Dorset, George insisted that Caroline spend the evening with him. They had been out separately and then, when she appeared at the appointed meeting place, there was no George. His sister-in-law's brother Fitzroy Campbell waited with her and was about to escort her home when George arrived, drunk and petulant, accusing Caroline of cavorting with Campbell. Caroline fought back. 'Tomorrow I am <u>gone</u> and it shall be long before you see me back again at Storey's Gate!' she later recalled saying. George's response had a kind of terrible inevitability: 'I think I have a way still to govern <u>you</u> my lady, – you may go to the d[evi]l if you like but you go <u>alone</u>.'[18]

This seems to have been the impulse of an angry moment. Surely anyone who had planned it wouldn't have shuttled his children between three different houses in London before sending them to his brother in Guildford? We don't have George's perspective on what he was doing, taking the children like this. Presumably he had convinced himself that Caroline was a bad mother as well as a bad wife, or simply that she was out of control and needed to be chastened. Or perhaps he'd realised that they had both made a terrible mistake, and saw this as the way to be free of her: she would be easier to negotiate with if he had the children.

And so he seized his three sickly and unhappy boys, sent them to his brother's house and set himself to punishing his wife. For days, he shocked the servants by interrogating his boys for information about their mother's behaviour. What had her relations been with Trelawny? The anxious servants reported to Caroline that he had threatened to lock Brinsley up for a whole week if the four-year-old didn't reveal lurid details about his mother. 'Mamma won't <u>let you</u> lock little Brinney up,' the brave little boy apparently responded. George went against Caroline's wishes in getting a dentist to wire up Fletcher's jaw to straighten his teeth – 'I can do what I please now with you, my boy,' he was reported as saying, making it clear that his son was a pawn in a parental battle. And he decided to sue for 'criminal conversation' – as adultery was known with a weird mixture of the coy and the lurid – with Melbourne. If Caroline lost, she would no longer be a mother in anything but name. Even if she won, she was coming to see that her hold on the children was shaky. The terrible truth was that the boys belonged to George.[19]

II. Custody

'The law is clear that the custody of a child, of whatever age, belongs to the father'

Custody: the prerogative of care. She'd been told during the brief separation in 1835 that the children were effectively George's possessions, but she hadn't fully believed it. They were her children – the gift of her otherwise unsatisfactory marriage – and George had always left their care to her. One thing that made the custody laws of the 1830s so bizarre was that most people didn't know how they worked.

Nineteenth-century society assailed women with ideals of motherhood. Take *The Magazine of Domestic Economy*, founded in 1835 to celebrate the home. In September 1835, amid recipes for 'hunting-beef' and Irish plum cake, and advice on the correct conduct on omnibuses (keep the flaps of your coat from being sat on by the person next to you), the magazine included a lengthy article on 'The Woman in Domestic Life', urging mothers to devote themselves to their young because 'the mother has the formation of the minds of the children, in that early age when impressions are most easily made'. The character of 'the whole of society' was apparently lowered by mothers who neglected the 'sacred duty' of creating moral children, so it's not surprising that mothers expected to continue with this duty if their husbands tired of the marriage. And there was a law granting mothers of illegitimate children under seven the right to custody. So married women might expect to have the same rights, but it had turned out, in a series of landmark cases, that they did not.[20]

This was the era when the law first entered people's intimate lives. Previously, separations were generally settled informally, with family members and local clergyman helping to arbitrate. From the seventeenth century onwards, for those with landed estates to inherit, there were complex legal custody arrangements giving the father full legal custody of his heir. For other people, custody tended to be more casually shared, with mothers being given the pleasures and burdens of child-rearing. In the eighteenth century, there was a handful of cases where custody was given to mothers by Chancery judges who saw fathers as forfeiting rights through extreme negligence or cruelty. Then, as agrarian society gave way to industrialisation, families began to splinter in more directions and the law took on a new role. Judges in all the courts were required to interpret legal principles that had not been much called for, and in doing so they brought to light the patriarchal nature of the law. The whole legal system at this point was built around the task of assigning property to this or that man. So the judges used the only laws they had at their disposal – laws that assigned children to men as property – both unwittingly and wittingly to shape a society in which men relied on women to mother their children but reserved the right to seize those children from them, shoring up patriarchal authority as they did so. Women who claimed some kind of maternal right to custodianship were rejected by courts fearful of the whole notion of women's rights coming into vogue.

The first landmark case was the 1804 dispute where Margaret de Manneville's baby daughter was forcibly abducted by her estranged husband, a French national. He'd been trying to challenge the marriage settlement that kept her money in her name. Frightened when he threatened to take their daughter abroad, she escaped to her mother's house, only for her husband to force his way in. Accounts from the time describe the husband snatching the baby girl away as she suckled from her mother's breast. It's a brutal image that illustrates the extremes of desperation and cruelty that characterised custody in these decades.

Margaret De Manneville applied to the Court of King's Bench for a writ of habeas corpus: the legal procedure that allowed a summons to be made demanding that an unlawfully detained person (usually a prisoner) should be released. This got her nowhere, so she applied to the Court of Chancery, claiming that Thomas De Manneville was guilty of 'ill usage' and of threatening to take the child out of the country. The father's lawyers insisted that the law was clear on the husband's right both to custody and to 'the society of his wife'. Therefore, they cunningly suggested that if Lord Eldon allowed the baby to be returned to her mother, the Lord Chancellor would 'indirectly pronounce a sentence of divorce'.[21]

These laws had never been required to apply so nonsensically to an actual situation. Musing on this challenging case, Eldon determined that the wife was presently living 'under circumstances, under which the law will not permit her to live', breaking the obligation of the marriage contract to remain with her husband. Because De Manneville had not sued to have his wife restored, Eldon could do nothing on that count. 'The single question is, whether this Court has jurisdiction against the legal, natural, right of the father to have the custody of the person of his child.' There was the danger that De Manneville would remove his daughter from the country, and with that in mind Lord Eldon ordered the child to remain in England. But the baby was to go to her father. 'The law is clear that the custody of a child, of whatever age, belongs to the father,' Eldon stipulated. In subsequent decades, Eldon emerged as a determinedly conservative judge, terrified of allowing the legal system to initiate change. He was right, in a way. Few people think that judges should be activists; they are there to apply the law, not to change it. And he applied the laws correctly, because the British legal system, unlike those in America and France, was not built on rights. Judges were not able to think in terms of the rights of either children or mothers.²²

Gradually, the implications of the De Manneville judgment became evident. Men like George Norton were dangerously bolstered by the knowledge that whoever they slept with, and however much they beat their wives, their children belonged to them. Judges were worried that if one mother got custody, mothers everywhere would leave the husbands they'd secretly wanted to leave all along. But the lawmakers don't seem to have considered the congruent danger. By granting custody uniformly to men, they gave men power of a kind that very few people can be trusted to use well.

Power and powerlessness mirror and distort each other. George Norton, burning Caroline's arm with a hot kettle and throwing her out of a carriage – it was frightening, but she was right to think that such flagrant assertions of power have powerlessness built in. She was better than him at day-to-day power games, but when it came to sheer power, he had the ultimate advantage: he was male. A man blanked as a boorish buffoon in her social circle had power over the lady everyone was eager to be noticed by.

This had been the case also for Emily Westmeath, whose custody battle had been the talk of upper-class drawing rooms a few years earlier. Lady Emily Cecil had married another cash-strapped George, the soon-to-be Marquess of Westmeath, in 1812, to find that her husband had a child with his mistress soon after and was funnelling Emily's money to her. In 1817, Emily took their three-year-old daughter Rosa and sued for legal separation. There was a brief reconciliation, with the usual promises of change, and then in May 1818 Emily demanded a full separation. Angry now, George sued to remove Rosa and their baby boy.

Lord Eldon was more troubled than he'd been by the De Manneville case. He asked Emily's mother to look after the children for a few days while he reflected on the situation. But shockingly, the grandmother replied: 'My Lord . . . I will keep no children from their father,' determining the fate of her grandchildren. George won custody and took the children to Ireland where, in the summer of 1819, their baby son became dangerously ill with hydrocephalus. Emily arrived to find the baby dead. George returned Rosa to Emily, while insisting that 'the power over my child I do not surrender, nor ever will'. Then in March 1820, George refused to let six-year-old Rosa return to Emily after visiting him. Emily sought a writ of habeas corpus from the Court of Common Pleas to recover her daughter, whose health was weak. But Lord Chief Justice Dallas declared that 'the father is in point of law entitled to the custody of the child'. Emily managed to smuggle a few letters to her daughter in a laundry basket and went to humiliatingly absurd lengths to see her, forcing her way into the house of her daughter's dancing teacher. Here she tried to persuade eleven-year-old Rosa to escape, but the girl refused even to kiss her mother, saying that her father had 'pointed out to me what sort of woman' she was, before adding: 'I never wish to see your face again.'[23]

The cases accumulated – and so did the children violated by these exercises of power. In 1824, a five-year-old child ended up in the custody of their father's mistress when the father asserted his right to custody even though he was in prison for debt. Many judges didn't like making these decisions. 'I know of no act more harsh or cruel, than depriving a mother of proper intercourse with her child,' said the Vice-Chancellor of England, Mr Shadwell, in 1827, forbidding the mother in *Ball v Ball* even to have visitation with her daughter, but he was convinced he had 'no authority to intervene'. In 1835, shortly before Caroline Norton's crisis, Henrietta Greenhill had a judge rule that her three daughters, all under six, should live with their adulterous father – a man so absent that one of her daughters had asked her mother's uncle if he was her father at a family gathering. Henrietta Greenhill managed to escape abroad to avoid giving up her children. This was a desperate act that counted as abduction. But when judges are bemoaning the cruelty of the laws they enforce, just this kind of desperation may be necessary.[24]

This was custody as ownership, justified in the name of custodianship, or protection. The judges were as bewildered by the contradictions of nineteenth-century gender as George Norton was. Lord Eldon, describing the legal paternal right as 'natural', seems to have somewhat enjoyed pronouncing these judgments. But Mr Shadwell, describing his own judgment as 'cruel', felt lost in a system impervious to the needs of children. In their own nurseries and drawing rooms, these men extolled the sacredness of motherhood. But for a man like Eldon, it was precisely his devotion to motherhood that made him so afraid that the whole institution of marriage was going to be undermined if he made even tiny changes to the arrangements around divorce. It related to the fears around the Reform Act: allow a handful more men to vote and usher in a revolution. The commitment to conservativism was a commitment to safety and to a rigid notion of stability.

The only two men to lose custody during these decades were Percy Shelley, in 1817, and William Wellesley in 1828. Both mothers were dead, and the fathers were judged of unsound moral character. Shelley had been living in unrepentant sin with Mary Godwin while still married to Harriet, the mother of his children, but this was the case with so many men who did get custody. The judge was more disturbed that he had written atheist poetry and called for the abolition of marriage and for social revolution. Shelley told Byron after losing the case that he had been 'dragged before the tribunals of tyranny and superstition, to answer with my children, my property, my liberty, my fame, for having exposed their frauds, and scorned the insolence of their power'. Eldon had declared in his judgment that: 'This is a case in which, as the matter appears to me, the father's principles cannot be misunderstood, in which his conduct, which I cannot but consider as highly immoral, has been established in proof' and was all the more disturbing because he wasn't ashamed of it – he saw it as 'worthy of approbation'. Shelley in turn denounced Eldon as a 'slave' of Hell in his poem 'To the Lord Chancellor': 'Thy country's curse is on thee! Justice sold,/ Truth trampled.'[25]

Shelley's conduct had been highly irresponsible. He'd cut himself off entirely from his children after falling in love with Mary, and had not even bothered to meet his baby son before Harriet's death. Arguably, it was because he was negligent in forcing them on exhausting journeys round Europe while they were ill that two of his children with Mary subsequently died. He was by no means an ideal father, yet he lost custody to his wife's family primarily because of political principles deduced from his poetry. And Eldon paid as little attention as ever to the needs of the children. This is a judge punishing a man by removing his possessions, rather than a custodian protecting children from their father.

It may be that we can never entirely avoid thinking of our children as our possessions; it may be that we shouldn't entirely avoid it after all, the feeling of possession is involved with the impulse for care. 'My children,' Caroline Norton would lament repeatedly in the months that followed George's flight. But in these court cases, children come across as a possession much like any other, requiring no special kind of love or care.

III. Struggle

'A woman is made a helpless wretch by these laws of men'

The trial took place on a muggy, drizzly day in London on 22 June 1836. Caroline Norton felt on trial as a mother. There was no possible future where she could retain her children as a known adulteress, so if she lost, three small children were going to be deprived of a mother indefinitely. Yet this was not a custody case. It's somehow characteristic of the British legal system that the court case that should have finally precipitated change in the custody laws should not have been a custody case in the first place.

Unlike the mothers in custody cases, Caroline had no voice here. The fight was between her husband and Melbourne, as though Melbourne was a thief who had stolen George's horse rather than his wife. Because married women had no legal standing, they were represented by their husbands in courts of law, which meant only Melbourne had the right to defend himself. None of the parties – Caroline, George, Melbourne – attended; George waited with his family in Mayfair, Melbourne got on with his duties as prime minister, and Caroline was in her mother's apartment in Hampton Court, waiting anxiously for news. In their absence, the rest of London thronged the court. The hearing was held in Westminster Hall, surrounded by the charred ruins of Parliament, which had burned down dramatically in 1834. This was always a favoured destination for anyone wanting to witness the aristocracy brought low. That day it was so crowded that even gowned barristers failed to get in. Reporters for every newspaper were there, including Charles Dickens for the *Morning Chronicle*. The following February, Dickens would write an exuberantly satirical parody of the case, bringing out all its cheap spectacle. Setting the scene of the courtroom, he described the 'numerous muster of gentlemen in wigs' in the barristers' seats, and the crew of lawyers moving around restlessly before the trial began, 'chatting and discussing the news of the day in the most unfeeling manner possible – just as if no trial at all were coming on'.[26]

This was one of the strangest, most horrible days of Caroline's life. She was in the uncanny quietness of Hampton Court while a lurid image of her was brought into synthetic life in the courtroom and newspapers. The newspapers generally sided with Melbourne and Caroline, wanting George Norton to fail. But they were also fully convinced of her guilt, and had no need to pretend to a stance of innocent until proven guilty. Cartoons proliferated showing Norton as a horned goat and Caroline as a shepherdess tending to her beloved lamb (Melbourne's family name was Lamb). Caroline was known by *The Satirist* as 'the unblushing one'. [27]

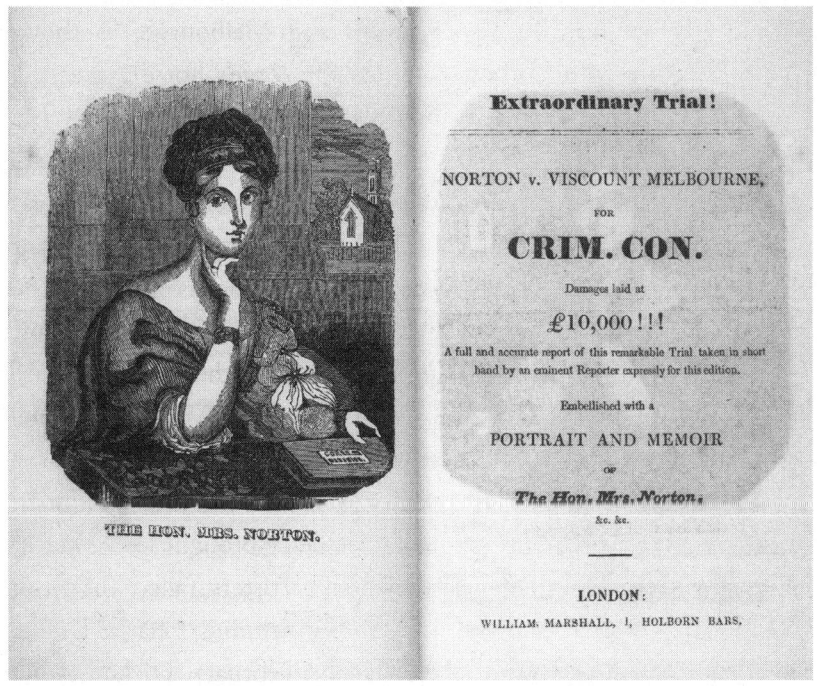

Extraordinary Trial! Norton v. Viscount Melbourne

Caroline went through this without Melbourne. He was the man she relied on for the kind of shared understanding that other people find in marriage; he was the man who had got her into this mess; but he was not there for her, and had not been since George removed her boys in March. It's impossible to know for certain if the two were lovers during the years of his daily visits. Many of Caroline's letters read like love letters; after the trial she would tell him that she believed 'no one, young or old, ever loved another better than I have loved you'. But during Caroline's pregnancy with William, the two joked in their notes to each other that Melbourne would eventually marry the baby daughter she hoped to have – this would have been in appalling taste if it had been Melbourne's child. What took place during these years may have been some kind of physical intimacy short of penetrative sex; not technically adultery, but enough of a love affair for Caroline to depend on Melbourne now. Yet he stayed away, sending his advice in bland and pallid letters. Brace yourself. Put up with his behaviour for the sake of staying married. He'd already been involved in one accusation of 'criminal conversation' and his deceased wife had been a known adulterer. It would be so bad for him as prime minister to have another scandal that some thought that the whole court case was the brainchild of George Norton's Tory MP brother, wanting to bring down the Whigs. For Melbourne, winning the case meant staying away from Caroline, but his coldness went further than that. Panic seems to have numbed his feelings; or perhaps he really did come to dislike the woman who'd transfixed him a few months earlier.[28]

'The fault is in <u>me</u> – I do not <u>attach</u> people,' Caroline reflected in one of her unanswered letters to Melbourne, a couple of weeks before the case. There was a sad truth in this. She may have just chosen the wrong men to attach to. Or she may have been too much for men in general: too open in her feelings, too full of her own personality, too determined to make a mark on the world. It was what she and her mother feared all along: she was too witty and self-possessed to inspire men with a desire to protect her. At twenty-seven, she didn't have the inner resources to withstand abandonment on this scale, especially as the people who really were attached to her – her children – were kept away.[29]

Messengers brought Caroline news from the trial. The judge was Sir Nicholas Conyngham Tindal, the Chief Justice of Common Pleas, a former Tory MP and lawyer known for his erudition and his sympathy for underdogs: he had successfully defended Queen Caroline against King George IV's accusations of adultery in

1820, and would successfully campaign to introduce insanity and self-defence as mitigating factors in murder cases. There was also a jury of twelve men. George's counsel was Sir William Follett, another Tory MP-cum-judge who urged the jury to consider whether Melbourne had merely pretended to be a 'benefactor, a patron and a friend' to Norton, and went on to claim that the blinds were drawn during Melbourne's visits and that Caroline had once been discovered by the servants 'lying on the floor, her clothes in a position to expose her person'. He produced letters from Melbourne saying innocuous things like: 'How are you?' and 'I will call . . . about half past four, or, if you wish it, later', claiming that there was 'something in the style even of these trivial notes to lead at least to something like suspicion'. Dickens, delighted by the absurdity, parodied it in *The Pickwick Papers*, where the corpulent, red-faced barrister, Sarjeant Buzfuz claims that a letter saying: 'Dear Mrs B – Chops and tomato sauce. Yours *Pickwick*' is a 'sly, covert, underhand' communication, intended to delude anyone who comes across it.[30]

Witnesses were summoned to corroborate Caroline's iniquity. George Norton's friends, including a man called George Derby, who stressed that Caroline was 'remarkably fond of her children . . . and was an excellent mother in every way'; and various servants. The housemaid Eliza Gibson described Caroline rouging her cheeks and tidying her 'dishevelled appearance and tumbled hair' between bouts of lovemaking. John Fluke, a coachman who'd been sacked for drunkenness, claimed to have once seen 'as far up as the thick part of the thigh', encountering Caroline lying on the rug with Melbourne. It was easy for Sir John Campbell, Melbourne's counsel, to dismantle Fluke, who played to the gallery, admitting his own drunkenness on each of the occasions he'd recounted. In Dickens's later parody, witnesses proliferate talking more and more about themselves and less and less about the case, with their evidence amounting only to occasional admissions that Pickwick has called Mrs Bardwell a 'good creature' and suchlike.[31]

The jury found Melbourne not guilty. Shortly before midnight, the court closed, and a couple of hours later Caroline heard the news. Her first thought was for her children, glad they wouldn't have to grow up with their mother's name blackened. But the truth was that her name had been blackened, and she was slowly taking in what this meant. In the blank, unhappy days afterwards, she used all her old determination to attempt to resurrect her life, while half-understanding that the court case had been a moment of rupture after which nothing could be the same again.

For Caroline and for so many since, the effect of a court case is to make our habitual world feel somehow unreal, and to leave us alienated from language because words have been weaponised against us. In the aftermath of my own case, I came to distrust words. Hearing the words of the barrister and of the judge in my head all the time, I wanted to eliminate language, so I sank into the wordless world I could inhabit with my two-year-old daughter. Caroline Norton couldn't do this – her two-year-old son was kept away from her. She was left isolated and uprooted; her only form of communication was letters, and so she wrote pleading, disbelieving, repetitive letters, circling round the lies and betrayals and confronting the vision of herself that had been brought into being in the press.

She was a woman who painted her face; a woman brazen enough to rise, dishevelled from her lover's embraces to order dinner from the servants. It didn't matter that these stories had been discredited. These words now had an existence of their own. The characters in her own books sometimes felt more real to her than the people around her – more real to her readers than the people around them. The same was going to be true of the version of Caroline Norton crudely delineated in the newspaper and in the souvenir pamphlet published after the case. She was horrified especially by the maid's accusations and wrote to friends contradicting these: 'The girl <u>Eliza Gibson</u> deposes that every day, or <u>generally</u> every day, during the months of July August & September 1833, I was occupied <u>painting</u>

& sinning – In that August my youngest child was born, and during that September I was on the sofa!'³²

She wrote this in a letter to Mary Shelley, who became her main confidante during this period, and remained her closest friend until Mary's death. It's a sign of Caroline's ultimate talent for survival that she knew, at this moment when she felt abandoned by most friends, that Mary was a woman with a large and tragic enough vision of the world to support her.

Mary was ten years older, and had told Trelawny in 1835 that she had never seen a woman she thought as fascinating as Caroline. 'Had I been a man I should certainly have fallen in love with her, as a woman, ten years ago, I should have been spellbound,' she wrote, disarmed by her 'eloquent colour which ebbed and flowed' and fine eyes. Caroline had been receptive to Mary from the start, and curious about her new friend's dramatic past. Mary had eloped with Shelley aged sixteen and lived an exiled life made up of strange mixtures of frantic excitement and day-to-day grimness with his circle of poets. She had been part of the Romantic experiment with new kinds of life and love and sensibility that Caroline, in more modest ways, was taking inspiration from. Caroline was impressed by Mary's own writing – her 1818 *Frankenstein* was arguably the most electrically powerful novel of these pre-Victorian decades – and by her lineage. Her father, William Godwin, had fuelled Caroline's own dreams of revolution with his *Caleb Williams*, while her mother, Mary Wollstonecraft, had stated decisively in her epochal *A Vindication of the Rights of Woman* that though women were 'convenient slaves', slavery degraded both the master and 'the abject dependent'. Caroline hadn't expressed herself in these terms before, but now in this letter to Mary Shelley, she went on to express feminist outrage at the whole legal situation of women: 'A woman is made a helpless wretch by these laws of men – or she would be allowed a defence, a counsel, in such an hour.'³³

Legally, Caroline was in a peculiar limbo. Melbourne had won her case on her behalf, but that didn't lead either to a restoration of her marriage or a divorce. Both Caroline and George now wanted rid of each other but having lost his case, he couldn't divorce her on grounds of adultery, and her willing return from their 1835 separation meant that she'd already 'condoned' his cruelty (any sign that a spouse had condoned bad behaviour would, ludicrously, continue to make divorce impossible for the rest of the century). Painfully, she wriggled against the snare like a trapped fox, finding that the wire held her however she turned. George was now doubly humiliated: he'd announced himself to the world as a cuckold, yet failed to win the court case that functioned as a kind of duel. He was not going to relinquish his children and lose his chance to continue and compound his wife's misery. Yet she wrote a plaintive, hopeful letter, asking for the chance to care for her younger boys.

> It is my earnest wish to pursue the plans intended for this year before these deplorable events; – to place the eldest at Mr W's (sharing such portion of his holidays as suits you), and to keep the two younger ones under my own eye. In conforming to this plan you best consult the welfare of the children, which is our mutual object. The little one is too young to leave its mother, and the impediment in Brinsley's speech makes me anxious to teach him myself.

She assured her husband of the truth she had painfully discovered: she understood that they were primarily his children: 'I merely wish to have these few first years of their lives at my disposal, seeing that much of their future well-being, whether as regards the exercise of their talents or the guidance of their dispositions, <u>must</u> depend on a mother's care and instruction of their infancy.'[34]

Caroline Norton half forgot who she was dealing with here, and assumed a reasonableness she had little reason to expect. Or perhaps she merely imputed this reasonableness to him in the hope of flattering him into acting the part of a reasonable man. 'I took great pains with Fletcher,' she said, reminding him how well-educated and intelligent he was for his age and assuming that George would therefore not deny the other boys these advantages or deprive her of the chance to fulfil her great duty in life; 'and of the affection of those little beings, to whom the agony of their birth, and the anxiety for their future, makes every mother think her claim so strong.' She promised she would not forget 'that it is of your children I have the charge'. It's unthinkable that she would have said this a year earlier. If George had set out to subdue her, he had succeeded. Unfortunately, he'd acquired a taste for it. He continued to withhold them, triumphing in the sheer fact of his rights: 'Whether access or not, and the quantum of it, shall be entirely within my own breast in all future time to determine.' All future time! He laid his claims on the future she had once looked into so confidently.[35]

Day after day, Caroline imagined her boys' bewilderment. Had they stopped asking for their mother or did they continue to ask futilely? It was summer now and the sun shone imperviously, turning the grass in the parks from green to yellow. London stank, as always at this time of year, with sewage rotting in the overflowing privies shared by whole streets in the slums, and rising from the River Thames. Caroline could have gone to Dorset but she knew that her boys were in London so she took to lurking in Storey's Gate, seeking pockets of shadow in the lurid August sun outside the home she'd once taken for granted. One day she managed to follow, when their nursemaid took them around the corner to Birdcage Walk, home of the royal aviaries, and into St James's Park. There she revealed herself, wretched and fearful – it was possible that George would have convinced them with his lies. But Fletcher rushed over when he saw her and handed her a crumpled letter he'd been saving in his pocket. Caroline told the seven-year-old boy what had happened, begging him to remember her. 'He was so dear and listened so attentively to everything I said to him,' she told Edward Ellice. 'I know he will never forget me . . . Let them do all they can about the children, I will undo in two hours what they shall have laboured to do for ten years.' She didn't manage to see them again like this. George agreed to one encounter, supervised by his lawyer, but it ended before she had the chance to relax into being with them. Presumably Fletcher did remember her; perhaps he had another note ready, in case she managed to come upon them. But they were moved yet again – it was so long since they'd been able to settle anywhere – this time to Scotland to live with George's sister. Caroline was frightened. The Nortons were an old-fashioned family who believed in corporal punishment for children, as so many of their class did.[36]

In 1831, in one of her flirtatious tussles with Melbourne, Caroline had questioned his enthusiasm for whipping children. He may have benefited from it, she said (indeed, he was rumoured to incorporate it in his sex life), but other children did not. 'I can recollect no single instance in which I was subdued by harshness and I think it is a general mistake, governing children by "force of arms" which restrains the weakest only till their strength & yours are nearly on a par.' She stood by this view but her husband and his relatives did not. She heard that during this stay, five-year-old Brinsley had been chastised by being stripped naked, tied to a bedpost and beaten with a riding whip. It was clear that Norton's custody was going to involve his seeing little of the children himself while subjecting them to the coldest forms of nineteenth-century fatherhood. This was a man driven to despotism by extremes of confusion and rage, engaged in the kind of parenting likely to create another generation of despotic men in turn. One of the worst aspects of losing custody is the resulting fear that your child is going to grow up more and more like the other parent. The knowledge that you'll have the chance to see them again when they're older is little comfort when you fear that by then they will be a person wholly other than the one who they'd have become with you.[37]

IV. Campaign

*'The whole and sole claim rests with him,
who has slept while she watched'*

Caroline was broken by the events of 1836. She could never again be that vibrant, unabashed young woman. George Norton had lost the case, but she'd lost her children, the man she had come to rely on, her income (absurdly, George remained entitled to the money she'd made from her writing) and her home. Even her clothes belonged to him, and he repeatedly threatened to sell or burn them. She was hardly welcome anywhere. She'd been too set on her own impetuous course to see this coming, but during these years, the subservience of women had become more entrenched. She can't have been surprised to find herself disliked – that was the wager, when she kicked Melbourne's hat around at parties. But she was surprised to discover how much it mattered.

She was often ill now, and found herself spitting blood. She worried she was going to die of consumption, as her father had done. 'My father was as strong a man as I was a woman,' she wrote, with sad anger to Melbourne, who was hardly in touch; '& yet he died after the same sort of accident – I hope I shall go too – & so relieve you of your fears of committing yourself by too kind a correspondence with me.' She feared death, and she feared madness. It's likely that she would have read *Maria, or the Wrongs of Woman*, Mary Wollstonecraft's posthumously published novella about a woman who is locked up in a lunatic asylum after her husband tires of her, and spends her days yearning for her baby. The danger here is that Wollstonecraft's heroine really will go mad, bullied into inhabiting the version of herself her husband foists on her.[38]

Maria escapes, and Caroline was going to as well. There was some uncertainty, in the months after the court case, about what kind of person she would be now that her life was shadowed by loss and failure. But it turned out that her courage hadn't just been youthful bravado. The autumn of 1836 brought about a transformation that I find astonishing now, and that the people around her must have been astonished by then. She had been condemned in court for being too independent and too publicly shameless. Rather than retreating into a more private incarnation of herself, she doubled down on becoming an even more outrageous kind of public figure: a campaigner. She was going to fight to entitle married women to custody of their children, committing with careful gentility to the women's movement.

'It is an unjust law which makes a mother's claim so vague!' Caroline had written to Mary Shelley in April. 'I do think if ever there was a hard and unjust law, it is that which enables a man to take such young children from the care & superintandence [sic] of their Mother,' she wrote to her novelist friend Catherine Gore in October 1836. 'My boys are <u>three, five</u> & <u>seven</u> years of age[.] at such a time they are only fit for the guardianship of a woman and it is surely hard that the man can take them from the woman who bore them, & loves them better than all the world, and give them to the care of any other woman he pleases.'[39]

Caroline allied herself with a movement for the rights of women that already had a lot of momentum, though not among upper-class women. When she had marched with the Tolpuddle Martyrs, she may have been the only 'lady of fashion', but she had marched alongside plenty of working-class women who had been active in the trade unions for decades. A rising number of political radicals were also feminists (though they didn't yet use the term, thinking of themselves instead as part of the 'Women's Rights Movement'): William Thompson and his collaborator Anna Wheeler, Robert Owen and his follower Frances Morrison, Richard Carlile and his lover Eliza Sharples (a self-styled 'General') were all actively campaigning for a change in the marriage laws and for larger rights (including the right to vote) for women. 'A contract implies the voluntary assent of both the contracting parties,' Thompson and

Wheeler wrote in their *Appeal to One Half of the Human Race, Women, Against the Pretensions of the Other Half, Men* in 1825. 'Have women been consulted as to the terms of this pretended contract?' Caroline didn't think of herself as part of the larger Women's Rights Movement. But it was precisely the secrecy of the terms of the marriage contract that she was objecting to.[40]

Caroline's pamphlet was entitled *Observations on the Natural Claim of the Mother to the Custody of her Infant Children as Affected by the Common Law Right of the Father*, and was intended to ignite a campaign to change the law. This was Caroline Norton at her best: emotive, passionate, but also smart, witty and irrefutably logical; prepared to play rhetorical games with men. She began with the absurd distinction between legitimate and illegitimate children, complaining that married men had excessive power that they exercised with vengeance and cruelty. She went on to give brief, evocative accounts of the key cases in the preceding decades, and ended with a passionate repudiation of the current situation. A separating husband was angry and often 'eager to avenge his real or fancied injuries'. Could it really be that such a man was given 'despotic power', while the woman, 'however wronged, however innocent', was not even allowed to appeal in court against 'the tyrant which oppresses her'. Against the laws of men, she set the laws of nature, committing to the natural ties between mothers and their babies that the conduct books and magazines liked to celebrate. A woman endured the 'tedious suffering' of pregnancy and then 'from her own bosom' nourished her child. 'Does *nature* say that the woman who has watched patiently through the very many feverish and anxious nights which occur even in the healthiest infancy, has no claim to the children she has tended? And that the whole and sole claim rests with him, who has slept while she watched.' She insisted – in ways some women's rights campaigners avoided, worrying about playing into the hands of the patriarchy – on the feminine capacity for care. 'The daily tenderness, the watchful care, the thousand officers of love, which infancy requires, cannot be supplied by *any* father, however vigilant or affectionate.' In a clever rhetorical move, she reminded her readers how quickly they would castigate women who voluntarily withdrew from their children. 'Would not the mothers (*even though* THE FATHER *remained in charge of his offspring*) be stigmatised as monsters?' Why, then, should women be forced into this monstrous position?[41]

She was fighting, and revealing to herself that she was going to be capable of fighting even when broken by George. But the exhausting grief of those months comes through in the pamphlet's closing description of the anguish suffered by mothers destined to 'dreary silence' day after day. So much of looking after children is about the hourly rituals and routines of their days, and Caroline Norton powerfully describes here the bitterness of each of those hours in their absence. There's the hour, day after day, when she would normally be putting her children to bed. And there are the nights of fitful sleep that follow, 'disturbed by the indistinct, yet heavy consciousness of sorrow'.[42]

By December she was ready to send the book to John Murray, her new publisher, telling him she saw its publication as 'a necessity'. There were people in her family, her mother among them, who disapproved of women writing pamphlets. To publish it would be to announce herself as 'unblushing' as much as her intimacy with Melbourne had done. But she had already lost her reputation, so she was not writing this book as a lady – no longer writing as an eighteenth-century debonair wit or Romantic woman poet. She understood that a different, more political kind of writerly identity might be needed. The pamphlet suited her as a form because it was direct but also modest in its literary claims. And she knew that she had the future on her side, knew that the laws that made her suffer would soon be seen as an ill-fated past mistake, even if independent women were going to continue to be punished through their children by vindictive husbands.[43]

Worried about being sued for libel, Murray only published the pamphlet for private circulation and Caroline Norton sent it to friends and MPs. It was brave of her to publish this under her real name, at a time when hardly any women of her class were standing up for the rights of women. It's evident throughout the pamphlet that she's constantly having to decide whether to be as rhetorically persuasive as she can or to get her message across in a more coded, meticulous way. She was charming and cajoling rather than lambasting, and this meant that she didn't make feminist claims for women as people with equal rights to men, instead making more conventional claims for women simply as needing better male protection.

This was easy for her because she had always seen herself as needing just this protection. Though she was brought up in a robustly matriarchal household, she was surely seeking a father figure when she identified Melbourne as a man to love (a few years later, the young Queen Victoria would choose the same man to advise her on a daily basis). 'You ought to come down and protect me', Caroline wrote in a letter to George in 1831, complaining about sleeping alone. She was trying to seduce him with her need of him, but this was indeed where she thought he'd failed her; not by being too patriarchal but by not being protectively patriarchal enough. Now, six years later in her pamphlet, she wrote that there was much talk of protecting the child from ill usage, 'but is there no way of protecting the *mother?*' She insisted that no one could read about these cases without 'admitting the necessity of some such alteration in that law, as shall afford a reasonable protection to the weak and helpless of the other sex'. And in asking for protection, she was prepared to say that there were women too morally transgressive to be allowed to look after their children. She was not able or not willing to allow adulterous mothers to join the fight alongside her, though in the hands of a different jury she might by now have joined their ranks. These women had already 'balanced the affection and society of her children' against other kinds of pleasure, she wrote.[44]

Did she have to insist on the female need for protection? It can feel, reading about the Victorians, that they were all benighted, and that we would have all somehow done better. But there were plenty of otherwise rational and generous men and women failing to challenge the status quo. They valued stability, and thought that marriage made society stable. It's possible that Caroline was genuinely torn, and thought one thing when with Melbourne and another with Mary Shelley.

Most judges and lawmakers of the time – Melbourne among them – believed that marriage relied on unity. Husband and wife could not have separate wills, so had to have only one, and it made sense for this to be the man's, given he was stronger, more worldly, and less consumed by pregnancy and childbirth. Hence single women (including unmarried mothers) were allowed relatively more freedom and rights than men, albeit without the social prestige of married women. Arguably, they were wrong; arguably, life is more stable when it's flexible and polyphonous than when it's rigidly linear.

But Caroline Norton was the kind of feminist, common among her generation and not uncommon since, who cared more about practicality than principle when it came to the rights of women. So she may not have been especially preoccupied with the rights and wrongs of these debates. She didn't need women to be acknowledged equal as some of the so-called 'Petticoat Reformers' gathered around the socialist Robert Owen did; she just wanted to be given the chance to get on with her life in ways that presumed a de facto equality, as she always had.

At any rate, the pamphlet worked. By February 1837 she could inform Mary Shelley that the MP Thomas Talfourd was giving notice in the Commons of a motion to change the law to allow women to be granted rights of access to children under seven (hardly a very radical demand). Talfourd was a poet and playwright-cum-lawyer who had been on Melbourne's defence team during the trial; he had also acted for the adulterous Greenhill in his successful attempt to wrest custody of his three small daughters from his wife, and had felt uncomfortable fighting to implement a law he regarded to be unjust. Caroline knew Mary would be pleased, for the sake of women, 'whom you have not the "clever woman's affectation" of thinking inferior to men', and of Caroline herself – she had the chance of seeing at least two of her boys.[45]

While Caroline waited to find out the fate of Talfourd's bill, George dangled the children before her, promising they would be brought from Scotland to live with her, only to fail to bring them on the appointed day. 'I am hungry for the children,' she wrote to him, and she meant it, but her desperation spurred him to further cruelty. This is the desperation of Emily Westmeath and Henrietta Greenhill: a desperation engendered by the terrible, whimsical imperviousness of the law.[46]

When they met, George lectured her, insisting that, as Caroline reported to Melbourne in their intermittent correspondence, 'his principal objection to giving me the boys was the dread of opposing God, who had made him the humble instrument of sobering one of the lightest & most thoughtless hearts in the world, which he trusted grief & disappointment would eventually bring round to the Throne of Grace'. Presumably what George actually said was less hyperbolic and it's possible that these were genuine sentiments. Men of this era were told that they were responsible for the moral and godly character of their families. It was their task to keep the characters of their wives and children steady.[47]

Meanwhile, William and Brinsley were both ill in Scotland, and Caroline worried that George's sister wasn't sending for the doctor. But in June 1837, George finally brought the boys to London and for a while, Caroline and her sons were able to see each other every day. The boys were seven, five and three now and it had been over a year since they'd seen her for more than a few minutes. Had they talked about her often in her absence? Certainly, they would have been subjected daily in stories, prayers and lesson books to the idea of the perfect mother, and must have thought of their own mother sadly at such moments. Now, faced with the reality of the 29-year-old woman who they may have remembered as more exuberant than she now appeared, did ideal and actual motherhood come comfortably together? There was probably simulated gaiety all round, but out of such simulations, real experience can emerge.

She found them well, except five-year-old Brin, who was anxious and, she thought, dangerously thin – she also worried that he was 'growing crooked'. 'They were very happy at returning, but cannot understand going away in the evening,' Caroline told Melbourne. There was a lot of sadness for her in these encounters: sadness at missing the taken-for-grantedness that is itself a characteristic of motherhood; sadness because she felt she still missed a child: the 'sharp talkative' three-year-old William didn't resemble her 'fat fair baby', and she had missed that crucial year when he'd changed from creaturely bundle to child; and a rueful sadness that her oldest and youngest sons talked incessantly about the sixpences in their purses – George, who had brought them to see her with the chief object of gaining a financial settlement, was bringing them up to care excessively about money.[48]

There was talk about Caroline going with the boys to the seaside, but then everything changed. After only a few days, George suddenly sent them to his brother's house just as the debate scheduled for Talfourd's bill was cancelled because William IV had died and the eighteen-year-old Queen Victoria ascended the throne, suspending Parliament. For a few months, Caroline's life had had a new frenetic energy because of the political campaign; for a few days, she'd had the promise of a life that included her boys. Now she was left with an empty house and an empty year. It's not surprising that she became frantic.

She went to Guildford and attempted to abduct the boys. She found them in the garden and carried Brin to the gate but couldn't open it; servants appeared and snatched him back. She can't have expected it to work, but she wasn't strategising rationally. She had always acted for effect, always found satisfaction in the sheer bravado of a bold action. And she was close to despair, so perhaps there was a satisfaction in enacting her own desperation. Passivity itself is gruelling when you are someone who is active by nature; George must have known this and known that these months of waiting and uncertainty had been the most effective way to punish her for living more fully and happily than he had during the years of their marriage. Now, if only for a few hours, she was acting wilfully again.

Afterwards, she responded bitterly to those with agency. She was angry with Melbourne, who she believed had a duty to continue to see her, and this anger became political anger with the Whigs, who she felt were fast losing the credibility and glamour they'd had in her father's and grandfather's day. Their majority narrowed in the July 1837 election, and she accused them of being complacent and lazy. Trauma and unhappiness always took bodily forms for her, and she was suffering from gynaecological complaints and panic attacks. One not obviously well-meaning friend said she was so sorry about Caroline's altered looks that she 'prayed to the Lord to take you'. She got through another arduous autumn and winter without her boys, and then Talfourd's bill was read again; this draft more bravely gave women the right to custody of children under seven, and access to older children. The debates took place in a Parliament as makeshift as Caroline's current life. The House of Commons was camping out in a rackety corner of the old Palace of Westminster while they waited for their new home to be built.[49]

This was the first legislation brought into Parliament on behalf of women – not an auspicious fact. The bill was opposed by a faction led by Edward Sugden, the self-taught barber's son who had opposed the Reform Bill and seemed determined to prevent anyone else overcoming the limitations of their birth as he had done. He condemned Talfourd's bill as 'directly immoral, antichristian', and claimed that it actively encouraged women to separate from their husbands, opening 'a door to divorces and to every species of immorality'. For Sugden's supporters, the whole future of society was at stake: immorality and revolution waited outside in the ruins like the fire they had recently escaped. Nonetheless, Taulford got it through, with a robust vote of 91 to 18. Caroline's confidence had been justified so far. The House of Lords was always going to be more of a challenge, though, and what made its opposition most frustrating was that it was led by Lord Brougham, a former Lord Chancellor who was famous for supporting electoral reform and calling for the abolition of slavery. In Brougham's shallow reasoning, women had so many legal hardships that there was no point mitigating these. And he worried that the 'one thing which more than another tended to protect the sanctity of the marriage vow' was 'the love and affection which women bore to their children'.[50]

Caroline despaired, hearing news of Brougham's complaints. If it was voted out, she would have to wait a whole year to try again – a year when her children would become less familiar month by month. The Lords voted the bill down, by 11 to 9. This was a small proportion of the House (a vote on prison reform in August got 65 votes in total); the others stayed away, perhaps overwhelmed by the disjunction created by their fear of encouraging divorce and their conviction that children did indeed need their mothers. If only Earl Grey had carried through his 1832 threat to pack the House of Lords with reforming peers, Caroline would have an easier time now. 'It makes me smile to hear the same men who cry out against our New Poor law, on the plea of its separation of families, defend to the utmost this one most bitter separation,' she wrote to Lord Brougham, regretting that he had cast his vote in support of 'gross oppression & injustice to persons in a helpless position'.[51]

After another long year, Caroline and Talfourd could try again. She was now circulating her new pamphlet *A Plain Letter to the Lord Chancellor on the Infant Custody Bill* – published under the pseudonym 'Pearce Stevenson', though it must have been obvious to her friends when she circulated this 'letter by a friend of mine' that she had written it herself. This time, she added the sad story of the Norton marriage, describing George's violence and sudden withdrawal of the children and the indignity of the trial. She distanced herself explicitly from feminist campaigners such as Eliza Sharples and Frances Morrison. The Custody Bill had been connected, she wrote in her new, masculine guise, with 'the ill-advised public attempts on the part of a few women, to assert their "equality" with men; and the strange and laughable political meetings (sanctioned by a *chair woman*), which have taken place in one or two instances'.[52]

Caroline would have considered herself fully up to the task of chairing a political meeting. But this distancing wasn't just expedient, and wasn't just because she was pretending to be a man. Her whole argument was predicated on a view of women as 'natural' caregivers, and she believed passionately that she'd have been able to care for her children better than George was doing. Feminism, then as now, was painfully divided on motherhood. Feminists like Eliza Sharples ventured everything on women being just the same as men, and therefore entitled to an equal education. It was hard to make this compatible with Caroline's argument about women's superior capacity for care. The political landscape wasn't – still isn't! – conducive to the kind of nuance needed to develop a sophisticated argument about how women can be both emancipated and caring. Instead it was men who set the terms of the argument, which pushed campaigners either into idealising motherhood as the apotheosis of womanhood or insisting on contemporary Victorian manhood as the model that all rational and capable beings needed to follow. Caroline didn't especially mind distancing herself from feminism, because she saw these women as humourless, badly dressed bluestockings who she couldn't conceive as friends. Over the next decades, upper-class rebels and middle- and working-class reformers would come together, but for now Caroline felt no compunction in rather cruelly laughing away their cause.

She urged Talfourd to be optimistic: 'Do not believe that if you can send it up with a good majority from the Commons it will again be thrown out in the Lords.' She had gathered more promises of support. This wasn't just blithe optimism about her ability to charm the world into changing; every year of failure made her more realistic. The bill was passed and on 17 August 1839 Queen Victoria gave Royal Assent to the Custody of Infants Act, the first piece of feminist legislation ever passed in England. It marked the beginning of a century-long fight for the rights of mothers and, crucially, the rights of children to maternal care. Caroline Norton had used all her powers as a writer and lobbyist to carry this through.[53]

The fact that feminist change was wrought under the star of an 'Angel in the House' vision of womanhood would come to plague and punish women in the century that followed. In the meantime, Caroline Norton doubled down on her vision of beatific motherhood. She published a poem, 'The Dream', and sent it with a special tribute to Queen Victoria. Her poetry was always more forced than her prose, and this reads as a kind of play-acting of the self-sacrificing, caring mother who the law had been changed to help:

> Sweet is the image of the brooding dove! –
> Holy as Heaven a mother's tender love!
> The love of many prayers and many tears,
> Which changes not with dim declining years, –
> The *only* love which on this teeming earth
> Asks no return from Passion's wayward birth;
> The only love that, with a touch divine,
> Displaces from the heart's most secret shrine
> The idol SELF.

Caroline may have hazarded everything on brilliance and courage once more, but there was no danger her readers would regard her as a wit.[54]

V. Aftermath

'There is justice to be had'

Again, she had won, but again she didn't know what the winning amounted to. She had revealed herself to be more powerful than any other wronged mother of her day. But still, the balance of power in their never-ending marriage was with George.

She wrote to him with new confidence. William was now six and the others were no longer of so-called 'tender age', but she had the right to petition for access if not custody. 'I would far rather receive permission from <u>you</u> to see them, than obtain it under the authority of a court,' she stated, with the plea now barely concealing a threat. George had an answer – he always did. The children were in Scotland, so he insisted they were outside the jurisdiction of the new Act. Her lawyers told her she still had a case. 'The law presses a little hard on women,' she told George, 'but there is justice to be had; do not drive me to seek it, but let me owe it to you <u>at last</u>.'[55]

In June 1840 Caroline was presented to the queen at court. She'd wanted this for some time – she hated feeling ostracised – but afterwards she told Mary Shelley that though she had enjoyed it, 'the petty successes so valued while one is very young & eager & vain, fade into vapour afterwards'. She was only thirty-two; in other circumstances she might have had plenty of enthusiasm for petty success. But the flighty young woman, dallying with several great men a day, really had turned out to be defined most of all by her feelings as a mother. This was the truth of her poem for the young queen; love had indeed displaced 'the idol SELF' from her heart's most secret shrine.[56]

The terrible mismatch between George and Caroline in these years was a mismatch of feeling. George seems to have viewed his children as endlessly robust. Therefore, he could change tactics month after month, wheedling his way free of any trap his wife set. What

I find most painful about all of this is that George seems always to be preoccupied with punishing her, rather than thinking about the boys, whereas I think there was a genuinely selfless aspect to Caroline's desire for them. Not that we ever are fully selfless; it's more that her selfishness took the form of desiring selflessly to devote herself to the children.

Meanwhile, the years passed, and soon they wouldn't need her anyway; she accepted that they should be sent to boarding school at eight or nine. 'I fret less,' she told Mary. 'I struggle less but I also hope less. What in fact is any thing worth in this life, if the strongest of all ties is made the one means of poisonous discomfort? I have not seen the boys and I dare say the summer will slip by without my doing so, now I have allowed that shuffling man to put off so much time.'[57]

George stopped her from taking the case to Chancery, refusing to contribute to the boys' education if she did so. Perhaps he was right on this occasion. They had tested their family in court once already and had all been damaged by it, pushed into positions more adversarial than when they had begun. A law case, as they had seen, has its own momentum.

This was the era when it was first becoming clear quite how cruel the vilification involved in a court case was when it came to family law. No family can fully withstand the appalling pressure and disturbance brought on them by the adversarial nature of the courts, even if it may be clarifying for the law at large, as the common law tradition relies on finding out what the law means case by case. Their society – and ours in turn – could not resolve its difficulties without recourse to law, but the law courts exacerbated the difficulties.

Perhaps Caroline understood this, because she gave up her legal threats and instead just pleaded with George to let her have William for six months before he started school: 'I have seen nothing of him since he was a mere baby, and I am quite able to continue his lessons without any master.' She wanted them to go to Eton, but George sent them to Buckland's at Laleham, Surrey, which frightened her because of its reputation for severe discipline. And then in September 1842 tragedy struck.[58]

The boys were in West Yorkshire, at Kettlethorpe Hall, George's family estate. George was away and they were left to play on their own with the oldest, Fletcher, doing his best to supervise the younger boys. Willie, now nine, went out riding alone and fell off his pony on Saturday 10 September, injuring his arm. There was no one to care for him except an old woman, the gamekeeper's wife. She took the boys to Chapel Thorpe Hall, a house nearby, where the owner was also away but there were more servants to help. They tried to care for his arm, but he got blood-poisoning. George returned the next day with some other guests and did his best belatedly for his son, but Willie deteriorated rapidly. A message was sent to Caroline in Tunbridge Wells. She rushed to the station and managed to get a series of overnight trains to Yorkshire, where she was met by Lady Kelly, a guest at Kettlethorpe Hall who Caroline hadn't met before.

'I am here,' Caroline said. 'Is my boy better?'

'No, he is not better. He is dead.'[59]

At the house, Caroline was finally reunited with her two older sons. Sobbing, they told her what had happened, and told her that Willie had died praying and asking for his mother.

Caroline blamed George entirely for his death. 'The accident would not have happened if they had the commonest attendance, granted to gentlemen's sons,' she wrote to her sister. People could say that it was God's will, but on those grounds they would never call a doctor. 'He died – because he was too young to rough it alone – as he was obliged to do.' She wished that a quarter of the sum lavished now on his purple and silver coffin could have been paid to a servant to look after him while he was alive.[60]

In the days after Willie's death, Fletcher pleaded with her not to blame his father for what had happened and gave his mother Willie's Bible. Perhaps Fletcher's concern for his father does suggest some real emotional relationship between father and son, which George may have helped to engender. At any rate, Caroline was comforted by her son's kindness – 'I never saw so dear & gentle a disposition' – and reassured that George seemed now to want her to be close to her elder boys. In her letter to her sister, she wrote that she believed 'I <u>should</u> be thankful it is neither of the others – I believe it <u>would</u> have been worse to bear – if it had pleased God to take either of them.' She didn't elaborate, but perhaps she felt that William was the child she knew least, and she seems to have thought that he had more fortitude in the face of suffering than the others. 'He was such a patient little creature – even I, who saw so little of him, saw that, & praised him for it,' she told her mother. The doctor said he had rarely seen as much courage or patience in a young child.[61]

The change in the custody laws had come too late for Caroline and for William. Change had begun, but it would become clear that it was riddled with contradictions, predicated on models of womanhood urgently in need of critique. And already it was evident that as the family was put on a higher and higher pedestal, the forms of family life that made their way to the courts were ever less coherent, and the legal system was ever less equipped to help. No child was going to emerge from a court case unscathed, any more than their parents were. This was true even when the mothers won – it would be true for George Sand. For her part, Caroline consoled herself with the hope of meeting her youngest son in another life: 'He prayed – & died without fear: so young as he was, I can feel that he is in Heaven – I saw little enough of him in this life – God grant I may meet him in another!'[62]

2

GEORGE SAND

July 1836. Caroline Norton's name has just been cleared in court and she is writing letter after futile letter, pleading for her children. George Sand is where we last saw her, racing, pushing her sweaty, soggy body along the riverbank, and plunging again into the Indre.

This is the same river where in adolescence Sand once launched downstream on a cherished horse, succumbing to the lure of drowning. She still yearns for oblivion, tempted to turn each immersion into eternity. But she lives on for the children she's fighting for – beloved bodies she's nursed painstakingly through fevers and held on her lap as she's taught them to read. Maurice, Solange. Her children. Instead of drowning herself she covers one more mile of the yellow-green meadows under the pulsing sun. And then she prays. 'There is a way to pray. Praying is an important and difficult thing,' she informs Marie d'Agoult – another aristocratic woman living separated from her husband and writing under a male pseudonym.[1]

George Sand is the triumphant heroine of this book: a woman who, in a century where she had no rights, managed to gain custody at three separate court cases. But this is a woman forged by suffering, who brought suffering to her children in turn. And this is a tragedy, like every other custody case.

CUSTODY

I. Beginnings

'Promise not to sell me'

Her life began with questions of custody, though there were no lawyers involved. Her mother had sold her to her grandmother, as her great-grandmother had sold her grandmother to a cousin. Children were passed around, as in the fairy tales Aurore – as she was then known – would grow up reading. Isn't 'Rapunzel' a custody story, at heart; and 'Rumpelstiltskin'? But it was only as the turbulent century came into its own that these family battles were decided by judges.

In 1789, as church towers had been toppled by revolutionaries, the world of priests had become a world of lawyers. A group of intellectuals tried to make a society from first principles; with his Civil Code, Napoleon initiated governance built on legal rules. The new rituals were the rituals of the courtroom and George Sand, who fused the energy of Romanticism and revolution and the iconoclastic intelligence of the Enlightenment, became a test case for parenthood in the new era. She was a woman at the forefront of change, prepared to redefine what being a woman was; she was also a mother, responsible for the vulnerable bodies of others. Hers would become the custody case of her era, and in the background were a set of custody decisions made before most people saw custody as a win-or-lose legal issue.

When George Sand's father, Captain Maurice Dupin, great-grandson of the King of Poland, married Sophie-Victoire Delaborde, a former prostitute, he knew he was creating an embattled future for his children. This was an emotionally incestuous family in a culture preoccupied with incest, and Dupin's mother was fanatically jealous of her son's lover. So they were estranged until his baby – black-eyed Aurore Dupin – was presented to the grandmother, whose name she shared, in a scene Sand later wrote up as a fairy tale. The concierge of her building was persuaded to claim the crying infant as her own granddaughter until Mme Dupin recognised the dark eyes and snatched the child. As the cries subsided, the older Aurore Dupin declared the bloodlines clear, slipped the large ruby ring from her finger and placed it into the tiny infant's hand. The older and the younger Mme Dupins now fought for the affection of the little girl and when Maurice died in 1808 this became a fight for custody.

Aurore was four when her father died. They had just buried her baby brother, burying him twice because Sophie-Victoire couldn't believe he was dead and sent her husband to dig him up. His death was especially appalling because she felt guilty about his illness. Heavily pregnant, she'd agreed to take three-year-old Aurore on a hazardous journey through the Pyrenees to Spain, to visit Maurice on the battlefield where he was serving with Napoleon's armies. The baby was born there and, although he was weak and probably blind, they set out on the long return journey to France when he was just a couple of weeks old, because the French were retreating from Spain. They slept in the carriage in oppressive heat as villages burned around them and cannons boomed. Aurore and her baby brother contracted scabies and rarely had enough to eat or drink. Back home at Nohant, he became colder and colder and then died.

Now Maurice, loyal to the whims and terrors of his beautiful wife, did as instructed, and brought the tiny boy to his mother for one final bath and a peaceful sleep in his cradle in their bedroom. The next day they buried him again in secret under a pear tree. They spent five September days creating a magical garden around the tree, with a miniature knoll that Aurore could climb up; Aurore and her older (illegitimate) half-brother Hippolyte cavorted around their father, riding on the wheelbarrow as he went to collect more earth. It was a bucolic idyll with a corpse at its heart.

This all happened at Nohant, the small, unostentatious chateau that Marie-Aurore Dupin had bought during the French Revolution, wanting to retreat from Paris and trusting that as a revolutionary and an illegitimate daughter she was exempt from the hatred of the aristocracy. The house was nestled in an unprepossessing valley in the Berri region, in the middle of France. Across the fields, there was the river Indre, which connected Nohant to La Châtre, the small city on a hill that Sand found remarkable 'for the quantity of very intelligent and educated people numbered among its population' – many of them Maurice's friends, and hers in turn. Maurice and his mother loved the countryside all the more because it wasn't particularly beautiful, and soon Maurice's daughter would celebrate 'the furrows of dark, rich land, the great round walnut trees, the little shady paths, the untidy thickets' that surrounded her.²

Chateau de Nohant

A week after his baby son's death, Maurice accepted an invitation to dinner in La Châtre, galloping five miles on the wild horse he'd been given by the Spanish in his last military campaign. On the way home, he rode so recklessly that the horse hit a pile of rubble in the dark and threw him off.

'When my Papa is finished with being dead, he'll come back to see you,' Aurore later recalled saying to her distraught mother.[3]

Eventually she understood that he was not coming back, and that she was in danger of losing her adored mother too. Maurice's mother was prepared to pay for the education of her granddaughter and make her heir of Nohant. But there were conditions. She was to be weaned off her mother and never to see her sister Caroline, Sophie-Victoire's older illegitimate daughter, who Maurice had been prepared to bring up as his child. This was a cruelly harsh bargain offered by a woman whose childhood had been blighted by a similar arrangement – aged two, she had been removed from her own actress mother and given to her father's niece.

Sophie-Victoire had two children to support and no way of earning a living. Her passion for her daughter was visceral and mammalian, but she was prepared to give her up.

'Promise not to give me away to my grandmother for money,' the little girl pleaded.[4]

Sophie-Victoire exchanged custody for an allowance. But the four-year-old girl defied them both by adoring her mother and becoming ill when separated from her. Each time her mother visited her at Nohant, she would climb into her bed, feeling the comfort of 'a baby bird nestling in its mother's bosom'. Each time, she was pulled away.[5]

She missed her mother's easy affection and cuddles – she had to address her grandmother in the third person ('Will dear grandmama permit me to go into the garden?') and to deport herself well. She missed her sister Caroline too. Once, Caroline came to visit Aurore at her grandmother's apartment in Paris and was turned away. Aurore heard what she'd later describe in her autobiography as 'a stifled but heartrending sob' from outside the gates. The younger sister was put to bed, where she moaned and sighed all night. The next day, her grandmother bought her a doll she had craved in a shop window. At first, she was joyful, cradling the doll 'like a young mother holds her newborn'. Then memories of the previous night made her feel perfidious, so she threw the doll across the room. Now it was the innocent doll who suffered, lying helplessly smiling on the floor. The girl grabbed the doll back and soaked her with guilty tears, 'abandoning myself to an illusion of maternal love which further vividly intensified my aggrieved feelings of filial love', in an extraordinary prefiguring of her later experiences as a mother. As always during periods of intense feeling, Aurore became ill: the sobs giving way to vomiting and fever.[6]

What does it do to you to love an absent mother this much? The unmet needs would shape the rest of her life. In adulthood, George Sand would be a woman tied just about securely into the generations of her family who filled the history books and graveyard at Nohant, yet entirely alone, making her life from first principles, and trusting fully in no one. Meanwhile there was the bond with her mother that was coiled so tight by the custody situation that it became unbearable. 'I felt myself physically and morally attached to my mother by a chain of diamond hardness that my grandmother sought in vain to break but that only kept tightening around my chest, to the point of suffocation.'[7]

The solution proposed by her grandmother – a solution George Sand would later propose for her own wilful and uneasy daughter, and which was the usual recourse for the French upper classes at this time – was a convent. Marie-Aurore had been sent to a convent at the age of two. She had kept her granddaughter at home for a lot longer, but now, aged thirteen, Aurore was sent away for two years. During this time, she would become self-reliant, make friendships that could take the place of family bonds, and develop an intense commitment to reading that would sustain and sometimes derange her in the years to come. By the time she emerged from the convent, she was weaned from her mother and ready to learn what she could from her grandmother, whose love of books she now shared. She also identified more and more with her dead father – to the point that she could write in her autobiography, in all seriousness, that she was an exact reflection of the man she'd last seen aged four, and was sure that if she'd been a boy and born in the same year as him, 'I would have acted and felt in all things like my father.'[8]

Her grandmother allowed her greater freedom now, less fearful of her granddaughter's bluestocking and 'tomboy' sides. Aurore galloped across the Berri countryside with Hippolyte, sitting astride her horse in boys' clothes. This was the custom for girls here, but Aurore was unusual in passing as a young man. And she read through the night: reading her grandmother's beloved Voltaire and Rousseau; reading Chateaubriand and renouncing the dogmatic, self-flagellatory religious faith she'd adopted at the convent in favour of a more life-embracing spirituality; reading Montaigne, Shakespeare, Molière and Byron and taking snuff so she could stay up ever later to read more. She had a tutor now, Deschartes, who had also been her father's tutor, and for a while she felt secure in relation to the various adults who had taken it upon themselves to care for her – until she confronted the question of marriage.

II. Union

'Marriage is beautiful for lovers and useful for saints'

Her grandmother wanted to settle seventeen-year-old Aurore's engagement before she died. She feared that otherwise Aurore would become subject to Sophie-Victoire's whims. Various unappealing suitors were summoned, and one proposed on condition that she refused to associate with her mother. She said no. She rode out on horseback, gasping for breath in a world that seemed determined to constrain her. Longing suddenly to drown herself, she drove her horse into the Indre. Spluttering back to life, she learnt from her tutor that her father had suffered from the same deathly urges. And then it became clear that her grandmother was dying. Aurore's days became a vigil, reading to the old woman, who took in less and less, until death sliced through her life again. She lay beside the bony corpse and pressed her lips to the face. Almost as grief-stricken as his pupil, her tutor came to her in the night with a plan. Her father's grave in the garden cemetery had been opened up in preparation for the new corpse. This was her chance to embrace him as an adult for the first and only time. 'Are you brave? Don't you think the dead deserve a service even more tender than prayers and tears?'[9]

And so – the stuff less of fairy tales than of horror stories – a night-time visit to the graveyard on a snowy night, slipping as she skid across the ice, and a descent into the grave, watched over by her macabre tutor. There she found her father's skeleton intact, though the head had come away. She lifted the head and kissed it. Her childhood was over.

What should we make of this extraordinary scene? As George Sand, Aurore Dupin's life would unfold as a series of stories. She could seem determined to make narratives out of her life. But in fact her life tilted into narrative patterns from the start, as it did here. It's not a coincidence that this era saw the frenzied birth of the realist novel; the period lent itself to narrative, because as one revolution followed another, and poverty turned into wealth and back again, lives changed so rapidly, proliferating possibilities of self-reinvention. Novels on the scale of Hugo's or Stendhal's were required to make sense of them.

George Sand would inhabit the institutions of modernity: courtrooms, political debating chambers, grand salons where those of humble and noble origin could mingle. Yet it's fitting that her life also included the macabre and the gothic. Courtrooms and graveyards neighbour each other, and in a life as intense as Sand's, this comes to the surface. If the gothic became a favoured form of these tumultuous years, it wasn't only because people were looking back. The gothic was peculiarly suited to the demonic ambitions of the modern. Mary Shelley had seen this in *Frankenstein*, and Sand would make use of it in the underground tomb scenes in *Consuelo* – a historical novel, published from 1842, which was bent on uncovering the roots of modernity. Sand embodied the modern precisely because she could climb into a tomb and embrace her long-dead father's corpse; she had every genre of experience at her disposal and could move freely between the intellectual and the domestic, the gothic and the sublime.

The deceased grandmother had been right about her younger namesake. This was a mother who'd claimed too little from her daughter and now claimed too much. Sophie-Victoire felt threatened by books and forbade Aurore from reading. She was annoyed that she seemed to care little about her appearance and wasn't more vain. How was she going to find a husband? The only way to escape her mother's petulance was through marriage, but they hardly met any new men. Then Aurore was invited to stay with friends of her father's – the Roëttiers – a couple she liked so much that she took to calling them mother and father and to thinking of herself as another of their five daughters (who all dressed as boys because Père Roëttier was sad not to have a son).

Here, suitors presented themselves, but the man she liked best was another surrogate child of the Roëttiers. They could be more like brother and sister; they could ride around on horseback and tease each other. She wrote excitedly to Hippolyte that she had 'a friend here whom I like a good deal, with whom I run and jump and laugh, as with you'. They took to describing each other as husband and wife. It was a joke, but it stuck. There was no courtship, no mention of love or desire – indeed, he assured her that he found her 'neither beautiful nor pretty' and was impressed instead by her 'good and sensible manner'. But by the summer of 1822, eighteen-year-old

Aurore was engaged to twenty-seven-year-old Sublieutenant Casimir Dudevant. When Sophie-Victoire tried to oppose the match (she thought he wasn't handsome enough), it pushed Aurore further into his arms. Sophie-Victoire did insist, to Aurore's distaste, on a prenuptial settlement that Aurore would be grateful for a decade later.[10]

Marriage. She was pregnant almost immediately. They were back at Nohant and it was freezing. Birds were dying of hunger in the snow, so Aurore, whose maternal grandfather had been a bird-seller, took the birds into her bedroom and tied fir branches to her bedposts to make them feel at home. She lay in bed while chaffinches, robins and sparrows ate out of her hands and warmed themselves at her knees. 'You cannot conceive of the pleasure one experiences, feeling your child stirring within your being,' she wrote to a friend from her convent days. But the happiness didn't include her husband. Casimir was always out hunting when she wanted to sit at home together and talk and read. 'In marrying, one of the two must renounce himself or herself completely,' she explained to her friend, 'abnegating not only their will, but even their opinion, in order to see through the eyes of the other, to enjoy what the other enjoys.' So who was this going to be – the wife or the husband? 'As it is the bearded party that is all-powerful, and in any case men are incapable of such commitment, it is necessarily incumbent on us to bend compliantly.'[11]

It was true. The bearded party was all powerful, in France as in England – this belief united conservatives and revolutionaries. 'Woman is made . . . to be in subjection to a man,' readers had been informed by the disputatious, stridently brilliant philosopher Jean-Jacques Rousseau in 1762, decades before the revolution that he inspired without living to see. 'The man should be strong and active; the woman should be weak and passive.' Denis Diderot, that passionately devoted father of a daughter, had called for improved education for girls, and during the revolutionary years, women had published treatises asking for the new era of equal rights to extend to them. 'Women have the right to mount the scaffold: they must have the same right to mount the tribune,' pleaded the low-born, high-reaching playwright and revolutionary Olympe de Gouges in her 1791 *Declaration of the Rights of Woman and of the Female Citizen*. But her views remained outliers and she was indeed to mount the scaffold in 1793; according to the press this was just punishment 'for having forgotten the virtues that belong to her sex'. The revolutionary laws did allow wives to divorce unfaithful husbands (radically, divorce was allowed even by mutual consent) and daughters to inherit (new inheritance laws enforced parity between all children). But the 1793 Constitution excluded women from universal suffrage along with children, the insane and the condemned.[12]

Over the next decades, it became clear that every form of progress was going to go hand in hand with atavism. These decades of modernisation were characterised by constant gyrations, because everyone disagreed on what modernity entailed. Feminists made progress, only to have their new rights almost arbitrarily revoked. In his 1804 Civil Code (still the basis of French law today), Napoleon excluded women from citizenship while guaranteeing equal rights for all citizens. Now there was no divorce by mutual consent and men could divorce wives on grounds of adultery, while wives could only divorce husbands if the concubine was resident in her home. Wives were treated punitively throughout the Civil Code. Married women couldn't manage property or sign a work contract, and only gained parental power when widowed. 'The husband owes protection to his wife, and the wife obedience to her husband,' stated Article 213, enshrining the patriarchal nature of marriage in the law. All this was taken further with the restoration of the monarchy in 1816: Catholicism was reinstated as the state religion, divorce abolished, and equality forgotten.

Aurore had to subdue her own tastes. Marriage guidance books proliferated, advising this. That same year, the 'Vicomtesse de G' published *The Art of Being Loved by One's Husband*, directing wives to be simple and honest and to fulfil their husband's every desire. A few years later Charles Chabot would subtitle his *Conjugal Grammar* with *General Principles through which Wives Can be Trained to be at Your Beck and Call and Rendered as Gentle as Lambs*, listing twelve commandments for wives, who were instructed to 'promptly obey' their husbands, 'shun coquetry and affectation', and be 'sweet, lovable and kind'.[13]

Even if Aurore wasn't prepared to follow this advice, Casimir had the right to control her. Nohant, her family home, was now his. He wanted to renovate the house and garden and didn't need her permission. Within months, she lost the sites of her childhood games and reveries.

Her new life was redeemed by motherhood. A child, Maurice, was born in Paris in June 1823. She breastfed him, following the example of her mother and grandmother, both adherents of Rousseau's calls for humanity to imitate nature.

It was expected that French upper-class women would devote more time to educating their offspring than their English counterparts. Mothers were required to train up the new personnel for the French bureaucratic republic. And with the birth rate falling more quickly than elsewhere in Europe, children were extravagantly idealised. The Napoleonic code called the family the 'nursery of the State' and a lot of revolutionaries happily endorsed this. Rousseau had pleaded for childhood to be drawn out and celebrated, which wasn't an available luxury for families living in poverty, but revolutionary intellectuals convinced themselves that idealising childhood furthered the people's cause. Jules Michelet, who pioneered new ways of writing French history through the lives of workers, extolled the child as 'the interpreter of the people'; the child, he claimed in his sometimes acute, sometimes misguided 1846 essay *The People*, was 'the people themselves, in their native truth, before they are deformed'. To avoid deformation, these precious children needed careful mothering. 'O the love of a mother! love that no one forgets!' intoned Victor Hugo. 'Perhaps there are no bad children without bad mothers,' Balzac's narrator observes pompously in *La Grenadière*. The eighteenth century had seen a new enthusiasm for loving, hands-on fathers, but now such fathers were satirised. An 1824 lithograph entitled *The Vicissitudes of Paternity*, probably by Frédéric Bouchot, shows a woman reading negligently while her angry and alarmed husband trundles around a clenched, squalling infant. It was good mothers who were extolled and contrasted with bad mothers, who neglected their children and took lovers.[14]

Aurore had a nursemaid to help, but she wasn't unusual in making herself responsible for every cough, tooth and tantrum. She was proud of her baby, but still solitary, as she reported to her schoolfriend – adding dutifully that it was hardly possible 'to believe oneself to be alone in the company of a husband whom one adores'. Claiming her husband as father and protector, while covertly probing the prevailing notion of ownership, she referred to Maurice as 'your child' in letters to Casimir. 'Your child is getting bigger and nicer every day,' she told him in August 1823. 'Your son is mad as the moon, he learns every day and has a new antic every hour,' she wrote a year later. It was easy to be affectionate when writing to her husband – 'I press you in my arms, I eat you, I adore you,' she assured him – but it was increasingly difficult in his presence. When Casimir felt angry, he didn't choose to hide it. One day Aurore was playing noisily with visiting children. He asked them to play more quietly, but Aurore didn't hear, so he strode across and slapped her cheek. She fled, humiliated, and would look back on this as a moment of rupture.[15]

They went to the Pyrenees, seeking healthy air for Aurore, whose unhappiness turned to ill health, and the similarly sickly Maurice. There she found the frenetic energy of her youth, leaping across precipices on horseback, and a new realism about marriage. 'Marriage is beautiful for lovers and useful for saints,' she wrote in her journal, but 'if love is no longer, or never was' a part of marriage, 'what remains is sacrifice'. There was no middle ground between the renunciation of saints and the 'comfortable stupor' of small-minded people who got through by blunting feeling. 'Ah, but there is a middle ground – it is despair.' She turned away from despair, she pulled back from the ravines – she fell in love. There was Aurélien de Sèze – a brilliant young conservative lawyer in the making; and there was the 'wildly courageous', rebelliously unmarried, 28-year-old Zoé LeRoy. With Zoé she discovered that all her thoughts could be shared; with Aurélien she discovered desire – anguished, chaste desire, all the sweeter for being unconsummated.[16]

Back at Nohant, she and Aurélien wrote tortured, passionate letters and Aurore wrote long letters to Zoé too, often about Aurélien. This was when she discovered herself to be someone who wanted to pen page after page, turning thoughts into words; eventually her collected letters would run to twenty-four volumes. When Casimir interrogated her, she confessed everything, but then in November 1825 she tried to incorporate him into the writerly selfhood she had discovered alongside Aurélien and Zoé. She wrote her husband a long letter, attempting to turn their marriage into something more profound: to be loving again, rather than saintly or small-minded.

She went back to their courtship. 'I was lively, mad, frivolous, apparently dazed, deep down I was serious, sad, horribly unhappy.' She'd play-acted the joyful young woman he'd wanted to see – but then she had to grow up. So many young women have done this, before and since, and men have fallen for them, perpetuating unsustainable models of femininity. It's the fault neither of the women nor the men – both have been told by their culture that this is how to be. My own husband's favourite adjective from our early years together, I remember, was 'cheery'. I took it as a compliment. By the time we both realised that I had no desire to be cheery, it was too late.[17]

Casimir liked to jump and laugh with her; at first, she appreciated this and didn't ask herself if he liked studying and reading as well – she was in the mood for self-abnegation, anyway. Then it became clear that he had treated her ideas as 'follies, as exalted and romantic feelings'. She became bored, but he didn't notice. 'My son was born,' she went on, claiming Maurice determinedly now as hers. 'Filled with joy I fed him,' but still she was bored. Then came Aurélien and Zoé – an exhilaration of happiness that was compatible with chastity. Now, she was prepared to give Aurélien up, and only to write him monthly letters that Casimir would be free to read (it was the writing itself she couldn't bear to give up, as much as the lover). She just asked that Casimir should read alongside her – books 'which are in your library and which you do not know' – so that they could share thoughts and pleasures. From now on, he would stop being angry with her, and if he lost his temper she would show she was hurt; and thus their estrangement would end.[18]

It didn't work – it couldn't. Though their world was changing so fast that no one knew quite what kind of a culture they inhabited, it was still the honour culture of the eighteenth century, and Casimir's honour had been wronged. It was all the more confusing that the affair with Aurélien was unconsummated. He'd grown up in a world where desire existed mainly outside marriage. He would reveal, soon enough, that he could put up with a wife's discreet affairs. But he'd married a woman committed to a new vision of companionable, loving marriage, and this brought its own humiliations. He was being told to improve his education if he wanted to retain his wife's interest.

A few years later, in *Valentine*, George Sand would satirise a husband who, faced with a wife burning almost to death in a passionate, chaste affair, talks to her as a fellow man of the world. This was the best Casimir could do. Aurore gave up her sexless love affair and found herself in a more sophisticated liaison with an old friend, Stéphane de Grandsagne, a gaunt, atheist scholar, who it's quite likely was the father of Solange – born in September 1828, 'as handsome as a cherub, white as a swan and meek as a lamb'. Aurore had lost her idealism and needed to stake out her territory. In 1829, angry about a business deal Casimir had conducted while drunk, she made her position clear: 'I am a mother first and this concerns my children.'[19]

She moved to Paris, leaving her children behind. On a bleak December day in 1830, she'd found an envelope in Casimir's desk 'to be opened only at my death'. Inside was a list of her faults. 'Curses for me and nothing else!' she told a young admirer from La Châtre, Jules Boucourain, who she'd asked, a little exploitatively, to tutor Maurice in her absence. 'He had collected therein all his impulses of temper and ill-humour against me, all his reflections respecting my *perverseness*.' Meanwhile Casimir had begun an affair with the maid of Hippolyte's wife.[20]

George Sand, portrait by Luigi Calamatta, 1837

She'd had enough. She was twenty-six, brilliant, beautiful in many moods and lights, trapped with an intellectually inferior man who castigated her as stupid. She loved her children, but she was often ill, often unbearably sad; she needed to find some other purpose in her life. She told Casimir that she was planning to alternate three-month stints alone in Paris with three-month stints at Nohant, assuring him she would take hardly any money. By costing him nothing, she'd be free. And she'd be obliged to earn a living, which was what she most wanted to do.[21]

The suddenness with which she formulated this vision of freedom is breathtaking. At twenty-six, she had come up with a new model of life as a wife and mother, claiming the right to reinvent herself on a vast scale. The confidence came from her family – from the father she idealised as courageous and free-thinking. She took on the self-assurance of her father and grandmother's world, while emptying her purse and rejecting the conventions governing upper-class behaviour. This is the fusion of Enlightenment and Romantic possibilities we saw in Caroline Norton, acted out on a larger scale because of the change and turmoil within French society. George Sand – as she would soon be known – had the free-thinking ease of the Enlightenment, without adhering to the full Enlightenment programme (though she was anti-clerical, her belief in God was unwavering); she had the Romantic capacity for self-invention and passion, without the alienation or egomania.

Paris in 1831 was convulsing with revolution after the king had been overthrown in July 1830. Charles X, who'd succeeded his brother Louis XVIII, had been unpopular for violating the constitution and going against his Chamber of Deputies (the French Parliament). His catastrophic mistake was to issue the July Ordinances, dissolving the chamber, radically suspending the liberty of the press (denounced as 'an instrument of disorder and sedition'), and diminishing the electorate. This prompted three days of fighting in the streets, ending with a new constitutional monarchy led by Louis Philippe of the

House of Orléans. The electorate was enlarged, censorship abolished, and tricolour flags draped across the Palais Royal. Paris became known as the 'New Jerusalem' because of the revolutions it sparked across Europe. Now the fighting on the streets continued as students, workers and disappointed revolutionaries protested the clericalism of the monarchy, the failure of the French regime to support revolution in Poland, and the introduction of machines in factories.[22]

In the evenings everyone – rich and poor – went to the theatre, which was still charged with the energy of the revolution it had helped ferment. Aurore Dudevant moved between plays and salons with a sense that her times mattered and she was finally at the centre of them. She'd left her grandmother's airy, aristocratic Paris, and moved to a small furnished apartment in the studenty Latin quarter, hunched between depleted aristocratic Faubourg Saint-Germain and the woebegone, overpopulated workers' district of the Faubourg Saint-Marceau.

There was a lover there, of course. She'd met the nineteen-year-old would-be writer Jules Sandeau in La Châtre and now began her first all-encompassing, happy love affair. She'd been so young when she married – eighteen; she hadn't known about the body's wants. Now, with the young man she often addressed as a son, she was discovering herself to be desirable and desiring. Sandeau later based a character in his novel *Marianna* on his lover, detailing 'the expressiveness of her eyes, at once burning and . . . throwing into relief some inner turmoil'.[23]

She didn't entirely forget about her actual son, or baby daughter. This new embodied version of her had been forged through the blood and milk of motherhood. If she knew herself to be capable of extremes of bodily love, she had learnt this in the nursery with her infant son. She missed her children now, and knew that she was causing them pain. Maurice was seven, and Solange two. She remembered her childhood separations from her mother as periods of devastating loneliness. Yet she was sure that she couldn't retain her health or sanity living alongside Casimir, and she couldn't separate from him without making a life for herself first. So she was able to tell herself in fairly good faith that she was doing this all for them.

'I should be most happy to see you dear child,' she wrote to Maurice after a month, 'but very sorry that you should be here now. People are quarrelling, murdering one another in the streets, pulling down the churches, and beating drums all night.' It's a painful letter to imagine Maurice reading, but it was true. The previous day demonstrators had marched on the archbishop's palace, pillaging and wrecking it. To the tutor Jules Boucourain, who she addressed as yet another son, she wrote long letters issuing instructions on how to bring up Maurice ('do not spoil him, and yet do your best to make him happy') and how to navigate Casimir's strictness ('you should affect to adhere to all he may say to you . . . being fickle in his ideas, he does not care whether his advice be followed or not'). It was upsetting getting a letter from her brother informing her that her son was miserable. 'Your son is the best thing you ever produced,' he told her after two months; 'he loves you more than anybody in the world. Take care not to impair that feeling.' But she was rightly suspicious of her brother, whose loyalty was ultimately to her husband.[24]

She had decided to become a writer, turning the graphomania she'd discovered with Aurélien to financial gain, and seeing where it might lead her. 'Oh yes, I suffer from being separated from my children,' she wrote to Boucourain. 'But it's not about lamenting; one more month and I will hold them in my arms. Until then I must work at my "enterprise".'[25]

Her enterprise was literature and she didn't care in what form it came. She was contented with journalism, and the newspaper industry was charged with energy now censorship was abolished. It helped that she was a true democrat – she believed that the power of the people would win out in the end and trusted them to behave wisely – so she thought that popular taste was worth catering for.

And in Paris, the people read: only a fifth of the population here were illiterate (the average elsewhere in France and across Europe was about a half) and English visitors were amazed to see flower-sellers reading on pavements. 'The French read with avidity whenever they can snatch the opportunity,' observed a visiting English captain. 'They read standing in the open air . . . They read at one end of a counter when a person is hammering a lock or a piece of cabinet work at the other without taking their eye from the book.' There would be 200,000 subscribers to Paris newspapers by 1848, out of a population of about a million.[26]

She began by writing for *Figaro*, a satirical newspaper, and soon was the only woman on their staff, tramping the streets in search of stories. This was easy because she'd begun to wear men's clothes – dressing like a student with a thick grey jacket, a wide wool tie, and heavy boots. 'With those little iron heels, I felt secure on the sidewalks,' she later wrote in her autobiography, mythologising this moment of self-realisation. She could sit cheaply in the pit at the theatre because no one noticed her. She was no longer a lady and had not become a gentleman. 'I was jostled on the sidewalk like a thing that got in the way of busy passers-by' – an 'atom lost in the immense crowd', driven by a sense of her own destiny to be 'morally and artistically free' and to earn her '*pain quotidien*'.[27]

The mingling of bohemianism and aristocracy in Paris allowed her to invent a new kind of life. The aristocrats in her circle defied convention to pursue extreme forms of libertinism and sensuality, and the youthful bohemians and reformers subsisted under rafters, making art and writing pamphlets – fighting for the equality the revolution had failed to achieve. She slipped between these worlds, interested in attending neither the orgies of the aristocrats nor the meetings of the reformers.

The most popular reformers were a group of early socialists who styled themselves Saint-Simonians, in allegiance to the deracinated late-eighteenth-century aristocrat Henri de Saint-Simon, who had called for a reordering of society based on Christ's injunctions to love your neighbour and help the poor. After Saint-Simon's death in 1825, a charismatic banker called Prosper Enfantin set himself up as a Saint-Simonian messiah, leading church-inspired services and demanding a programme of collectivism, internationalism and the abolition of private property.

By 1831, Saint-Simonianism was becoming a focal point for French feminism; women spoke at their meetings and Enfantin advocated new, feminine forms of governance. It was here that the most progressive ideas about sexuality and marriage were found, though soon some female followers would break away, demanding fuller equality. Sand was sympathetic to Enfantin's ideas but avoided getting closely involved. She wanted to go to the theatre, to write through the night, and to wake up in the afternoon in the arms of her lover-son. She shared Enfantin's disregard of convention but feared that in joining a sect, she'd get tangled in new proprieties.

As a woman writer, she needed to defy convention because book deals were made and contracts negotiated amid the lime trees in the courtyard of the Palais Royal, the palace of the Orléans monarchy. This quadrangle, lined with arcades of shops on three floors, was the meeting point of many kinds of world-building and destruction. It was an important site of the 1789 revolution: it was here the radicals had made revolutionary speeches and subsequently paraded heads on spikes. Now those combinations of idealism, hedonism and recklessness had found new, opulent forms. It was the home, amid its unusually bright lights, of the city's most enticing brothels, cafés and gambling rooms, and of its luxury shops and publishing houses. Here you could buy an elegant watch, or opt for a pair of gold and pearl-set pistols firing perfume instead of bullets, or indeed buy an actual pistol; or you could flick through the latest novels or pamphlets in the booksellers, or sell your poems to an avaricious publisher, crossing paths with bare-breasted women selling other wares. There were risks involved for Sand, coming here – and it was a place that clarified the risks involved in writing at all: she too was laying bare the body and its desires, and she knew that however necessary this was, she risked harming her children if she failed.

In April 1831 she returned to Nohant, where the reunion with her children was painfully ecstatic. 'I am very happy,' she told a friend in La Châtre. 'I kiss them from morning to night. That's all I can tell you about myself. I have been deprived of them for so long that I am like an imbecile in my happiness at finding them again. I don't know if there is anything on earth other than Maurice and Solange.' At Nohant, she took in the extremity of the gains and losses in her new life. It was clear how much she needed her children and how much she needed the Parisian life she now pined for. She wrote to Emile Regnault, a medical student – who seems, like everyone in her circle at this time, to have been more than half in love with her – that though the countryside surrounding her was beautiful, with lilacs puffing their perfume into her bedroom and nightingales singing under her window, she was dreaming of vaporous evenings in Paris, of pink clouds giving their sheen to the roofs.[28]

For a few years, she would always long for the place she wasn't in. She was cross with Regnault, who asked why she couldn't just come straight away. Couldn't he see that she was struggling? 'Would you love me so much if I could be rightly reproached for being a bad mother? If I didn't love my children?' And she was cross with her own mother, who disapproved of her daughter's new metropolitan freedom and, as ever, misunderstood her. It wasn't society or performances that she needed, she told her, but freedom. 'The freedom to think and to act is my primary need.' This was partly the irritability of guilt. She knew she was hurting her children with her absences; Jules Boucairain and the maids were hardly mother substitutes. 'I really feel the courage to bear the deprivation of my children,' she told Regnault; 'what hurts me, what tears me apart is the idea of the grief they may feel.' It was all the more aggravating to be reminded of this grief by the mother who had allowed herself to be separated from her daughter and left her fearful of family ties. 'Our home is a model of a home,' she informed her sardonically; her husband kept mistresses or didn't, as he pleased (Claire, the maid, was now pregnant with his child), spent money or didn't – it was only right 'that the great freedom enjoyed by my husband should be reciprocal; were it not so, he would become odious and contemptible in my eyes'.[29]

She departed once more for Paris full of sad delight at young Maurice's kindness. He'd been ill, and when he woke in the night and found her watching over him, he was 'tormented, sick as he was, to see me worried and deprived of sleep'. Away from him, she was anxious about his health, writing to urge him to run and jump around the garden, rather than staying in the same place – that was the way to avoid getting ill again. In Paris, she found a new flat with Sandeau on the fifth floor by the river, where they spent days looking at each other 'in this perfect state of imbecility that does not even allow speech', and looking out over the Seine from their bed. She began a salon where she was gratified to receive Balzac, and styled herself 'J. Sand', a temporary pseudonym she shared with Sandeau, with whom she was writing a novel.[30]

Another departure that was also a return: Nohant, in January 1832, was full of children – friends' children joined hers racing around the house and she organised games of blind man's bluff and shuttlecock. 'My big daughter is as beautiful as a rose and always hanging around my neck or clinging to my hands', she wrote to Regnault. She attempted to write a letter to her mother while Maurice jumped on her back and Solange climbed on her knees. Then she became ill once more, frightened by her own lack of breath, pining for Sandeau. Through all of this she wrote: pages and pages every day, setting the pace for the rest of her writing life. She'd started her first proper novel, *Indiana*, about an unhappily married woman, her controlling husband, her risibly Don-Juan like lover and the cousin she's loved since childhood.[31]

She wrote her way out of her marriage. Nohant had meant home to her for decades but now didn't. Casimir made her feel like an unwelcome visitor, forbidding the servants from following her instructions and accusing her of madness and immorality. So she had to find a way to make her new life in Paris include motherhood. As a child she had thrown that doll across the room and then covered her pretend baby in guilty kisses. She had understood the ties of love by stretching them thin and then feeling herself caught as they pinged back. She may have been right: being a parent is ultimately a process of giving up custody as the child ages, so you can practise by nourishing your child's freedom. But acting out the push and pull of love made her sicken now as it did then, and she half-knew how bad it was for her children.

So she decided to take Solange to Paris. They would be a little family, she told Regnault, who she styled both as her own son and as her daughter's fiancé, warning him that one of Solange's 'sweetest pastimes is to ride on the backs of her lovers and snatch their sideburns'. It might be difficult to write, but 'the happiness, the gaiety, the health' of Solange were her most important 'work'; if her daughter wilted in her absence, she'd regret it more than anything. She couldn't take Maurice – her husband got to make the decisions about him – but soon he would go to boarding school in Paris.[32]

Her time with Solange in Paris may have been the happiest period she spent with her daughter. The city was still in chaos. There was cholera, covering the Pont Neuf with corpses and patients on stretchers, and leaving the city smelling of the chlorine used to disinfect the houses of the dead. And there were more protests, with rioters blaming the unpopular king for poisoning the wells with cholera. She assured her three-year-old that the shooting under their window was a comedy staged for their benefit, and when Aurore got sick she wrote home blithely to Casimir that she'd had 'a small attack' of cholera, which she'd surmounted with tea and woollen blankets. Meanwhile she taught her daughter to read, earlier than she'd managed with Maurice, and the child played alongside her every morning while she finished her novel. In the afternoons, they explored the gardens of Paris and made the acquaintance of the elephants and giraffes in the Jardin des Plantes. 'She eats enough for six, and goes to sleep in the omnibus,' Aurore wrote to Maurice, appealing to his shared pride in his sister and assuring him that they talked about him all the time: 'She wakes up on alighting, and walks alone without grumbling. It is impossible for any child to be better. I am very glad to have her with me. If you also were here, my dear boy, I should be perfectly happy.'[33]

This was the spring she became George Sand, publishing *Indiana* in May 1832 under her new, sole pseudonym to astonishing overnight acclaim. The novel was the hit of the year – the hit of the decade. 'You have never witnessed a more penetrating analysis, a more exquisite dissection . . . of the human heart,' wrote a reviewer in *L'Artiste*. It delighted the world so much that it left Victor Hugo insecure. Reading it described as 'the finest novel of manners that has been published in French for twenty years', he published a counter-attack. 'What about mine, then?' he asked. 'Do you take *Notre Dame de Paris* to be a whore?' Aurore Dudevant had become George Sand, a woman with a man's name and influence – from now on it was the name that her friends and soon even her children would call her. 'In Paris Madame Dudevant is dead. But George Sand is known as a lively fellow,' she wrote to a friend. This was a transformation she underwent with her daughter by her side. It was possible to be both an emancipated woman and a mother.[34]

Indiana, and her next novel *Valentine*, both written in frenetic bursts over a few months, are novels where Sand is furious about marriage and the power it gives husbands, but also curiously determined to present her heroines as chaste adherents of convention. Both heroines are terrified of desire in ways that few grown-up women in Sand's social circle felt the need to be. She was writing for money, so perhaps she thought only chaste novels could sell.

But perhaps too she wanted an idealised version of herself to exist – the meek, charming woman her grandmother sent her to the convent to become. It can be easy to forget how compelled she always was by the desire to comply as well as the desire to protest.

Unexpectedly, there's a striking sympathy towards husbands, in *Indiana* especially. Looking at Indiana, the narrator says, beside her old husband, 'like a flower of yesterday that had bloomed in a gothic vase', you would pity her, but would pity the husband even more. Marriage becomes as constricting for husbands required to perform versions of protection that transmute into versions of control as for the wives unhappy in their obedience. Sand rejected any notion that she was a Saint-Simonian at this time. She didn't identify with the feminists who were becoming more articulate around her, but she was showing with her writing what was wrong with the position of married women, and showing with her life that another kind of life was possible.[35]

Despite her interest in illuminating the world she lived in, Sand's endings would always be idealistic, with her lovers tied more indissolubly than anyone she'd encountered in life. Balzac wrote a review of *Indiana* praising Sand for her realism: 'Here is a book in which truth takes its stand against the fantastic.' But in conversation, he told her that she was an idealist while he was a realist. She wrote characters as she wanted them to be, where he wrote them as they were. In fact it was precisely Sand's combination of realism and idealism that allowed for the complexity of her depiction of marriage. The protagonist Indiana's predicament is horribly realistic and she comes to recognise the unfairness of her situation and to lay claim on the freedom of her spirit. 'I know that I am the slave and you the master,' she tells her husband. 'The laws of this country make you my master . . . but you cannot command my will, monsieur; God alone can bend it and subdue it.' But what separated Sand from the stricter realists was that she didn't want to settle for the world as it was; instead she was fundamentally a romantic who wanted to bring another, better world into being in her fiction, and to offer it as an ideal for readers – perhaps as a call for radical change. So Indiana tells herself that: 'A day will come when everything in my life will be changed.' For Sand, this was something between compensation for the grim present and a call to arms.[36]

Things moved fast. By July 1833 Sand had published *Lélia*, the book that thrilled and scandalised French society ('If you have a daughter, a tender flower whom you want to protect from the breath of vice,' then send her away while you read this book, warned one review) and gained such a huge reputation internationally that by 1834 Caroline Norton was signing herself 'Lélia' in letters. Sand wanted to write about women who protested and women who complied, and she found a unique solution here. She split the narrative between the tyrannically chaste Lélia and her courtesan sister Pulchérie, and staged a dialogue where they compare the virtues of their lives. 'Unlike you, I haven't lived with deceptions,' Pulchérie tells her sister; 'I haven't demanded more of life than it could give me . . . to face shame is my virtue, as it is yours to avoid it.' For Pulchérie, sexual freedom is a way to reach beyond the pettiness of received opinion, obeying the dictates of God rather than society.[37]

Sand's own reputation was based more on Pulchérie than on Lélia. This was unhelpful for Maurice, who now started boarding school in Paris. He and Sand had remained as close as before, despite her absences, even sharing a bed on her trips back to Nohant. Now he was so unhappy at school that during his days off in Sand's apartment he wept instead of eating dinner, fearfully counting the remaining hours. There was very little Sand could do about this situation: boarding school was the conventional way of educating upper-class men of their day and Casimir would not have agreed to remove him, even if Sand had suggested it.

The affair with Sandeau ended and there were new lovers. There was a passionate, consuming friendship with the actor Marie Dorval that it seems very likely was sexual ('You are the only woman that

I love, Marie – the only one that I contemplate with admiration and astonishment'), and certainly appeared so to titillated acquaintances. And there was the era-defining affair with the libertine and sickly poet Alfred de Musset, who identified himself peculiarly with Stenio, the Don Juan of *Lélia*. In December 1833, she accompanied Musset to Italy. She'd been suffering from rheumatism all winter and hoped the warmer climate might help, but she was also ready for another adventure, still in search of freedom. This adventure wasn't going to include her children: Solange was dispatched back to Nohant with her maid; Maurice would spend his free weekends with Sand's mother.[38]

By February, Musset was dangerously ill, and she was so fed up with his feverish rage that she transferred her affections to the Venetian doctor who was helping to save his life. Her marriage rolled on unsteadily in the background, with Casimir asserting himself by making vague threats to send Solange to boarding school and by trying to turn the children against her. 'Do the same as me and tell [Maurice] what I told him,' she begged Casimir, 'that he must love us equally, because we are his two best friends.' She pleaded with him not to send Solange to school until she returned in April, insisting that the girl was still too young. Casimir acquiesced and – this was not her finest hour as a mother – Sand decided to stay longer in Venice, telling friends that she had to wait out Musset's recovery.[39]

She did miss her children, as always, but it's striking that she was sometimes more preoccupied by her own extravagant feelings than by the needs and feelings of the children themselves. 'I'm sad not to have my daughter with me,' she told Musset in May. 'What is this love that mothers have? It's still a mystery to me. Care and worries a hundred times sharper than in the love of a lover and yet less joy and transport in the possession. Absence which isn't felt for the first few days and which becomes cruel and burning like a fever the longer it goes on.' Maurice hadn't written to her for over a month at this point, perhaps punishing her for her protracted absence. She wrote apologetically but a little callously to him, telling him that she woke up crying from dreams where she was holding her children in her arms, but she couldn't yet leave Italy: 'I don't do what I want, and when you're older, I'll tell you all the reasons that forced me to leave you often and to stay away from you for many months.' He was lucky, she told him, that he didn't feel the sorrow of their parting as much as she did. Once she'd acknowledged that her absences pained the children as much as they pained her; now she seems to have refused to acknowledge that Maurice's silence might have been a response to precisely that sorrow.[40]

In the children's absence, she proliferated family as always, insisting to Musset after she'd left him for his doctor that she loved the doctor as a father and that Musset was their child. There is something odd about her need to produce surrogate children all around her, even as she separated herself from her actual children, and something striking about her casual enthusiasm for conceptualising her life in such incestuous terms. She seems to have been drenched in her need of family, but also distrustful of it, so surrogate families provided a safer alternative. And these were decades in France when a remarkable number of writers wrote about incest, inspired by Chateaubriand's 1802 novella *René* and drawn to the particular possibilities of transgression within a wild travesty of conformity that incestuous relationships involve.[41]

She missed her house as well as her children. Nohant was still as much a family as a house for her, with her father and grandmother awaiting her in the garden cemetery. Returning from Italy, she agreed to send Solange to a small boarding school in the autumn and became determined to reclaim Nohant for the school holidays, without having to hide away from Casimir's petty rages. They drew up a separation agreement, where she gave him more than half her income in return for the house and the children. But Casimir immediately became disgruntled and she knew the agreement had no legal standing. 'Marriage allowed him this right,' she later wrote; 'under our laws, the husband is master, and the master is never obliged toward the one who is master of nothing.'[42]

The crisis came in October 1835 when Casimir criticised Maurice, and Sand responded by defending him. She sent her son to wait for her in her room. Casimir was sure he'd heard her say 'your father doesn't know what he's saying', so threatened to hit her. She cried out, and their friend, the older married lawyer Alexis Duteil, seized Casimir, who persisted in trying to hit his wife, throwing himself around wildly until he escaped and seized a gun, shouting: 'You'll see what I'm going to do to you.' Duteil disarmed him and Sand retreated. She could no longer live alongside her husband.[43]

III. Fissure

'I shall recover my freedom and dignity'

She spent a day with the children, deciding what to do. She drove them to the woods herself in a dilapidated cabriolet. Maurice helped unhitch the little horse and they picnicked in the shade of old oaks, looking out onto the valley, where the heather glowed in the autumn sun. For Sand, as for Wordsworth, the oaks and heather seem to have been a sign of the resilience of a nature figured more as tenacious than transcendent. And the children were energetic, enthusiastic – it reminded her of her happiest days with her own mother.

They returned at nightfall and the next day she consulted friends, who advised her to seek a legal separation. If her husband didn't challenge it, she'd get a decision by default, hopefully based on their informal separation agreement, and she'd be spared the publicity of a full hearing.

Luckily her latest suitor was one of the most eloquent lawyers of his generation. Louis-Chrysostome Michel was a militant republican who she'd met that spring, when he was involved in a highly publicised case defending 121 workers for conspiring and provoking disturbances. She fell in love with this powerful, though ailing man, struck by the extraordinary shape of his head (it seemed to her that he had two skulls soldered together, which she saw as an entwining of soul and intellect) and by his passion for democratic justice. He played into her ongoing family romance, imagining her as his son. She in turn imagined him as a king, signing herself his 'most humble servant and faithful subject'.[44]

Michel was at this time in prison because he'd published an article denouncing the authorities (in language which Sand interpreted as being misguidedly reminiscent of the bitterest periods of the 1789 revolution). The prison was in a setting worthy of the more gothic scenes in Sand's fiction: the ancient chateau of the Duc de Bourgogne. Now Sand and her friend François Rollinat (a lawyer in nearby Châteauroux) went to the prison by night to consult Michel on her separation. They persuaded a jailor to lead them in through a break in the wall, following him through chilling halls and stairways to Michel's gloomy cell. His answer echoed out from the stone walls: Test yourself against the law. He told her to fight. Thankfully he'd soon be out of prison and able to represent her in court.

To maintain her rights, she couldn't return to her marital home – she had to stay with friends until the judge ruled on her temporary domicile. So she went to Duteil's house in La Châtre. It would be months before she could see her children again.

She would have preferred a divorce to a separation, but French law still didn't allow for it. Following the 1830 revolution, the Chamber of Deputies had passed a bill reinstating divorce, but it had been rejected by the Chamber of Peers. The codicil now attached to the Napoleonic Code stipulated that the rules governing fault-based divorce should remain as they were, with divorce changing to separation, but there would be no separation by mutual consent. The custody laws remained unchanged, however, and here French mothers were better off than English mothers. Day to day, French men owned their children, so a French wife could not flee with her children. But when it came to a legal separation, an insistence on rights which was the legacy of the revolution helped children and mothers. The revolutionary laws that had declared divorce one of the 'natural, inalienable and sacred' rights for men and women, stipulated that in cases of divorce by mutual consent, girls went to their mother and boys over seven to their father. However, the law also specified that 'the father and the mother will be able to make such other arrangements on this subject as they see fit', and that in cases of fault-based divorce, the decision would be based on 'the interests of the child'. Later on, modifications could be made, again in 'l'intérêt de l'enfant'.

It would be a hundred years before children in Britain had legal interests, yet here they were, enshrined in law. It was so unpredictable where the confused and conflicting drives towards progress and atavism would lead at this stage in French history that it's not surprising to find progressive laws about parenthood patched in among regressive laws about separation. Initially, the arrangements were decided by informally constituted family assemblies. With the Napoleonic Code and the shift in governance from priests to lawyers, divorce became a matter for a court hearing. Here again, children were to be entrusted to the spouse who had obtained the divorce, unless the court ordered, 'pour le plus grand avantage des enfants', that 'all or some of them will be entrusted to the care either of the other spouse or a third person'. 'The greater advantage of the children.' This too would have sounded strikingly progressive to English ears. What was more, the Civil Code enshrined the 'droits' of the children to the advantages assured by law. These clauses had remained in the code even after the 1816 restoration of the monarchy.

All this allowed individual judges the power to grant custody to mothers, and especially to mothers suing for separation, even if they were adulterous. Sand knew Casimir could destroy her reputation if he chose to fight – she was a woman with lovers and a writer grubby with commercial success – but she was sure that it would be in her children's interest to live with her, so she risked it. It helped that Casimir had bedded his brother-in-law's maid at home; Article 339 of the Penal Code stated that husband who kept concubines in the conjugal dwelling lost the right to charge their wives with adultery.

'I shall recover my freedom and dignity,' Sand told her mother, explaining her demands, which were to have full custody of her daughter and half custody of Maurice during his holidays. She knew Sophie-Victorie would worry about the publicity, but she made a stand: 'I am my father's daughter and do not care a jot for prejudice when my heart dictates to me courage and justice.' She was indifferent to scandal, she claimed; 'all I care for are Maurice and Solange.'[45]

In January 1836, she waited at Nohant for the court case. She'd sent the servants away so was alone in the house, with just the gardener and his wife bringing food. It was so quiet that she could hear the town clock three miles away. She spent her evenings writing humiliating letters, begging friends to appear as witnesses in court. Casimir had assured her he wasn't going to attend, so she was hopeful it would be an easy verdict. The hearing took place from 14–22 January and she managed to produce seventeen witnesses – mainly local friends and servants – and then awaited the judgment.

While she waited, she read Musset's *The Confession of a Child of the Century*, which had been published on 1 February. Musset had distilled their love affair into the story of a disillusioned libertine who finds himself in the countryside after his father's death. He meets an older woman, modelled on Sand but without her writerly bohemianism; Brigitte is a chaste do-gooding widow, possessed of fine black eyes and unusual piety, who's happy with her narrow life until Octave startles her into passionate, mutually destructive love. There's much to dislike in this rather repetitive, self-consciously misanthropic and misogynist novel. But its energy and brilliance come from its diagnosis of Musset and Sand's generation: 'During the wars of the Empire, while husbands and brothers were in Germany, anxious mothers brought into the world a generation that was ardent, whey-faced and morbidly sensitive.'[46]

Sand was captivated by his sense of theirs as an irreligious century that turned love into an illusion and divided society between anguished idealists and sensual materialists (and often, as in Musset's case, leaving them fatally confused about which they were). 'I started to cry like a child when I finished the book,' Sand told Marie d'Agoult. She thought it told the exact truth about her, 'from the "sister of charity" to the "stubborn, stiff-necked goose"'. And it brought back a time when she believed in passion as an ideal, which she found painful amid the disillusionment of the end of her marriage. She wrote to Musset that she had loved him a great deal, had forgiven him everything, and never wanted to see him again.[47]

On 16 February she finally obtained the judgment she'd hoped for. Nohant and the children were hers, in exchange for an income for her husband. 'I am savouring for the first time since my grandmother's death the calm of contemplation,' she wrote; 'no conflicts surface.' She remained alone there, moving around the house lit only by the dying fire, aware of this as another rupture.[48]

The problem with custody cases is that there are winners and losers. Amid the mess of human failings and feelings that characterise marriage and family life, the courtroom is the one place where it's possible to win. Casimir Dudevant, humiliated and confused, tried to regain control. He appealed, claiming that he hadn't been notified of what was going on. This was a system set up for men to exert power in – especially the husbands of emancipated wives – so it was worth trying his luck. Another hearing was scheduled at La Châtre and Casimir drew up a list of recriminations for his lawyer, including his wife's infidelities and, most pernicious of all: 'September 1830. She writes novels.' He described her as 'affecting the manners of a young man, smoking, swearing, dressed as a man and having lost all the feminine graces, with no understanding of money'.[49]

Casimir Dudevant, drawing by unknown artist

They returned to court in May. A contested separation hearing was a major social event, as Caroline Norton's adultery trial had been, and all the more so because of Sand's fame. The legal newspaper *Le Droit* detailed excitedly the huge crowd squeezing into the narrow tribunal. Casimir's lawyer, Louis-Antoine Thiot-Varennes, came up with his charges, delineating Sand's debauchery to titillated gasps, but Michel easily trounced him, insisting that Dudevant's cruelty and adultery had made the marital home uninhabitable for Sand. She felt self-righteous pleasure and relief, watching her husband listening to Michel's 'lightning lessons', and then waited for the judgment. Everything could be about to change. If she lost, she planned to flee to America with the children and had borrowed 10,000 francs for this purpose. The 11 May judgment annulled the first decision on the grounds of faulty procedure, but upheld the judgment. The judges didn't believe that Dudevant wished to renew their union. He went home quietly, but not before threatening to denounce Michel as Sand's lover and to drive thirty sabres into him. She had won again but it wasn't over – Casimir was going to appeal in Bourges.[50]

She waited. Distraction came from another lover: Michel had been too busy to see much of her, except in court, and she succumbed briefly to the idealistic but dissolute Swiss poet Charles Didier. He had fallen in love with her through reading *Lélia*, as Musset had done, but he found the actual woman cold and she found his gallantry irritating. 'I do not ask for the support of anyone,' she wrote to him, 'whether to kill someone or pick a bouquet . . . when I want beautiful flowers I gather them on my own, barefoot.' She sent him on his way and as June turned to July, she slept mainly at the houses of friends in La Châtre, frightened of confronting Casimir at Nohant if he came to make a show of power. By day she exhausted herself, walking and swimming in the heat. 'Not a beetle passes but I run after it,' she told Marie d'Agoult. Her happiest moments were when she was tired enough to sleep. She would lie on a meadow in her wet clothes and escape her suffering for an hour in the sun. 'You will perhaps think that it is better to indulge in such amusement than in blowing out one's brains,' she suggested to Marie, admitting that she still had fits of melancholy. She missed her children and she missed the home she'd supposedly won back. She couldn't publish her new novel, *The Master Mosaic Makers*, because its republican stance would be bad for the case. Everything was on hold and it felt like Casimir would find ways to extend the appeal indefinitely, leaving the children in their unsettling limbo. You can turn the law into a way of life. A lot of parents have done it, and, in the wake of a revolution made by lawyers and journalists, French society was revealing how the machinery of the legal profession could become central to every aspect of political and domestic life.[51]

Sand was uneasily aware what this process was doing to her children. Maurice continued to assure her that he was defending her at school and wanted her to 'win', thanking God for 'having given me a mother like the one that I possess'. But no matter how bravely loving he was, he remained a twelve-year-old boy who wished that his parents could be together and not featured in newspapers. 'If I could reconcile you – what happiness,' he wrote, threatening that when his parents were old, he would catch them by both ears, 'as one does to little children who have argued, and I will make you approach each other'. This boy, who had watched his father hold his mother at gunpoint less than a year earlier, assured her that one day his father would attain her forgiveness.[52]

Maurice's letters were painful to receive, and so were Solange's more laborious but loving missives about school life. Solange knew nothing about the case but may have noticed her teachers' precautions: they'd been asked to forbid her to go out with her father's acquaintances. Sand wrote to thank her daughter for one of her letters, hoping her greatest reward was 'to give happiness to your old mother who thinks of you all day and dreams of you all night'. It was true. She hadn't always been preoccupied by her children since the first move to Paris, where writing and love affairs had often consumed her. But it was her children she thought of now, swimming in her clothes, racing along the bank, sleeping in the meadow.[53]

In her autobiography, she would angrily indict the prevailing, public and adversarial system for marital separations. 'The law's principal fault is the publicity it accords to debates,' she wrote. Women accused of adultery were stigmatised, dishonoured in the eyes of their children. 'What a solution to domestic misery! It is savage. It can kill the spirit of the child condemned to watch the prolongation of his parents' discord or to experience its outcome.' In custody cases we pursue a vision of our children's lives we believe to be right for them; we go to court because we want to protect them; but so often in the process we make their lives worse, damaging the children we are attempting to care for.[54]

She was still optimistic that she'd win, if she could ever get a judgment that wasn't open to appeal. But she knew that there were other wronged women with abusive husbands who had no hope, because they didn't have the money for a lawyer like Michel, or the energy or self-possession to put a case together. And she knew – these were the class of women who would soon populate her fiction, most memorably the miller's wife trapped in a controlling and violent marriage in *François le Champi* – that these women wouldn't be able to borrow 10,000 francs to steal their children to America; they were stuck watching their husbands abuse their children.

One such woman was Flora Tristan, who would soon emerge as one of France's foremost feminists. Tristan had come to Sand's salon a year earlier and been rather resentful of Sand, holding court on an ottoman. Tristan was envious of Sand's separation from her husband – which at her distance looked easy – and of her literary success and inherited wealth. She interrupted the salon chatter to ask Sand why she donned a male pseudonym and male clothes when she could be asserting new possibilities for womanhood. Sand responded that she just wanted the freedoms that men had, and nothing stopped other women dressing as men. Later, Sand said that she didn't much like Tristan, despite her courage and conviction – she was too vain. But both women might have found more cause for sympathy if they'd known about the casual brutality of each other's husbands.

The illegitimate daughter of a Peruvian aristocrat, Flora Tristan had grown up in desperate poverty, which she escaped by marrying Andre Chazal, her boss in a lithography workshop. Chazal drank and gambled and in 1825 Tristan had fled with her three children. In 1828 the Civil Tribunal of the Seine had granted her separation of property but not of body, so her husband still legally owned their children, and repeatedly tracked her down as she moved between boarding houses. One son died of cholera in the 1832 epidemic that Sand weathered more easily with Solange, and shortly afterwards Chazal demanded custody, arriving at the house Tristan shared with her mother with the mayor and a police officer. When Tristan attacked Chazal with furniture, she was subdued by force, and eventually she agreed to give up their son Ernest in return for Chazal agreeing to a full legal separation and allowing her to keep their daughter Aline, who he had never known. These were the precarious arrangements still in place when Tristan and Sand met.

Since then, the situation had deteriorated. Chazal had continued to harass Tristan, and decided to kidnap Aline, encouraged by a Montmartre police commissioner who advised him that she was his stolen property. Early in 1836, Tristan managed to rescue her and to arrange a custody hearing in a Paris court. Aline pleaded with every official to be with her mother, and Chazal was seen to have forfeited his right to fatherhood with his long absence, but the judges decreed that the mother was a harmful influence: she'd made a scandal of herself with her public demands for divorce and equal rights. Aline was to be placed in a boarding school.

'Don't come and tell me that you love me,' Aline wrote with misguided courage to her father in the spring of 1836, while Maurice Dudevant fantasised about reconciling his parents. 'I will answer that it is not true, because if it was true you would prove it to me by not making me unhappy.' Her courage was misplaced. Chazal arranged for her to be placed in an institution for juvenile correction and then, when she escaped, kidnapped her. A few months later Tristan received a letter from Aline saying that her father 'did things' to her in their shared bed. Eventually in 1838 Tristan attained custody of both her children, only for Chazal to shoot her. Thankfully she survived and Chazal was finally imprisoned.[55]

In Aline Chazal's case, the law had not prioritised the 'advantage' of a child with an emancipated mother. George Sand had better luck: she had the money to buy her husband off, or to escape if this failed, and she had one of the greatest lawyers of her century on her side.

The Bourges court was packed on 25 July 1836. Press reporters hoped for a woman in a man's frock coat, reeking of the perfumes and cigar smoke of the Palais Royale, but she was wearing a demure white dress with a flowery shawl. She'd arrived in Bourges two days earlier, accompanied by Solange (in readiness, again, to flee), who spent the days playing with dogs and chickens in the garden of Duteil's parents. The little girl was still supposedly ignorant about why they were there, though she was now almost eight and must have overheard conversations and noticed her mother's intense anxiety.

Bourges law court in 1836

Casimir's lawyer, Thiot-Varennes, began by saying that his own speeches were dictated by personal conscience, and 'in conformity with the purest morality, and not with that morality of convention which one finds in some novels'. He went back into the early years of the marriage, presenting Sand as some sort of precursor to Madame Bovary, beset by 'a deep boredom, a distaste for all things'. He read out sections of the 1825 letter where she tried to understand their mutual unhappiness. He described her life in Paris where she'd succumbed 'without restraint to her prodigal and ruinous tastes', and characterised her novels as works 'filled with bitterness and regrets that devour your heart'. Despite this assassination, he claimed that Dudevant wanted to forgive her and welcome her back into his home, for the sake of the children she was trying to snatch away.

It was an easy argument for Michel to demolish. He began by addressing the judges directly. 'Why this eager crowd around you?' he asked. Was it a matter of state importance? No, instead: 'A woman wants to reclaim her outraged freedom, her trampled independence. She comes here to ask for an asylum for her old age; and, as a consolation for the calumnies with which she has been heaped, her children, the fruit of her womb!' Throughout, he celebrated Sand as a novelist, rather than denying her writing. 'This woman is the glory of our time.' The day was a great one, he said, because they had the chance 'to proclaim the innocence of the persecuted genius.'

He then addressed Dudevant. 'The marital home is profaned, and it is you who have profaned it: you have introduced debauchery and prostitution into it.' He took the 1825 letter that Thiot-Varennes had introduced as evidence of Sand's debauchery, and read more of it, turning it into evidence of her tenderness and honesty. He read out enough about Aurelien to make it clear that this passion was, in the end, chaste, and he read out the passages where Sand had begged her husband to help her to redeem the marriage. *Le Droit* reported that this letter, with its 'magical' style, profoundly moved all present. Michel then detailed Dudevant's cruelty to his wife and son, describing the confrontation with the gun that had led her to court. 'The forgiveness you offer is an outrage,' he admonished. 'You are the one who offended.' If Casimir Dudevant wanted instead to obtain Sand's forgiveness, he needed 'to present yourself in this sanctuary of justice with your heart humbled and repentant, your head bowed with pain, and covered with a veil'.

Again, he pointed out the contradictions in Dudevant's position: if she was this pernicious, why would he want her back? And he celebrated her as a woman who loved her children, insisting that her writing made her more moral rather than less so. 'Because a woman yields to the whims of her lyre, to the inspirations of a creative spirit, you would think her incapable of bringing up her children?' But that, he added, would be to condemn Diderot, who was such a tender father. And Sand's children would 'walk under the supervision of their mother, in the path of honour and duty'. To prove this, two of Maurice's letters were read out, demonstrating his love for his mother and his dutifulness as a son. And he read out a letter from Sand, exhorting Maurice to 'pray to God for your father and for me'.[56]

Michel emerges in these hearings as the lawyer every woman in this book needed. He fought fiercely against the punitive injustice of Sand's husband and honoured her as a mother, a writer and a free-spirited woman. And he showed himself to be a feminist in ways that had urgent, practical value for Sand and perhaps for some of the women watching or reading about her case and gaining courage to separate from their own husbands in turn. He'd wrested Sand's words away from Dudevant and his lawyer. He didn't deny them; he simply quoted them more fully, bringing out her precision and honesty and making a space for this kind of thinking in the courtroom – a precedent that would not be followed over the centuries. Her writing was her threat to the patriarchy: she had told the truth about women's experience. Michel validated this, defending her as a persecuted genius. He hadn't bothered to deny Dudevant's charges of adultery; he just made it clear that Sand was a complex, feelingful woman and that this made her more deserving of her children rather than less so. And he was convincing enough that, in an age when the legal system was set up to scourge adulterers, his strategy worked.

The judges were stalled at a 5:5 verdict. Five of the most upstanding men of Bourges were on Sand's side, prepared to give two children to a known adulteress – a move unthinkable in England, where even Caroline Norton stipulated that tiny infants should be removed from adulterous mothers. The larger mood of the courtroom was with Sand and there were hisses when the judgment was suspended. This was a room full of readers who had been moved to tears by Sand's stories and were now moved by the tales of her suffering in her marriage. Dudevant saw that his case was doomed and agreed to settle, asking for money in exchange for the children and his wife's house.

Custody dragged its way down the generations. The immediate effect of the court case was to make Maurice ill. He had dangerous fevers and heart palpitations, which were diagnosed as an aneurism. Dudevant was sceptical at first, but then sent him back to Sand after a mutually sleepless night with his son. The doctor played into Sand's fantasies of a complete and exclusive mother–son bond by claiming that only the mother could cure the child; if she died, the son would immediately follow.

Maurice's illness and frantic need for his mother was a response to the custody case. If motherhood and the law traumatise each other, because the somatic feelings of motherhood are incompatible with the linguistic precision of the law, then in Sand's case, Michel had found a way around this. He had forced the mother's feelings and her bodily life with her children into the courtroom. But the structure of the case was still one with winners and losers, and the children were caught between the two combatants. And so Maurice was left traumatised, living out the case in his body, fearing the absence of the mother he felt he had almost lost. He spent his fevered nights at school crying out: 'Nohant, Nohant!'

During this period of victory chastened by suffering, Sand wrote one of her most overtly feminist texts, a series of 'Letters to Marcie', published in *Le Monde*, which she presented as a man offering advice to a young woman. Here she advises the fictional Marcie to educate herself, warning that 'women receive a deplorable education' and that this is the 'great crime of men against them'; men fear that educated women will have moral ascendancy over their households.[57]

Embarking on these letters, Sand doubted whether she could encapsulate her thoughts about women's lives, but in the wake of the court case she wanted to try. The project was abandoned after the editor, L'Abbé de Lammenais, made cuts to her third letter without consulting her. She told him that she would withdraw the letters if he was going to edit them, and that she wanted in particular to write about divorce. 'To sum up my bold ideas, they consist in claiming divorce in marriage. For me, the only remedy to the moral injustices, to the endless miseries, to the often incurable passions which disturb the union of the sexes, is the liberty of breaking up conjugal ties and forming them again,' Lammenais didn't respond enthusiastically, so she didn't write this letter. Without her views on divorce, this series of letters feel a little underpowered. This isn't the kind of feminism to impress Tristan and her circle of Saint-Simonians, who were now calling for the vote and for women to sit on juries and become lawmakers themselves. In the early letters, Sand is concerned most of all with motherhood, and with telling the virginal Marcie (in terms that Sand would surely find horrendously patronising if spoken by a man) that women, who are 'not fit for the jobs which the laws have hitherto denied them', are lucky nonetheless to have had 'placed in her arms and attached to her bosom the childhood of man', giving her 'joys ineffable whose power is a mystery to most men'.[58]

At a time when she'd risked everything for motherhood, and when her lawyer had convinced the Bourges courtroom that a child's need for his mother is absolute, Sand went on to say that a woman has two distinct natures: the lover and the mother. The lover may be sublime but may also be unjust and unfortunate; the mother 'is all fairness, all goodness, all serenity'. As always, she idealised motherhood, but this time the idealism went alongside real, practical efforts as a mother. She was busy trying to nurse her son back to health, all the time frightened because Casimir was determined to revenge his humiliations, as Chazal soon would be. He threatened to kidnap Maurice, so Sand took her son to Fontainebleu. Here they hid at an inn, horse-riding and catching butterflies by day, with Sand dashing back and forth to Paris to witness the death of her once so painfully beloved mother. Embracing her mother's corpse as she'd long ago embraced her grandmother's, she thought back to their awful early separation and found that 'what they say about the power of blood-relationships and the voice of nature is not a dream'. While she was there, Casimir descended on the child who remained an easier prey, kidnapping Solange from Nohant in October 1837.[59]

Another girl, pleading with her father not to hurt her. He'd struck her governess and now he was carrying his daughter to his carriage. In letters at the time, Sand reconstructed the scene with perhaps a little embellishment, based on the accounts from the servants. Solange apparently threw herself at his knees crying: 'I love you, Papa, I love you, but don't take me away, I love you but I don't want to leave Maman and Marie!' He took her to his stepmother's house in Guillery – an exhausting 350 kilometres away. For Solange, there were several arduous days of travelling and then a wait, while Sand gathered the necessary papers to come to the rescue, leaving behind her still-sickly son. 'All out of paternal love according to him,' Sand wrote to a friend. 'This conduct is as absurd as it is odious.'[60]

Sand was heroically competent in the crisis, as always. She rushed to Paris, summoned the police, and got proof of custody from the ministers. She spent three days and nights in a post-chaise to Nérac, accompanied by the children's new tutor who was also her latest lover – the young, self-abnegatingly adoring playwright Félicien Mallefille – and by her solicitor's clerk. In Nérac, she found several policemen, a subprefect and a bailiff to accompany her on the 10-kilometre journey to Casimir's door, arriving at Guillery with this full escort on horseback. Casimir was preparing for flight, but now the house was surrounded he became 'gentle and polite', and led Solange by the hand to the threshold. 'Solange was placed in my hands like a princess on the border of two states,' Sand told Duteil. 'The baron and I exchanged a few pleasant words. He threatened to take my son back by authority of justice, and we parted charmed with each other.'[61]

She then decided to take Solange on a peculiar pilgrimage, further south to the Pyrenees, where she had last gone with Aurélien and Zoé LeRoy, and where she had travelled as a three-year-old with her mother on that ill-fated journey to visit her father on the battlefield. They rode on horseback 200 kilometres to the border of Spain, crossing the mountains known as the 'Frontière sauvage'. This was the landscape she had found exhilarating when last there, but also 'monstrous' – not a 'land of men' but of mountains whose 'eternal barriers' shut out light and air. As they entered the Pyrenees, the weather became abysmal: there was snow and fog and ice and there were patches where they could barely see. Sand described her eight-year-old daughter 'trotting like a devil, defying the rain and laughing with all her heart, on the edge of the terrible precipices which line the road', riding 70 kilometres in a single day. Within four days, they were back in Nérac, where they recovered for a couple of days before travelling the 350 kilometres back to Nohant.[62]

The image of Solange riding huge distances along precipices in the snow projects the full triumph and tragedy of this custody case. I think Sand was absolutely the right person to have custody of these children, but she was an imperfect mother. Indeed, Sand is a reminder that mothers shouldn't have to be perfect to get custody: for once here, the judges were able to see that a flawed and transgressive woman was nonetheless the best person to bring up her children. And yet, I find Sand's decision to prolong her journey at this point bewildering. Sand and Casimir seem to have been caught up in a kind of folie à deux, whipped up by the court process to incite each other to ever more extreme acts, with their children rendered ever more passive by their parents' tumultuous combat.

Sand experienced her life as narrative, and seems to have got dangerously caught up in her own story. This journey became the apotheosis of romantic freedom: she was acting out of her own excess of strength, daring herself and Solange not to show weakness. She wanted to celebrate her triumph with her daughter, making something of her needless journey and turning the kidnapping into an adventure. Solange went along with it, apparently joyfully, glad to be reunited with her mother, glad to prove to her that she shared her courage and strength. But this was surely too much to require of her: this was an eight-year-old, riding along deathly precipices in the snow as a result of a dispute between parents she was powerless to affect. For Solange it would create an ideal of mother–daughter closeness it was impossible to recapture, a model of strength she could never live up to, and a sense of life as a constant process of frenzied strife that made it hard to settle into any quieter version of domestic life.

Maurice deteriorated again after the kidnapping of his sister. 'It can kill the spirit of the child condemned to watch the prolongation of his parents' discord or to experience its outcome.' Sand knew the truth of that line when she later wrote it in her autobiography. She'd watched her son languishing almost to non-existence in the years after her legal case. 'Gaubert says he will recover, but it is very sad to see childhood pass by without joy, without strength, and without work,' she wrote in a letter in May 1838.[63]

It was partly for Maurice's sake that she made the journey to Mallorca in October 1838, accompanied by her children – Maurice was now fifteen and Solange ten – and by Frédéric Chopin, the brilliant, frail composer with whom she would spend the next decade. She'd begun her love affair with Chopin in June, seduced in part by his music (Sand was a serious pianist herself and would devote many of her 1840s novels to music). Now his chronic tuberculosis was being exacerbated by the French winter and she headed south with him, to satisfy his and Maurice's parallel needs for the sun.

In Mallorca, after a grim journey, they briefly flourished. 'I firmly believe we will never leave Mallorca again,' she announced, describing the long walks the two young men she described as 'sons' were able to undertake. Solange was healthy as always, and was responding well to Sand's new attempt to be a less indulgent parent: 'Our family ties are more tightly bound and we press against each other with more affection and intimate happiness.'[64]

Then Chopin became seriously ill, and the 'family' were shunned because of his TB. It was with relief that they all returned to France in February, thus beginning a decade of Sand mothering alongside Chopin at Nohant and in Paris.

This was an era in which books proliferated, and children did too: in 1839 Sand made herself responsible for Oscar, the son of her sister Caroline, whose cries outside her grandmother's house had once devastated her, and in 1846 she formally adopted Augustine Brault, a distant cousin on her mother's side who she'd been looking after for a few years. Her enthusiasm for Augustine occasioned outraged jealousy from Solange and confusion from Maurice, who never quite managed to fulfil Sand's hopes that he'd fall in love with his quasi-sister and marry her. Part of the problem was Maurice's extreme love for his mother. He said that he didn't want to get married at all because he would never love a woman as much as his mother, who had told a friend in 1847 that 'nothing will be sweet enough after my treats', with slightly disturbing pride.[65]

Throughout this decade, Sand's relations with Solange deteriorated. Everything had been staked on the court case, and the court case had been staked on her love for her children, and of Solange in particular, because Maurice was always going to be shared with her husband. After the court case, Sand saw herself as sacrificing everything for her daughter, convinced that she wouldn't be able to marry her well if she didn't. She abandoned the more ostentatiously bohemian aspects of her Parisian life and tried to live as settled as possible a family life with Chopin, though after a couple of years their relationship was no longer sexual. This is a mother who loved her daughter with exuberant devotion. 'Solange is a lion, a leopard, an eagle, a charm, a boy, a devil, everything except a young lady. I love her in a foolish way,' Sand wrote in the same 1838 letter where she worried that her son's youth was wasting away in illness. And, partly because she resented the sacrifices required, this is also a mother who could never stop reprimanding her daughter, or looking down on her for the ways she was different from her. 'Solange is still superb in health and intolerable in character,' she wrote in 1841 to her brother. 'It's only the character that is sinful – whimsical, unequal, dominating, jealous and hot-tempered,' she wrote a month later to the head of the convent where she was sending her, though to counter these, she added, there was 'intelligence, generosity, certain innate greatness'.[66]

Again and again in her letters to Solange at school she told her off for her coquetry and laziness, accusing her of exaggerating her unhappiness. But Solange's pleas seem genuine to me – and too desperate not to be taken seriously. 'Imagine a daughter deprived of her mother for whom all the days, hours, minutes seem so long that she's desperate about the time she must spend before seeing her mother again,' Solange wrote to Sand, adopting her mother's own tendency towards hyperbole. Solange had gone to boarding school so much younger than Sand herself: she was seven, where Sand was thirteen. It's not surprising that she was anxious and insecure, and Sand seems to have forgotten her own periods of unhappy illness in adolescence – forgetting that she really did once drive her horse into the river in the hope of drowning herself. In 1841 she wrote to her twelve-year-old daughter that though she would always love her with the instinctive love that 'warblers have for their young', Solange was now old enough that she needed to make her mother love her as her friend, which she hadn't yet succeeded in doing. 'I was not very happy with your impertinence and your answers last time,' Sand told Solange in 1843.[67]

In 1846 Sand engaged her eighteen-year-old daughter to a local man who adored her. He was neither rich nor witty, but Solange said she'd played with dolls enough and wouldn't mind a quiet and rural life. Sand felt she was grateful to be offered a 'voluntary slave'. The engagement ended six months later when the famous sculptor Auguste Clésinger was commissioned to make paired busts of Sand and her daughter. He seems to have paid court to both of them, and to have proposed almost immediately to Solange, who was easily enchanted by this imperious artist, fourteen years her senior. They became engaged and, shockingly, Sand consented to it. She was apparently as powerless before his will as her daughter was and connived in setting them up together from the start, leaving her daughter alone for her sittings. 'It will be done because this man wants it,' she told Maurice, 'he does everything he wants immediately, at the minute, without needing either to sleep or to eat. He has been here three days, he has not slept two hours, and he is well. This tension of the will, without fatigue or failure, astonishes me and pleases me.' She hoped that his decisiveness would complement Solange's restlessness; she felt that the mutual adoration would form a good enough basis for a marriage, and wanted to hasten it before either of them changed their mind. What did she fear? That Solange would be unmarriageable if she was known to have ended two engagements? It doesn't seem enough to justify allowing this marriage to go ahead on so short an acquaintance, in an era when marriage was irrevocable and when husbands had all the power, as Sand knew in every fibre of her war-wounded body.[68]

At least Clésinger was rich. 'I believe he will lead her well, and in a brilliant way, because he earns a lot of money,' wrote Sand. Except that it quickly became clear he wasn't rich at all. He was a gambler and, immediately after their marriage, he asked Sand to mortgage Nohant to pay off his debts. This was the house she'd unwillingly sacrificed her mother to inherit; the house she'd publicly humiliated herself to win back from her husband; the idea that she would mortgage it for her feckless new son-in-law was absurd, and Solange can't have seriously expected her to agree to it. But Solange took her husband's side and a summer of bitter confrontations ensued. In July 1847 there was an appalling fight when Clésinger raised a hammer to Maurice. Sand slapped Clésinger across the face and he responded by punching her on the chest. She sent the couple away, sure that she never wanted to see them again. In the weeks that followed, it was Solange who kept Sand awake at night in fury, rather than Clésinger. 'My God, I have never done anything to merit a daughter like her!' Sand told a friend; 'it's Solange who tears my entrails and who kills me.' She took the title of Musset's novel and applied it to Solange: 'This century is cursed and she is the child of her century,' she wrote, complaining that Solange had chosen the intoxication of pride and vanity as an alternative to religion.[69]

When Chopin attempted to mediate, Sand broke with him as well, becoming convinced, rightly or wrongly, that he'd been more in love with her daughter than he was with her. For his part, Chopin saw her as driven to destroy her most important relationships: 'Some kind of frenzy has come upon her; she harrows up her own life, she harrows up her daughter's life.' He was right that Sand was engaged in a frenzied act of self-destruction. And she shouldn't have been so surprised that this marriage between an egotistical, overbearing gambler and an eighteen-year-old virgin had gone wrong. Of course, Solange had been lacking in self-knowledge when she agreed to marry him. Yet Sand had allowed it to happen.[70]

Reading Sand's letters from this time, I keep thinking of two images. There is the 32-year-old woman swimming fully clothed in the river, exhausting herself because she is desperate – desperate with fear and longing for her children; a woman who would be astonished to be told that only ten years later she will repudiate the daughter she is fighting for, after letting her embark on a marriage even more obviously ill-fated than her own. And there is the eight-year-old girl, driving her horse through the snow at the edge of mountains, full of pride and courage because she is accompanying the mother she admires; the mother she's been snatched from and then triumphantly rescued by. They were fighting on the same side then; they were uniting in their bravery and escaping the grasp of the man who wanted to constrain them. What happened? Why did it have to end like this?

Perhaps their tragic separation was somehow written into those scenes – into the desperate energy of the traumatic custody case and its aftermath. The law courts had pushed them into extremes of courage and recklessness that perhaps there was no turning back from. Feats of strength had been required from Solange, yet then she was required to apply herself peacefully to her studies, on pain of being kept away from her mother. This unrealistic expectation had been hard for her to fulfil – so then, sensing her mother's withdrawal, she sought admiration from men instead. Why not Chopin? After all, as a child, her mother had jokingly engaged Solange to one of her own admirers. And why not Clésinger, given the peculiar act of mother–daughter display involved in being sculpted together? This was the sculptor Sand had selected to be admired by; there must have been a triumphant pleasure in seducing him, which could have been left at that, if Sand hadn't encouraged the marriage, apparently glad to hand over to Clésinger the daughter she had fought so hard to wrest from another controlling man.

Bewildered by family relations, Sand committed herself to revolution. The 1848 revolution left her ecstatic for a few months. She saw this as a victory brought about by the people. Musset had seen it coming in his *Confession*, describing a gang of masked roisterers bumping through Paris to a carnival, while drunk, ragged men look on, occasionally stepping forward to 'hurl a torrent of abuse in our faces and throw a fistful of flour'. Sand arrived in Paris on 1 March, a week after the king's abdication. She'd been writing for the socialist periodical *La Revue indépendante* and now could honour the memory of her mother and her grandmother by being a true revolutionary. She managed to convince the Minister of the Interior (an old friend of Michel's) to appoint 25-year-old Maurice as mayor of La Châtre, which helpfully kept him away from the dangers of Paris. 'Citizens, France is embarking on the greatest endeavour of modern times: the foundation of the government of *all* the people,' she announced in the government's *Bulletin de la République*. 'The new idea can take its place in Europe.'[71]

Sand's optimism was misplaced. In April, France held its first national elections with universal male suffrage: 7 million voters went to the polls. Sand herself came close to being a candidate, proposed by the feminist 'Club de la rue de la Taranne'. She repudiated this proposal with a derision that shocked the feminists who had looked to her as a sympathetic role model. She thought they were mistaken to call for female suffrage when women didn't have marital freedom or financial independence. And she fervently wanted the election to go well and didn't think putting herself forward would help.

It didn't go well. The assembly that was returned was so conservative that it included many landowners, three bishops and three nephews of Napoleon. The waves of revolution and reaction continued. A group of revolutionaries managed to invade the National Assembly and proclaim an insurrectionary government. Sand watched helplessly as the regime quashed the insurrectionists, killing thousands of civilians in what Victor Hugo described as the greatest street battle in history. Sand had proclaimed her allegiance to the revolution and now she was seen as an ally of the protestors. The shopkeepers of La Châtre descended on Nohant shouting: 'A bas Mme Dudevant!' –'Down with Mme Dudevant' – and 'A bas les communistes!' In July, Sand described her heart as broken. The government had killed the republic by 'arming its children against each other'.[72]

Meanwhile, Solange had given birth to a baby girl who died aged one week old. Sand felt some stirrings of sympathy, but even now she could tell Maurice that she no longer loved his sister: 'As far as I am concerned she is a cold rod of iron, an unknown being, a stranger in the world of ideas and feelings where I have my being.'[73]

In February 1851, Solange appeared at Nohant, accompanied by her new baby, Jeanne – known as Nini – and a maid, and won over the grandmother, in a re-enactment of the scene between the young and the old Aurore. After the visit, Sand embraced her daughter and her granddaughter tenderly in her letters; by July 1851 she had welcomed Solange and her 'ravissante' little girl to Nohant, and found that she hardly had any of her usual migraines, however hard she worked. Solange left her alone with Nini for a few days and Sand reported proudly that the little girl had laughed madly all morning. Another child had entered her heart.[74]

IV. Nini

'A marvel of grace, prettiness, cuddling, babbling'

There's a drawing by Sand from 1854 of four-year-old Nini looking still and contemplative. The artist's lines are careful and delicate; there's a tenderness in the button on the girl's blouse, the curl of hair around the neck, the dark eye. It's a drawing full of wondering love in which Sand grapples with the truth about children's experiences. In custody cases and in most novels, we describe the experiences of children in the language of adults. In the drawing, Nini's expression is allowed to speak for her; Sand seems to be asking herself what it means to represent a child, and requiring delicacy of herself as she does it.

All at once, Sand's life was centred around the little girl. Nini came and went, sent back to her mother in Paris with a 'poor little scratched cheek' that she'd acquired kissing her grandmother in the rose garden. Solange began separation proceedings against her husband, though Sand thought she should have waited longer to go to court, and then reconciled with him. Sand disapproved of her vacillations: 'one should get used to not holding her to what she says, poor child'. During marital arguments, Clésinger would place Nini with his parents. 'He takes this poor little girl . . . without clothes to change into,' Sand reported furiously, adding that the 'madman Clésinger' admitted that she cried for entire nights for her mother there. When Solange began separation proceedings again in June 1852, Sand thought of hiding three-year-old Nini with a nurse, but meanwhile she took the girl herself and their bond deepened. In letter after letter, she describes her as 'a marvel of grace, prettiness, cuddling, babbling', proud that though she is impetuous and prone to tantrums, she submits always to her grandmother. 'She's so nice to me that I don't need a maid for her. She stays with me all day, playing with her dolls without saying a word while I work on my novels and my plays. She is adorable, full of kindness and grace.'[75]

Sand was now living with the engraver Alexandre Manceau, and this was the calmest love affair of her life; he was thirteen years younger than her but lived alongside her with a devotion and steadiness very unlike her previous lovers. He acted as her secretary, organising her daily life, making sure she had ink, tobacco and sugar water ready every evening.

Around them, the century's underlying turbulence made itself felt in new explosions. Napoleon's nephew, Louis-Napoleon, had been elected president in 1848 and then seized absolute power in a coup in 1851, initiating a period of repression and censorship and exiling many of Sand's friends. Sand had been scathing about his standing for president in the first place, but it was in keeping with her mood during these years that she now presented herself as peacemaker. In January 1852, she took the astonishing step of writing to Napoleon III, insisting that she came to him 'broken' and 'timid', with her socialist friends now 'scattered to the four winds', accepting his leadership with 'the submission which we owe to the logic of Providence', and offering her services in helping him pardon her imprisoned and exiled associates. It's a sign that she didn't underestimate her stature within French culture, or the stature of culture within the larger political scene, that her attempt was successful: she met the man she had flattered as 'a Socialist genius . . . accepted by the people' and, through his favour, attained the release of hundreds of political prisoners.[76]

At home, a new kind of peace prevailed as well. Sand was becoming a contented matron; she'd gained weight and she wore comfortable dresses – her days of frockcoats and boots were over. Together she and Manceau incorporated Nini into their routine, with Manceau looking after her in the mornings and Sand taking her about with her in the afternoon. When Sand had to go to Paris, she left Nini with a neighbour, writing a schedule of the kind that so many anxious carers have written over the centuries: 'Should be washed head to toe in lukewarm water, in the morning and at 5 o'clock . . . Drinks red water, sugar-water and when she goes to bed a small piece of sugar in a third of a glass of water . . . Cut her toenails very little at a time, but every week at least.'[77]

In July 1853 Solange and Clésinger reconciled for the final time and took Nini back to Paris. Sand wrote a little aggressively to her daughter that she had 'the misfortune to attach myself to all those I take care of' and that she didn't want Nini to come and go – next time the child had to come for good. Nini returned alone in December, unpacking her dolls and toys with 'transports of joy' and announcing that she never wanted to leave. The marriage was definitively over and at Nohant, the little family of courtiers gathered around the redemptive child. Sand was making a children's rock garden she called 'Trianon', reminiscent of one of the most powerful memories of her childhood: the garden that she helped her parents concoct around her baby brother's grave. She wheeled stones and planted ivy while Nini rushed around with her wheelbarrow and Manceau sat and read to them. Maurice had a theatre now at the house and gave marionette performances in the evening. 'We are inseparable and it is impossible to make a better household,' she told Solange in Paris.[78]

'Isn't the childhood of a human being a mysterious state full of unexplained wonders?' Sand wrote in the autobiography she had begun in 1847. 'Where do children come from? Before being formed in their mother's womb, haven't they had some sort of existence in the impenetrable womb of the Divinity?' She was newly amazed by the passage from babyhood to sociability – the child naming objects and claiming those around her with love. Her writing from these years is constantly drawn to children, rescuing them from peril and often providing them with surrogate parents. 'Now I know something that I never believed in before it happened to me,' says the harsh beauty Brulette, given a child to bring up in Sand's 1953 novel *The Bagpipers*; 'it is that any child, however ugly and wicked, may be bitten by a wolf or trampled by a goat, but never by a woman, and that he will come to rule her, unless she is made of a different wood from the others.' These novels of rural life have a casualness, a waywardness, lacking in Sand's early novels; there isn't the feeling that everything is determined by the plot and, indeed, the plots are forgettable. It's the landscape that stays with you: the brooks, crisscrossing the woods in every direction and forming moist thickets where alders and willows grow; and also the feelings – and in this case the strongest feeling is the love of the woman for the child and of the child for the woman.[79]

While Sand wrote wonderingly about childhood, Solange was understandably unhappy. Her marriage was ending and she had no money – her husband had spent her dowry. Sand was more loving towards her daughter than she had been in a long time, and the two collaborated in making plans for Nini. But the admonishments continued, especially when Solange wrote to Sand during moments of anguish. While she waited for the first of her many custody verdicts in 1851, Solange went to a convent. 'Is this how I am going to spend the best years of my life?' she asked her mother; 'without a parent, without a friend, without a child, without even a dog to interrupt the void?' She insisted that this wasn't boredom, but despair, adding that she could see why poor girls without 'spirit' or education allowed themselves to be drawn into pleasure and vice. Sand knew what it was like to wait for a separation judgment. She knew what it was like to fear, as Solange did, that the judgment would mean nothing, because the husband would only appeal it, and then kidnap his daughter anyway. Yet she chastised her daughter for writing in 'an attack of spleen', saying that she had 'no grace' in complaining about a situation she'd brought on herself by going to court precipitously. She was also angry about Solange's implication that she found vice tempting; having been attributed with vice of this kind herself, this may have been too incendiary a subject: 'Do you know that if I were a judge in your trial and read your aphorisms today I would certainly not give you your daughter.' She told her to fetch her daughter and bring her to Nohant. Nini was a 'treasure' who could take the place of everything for her if she would allow it.[80]

Sand seized her granddaughter with a kind of eager greed reminiscent of her own grandmother, and she had the same incentives to offer the discarded mother: income, inheritance. Nini didn't cry for her mother as Sand had done; Nini's grandmother was more approachable, and Solange was freer to come and go. The family that emerged at Nohant did include Solange, but it's telling that Sand wrote that letter about the perfection of their household in Solange's absence. For her part, Solange does seem to have felt the needs for freedom and for motherhood as competing claims. She was only twenty-four when she brought Nini back to her mother. She was horrified by the thought of sending her to a convent, insisting (in what is surely a rebuke to her mother for her own childhood) that 'a child who grows up without kisses is a plant that grows without the sun' and would end up with a sad mind and a cold heart, 'like the flower that opens in the shade'. But she was happy to leave her daughter with her mother, and for her part Sand seems to have found being a grandmother easier than she'd found being a mother. She no longer had the urge to throw the doll away before guiltily reclaiming it. She no longer had either the compulsion to leave or the agony of absence. She was comfortable enough now in her identity as a writer and as a woman who had defied convention that these daily acts of maternal care came easily, leaving grandmother and granddaughter bathed in the light of their shared happiness. And so she loved recklessly – courageous as always. She seems to have forgotten, for a few months, how precarious their situation was.

Clésinger came suddenly in May 1854. He'd found letters exposing an affair of Solange's – hardly a surprise, given their lengthy separations – which he deposited with his lawyer. He then arrived at Nohant, demanding his child. Sand handed her over and cancelled the preparations she'd put in place for the girl's fifth birthday, three days later.

Yet another girl, powerless in the struggles of her parents, crying out for her lost mother and grandmother. It's not surprising that Solange should have ended up in her own custody case, or that the custody case should push Clésinger into extremes of brutality and cruelty. Clésinger did love his daughter, though he made a habit of kidnapping her, and had joked to a friend in his wife's hearing that he was bringing her up to be his mistress. Galvanised by the court case, he turned that love into a means to punish his wife and the mother-in-law who had refused to mortgage her house on his behalf.

Wretched, Sand and Solange wrote letter after letter asking where Nini was. The reconciliation between mother and daughter was genuine during these months; they were frantic for the same end: that the child should live with her grandmother. After a month, Clésinger put Nini into the Villeneuve convent in Paris. 'The mountains of pain that darken this side of my horizon would be too high, too sad to show you,' Sand wrote to a friend. Finally, in December, it was time for their hearing. Solange didn't plead for custody – Clésinger had clear evidence of her adultery, of a kind that Casimir Dudevant hadn't managed to obtain in Sand's own case. But the judge saw that Clésinger wasn't capable of looking after a child and, in another move that wouldn't have been possible in the English courts of the time, granted custody to Sand.[81]

'The child will come back to me, the great sorrows are softened and effaced,' Sand announced. She urged her daughter to collect her immediately from the convent, and then not to leave her defenceless for 'a day, an hour – he can take her away'. However, Clésinger had announced his intention to appeal, and until the new judgment was in, the girl could not to be released. Furious, Sand wrote to his lawyer, Eugène Bethmont, demanding that the child at least be moved to a better convent as the Villeneuve convent was dirty, and she was badly cared for: her winter clothes hadn't yet been unpacked, though it had been an icy winter. Manceau went to Paris to visit Nini at the convent, but was told that she had scarlet fever and could not see him. The next day, he was told the same thing but, walking past Clésinger's apartment, he saw Nini with her father, standing at the window in a summer dress.[82]

'If Mmes Villeneuve did not tell a ferocious lie, the child seen at the window with scarlet fever would be in mortal danger,' Sand wrote to Bethmont, outraged.[83] Bethmont himself was a substantial figure in their world, and she feared that he was sacrificing her granddaughter to his own determination to win the case. She felt that Clésinger was malleable enough that the right lawyer could have persuaded him to give up and concentrate his energies elsewhere. But Bethmont was a disillusioned politician who'd had a brief moment of glory as Minister of Commerce and then Minister of Justice in the revolutionary government of 1848. Now he was clearly irritable at finding himself responsible for the warmth and linen of a five-year-old girl, but he was going to see it through; if the battles in his life had become more trivial, that made him all the more foolhardily resolved to win.

Bethmont insisted that everything was fine and that all parties had agreed for the child to be at the convent, visited by the father and mother. Incensed, Sand retorted that this had not been agreed at all, and that Bethmont himself had admitted that the convent was insufficiently clean or warm – he had gone there to try to improve things: 'You add, Sir, that Mr Clésinger is very determined in his resolution. So am I in mine.'[84]

But nothing was changed, and Nini was sent back to class, though she had not fully recovered from her scarlet fever. In January, she deteriorated rapidly and Solange was summoned. She found her daughter disfigured by swelling, and suffocating, though not in pain. The girl played on her bed bravely, sewing together little rags. Solange watched over her until the next day, when Nini put away her toys in little boxes and took from her neck the medallion containing a lock of her mother's hair. She tried to smile as she handed it to her mother, and then she fell weakly asleep and died.

At Nohant, Sand cried all night. Solange brought home the little body to be buried in the garden cemetery, beside Sand's father and grandmother, under the cypress trees. 'You won your case,' Sand wrote in bitter fury to Bethmont, who she described to all her friends as an 'assassin'. 'My little girl is dead. I'm waiting for someone to come and desecrate the grave where she rests with my father and grandmother, after six months of moral and physical distress.'[85]

There were weeks of devastated grief, shared with Solange. In the midst of this, Sand wrote a poem to her daughter, resurrecting their love among the ruins:

> Pour ma Solange en
> Ce beau jour,
> J'ai retrouvé tout mon
> Amour,
> Puisqu'elle veut être bien
> Sage
> Pourvu qu'elle en ait le
> Courage![86]

> *For my Solange on*
> *This beautiful day,*
> *I found all my*
> *Love again,*
> *Since she wants to be*
> *Wise*
> *Provided she has the*
> *Courage!*

Together they spent a day collecting the toys scattered around the house. Everywhere, Sand had placed things where Nini would find them on her return: the wheelbarrow and little watering can; the books and needlework; the dolls that Sand had dressed every night the previous winter in a new dress, so that Nini would be surprised by them on her pillow when she woke up. There were even toys waiting on Sand's writing desk.

Sand told her friend Édouard Charton that though she wanted to resume writing, she was not sure that 'that phase of life' could ever return: 'my whole life during the last two years was absorbed by that little child. She caried away with her so much of my being that I do not know what is left to me, and I have not yet had enough courage to make the examination.' Charton had advised her to read *Terre et Ciel* by Jean Reynaud, a Saint-Simonian mining engineer who had recently come up with a new religious philosophy about the transmigration of souls. Sand read Reynaud, envisaging souls passing from planet to planet alongside him, and read Leibnitz, whose faith in the immortality of the soul and of some form of bodily life had always consoled her. Her faith in God remained as strong as ever and she was able to affirm to Charton that she could now see 'future and eternal life' before her as a certainty: 'I know full well that my Jeanne is not dead; I know well that she is better than in this miserable world, where she was the victim of the wicked and the foolish. I know well that I shall meet her again, and that she will recognise me, even though she will not recollect me, nor I her.'[87]

All this because a father had taken a daughter he was unable to look after himself away from a home where he knew her to be loved. In her autobiography, which she eventually brought herself to finish a few months later, Sand wrote that there were events she had not recounted; events she 'could not excuse, because I could not yet explain them to myself', and people she had not forgiven. 'My heart is a cemetery,' she wrote here. It was partly a homage to her beloved Chateaubriand, but the reverse was also true: the Nohant cemetery was now the heart of her emotional world.[88]

It was a hot summer day when I visited Nohant, in search of little Nini and of the mulched bones of Sand's ancestors. I wanted to swim, but the river I'd imagined to be close by the house was several fields away, and I didn't have Sand's hectic energy that day. Instead

I sat in the woods, by the remains of Trianon, guarded by a tall oak tree. This corner was dark with shade, with sunlight creeping in from the nearest path. The moss-covered stones felt arbitrary in their assemblage now, and seemed too heavy to have been carried by a fifty-year-old woman and a four-year-old girl, though anything was possible with Sand. It was easy to imagine Nini with her little wheelbarrow, going back and forth. Love here was their slow and careful daily work; the passing of time side by side. And I sat in the dappled graveyard, where Sand once climbed in to embrace the bones of the father who had died before he had time to see her grow up. I touched the cool stone of the twinned, ivy-covered graves: Marie-Aurore and Maurice Dupin; Jeanne and Solange Clésinger – united now as they were at the moment of Nini's death.

I missed my own children uneasily, as I always do when away; they become somehow spectral. Between my wanderings around the garden, I talked to the friend who had come with me from Paris. I was thinking about Sand's life as a writer and her life as a mother, and about how for a while she had to separate these lives, leaving her children behind.

Was it possible to be a good writer and a good mother? a London friend had asked me before I came. What a stupid thing to say, my Paris friend said now. What a privileged question, when there are plenty of mothers who can't give all their time to their children because they are busy cleaning offices for twelve hours a day. But the London friend knew that she was privileged. She was worried that she enjoyed writing too much, and that she wasn't meant to be so happily absorbed in something that took her away from her children. Isn't that what Solange minded about her mother? – she had too good a time.

Does motherhood always mean self-sacrifice, or are there ways of having it all? Michel made it possible for Sand to be a mother and a writer, defending her in court. He made it possible for her to be proudly emancipated and yet to pride herself on her care-giving.

She didn't ask herself if she could be a good writer and a good mother. Instead, she brought the two identities together with her characteristic combination of wilfulness and grace; she wrote while Nini played on the floor beside her, as Solange once had. It was only when Nini died that she couldn't write.

'My heart is a cemetery.' But if it was this cemetery, was it a bad place to be? It is a place of peace, where even on the hottest of days, the trees shade the dead, who are serenaded by birdsong, with the sky shining brightly through the canopied leaves. While I sat there, a French couple wandered in and tried to work out who was who: three generations of Aurores, Maurice Père et Maurice Fils. It's a lineage shaped by questions of custody and by the dead; each generation in turn forged in the furnace of their dead relatives. 'The dead, we are them, without doubt,' Sand wrote in a letter in 1848; 'there is a mysterious link that explains how our lives are sustained by theirs.' Walking around Nohant, I felt that it was a house that made both the loss of custody and the death of loved ones curiously sustainable, because each generation felt that they would be connected to their dead in the end.[89]

Love powers you through the world, my Paris friend said, over lunch in La Châtre, while we did our best to ignore the screaming child across the way. As we watched the little girl throw her pizza on the floor, we recalled that when we were younger, scenes like this made us determined not to have children. Yet we found ourselves having them all the same. And then the miracle, the 'unexplained wonders', the first shared 'I love you'. Children flourish, my friend said, when they know they are loved. I thought of my absent children, and felt at peace, knowing that they knew they were loved. 'I love you, I'll miss you' my usually reticent eleven-year-old son had said to my partner for the first time, the week before. Without love, it is just survival, my Paris friend said now. Did Nini know she was loved, in her convent, I wondered? Did Solange, when she was taken away from her governess by her father? Did Aline Chazal, when her father slept beside her at night in their enforced proximity, shaking with alcoholic tremors?

I had been thinking, before I came to Nohant, about the differences between the love we feel for our children and for our lovers – about the split selves that Sand described to Marcie, and the differences between maternal and sexual love she described to Musset. That same London friend had said that our love for our children, at its best, has a fulness, an intensity, that it's hard to allow ourselves with lovers. With our children we go all the way, not fearing rejection. There are other disasters to fear: loss of custody, betrayal, death. But Sand's grief in 1855 was not the grief of a woman who had held anything back. And she would love again: Maurice's daughter, the third Aurore.

'My dominant passion on the whole is my Aurore,' she wrote to Flaubert when the girl was six. 'My life depends on hers.' This granddaughter would be with her until she died, and was eventually buried beside her in the graveyard that was also a heart.[90]

Sand was a woman who multiplied the possibilities of how a woman could live. She valued freedom above almost everything else, yet she repeatedly staked everything on motherhood and she somehow, in a stubbornly patriarchal legal system, retained her right to mother her children and eventually made them a part of her freedom. Maurice and his children took 'Sand' as part of their names, sharing the identity that she had invented for herself. Maurice's father wasn't happy about this: before he died, Casimir Dudevant wrote to the Emperor Napoleon, hoping to solicit the Grand Cross of the Légion d'honneur, as compensation for the hardships he'd endured as the husband of the notorious George Sand.

Underground, in this corner of a garden in a forgotten valley in the French countryside, love that has taken the form of loss now takes the form of bones brought together in the soil – parents and children separated in life but joined again. To love here is to have roots that drive into the ground as the trees' roots do. Every moment in Sand's life has a kind of parallel existence in this garden: it was here that she came, dripping with sweat and water, after submerging herself fully clothed in the river; it was here that she and Solange returned, exhausted, after the triumphant rescue by a mother of her precious daughter. All the ferocity and energy of those days is here still, making itself felt, so that sitting in the graveyard, it isn't hard to make out the horses' hooves, as that child of her century and of ours, plunged so determinedly into the future she played a part in creating, even as it became ever more fully an age of lawyers.

3

ELIZABETH PACKARD,

with a Guest Appearance by Britney Spears

Custody is always a battle for control, but sometimes it's a small element of a larger attempt to control someone using all the institutions around, albeit the element with the most collateral damage.

June 1860. Five men bang on the locked door of the bedroom a woman shares with her three youngest children. The children have been stealthily got out of the way and now it's time to remove the mother. She's known it was coming – a month earlier, thirty-nine of her pastor husband's parishioners petitioned for her to be 'placed in an Insane Asylum, as speedily as can be conveniently done' – but she knows her rights. She's a free woman, protected by a constitution granting rights to every democratic citizen. She tells her husband confidently through the door that he doesn't have the power to incarcerate her without a jury trial.[1]

'I am doing as the laws of Illinois allow me to do,' he responds.

It turns out that she's married away her freedom: in the state of Illinois husbands can declare their wives insane without a trial.

'You have no protector in law but myself,' he continues, 'and I am protecting you now! It is for your own good I am doing this,

I want to save your soul – you don't believe in total depravity, and I want to make you right.'²

He's saving her soul, and hopes to save his children's souls in the process. She's been telling them that they're godly creatures when he knows them to be sinful – born in depravity. Eventually, he convinces her that she has no choice.

Next to her, the bed of six-year-old George has only just been made. An hour earlier he was waking beside her, warm with sleep, and rushing off to bring her strawberries. Last week she was awake night after night, tending to the boy's fever, wiping him down, persuading him to drink. It doesn't seem possible that she's going anywhere without her children, but she goes through

'Kidnapping Mrs Packard' (from Modern Persecution)

the motions, dressing neatly, tying back her long brown hair, leaving her face framed by trim ringlets. And then she opens the door and instructs the men to make a saddle with their hands; she's not going to walk out on her own accord, but she's going to remain dignified, a small, upright woman carried down her own stairs by men she knows to be relics of the past, while she is a woman of the future.

There's a crowd at the station, but no one protests on behalf of Elizabeth Packard as she's forced onto a train. After she's gone, two of her children arrive at the station – George and his sixteen-year-old brother Isaac, who their father got out of the way earlier by dispatching them both to the store where Isaac works. When they discover what has happened, they cry out for her: 'We have no mother!'

Outraged – so her neighbours later report to Elizabeth – the older boy asks why no one protected her. 'I knew your father was determined, and he would put her in at any rate,' his boss at the store tells him.

'*George, we have no mother!*' (*from* Modern Persecution)

George runs down the train track, determined to rescue her: 'I will get my dear mamma out of prison!' he tells some onlookers, who pull him back.

Over the next few days, neighbours hear Elizabeth's daughter, eleven-year-old Libby, crying day and night. 'Her plaintive moans could be heard at quite a distance from her home,' Elizabeth Packard wrote later, maternal pride mingling with sadness. '"O! mother! mother! mother!" was her almost constant, unceasing call.'[3]

January 2008. A mother and baby are locked in a high-spec LA bathroom. At sixteen months, the baby is still soft and chubby. Not long ago, he was inside the body of the woman who now clutches him, sobbing. He was safe in her womb; so safe that she sometimes wishes she could hide him there again. People tell her she's not fit to protect him from the world's assaults, but can't they see that she shares their fears?

Her older son, the two-year-old, has been handed over – not to his father but to the security guard sent to collect him. She was about to hand over the baby but then she ran in and locked the door. She's terrified that if she gives him up, he'll never return. Already, she only has visitation rights; soon, in this world controlled by lawyers and judges who seem to be always on her husband's side, she may even lose those.

Does the baby cry in the bathroom? Perhaps initially he's just happy with this sudden intimacy with his mother. But then there are noises from outside and the mother can't hide her terror. This isn't a womb and they both know it; it's all corners and gleaming tiles and bangs and shouts and a woman shaking with fear. She has a friend visiting, who shouts that she can take her time, the security guard has said he'll wait.

She has to relinquish him. She prepares herself, cuddling him and crying. Then suddenly the bangs are louder and there's a SWAT team in black suits, crashing through the door. The baby is snatched, and the mother tied onto a gurney and taken to a psychiatric hospital where she's committed for seventy-two hours. At her next custody hearing she'll be told that she can spend even less time with her boys.

Britney Spears had had two babies within a year; her husband, the dancer Kevin Federline, was barely at home during her first year of motherhood; she was so hounded by the paparazzi that she kept her children's faces covered outside, and ended up driving away with a baby on her lap, only to be castigated as a bad mother. She went out drinking; she danced on tables and stripped in public – wasn't this what the world most wanted? And then, when her husband got custody and she could only see her children in front of a parenting coach, she was found wanting.

Lisa Hacker monitored four visits and filed a report saying that while she felt Spears 'loves her children and the children are bonded' to their mother, she thought this mother wasn't 'child-centred' in her interactions. The house ranged from 'chaotic to almost sombre with little communication at all'. Sometimes Spears failed to play with or talk to her children, though on the final visit she seemed 'much more engaged'. Lisa Hacker spoke in the admonishing language that judges and their representatives have used to mothers for over two centuries. 'The problem is that unless Ms Spears realises the consequences of her behaviour and the impact that it has on her children, nothing is going to be successful.'[4]

Elizabeth Packard and Britney Spears were both incarcerated in mental hospitals, separated from children they were seen as unfit to mother. And out of the books they wrote, over a century apart, pulses the agony of abused motherhood: Elizabeth Packard, recording her children's plaintive moans, and Britney Spears, imagining her boys 'not knowing where their mother was, wondering why she didn't want to be with them', and longing 'to get a battering ram to get to them . . . I was simply out of my mind with grief. My children had been taken away from me.'[5]

America. 'The land of the free and the home of the brave,' as Francis Scott Key wrote in the 1812 poem that would become the national anthem, celebrating the Star-Spangled Banner waving after military victory. This is the freedom of democracy; the freedom of the American dream that tells everyone to create themselves and to forge the largest life they can imagine. But what happens when the impetus towards change becomes so powerful that the forces of reaction set in, turning conservatism into patriarchal oppression? And what happens when the people seizing this freedom are mothers?

What made Britney Spears so appealing as a teenager, sliding between high-voiced sweetness and gravelly world-weariness, was that she was the exaggerated embodiment of the American dream, the sugary fruit of mass democracy. Here was the rise from rags to riches personified – the girl who loved to sing got to sing. And all this played out under the scrutiny of the mass media she seemed to accept as her due.

But then motherhood was added to the mix. Partying recklessly, driving around with her baby on her lap, she was every 'trailer trash' mother, exposing the faultlines in the system. How can you self-actualise as a woman at the same time as raising a baby? How can you captivate with your sex appeal when mothers aren't meant to be erotic? Britney's motherhood provided the revelation: the plurality of democracy is an engine of conformity rather than freedom. The judgements of the mass media piled in and there was a kind of inevitability in the breakdown that followed. She ended up unsafe to mother her children because the culture had refused to accept her as a mother. The asylum beckoned, as it always had.

For Elizabeth Packard, born in 1816 into an age of exuberant post-revolutionary optimism and growth, the constitutional promise of 'life, liberty, and the pursuit of happiness' was a birthright and a spur to action. Hers was an age instilled with the complex optimism of frontier living – of the mighty, often addled, desire to declare that this was a new sort of country, with unique claims to grandeur and goodness. Before her husband, Theophilus, escorted her to the asylum in 1860, it hadn't occurred to Elizabeth Packard that the rights proffered by Jefferson were not the inalienable rights of women as well as men.

Around her, feminists were campaigning with growing success for women's education and rights, and judges increasingly upheld children's right to their mothers – pushing American law way ahead of the English counterpart it remained complicatedly entwined with. It wasn't that she was a women's rights campaigner or aspired to a career of her own. She was happy to conform as a woman of her era and liked spending her days in her trimly organised home – making her children's clothes, and supervising their diets and conduct, and helping at her husband's church. She was producing six citizens suited for a new age, so motherhood itself required energy and improvisatory ingenuity. She understood her age to be different from the one she'd grown up in, and she wanted everyone around her to know that things were changing. So she exercised her freedom of speech by introducing her husband's Illinois parishioners to the most radical theological ideas. Her doctrine of universal love was rapidly becoming more accepted than her husband's doctrine of total depravity.

But she was now destined to understand how unstable all this was. Because it turned out that it was just this wave of optimistic progress that was leading to enlarged, federally funded mental asylums and to ever-increasing numbers of wives and mothers being incarcerated within their walls. And it turned out that the very energy and ingenuity required of mothers was the energy and ingenuity that necessitated their suppression when they exceeded the limits of a patriarchal age, and that the legal system was ill-equipped to enforce the rights of women. Elizabeth Packard set out to get her children back and to change the law. In doing so she would push the limits of her age as far as they could be pushed, revealing how powerful mothers were – yet also how powerless, when it came to protecting another generation of children from harm.

I. Marriage

'Wives, obey your husbands'

They had married, Elizabeth Ware and Theophilus Packard, in 1839, when she was twenty-two and he thirty-seven. She was the beloved, brilliant daughter of a Massachusetts Congregationalist minister and his wife: Samuel and Lucy Ware. Around them, girls' schools were sprouting, ready to instruct the daughters of Massachusetts; Samuel Ware educated Elizabeth exceptionally well and encouraged her rapid success as a teacher, but then married her off to an inferior man.

Theophilus Packard had grown up in the rectitudinous shadow of his own pastor father and looked up to Samuel Ware as a senior colleague. Aged ten, Elizabeth had begun listening to them deliberating on theology, never offering her own opinion, and she was surprised when this man, with his unappealingly huge forehead and shock of red hair, was proposed as a suitor. He was so undemonstrative – this didn't seem like love – but her father assured her that tenderness would follow.

It was a marriage that managed to be at once too cramped and too roomy: proximity without intimacy. She looked after the vegetable garden and the hens; he controlled her mail, her money and her friendships – but this wasn't unusual, and she deferred to his worldliness. There were three years like this and then, finally, their first child was born, and the other babies followed.

Theophilus was growing dissatisfied with Massachusetts. He was a co-pastor with his father at the prestigious Shelburne Congregationalist Church, but the Congregationalists were riven between Calvinists and Unitarians, and he wasn't on the winning side. He wanted a new start, and Elizabeth liked the thought of starting again in a wider, emptier land. She made elaborate travelling outfits for their five children – a black velvet tunic, lined with dove-coloured silk for her daughter, and a black silk-velvet cap with blue satin rosettes for her baby – and in 1854 they went west, first to Ohio, then to Iowa, then on to Illinois in 1857, to a village called Manteno, with a train station, a general store and a saloon, situated on the rich green prairie of Kankakee County, where Theophilus's sister Sybil had recently moved. Theophilus was the pastor of Manteno's First Presbyterian Church, which had formed four years earlier with eleven members and met in makeshift locations, including the Illinois Central freight house and the Manteno Methodist church. This was all a lot more provisional than the dignified, whitewashed church building in Massachusetts he'd begun his career in, but he hoped to oversee the erection of a new church building.

There was space here, and skies that made the earth feel limitless. Elizabeth Packard could open the green shutters of her bedroom and look straight out at the prairie. 'Action is the vital element out here,' she later wrote of the West; 'the prairie winds are always moving – no such thing as a dead calm day here.' There was so much space – why not take up more of it? 'Our mould in which we were cast has been broken up. We have had room for expansive growth. We were too conservative rut thinkers, there.' As a mother she had things to say and a voice to say them; in the West, this became a voice she wanted her whole community to hear.[6]

When Illinois graduated to statehood in the year of Elizabeth's birth, in 1816, it had become America's most westerly state. Even now this was frontier territory, makeshift and spartan, despite new transport and infrastructure, and though all state institutions were run by New Englanders along Yankee lines, it was radically more democratic than the world the Packards had left behind. Arriving in Illinois in 1846, one New Englander deplored the way that: 'Men who in the circles where they had their origin, would have ever stood back, relying upon others' opinions, are not infrequently, in a new settlement, thrown upon their own resources, and compelled to think and act.' Government here was treated as the public's servant rather than master. For decades, every adult male had been able to vote; admittedly, now you had to be a citizen and to have been there a year, but this was still more democratic than Massachusetts, where voters had always been required to be taxpayers and were now required to pass a literacy test too.[7]

Motherhood on the frontier offered new opportunities. Less than a decade earlier, women had arrived here on wagons and found themselves running hotels and schools, or riding bareback chasing runaway cows. Things had changed, but maternal resourcefulness was required and permitted, and this came easily to Elizabeth Packard. Cooking with her children in her tightly ordered kitchen, praying with them in the nursery, she brought to motherhood a combination of puritanism, freedom and inventive zeal fitting for her times. While breastfeeding, she was strict with herself – there were months of cold baths, fuelled only by graham crackers and water – but she let her babies nurse whenever and wherever they wanted. When her sixth baby was a week old, she cooked and ate the family Christmas dinner with him feeding at her breast – unimaginable among her class in England at the time.

'The home from which Mrs Packard was kidnapped'
(from Modern Persecution)

For the children, life was structured around chores and measured by merit points. Elizabeth only used a rod on Samuel, her third child; the others found 'a mother's reproof' punishment enough. Aged five, Samuel described their daily life to a visitor, and his mother recorded their conversation. His first task, he explained, was to fill his mother's wood box; then he played while she did her chores, entertaining the baby if necessary; when the bell rang it was time for his education – he read and recited his spellings and then practised sewing on his bedquilt. Off he went on his sled outside, until she rang the bell for dinner: 'Then I come in quick, for if I don't I get a tardy mark.' He enjoyed his food, he said, but his father never gave him enough. Then it was time to amuse the baby and play, before doing more reading and spelling and knitting, and playing outdoors until supper time. 'I like to play a great deal better after my stint is done, than before, and ma says the way to enjoy play, is to do our stint first: "duty first, and then pleasure", she says is the way God does, and ma says we must be like God.'[8]

After supper: prayers, a cold bath, and bed; sometimes they were allowed to listen to visitors talking in the parlour before bed, and Samuel tried not to plead to stay up longer. 'Objecting!' was the retort otherwise, accompanied by a bad conduct mark. These accrued easily, for offences like forgetting to take off his hat before entering the house, or speaking crossly. One disobedience mark counted as six common misdemeanours. And accumulated credit marks for completion of lessons resulted in sleds and wheelbarrows and gimlets and hammers.

It was a strict regime, but it does seem to have been suffused with love. 'Mother if you ever go out to the water, I want to go with you,' second-born Isaac once apparently said to his mother; 'for if you are drowned I want to be drowned with you, because I don't want to live after you die.'[9]

Reading this I think of my daughter, who, for a few weeks before she turned six, pleaded with me nightly to let her die at the same moment as me. It can feel frightening, to be trusted with this much love.

Setting up systems of merit marks, educating her children, supervising their diets (though note her husband asserting control over the size of portions), Elizabeth Packard was given freedom and autonomy she hadn't had since school-teaching. Here she was different from her own mother, whose role had been primarily to implement her husband's ideas about upbringing – which chiefly involved putting their children in the hands of Massachusetts's excellent schools.

At the turn of the century, child-rearing advice had been addressed to fathers, but now it was almost universally addressed to mothers, often encouraging them to extend their moral authority over their husbands as well. Why was this? There was the separation of the workplace and domestic sphere seen in England and France. But there was also a specifically American shift, following the 1783 revolution, which brought in its wake a new egalitarianism and a widespread aversion to unaccountable authority, including patriarchal authority.

In the early 1830s, as Elizabeth became part of the first generation of girls to get a full, scientific education at the newly founded Amherst Female Seminary, the French revolutionary Alexis de Tocqueville visited America. President Andrew Jackson's democratic reforms were in their early stages – the country was expanding west and moving towards full male adult suffrage as it did so – and Tocqueville wrote admiringly in his *Democracy in America* about the effects of Jacksonian democracy on American family relations: 'the several members of the family stand upon an entirely new footing towards each other . . . paternal authority, if not destroyed, is at least impaired'.[10]

Politicians now emphasised the individual's democratic worth; preachers in the growing Evangelical churches insisted on equality before God – speaking colloquially rather than in the language of theologians; economically, market capitalism allowed individual competitiveness to triumph. This all went along with a falling birth rate, here as in France, which made children newly precious. It was mothers who birthed the children and brought them up. Sons weren't going to replicate fathers; a new kind of man was required to lead the republic. 'Our children are born to higher destinies than their fathers,' announced influential magazine publisher Nathaniel Willis in 1827, launching *The Youth's Companion*, with readers like eleven-year-old Elizabeth Ware in mind. Parents with the right mix of affection and sternness – and mothers in particular – could shape virtuous, autonomous citizens. The advice manuals didn't specify whether these mothers should themselves be autonomous citizens, with their own needs and drives.[11]

These newly precious children came with rights, in the era of rights that followed the revolution, as it had in France. One of the most popular women's magazines, *Godey's Lady's Book*, campaigned for 'The Rights of Children', claiming equality between children and parents. John Locke's idea of the child as a tabula rasa, a blank slate, was sentimentally embellished, his emptiness transformed into an idealised innocence by writers like Lydia Sigourney, a married educator who gained a vast readership in the 1840 and 1850s. 'How entire and perfect is this dominion, over the unformed character of your infant,' Sigourney wrote in her *Letters to Mothers*. 'Write what you will, upon the printless tablet, with your wand of love.' Elizabeth Packard was bringing up her children in the wake of Lydia Sigourney, and of Lydia Maria Child, the influential magazine publisher who averred in her 1831 *Mother's Book* that children had no faults that weren't correctible by pure maternal affection: for children 'come to us from heaven with their souls full of innocence and peace . . . under the influence of angels'.[12]

Elizabeth Packard's children were so eager to please that she became sure of the truth of Maria Child's ideas: children were innately innocent; they weren't the depraved creatures Theophilus and fellow Calvinists condemned them to be. As a young girl, she'd listened to her father's conversations, not just with Theophilus but with Henry Ward Beecher, who taught Sabbath school at their church and would go on to become the renowned preacher of a 'Gospel of Love', questioning the existence of hell. Beecher's articles in the Congregationalist periodicals fuelled Elizabeth's new convictions. Her children weren't waiting to be saved by a dramatic conversion. She didn't want to awaken 'sorrow for sins' as the Calvinists commanded. She began to challenge Theophilus's views, and to spread her reading beyond Congregationalism to the more controversial 'Swedenborgianism', with its promise that anyone who lived well and had faith in God would be saved. It helped that she'd fallen in love with a local Swedenborgian, Abner Baker, a father of five from Manteno. She outraged Theophilus by engaging in a lengthy correspondence with Baker, expressing her chaste, godly but nonetheless passionate love and elucidating her more unorthodox views.

She was, in her way, as religious as her husband, though he might have found it easier if she wasn't. 'Ma says we must be like God,' said Samuel. As a baby, her first-born son Theophilus (known as Toffy) had suffered from croup, and Elizabeth had felt 'soul and spirit both quiver with anguish'. She prayed to God to let him live and felt God say: 'The child is Mine – not yours.' When Toffy lived, she felt that God was rewarding her for learning to love him more than her children. But it was because she loved God that she trusted in his munificence. And it made no sense that human nature was inherently sinful.[13]

These may sound like small differences but they weren't. Samuel, caught thieving, flung his arms around Elizabeth's neck, begging her not to give him up for hell: 'There is nothing can keep me from it but you, mother.' It mattered enormously that she could assure her fearful son that he could go to heaven, if he just prayed for forgiveness and behaved well. But for Theophilus this complacency would jeopardise Samuel's chance of being saved. He began to cast doubt on his wife's sanity.[14]

She gained confidence and some new, even more incendiary ideas after a trip back to New England in 1857, returning as a Spiritualist. For Theophilus, this felt like a bewildering personal attack. Yet at the start of 1860, when he went east to do a stint as a guest preacher, he recommended that his wife join his brother-in-law's ailing Bible class. Perhaps Theophilus wanted to expose her views, revealing her madness to his parishioners. Certainly, she attracted attention. There were six members of the class when he left and forty-six when he returned. 'God's work as he made it was perfect,' Elizabeth told them, reading out carefully crafted, eloquent essays. She split an already divided church, finding a receptive audience in other parents longing to assure their fearful children that they, too, were bound for heaven.[15]

'Wives, obey your husbands,' Theophilus quoted at her. But though she'd obeyed him in Massachusetts it was different here.

'I shall put you in the asylum,' he warned. But she didn't believe that he could, and perhaps she was bent on finding out just how far she could go.

'I never dare to do what I conscientiously believe to be wrong,' she later recalled telling him, with a self-righteousness that can't have helped marital relations.[16]

It was all especially difficult for Theophilus because Elizabeth's were no longer minority views. All over America, the Congregationalist Church was being overtaken by Unitarians, convinced that man was already close to God. The Unitarian Horace Bushnell published his book *Christian Nurture* just as the Packards' third child was born in 1847. Simply observe children, he wrote, taking joy in obeying their parents, flowing with 'ductile feeling' and tender sensibilities. Why not assume that the child was born a Christian, whose faith, nurtured by the right godly parents, was simply renewed with age?[17]

Around them, new sects spawned to rival the Congregationalists – Disciples of Christ, and the Latter-day Saints – and few of them believed in infant depravity or predestination. Theophilus had been born into a world where the Congregationalists were the most thriving denomination, but now the Congregationalists had only a tenth of the preachers of the Methodists. He still couldn't get a congregation of more than fifty and it was humiliating holding his services in the Methodist building, knowing that their services were better attended than his. Now his wife turned out to be an enemy within his congregation – a natural democrat who was sweeping their children into the mob-ruled world that he feared.

This was the plurality, the cheek-by-jowl convergence of people with different beliefs, that mass democracy was meant to encourage. Theophilus wasn't alone in finding the cacophony too much and looking back desperately to an earlier, clearer age. Wasn't the danger that the small-scale community democracy celebrated by Tocqueville would quickly give way to conformist majorities imposing their will on minorities? 'The elect, the elected . . . they come here bright as dimes,/ and die dishevelled and soft,' Robert Lowell would write a century later, casually aligning spiritual and political election and revealing the ways that mass democracy had repurposed Calvinist superiority for its elected masters.[18]

Elizabeth Packard's solution – to look inwards, staking everything on her own vision and powers – was the one proffered by Ralph Waldo Emerson, prophet of modern America. Emerson himself had been ordained as a Unitarian minister in Massachusetts in 1829, before he disavowed churchgoing, settling neither for the combined 'magnificence' and 'nonsense' of Calvinism, nor the 'effete' alternative of Unitarianism – but founding the Transcendentalist movement, which located God as immanent within us. In his foundational 1841 essay 'Self-Reliance', Emerson celebrated the integrity of the individual human mind in terms that must have given confidence to Elizabeth Packard, who was sure to have read it: 'Whoso would be a man must be a nonconformist. He who would gather immortal palms must not be hindered by the name of goodness, but must explore if it be goodness. Nothing is at last sacred but the integrity of your own mind.' Emerson promised that the single self could achieve total autonomy; his was a self who gained its power from motion – 'power not confident but agent', manifesting itself in transition 'from a past to a new state'. In Illinois, it was easy for Elizabeth Packard to feel Emersonian; to feel on the move alongside this rapidly growing state. If Emerson was saying that everyone had to be visionaries in this newly pluralistic world, then who could be better fitted for this than mothers responsible for creating the leaders of the new republic? Already Elizabeth Packard was a pastor's wife who was also a pioneer citizen and a democrat with her own opinions. These many roles required improvisatory energy and an extraordinary capacity for personal change.[19]

Fearing the excessive integrity and power of his wife's mind,

Theophilus asked an authoritarian parishioner, Deacon Josephus Smith, to take over the Bible class. The deacon told him to oust his wife. Elizabeth described a mutually humiliating scene where she, desperately attempting to shore up the patriarchal authority of a man she'd succeeded in exposing as weak, sat on his lap pleading with him tearfully to 'be a man' and tell his congregation that his wife had the right to her own opinions. When that didn't work, with her characteristic mix of primness and independent-mindedness, she said she wouldn't leave unless she could say she'd been forced to. Otherwise, she taunted, she'd be lying.[20]

Elizabeth's next move was to suggest publicly that the church should dismiss her so she could join the Methodists. Now many parishioners joined Theophilus in doubting her sanity, and in May 1860 39 of them petitioned to have her 'placed in an Insane Asylum' and conducted a mock trial of her sanity in their parlour. Theophilus began locking her in her room and boarding the windows shut so she couldn't cry out for help. He gave her the option of going to her brother's in Batavia, Illinois, instead. She said no because he wasn't going to give her any money for expenses there – though he was prepared to pay her board at the asylum – and because he wouldn't let her take all the children. And anyway, she didn't believe he could put her in an asylum, and she thought she'd win a showdown if it came to it. Perhaps, indeed, she wanted a showdown; there was certainly a frenzied quality to her in these years, though that didn't mean she wasn't fit to mother her children.

And so, somehow, it came to this: a woman being carried from a wagon into one of the most frightening institutions of the country, all because of a theological difference that was as tiny and pedantic as it was vast and destiny-defining: Were their children saved or damned?

II. Incarceration

'Calvin dared to defy God's authority in separating me from my children'

She had been incarcerated before. When she was nineteen, her father had sent her to the State Lunatic Hospital in Worcester, Massachusetts. She'd been working as a teacher when she developed what was then called 'brain fever'. She had migraines and couldn't tolerate light or noise, her face and eyes were red, she could become delirious. Her parents had tried looking after at home, but the bleedings and purges made her worse, so after three weeks of delirium they wanted her in institutional hands. A state asylum seems a rather extreme solution: Samuel Ware had to fill in a form saying his daughter was a 'Lunatic so furiously mad as to render it manifestly dangerous to the peace and safety of the community' to keep her at home. At the asylum, the doctor recorded that 'her mind is rational on some topics and greatly insane on others'. He proposed, of course, to make her more 'womanly': no more reading, no more mental labour. She was released after six weeks, better, but less trusting of her previously adored father, and with a medical history that would play into Theophilus's hands.[21]

Now, in the Jacksonville Insane Asylum, Elizabeth was greeted by the superintendent, Andrew McFarland, himself the son of a Massachusetts clergyman. The Jacksonville asylum had been established in 1847 as part of a wave of apparently progressive reforms, spearheaded by campaigner Dorothea Dix. After witnessing those patients who were deemed insane 'chained, naked, beaten with rods' in prisons, Dix had lobbied the government for so-called humane asylums set up on the Kirkbride plan, named after the reforming physician who wanted mental asylums to be places of beauty and wholesome rural life – complete with farms and pleasure gardens. 'Moral treatment' was the order of the day, and 'moral' insanity a common diagnosis. Here, aged forty-four, Elizabeth Packard was diagnosed with 'moral insanity with monomania on the subject of religion'.[22]

The physician, McFarland, was a product of the new system: more brilliant, more ambitious and better suited to the new America than Theophilus; a visionary dedicated to the new science of psychiatry, determined to make his mark by curing the insane. He met his match in Elizabeth Packard, as she met her match in him. Growing up, she'd wanted to marry a manly intellectual, so she was excited as well as outraged to find herself confronted by one. Immediately, she and her doctor began the conversational jousting they would continue for the next three years. He seems to have been half-seduced by her and yet convinced from the start that he would find something mad about her, if only he could understand her better.

He put her on the Seventh Ward, where she was put off by the 'horrid and sickening stench' and flimsy furniture, but glad to find other apparently sane wives and mothers whose husbands had had enough of them. This was the underside of America's perpetual Mother's Day. If mothers were sources of gentleness and perfection, then mothers who failed to be submissive and feminine had to be ousted from family life. Child's *The Mother's Book* commanded women to 'govern her own feelings'; it was crucial that children never saw or felt 'the influence of bad passions'. The mother was to be ruled by 'patience, humility and love', even when opposed in her godly mission by an ignorant or untrustworthy husband. Ignorant husbands whose wives failed to be loving and humble could incarcerate them with more self-righteousness than guilt. And men were all the more fearful of independent women because the women's movement seemed to be making easy gains. American feminists were ahead of their English peers, aided by the leading role women played in the anti-slavery campaign and by the new precedents set by women in frontier states – before the decade was over, Wyoming would give women voting rights.[23]

It was precisely because it was so good a time to be a mother that it could go so badly wrong – and in such disorientating ways. Elizabeth's strengths were the strengths of American motherhood writ large: ingenuity, energy, love. Her weaknesses were her own: an extreme investment in her own rightness, a disdain of the pragmatic compromises that may need to characterise marriage. The fact that these weaknesses led her into the asylum reveals the stresses and fragilities inherent in motherhood at this time. Indeed, motherhood itself was seen as a cause of madness; women who took to mothering with too much intensity could be diagnosed as insane. Just as Elizabeth was being committed, the assistant physician at the Southern Ohio Lunatic Asylum was publishing his findings that 1 in 11 of the almost 12,000 women incarcerated in American asylums had been diagnosed with 'Puerperal Insanity': 'Often it happens that, long before any attack is apprehended, the patient is exceedingly influenced by overwrought emotions. Easily moved by trivial circumstances, she weeps or laughs immoderately compared with the cause. Usually there is sadness, a tendency to look at the dark side of every thing, to fear evil in the future.' Fear of harm; extreme emotions; some of these women would have had what's now known as post-partum psychosis, but much of this just sounds like a description of what it's like to have a child.[24]

Though separated from her children, Elizabeth Packard began to conceive of herself as a universal mother to the women around her in the asylum, holding daily prayer meetings and discussion groups. She learnt the rules: they had to avoid lamenting their absent children, or they would seem as too fretful to be sane. 'We must *seem* happy when we are miserable, or we can have no chance for a release,' a new friend told her. She saw a woman constrained in a straitjacket – this could be in store for any of them. And so she began to conform, keeping her longing for her children private, to the extent that McFarland could write casually to her husband that the purported disease had 'erased from Mrs Packard's mind the sentiments or instincts of maternal as well as marital affection', and that 'at heart' she was 'really indifferent' to her children.[25]

'How can I live without my children?' (from Modern Persecution*)*

Every day, there were long talks with McFarland. He quoted Shakespeare and Burns; indeed, he described himself in a scientific paper as a 'benignant Prospero', controlling the many Calibans under his direction. They even danced together, at the regular asylum balls. She'd grown up thinking that dancing was a sin, but she changed her mind and took dancing lessons from an attendant. 'Is such ease and grace of figure and motion a sin?' she asked. 'Then the sailing of the fish is sin; the soaring of the bird.' But then two events undermined her confidence. She discovered that McFarland had been intercepting and hiding letters sent by her friends and children. And he kissed her. She'd gone to report a complaint: another woman had accused her of indiscretion because she allowed a male patient to push her on the swing. Promising to protect her, McFarland kissed her on the forehead. She withdrew.[26]

'Dr McFarland, men do not send their wives, nor fathers their daughters here, expecting that you will manifest your regard for them in *this manner*.'[27]

She began to write. She'd written before – essays and letters – but this was different. Now she found she could write about anything. Surrounded by the crushed physicality of life in the asylum, she insisted on her mind. She wrote to prove her sanity and to create herself, turning the authority of the Bible class essays into a new, visionary mode of being. Being untethered from her children when the stakes of motherhood had been so high, the strength required so frenetic, left her with vitality desperately in need of an outlet. As for George Sand, the endless creation of words on the page could become a release for a mind and body that needed to be continually in motion, even within the stasis of the asylum. She started by writing two documents: a defence of her sanity, and an admonishment of McFarland for the treatments she'd witnessed at the asylum. She was throwing her energy out into the world, beginning a campaign to improve her country on behalf of mothers everywhere. She had been thwarted by the promise of the American dream, which turned out not to apply to women; in response she began to dream more grandly, conceiving of her life on a new and immense scale.

She presented the first to McFarland on 26 October 1860. 'Have you not reason to fear that my case fairly represents a class of oppressed women, who have been unjustly imprisoned here, by unnatural men,' she asked him, urging him to 'be our protector, instead of our husbands' abettor in crime?' He could hear the truth in what she was saying. But there was something excessive about it. She described her husband as a 'perverted and unnatural man' and asked for him to be punished by God. For McFarland, there was something 'diabolical' about her hatred of her husband. This must be a clue to her madness.[28]

On 6 November, Abraham Lincoln was elected president of a divided nation, with a mandate for freedom. Elizabeth read the newspapers, day after day in the ward, and doesn't seem to have felt cut off. It helped that she was allowed special privileges, sent out into town shopping. She identified with the slaves she read about.

If they were soon to be freed, shouldn't women ask for the end of their oppression too?

Now she presented her second document, threatening to publish it if McFarland failed to respond. His treatment of the inmates, she wrote here, was 'contrary to reason, to justice, to humanity'. She was called by God to expose his actions 'unless you repent'. He was destined to see her 'rising and applauded as the world's reformer' because 'the time for downtrodden and oppressed women to have their rights, has come. Her voice and her pen are going to move the world.' She also ticked him off for inappropriately kissing her.[29]

Furious, McFarland seems to have panicked. He'd clearly been at least somewhat out of control; he'd given her hours of his time when he had an entire state asylum to run, and he'd kissed her. Now, facing his own weakness, he had to exert power. He kept away from her for five days and then he led her to the Eighth Ward. She was going to see what insanity looked like.

There were no carpets here; there weren't even any chairs. The smell was worse than anything she'd smelt before – a 'most fetid scent at the pit of my stomach' – and there was the constant noise of 'screaming, fighting, running hallooing', as unwashed women splashed around in 'unfragrant puddles' of their own urine. The punishments here were appalling: a desperate patient was held under water until she agreed not to scream; patients were put in near-boiling water with their hands and feet tied.[30]

It was a challenge to be a universal mother in these new circumstances, but after a few days she rose to it. Though there were no baths, she washed herself in her chamber pot and then washed the other terrified, scuffling patients one by one, as she had her own six children. On his ward round, McFarland looked with astonishment at the row of clean faces and combed hair.

'Doctor,' she later recounted saying. 'I find I can always find something to do for the benefit of others, and you have now assigned me quite a missionary field to cultivate!'[31]

It wasn't easy; some of the women turned violently against her. It wasn't sustainable; there would be dirty inmates in the Eighth Ward for years. It wasn't wholly sane: there was something excessive and desperate in her insistent cleaning, which seems to have been driven more by her own needs than by those of the other women. Nonetheless, it kept her alive, and so did writing, though she wasn't officially allowed to write – she had to hide tiny patches of paper to scratch away at. For most patients, the asylum had a 'sedative influence', she observed, but in her case 'this woman-crushing machinery works the wrong way. The true woman shines brighter and brighter under the process, instead of being strangled.'[32]

She missed her children, those 'dear fragments' of herself she couldn't bear to think of under Theophilus's wrathful care. He wrote announcing his plan to break up the family and send the younger children away. Who should he give the baby to? And who should have Libby? 'Elizabeth has had a fall and hurt her side, so that it pains her most of the time, and yet does all the work for the family, except when her aunt Dole comes and helps a day occasionally.'[33]

It was appalling. Libby had been doing well at the school she was no longer allowed to attend, and now her mother was powerless to stop this – or could only stop it if she repented and obeyed her husband.

After a year at the asylum, Theophilus visited. She treated him coldly, though he seemed to expect they would converse as husband and wife. He asked her advice about the children, telling another patient despairingly that he'd never seen 'children so attached to a mother, as Mrs Packard's are to her'. He couldn't persuade them to disregard her authority or even to eat anything she'd disapprove of.[34]

'He is trying to make me say, "O, husband do take me home! If you only will, I will think, speak and act just as you please,"' she told McFarland disparagingly.[35]

McFarland found her coldness towards her husband distasteful. If Elizabeth could have found it in herself to renounce her religious views and accept her husband's authority and rectitude, she'd have been allowed to go home. She could have done this: exchanged mental freedom for physical freedom, her voice for her children. Perhaps she would have done, if she'd been offered that choice the day they took her away. But she was stubbornly committed to her inalienable freedoms, waiting to rise as the world's reformer. She could go home and free Libby, but then what about Libby's daughters, and their daughters? If she stayed, surely soon she could convince McFarland of her sanity and go home as a free woman to set about ensuring that mothers would never be wrongly separated from their children again. 'Nothing is at last sacred but the integrity of your own mind,' Emerson wrote. Elizabeth Packard was staking everything on the God within, as he was (though Emerson's collusion in the incarceration of two of his brothers and his follower, Jones Very, in mental asylums has led some to note the peculiar parallels between the psychiatry movement and Transcendentalism).[36]

Meanwhile, Packard told herself that she remained part of a family: 'I am not childless. All God's sons and daughters are my brothers and sisters.' And in taking on Calvinism, she addressed her ire to John Calvin himself, assuring him that God would punish him for separating her from her children: 'Calvin dared to defy God's authority in separating me from my children; but God has him in hand for it now.'[37]

By 1862, civil war had erupted. America was riven by intractable questions of slavery. Even President Andrew Jackson had owned some 300 slaves; American freedom and democracy were predicated on the systematic denial of the freedom and rights of millions of the country's inhabitants. In the nation, as in the Packards' marriage, turbulent discussion had exploded into a violent act of rupture. In Jacksonville, where a tenth of citizens had enlisted for military service on behalf of the Union, Toffy – now known as Theo – visited his mother, lovingly declared her sane, and announced that Isaac was joining the Union Army. After this, Elizabeth looked anxiously for her son's name in the death lists, while congratulating Lincoln for espousing the cause of the oppressed: 'God holds him up, amid the crash of worlds.' That meant, surely, that God would support her too. The rhetoric of freedom and universal struggle powered her writing. 'The North may as well give up this civil war, and succumb to the South, and put their necks again under the yoke of the slave oligarchy, as [a woman] yield up her contest for "spiritual freedom" by returning to her husband and establishing the marriage union as it was.' She wanted a union based on equal rights and justice, as she believed Lincoln did, though in fact at this stage he primarily wanted to save the Union at whatever cost.[38]

Packard collaborated with rebellious attendants in writing letters to the newspapers exposing the conditions in the asylum. A natural democrat, she would always make enthusiastic use of the mass media. 'She gives us a world of trouble,' McFarland wrote to Theophilus in April 1862, 'which I only put up with under the thought, that she would give you, if possible, still more.'[39]

She gave McFarland trouble, but she fascinated him. He began their private colloquies again, determined to expose her madness. They argued about the Civil War and the death penalty, and she fixed on him once more as her protector – he was her only chance.

He let her write, hoping to trap her. So she wrote and wrote, a massive book called *The Great Drama*, where she luxuriated in the bodily details of motherhood: 'I never refuse to let my babies nurse me when they want to.' At the end of the first volume, she described her departure and her children's devastation in great, partly imaginative detail, and rather self-righteously blamed her husband's sister

Sybil for colluding in the plan by offering her to look after her baby just before the incarceration (ostensibly to give Elizabeth a break, after nights of nursing George). 'I don't thank you for taking care of my own, dear, little Arthur,' she told Sybil. 'No! I don't! I prefer to take care of my own children – for I know I can take *better* care of them than you possibly can. I excel you in family government. My children mind me better than yours do you. They love me better than yours do you, and they have reason to do so.'[40]

McFarland had promised to publish the book, and she hoped to inspire the government to change the laws to protect married women. 'Tell me not of the horrors of Southern slavery,' she wrote, 'when the child is torn from the mother.' In fact this was one of the worst horrors of Southern slavery, but her abolitionist fervour seems to have waned during these years. If it hadn't, perhaps she could have pointed out how many freed slaves were incarcerated in mental asylums (in the 1840 census six times as many Black people as white people were categorised as 'insane').[41]

Reading the book, McFarland was happy. He announced at a psychiatric conference that he'd finally identified Elizabeth Packard's delusion: 'She was the Holy Ghost . . . This delusion had possessed her', making her thwart her husband. In fact, she had been speaking somewhat metaphorically. 'Is not a spiritual woman a personification of the Holy Ghost,' she wrote. But McFarland was grappling with a genuine insight. The megalomania that had led her to announce in 1860 that God was commanding her to expose the asylum, had swollen to the point that she – in common with many men of her day – believed she had a mission from God, and it was a mission bestowed on her as a mother. She compared herself with 'Christ in prison'.[42]

Sane. Insane. Elizabeth Packard's biographers tend to commit fully to her sanity – as she did. She needed to: she was fighting for her life. But do we? Will it harm her case to acknowledge how frenzied and grandiose she could be? Mothers are required to be sane at all times, but often have good reason to feel mad. We're

Caroline Norton, portrait by George Hayter, 1835

Lord Melbourne, portrait by George Hayter, 1838

Fletcher Norton (b. 1829)

Brinsley Norton (b. 1831)

Willie Norton (b. 1833)

George Sand, portrait by Auguste Charpentier, 1838

Maurice Dudevant in
national guard uniform,
drawing by George Sand

Maurice and
Solange Dudevant,
drawing by Nancy
Mérienne

Solange Clésinger by her
husband Auguste Clésinger

Drawing of Jeanne ('Nini')
Clésinger by George Sand, 1854

Elizabeth and
Theophilus Packard

Elizabeth Packard

Britney Spears and her son Sean Preston at *The Late Show*, 2006

Britney Spears and her sons visit the Dodgers Stadium, 2013

encouraged to worry about irrational sources of danger, to conceal our own desires, to push ourselves to extremes of physical and psychological endurance. If we're going to fight on behalf of those with mental health conditions, or to challenge the banality of sanity with R. D. Laing, can't we allow that Elizabeth Packard's writings aren't always the fruit of a wholly reasonable woman? Surely the point is that you shouldn't have to live up to some ideal of absolute rationality to be allowed to mother your children.

America was a land of visionaries, as Emerson commanded and warned. But those visionaries were rarely wives and mothers. The same woman carefully spooning cold water to her child, doling out merit marks, scrubbing every surface – should she also have a new vision of heaven and hell? The godly fervour and maternal efficiency were closely connected in Elizabeth Packard. Her puritanism fuelled her sense of universal love. She contained multitudes, but they needed to be clean multitudes.

On 22 September 1862, Lincoln issued the preliminary Emancipation Proclamation: as of 1 January, all slaves in seceded states would be free. Hundreds of thousands of slaves in the Southern states still in the Union remained enslaved, but it was a start. And it was a fight fuelled by horror at the plight of slave children separated from their mothers – a fight fought by mothers, who found their collective voice in the writing of another Massachusetts woman, Harriet Beecher Stowe (sister of Elizabeth's childhood hero Henry Ward Beecher), whose staggeringly popular 1852 novel *Uncle Tom's Cabin* had captured the nation's imagination. For Elizabeth Packard, all this augured changes for women as well. 'We [women] do want equal rights at least with a colored man,' she told Lincoln in her many-volumed book. A month later *The Great Drama* was finished. McFarland failed to publish it, though she wrote him a plaintive but peremptory love letter, offering her heart to him as the 'first true man' she had met and demanding his help. Her son Theo had now taken over paying her asylum fees; before this she'd depended on state support because Theophilus had lost his job – the Church Fathers had let his contract lapse. With Theo paying, Elizabeth had more privileges; walking into Jacksonville on her son's arm, she could believe herself more guest than inmate. She was in no hurry to leave, especially as she'd heard that if she did, her husband would simply send her to another asylum.[43]

A century later: yet another mother, yet another asylum. Jean Spears was grieving the loss of her baby son, who'd died at only three days old. Her husband, June Spears, couldn't bear her grief. And perhaps she was out of control; perhaps she couldn't stop crying, or she was drinking, or running through the streets, or doing whatever a woman might do who had spent nine months gestating a child and brought him into the world and fed him, only to find herself cradling a corpse three days later, her breasts still full of milk. Think of George Sand's mother, digging up her baby son and giving him his final bath, tended by her loving husband. June Spears wasn't up for this; instead, he sent his wife to the Southeast Louisiana Hospital in Mandeville, another of Dorothea Dix's 1840s achievements. Their five-year-old son – Britney Spears's father, Jamie – was left at home, at the mercy of his police officer father, who made him exercise every day to the point of exhaustion.

The photographer Richard Avedon took photographs at the hospital a few years later in 1963. He was collaborating with James Baldwin on *Nothing Personal*, their book – somewhere between grim indictment and visionary dreamscape – documenting contemporary America. He stayed at the hospital for a week, living alongside the patients he photographed in states of degradation and despair. Images show women arrayed on the floor in ragged dresses and leaning on each other with rolling eyes. The most haunting picture is of a large woman in a white nightie, sitting on an unmade metal bed, the bars of a prison cell behind her. Her hair looks greasy and her face at once vacant and angry. But there's something vulnerable about her pose – she pulls back from the camera – and in her arms she cradles a child's doll, that stares out blankly, its hair as dishevelled as that of the woman engaged in this desperate, humourless parody of motherhood.

Jean Spears may have sat like this. She may have been given a doll to hold, to make up somehow for the loss of her baby. She was put on lithium; her eyes, presumably, came to roll as the other patients' did. And then she was released, and for a few years she managed to mother her son, but when she was thirty-one and Jamie was thirteen, she shot herself on her infant son's grave.

Britney Jean Spears thought of her grandmother when she was at the Beverly Hills psychiatric treatment centre that her father sent her to for four months at the end of 2018. This was more luxurious than the Louisiana ward with its metal beds. But the treatment was similar. She was forced to take lithium. She couldn't have a bath in private or shut the door to her room.

'I'm Britney Spears now,' her father had asserted a decade earlier, in a raw cry of power. This is the man who, as a small boy, had watched his mother being taken off to an asylum. For the last ten years it is alleged that he had controlled his daughter, convincing her that she was sick at the same time as he forced her to perform day after day, even when she was at her weakest. According to Britney, he controlled who she spoke to and when; the money he drove her to earn; and even her body. Was he wreaking his revenge in committing her to a psychiatric hospital, or was he somehow making sense of his own father's actions? Perhaps women really did need to be locked away in asylums; perhaps his father hadn't been responsible for his mother's death; perhaps this was what it would take for his daughter to be the capable, sane woman his mother had failed to be. And so the pain makes its way down the generations: from George Sand to Solange, from Jean to Britney Spears.

Britney Spears was desperately unhappy at that treatment centre. She forgot where she was and began to think that her 'little heart, whatever made me Britney, was no longer inside my body anymore'. She didn't spar with her doctors or complain to the ever-hungry press or claim her right to freedom. Ten years earlier, she'd made the deal that Elizabeth Packard had refused to make – obedience in exchange for her children: 'My freedom in exchange for naps with my children – it was a trade I was willing to make. There is nothing I love more – nothing more important to me on this earth – than my children. I'd lay down my life for them. *So*, I thought, *why not my freedom?*'[44]

Centuries had passed since the Founding Fathers staked American identity on freedom; the American dream was more about riches than self-determination now. Mass democracy has been the fulfilment of the American dream but also its undoing, leaving the field of action narrower and more stagnant.

For Elizabeth Packard, the vitality of motherhood could be channelled towards new forms of freedom and social change. For Britney Spears, the judgements of the mass media were too overwhelming; as Tocqueville had half-known in 1831, the views of the majority would eventually make genuine plurality impossible. Britney had been told that there was only one way to be a mother, and she acquiesced, enacting passivity and obedience, attending every therapy session and rehab programme (though this didn't preclude obediently parading her sexuality in the performances choreographed by her avaricious father). And her father, controlling her through the conservatorship, seemingly used Britney's determination to see her children to give her ever less freedom. This did and didn't come as a surprise – she'd grown up with the story of her grandmother Jean. The Christmas that she was in the treatment centre, she was meant to have her boys with her; they were now twelve and thirteen and she had been apportioned 30 per cent of their custody in the latest agreement with Federline. Instead, she was dosed on lithium in a clinic that bore a frightening resemblance to her grandmother's asylum.

Three years later, she finally fought back, hiring new lawyers and fighting to end the conservatorship and to gain a larger share of custody. She was powered now by the #FreeBritney movement that had emerged to challenge the mass media and the corruption of the courts. She had a chance of winning so, fearing defeat, Federline's attorney Mark Vincent Kaplan used her enforced treatment with lithium as evidence of her unfitness as a mother:

> Lithium is regarded as a very powerful psychotropic medication that isn't cavalierly – I would hope – prescribed by a medical professional out of convenience. So there has to be some reason for that, and we'd want to know – whatever that reason was – that the reason or condition wasn't still impacting Britney's judgement at the time the conservatorship, if ever, is terminated.

'If ever.' 'I would hope.' These are such casual assertions of power. Somehow the fact that she's been drugged gives those controlling her the right to use those drugs against her, proving her frailty so that more drugs will be required. And so it goes on, until you end up with a 31-year-old mother standing with a shotgun blowing out her brains on a baby's grave.[45]

Or, you don't. 'In the Bible it says your tongue is your sword,' Britney Spears writes in her autobiography. 'My tongue and my sword were me singing.' She sang, during her years of incarceration, to fulfil her endless obligations to her father, but also to survive – as Elizabeth Packard continued to write even in the Eighth Ward. Britney may have lost control of her public voice, but in private, she felt she still sang with God behind her – as Elizabeth Packard wrote with Christ guiding her pen. 'Singing took me into the presence of the divine,' Britney said of her childhood self. 'As long as I was singing, I was half outside the world.'

Having survived, both were able to fight – for their children and for their rights. In Britney's case this involved making a 23-minute speech to the court, detailing her account of her father's abuses in the same, informally passionate voice that the ghostwriter has managed to retain in her book, moving between a kind of gallows humour and devastation. 'I don't even believe in therapy,' she half-joked to the judge, complaining about the enforced therapeutic regime she'd been trapped in: 'I always think you talk to God.'[46]

Having gained her freedom, Britney released her unfiltered voice into the world, filming herself singing a lower, darker, a cappella version of her first hit, '. . . Baby One More Time', in 2022, ostensibly while doing the laundry.

Her voice has had so many metamorphoses over the years. Her childhood voice – that connection to the divine – became the artificial voice of the pop singer. Detractors saw this as the voice of a capitalist machine, but Britney felt it was hers – she had agency in choosing how to make it sound (she stayed up all night to make her voice more gravelly in the personally released version of '. . . Baby One More Time'), and the mix of authenticity and artifice was what made it so captivating, because it's troublingly unresolved. Then her father took over, and though she continued to sing, she lost control of the process, feeling disconnected from the nasally high-pitched, manufactured voice relentlessly piped out.

In the new, 2022 version, Britney comes to us in shadowy images, singing about her discovery that something is wrong in the world, in slow, soul-inflected tones, using the rawness that comes from pushing singing closer to speech. 'I haven't shared my voice in an extremely long time – maybe too long,' she wrote alongside the clip on Instagram. It may not be her most technically accomplished piece of singing, and its lack of filter doesn't make it authentic. No voice is authentic – not Elizabeth Packard's either, though her prose poured out with feverish ease. There's authenticity in the original 'Baby One More Time', just as there's artifice here (was she really doing the laundry?) It was part of the process of Britney reclaiming her voice from her father, as her memoir has been; and, crucially, it involved giving up on the overgrown teenager of her earlier work and inhabiting the voice of an older adult woman: the careworn mother of her memoir.[47]

III. Release

*'I want to live with my dear children, whom
I have borne and nursed, reared and educated'*

Elizabeth Packard was carried out, as she'd been carried in. When Theophilus came to collect her in June 1863, she refused to leave, frightened he was going to incarcerate her again. She was lucky. He sent her to the house of her cousin Angeline, warning that if she ever came near her children, the next asylum beckoned.

She was in another impossible situation. Freedom was of little use

'Enforcing the "Nonentity" Principle of Common Law for Married Women'
(Elizabeth Packard being carried to the bus, from Modern Persecution*)*

without her children. She'd been free to write in the asylum. She could have fought for divorce and custody, but she didn't think she'd win, and didn't want to be divorced. Still her father's daughter, she didn't see marriage as dissoluble; and she thought that by divorcing Theophilus she'd play into his hands: 'Would it not be becoming an accomplice in crime, by doing the very deed which he is so desirous of having done, namely: to remove me from my family?'[48]

Would she have had a chance, if she'd fought for custody? Maybe. America had some of the most mother-friendly custody laws in the world; far more so than England, though there too divorcing mothers supposedly had more access to their children than they'd had in Caroline Norton's day. Divorce itself had become easier in England with the controversial 1857 Matrimonial Causes Act, which moved divorce cases from the ecclesiastical to the civil courts. Women's rights campaigners failed to combat the profound inequality of the bill, which allowed husbands to divorce wives on the grounds of adultery, where wives needed evidence of a second misdemeanour (usually cruelty). But Caroline Norton, now the mother of grown-up children and the mistress – finally – of her own income, played a part in successfully campaigning for the Act to protect divorcing women's property. And the newly established Divorce Court ('the Court for Divorce and Matrimonial Causes') was empowered to make custody orders for children up to the age of twenty-one, giving judges wide powers. Women who could prove their husbands were adulterous and cruel could now get custody. This was promising but divorce remained prohibitively expensive, and therefore exceptional: there were about 150 divorces a year in a population of 20 million.[49]

By contrast, throughout America, every day in the mid nineteenth century, there were people going into courts married and coming out unmarried. There were about 38,000 divorces in 1860, among a population of 31 million. The revolution – that bitter but ultimately optimistic divorce between one nation and another – had been followed by decades of legislation making divorce easier across

America; most states now allowed divorces to be decided by ordinary circuit courts, and some included intemperance and insanity as grounds for divorce, alongside adultery and cruelty. The more straightforward divorce became, the more vehemently it was opposed: many Christians, like Elizabeth Packard herself, still saw marriage as indissoluble and feared that the new legislation encouraged the very sins it punished, and some feminists thought that divorce primarily advantaged philandering men. But there was now a straightforward and affordable structure for women to claim custody.

The success of mothers in custody cases in America was enabled by the new language of rights taking shape, leading judges from as early as the 1840s to conclude that children had rights – even if American judges remained ostensibly beholden to English common law, where children remained the possessions of their fathers. This was possible because the common law had been eroded alongside the traditional Church. Jacksonian calls for democratic reform were centred on the law and on the arcane precedents that had to be amassed in arguing a case. In courtrooms across the United States, judges began to address their audience directly, giving their judgments in frank, comprehensible prose. More and more judges discarded common law, speaking in terms of universal principles.

Inaugurated as Dane Professor of Law at Harvard in 1829, Joseph Story stated that the 'true glory' of the common law was that 'it must for ever be in a state of progress, or change, to adapt itself to the exigences and changes of society'. English law didn't always translate well to America. Tocqueville, celebrating American democracy, admired the 'immense political power' given to the judiciary (a power he saw as helpfully counteracting the collective will of the people): 'the Americans have acknowledged the right of the judges to found their decisions on the constitution rather than on the laws. In other words, they have left them at liberty not to apply such laws as may appear to them to be unconstitutional.' Tocqueville saw that if this was the great age of American law, it was because, for a while, it combined the best elements of mass democratic reform and old-world elitism. Thus these robed, wigged men in courtrooms had become the guarantors of the American dream, with its promise of all men being created equal, holding the judgements of the majority at bay. And with every judgment, these judges shaped the opinions of the people around them, because for every mother they reunited with her children, there were more men and women who saw this as a normal occurrence.[50]

Children gained, and so did mothers. Male judges may not always have cared about the legal rights of their wives, but they wanted to protect their daughters from domineering husbands. James Kent's influential 1830 *Commentaries on American Law* celebrated the new and 'Christian' era in America that had begun to provide 'equality and dignity' for women. This casually contradicted William Blackstone's 1765 *Commentaries on the Laws of England*, hitherto the legal bible on both sides of the Atlantic, with its assertion that wives were 'entitled to no power, but only to reverence and respect'.[51]

Mothers were idealised in England as much as America. But in the States, slavery had made the question of mothers' attachment to their children especially poignant and enflamed. When Abraham Lincoln credited Harriet Beecher Stowe as 'the little woman who wrote the book that made this great war' in 1862, he was crediting the war to a book that dramatised the grief and desperation of a slave mother whose son is about to be taken away from her. In *Uncle Tom's Cabin*, Stowe castigates the slaveowners, who imposed these separations, for killing the soul in both mother and child, taking them from God. 'I've hungered for my children, and thirsted for them,' says Cassy, a mother who's poisoned one baby rather than let him be sold into slavery. '"Here, Here!" she says, striking her breast, "it's all desolate, all empty! If God would give me back my children, then I could pray."' As abolitionists pleaded for slave women to keep their children, it became less thinkable to separate any mothers and children. For anyone committed to abolition, the only logical response was to award children to mothers in custody cases, and judges did this, again and again.[52]

In 1840, New York's highest court awarded a three-year-old daughter to her mother in *Mercein v People* on the grounds that 'the law of nature has given to [the mother] an attachment for her infant offspring which no other relative will be likely to possess in an equal degree', and that no court should 'violate the law of nature'. The decision was repealed two years later but set a compelling precedent. In 1843 in Tennessee, Judge William B. Turley explicitly discarded common law, with its 'stern and iron-bound principles based upon the manners, customs and thoughts of our ancestors', in favour of equity, which considered men and women as people created by the same power, with 'equal rights to all the enjoyments of life'. Thus, though he gave the eight-year-old boy to his father, the six-year-old girl and four-year-old boy were awarded to their mother, on the grounds that 'in all cases the interest and welfare of the child is the great leading object to be attained'. Similarly, in South Carolina in *Ex parte Hewitt* in 1858, the judge plainly asserted that a husband could lose his rights if his custody 'should be inconsistent with the welfare of his children, which is a paramount consideration'. And in 1860 Judge Joseph Baldwin of the Supreme Court of California – a lawyer who had tried out politics and published a book of humorous portraits of politicians before becoming a judge in his forties – restored a seven-year-old girl to her mother on the grounds that 'children, though younger in years, have themselves an interest, even more sacred than their parents, and more deserving of protection'. In an American twist, Baldwin added that 'the interests of the community and of the child necessarily harmonise'. These are children, then, of the new republican generation – with roles in the community beyond the confines of their parents' world. In an 1858 self-help manual entitled *Every Woman Her Own Lawyer*, attorney George Bishop explained that the law, across all states, empowered the judges to 'give custody to the party that, in the court's judgment, is most competent to bring them up with advantage to the children themselves and benefit to society'.[53]

And all along, there were reforming ladies – cajoling, peremptory, flattering, reproachful – taking tea with senators and presidents, reminding them of the need to protect their sisters and daughters from irresponsible men. They had more success with women's property rights than custody rights, but in 1860 New York brought in an Act granting that 'every married woman is hereby constituted and declared to be the joint guardian of her children, with her husband, with equal powers, rights and duties in regard to them with her husband'. It turned out to be too much too soon: the Act was repealed in 1862 and not reintroduced in New York until 1893. But New York had created a legislative and legal precedent, and other states would follow within a decade.[54]

If Elizabeth Packard had fought for custody, right then, in 1863 in Illinois, her lawyers would have found local precedents for maternal custody. In 1846 Ann Cowls had been granted custody of her six-year-old daughter and four-year-old son in Illinois, first by a lower court and then, when the father appealed, by the Supreme Court. The father here was 'vulgar, profane, frequently intoxicate', and lived with a woman 'of notoriously bad character', so this was a pretty extreme case, but the Supreme Court judge, John Caton, went beyond simply castigating the father and asserted that he was sure that 'no certain rule can be laid down for the government of the court in all cases, except that the best interests of the child must be consulted'. Three years later Caton granted an eight-year-old girl to her mother on the grounds that, though the father's conduct to the child was 'unexceptionable', and 'while the affection of parents for daughters may be equal, yet the mother, from her natural endowments, her position in society, and her constant association with [her daughters]', was better placed to give 'care, attention and advice' to them.[55]

Caton, who had arrived in Illinois in 1833 with only $14 – and had worked at the first law firm in Chicago in the days when sending people to jail simply involved tying the prisoners up in the cabinet shop while they waited for them to be moved on – was still a judge in the Supreme Court of Illinois in 1863. He might have sympathised with Elizabeth Packard. But alongside these hopeful cases there were adolescent boys handed over even to cruel fathers; exemplary mothers losing infant children to brutal husbands because some judges still felt bound by common law precedents; and adulterous women losing custody in all states. The judge of the 1854 case *Lindsay v Lindsay* in Georgia claimed that even though the mother had not known she was adulterous (she'd thought she was fully divorced, and it was her husband who had been adulterous while they were still married), it was not in the interests of her four-year-old daughter to be with so dissolute a mother:

> There may be no difference in the sin of the man and the woman, who violate the laws of chastity . . . But we do know, that in the opinion of society, it is otherwise . . . for when she sins after this sort, she sins against society . . . her associations are with the vulgar, the vile and the depraved. If her children are with her, their characters must be, more or less, influenced and formed by the circumstances which surround them.

'The opinion of society': this would continue to trouble judges in custody cases over the next century. Should judges merely reflect the opinions of society, which are admittedly going to affect the children, or should they lead the way in shaping those opinions? This question still remains unresolved, and in the *Lindsay v Lindsay* case, as in many cases since, the judge had it both ways, presenting his hands as tied by the opinion of society only to uphold just these opinions in stridently moralistic terms.[56]

A judge may not have looked favourably on a woman who had been in asylums for the insane not once but twice. It wouldn't have helped, either, that Theophilus had said she could come home, if only she would obey him. Could she get custody as a disobedient woman? Might she be seen as vulgar and vile and depraved? Elizabeth Packard was probably right not to fight for custody. She needed categorically to prove her sanity first. But there was another reason not to. Her time as a universal mother in the asylum had left her hungering to test herself on the world's stage. She told herself that the only way to get her children was to improve the legislation on behalf of all married women. If this wasn't quite true – if she could have tried out simply taking Theophilus to court – it was a useful way of not quite admitting how much she desired to become a campaigner, as she launched herself into a literary career.

Around her there were other campaigners making the connection between freeing married women and freeing slaves. Packard knew that her book would be helped by the groundswell of the larger movement. Women's rights campaigner Susan B. Anthony was conducting a high-profile, risky campaign on behalf of Phoebe Phelps, an author of religious children's books and the wife of a Massachusetts state senator. When Phelps had confronted her husband with proof of his adultery in 1858, he'd deposited her in the McLean Lunatic Asylum in Belmont, MA. Her brother secured her release a year later, but she was kept away from her three children. Eventually, she managed to see one daughter, and to escape with her to Susan Anthony's protection. Senator Phelps then kidnapped his daughter back and threatened to have Anthony arrested. It's astonishing that a man in his position was so blatant in his ill-treatment of his wife in an era when white American wives and mothers were, on the whole, revered. Nonetheless, he managed to turn some of Susan Anthony's allies against her, making them fearful that he'd succeed in alienating their supporters. Bravely stubborn, she continued to campaign, reaching for the same rhetoric as Elizabeth Packard. 'Trust me,' she said. 'I ignore all law to help the slave, so will I ignore it all to protect an enslaved woman.'[57]

Elizabeth Packard had the chance to recuperate, living with Angeline – the cousin she'd been brought up with as a sister, whose brown eyes and hair and long nose resembled her own – and to try to get her book published. Publishers rejected it (they didn't want asylum patients as authors), so she self-published a thousand copies of a pamphlet on the subject of Jacksonville. Then it was time to see her children. She'd risked everything to be disobedient before and was going to do it again. Several of her cousin's neighbours helped fund the train fare back to Manteno, where it had all begun.

It was only October but there was snow – just starting to melt. She left her trunk at the station she'd last seen when forced to board that train over three years ago, and then walked carefully down the sloppily wet platform towards the house she still knew as home. At the end of the platform, she began to worry about Theophilus, fearing that once he'd seen her, he'd intercept her luggage and read her papers. She saw a small boy with a cap pulled down, walking behind her, and asked him to run to the stationmaster to tell him that Mrs Packard wished him not to let Mr Packard take her trunk. The boy hesitated.

'An't you willing to do this favor for me?' she later recalled asking.
'It is so wet I don't like to go back.'
He wriggled: 'I don't want to say anything against my Pa.'
She pulled back his cap. It was her son George. She dropped to her knees in the snow to embrace him, but he held back, and she let him go.

It's a heart-breaking image. The six-year-old who had loved serving her strawberries and had run along the tracks, desperate to rescue his mother, had become a ten-year-old, fearful of displeasing his father. 'My Pa has done right,' he insisted, when she promised him that he'd never be separated from her again. He needed more time.

She found Theophilus, with four-year-old Arthur on his lap in the kitchen.

'Good morning, Mrs Packard,' her husband said. She took Arthur and sat with him on her lap. George and Elizabeth came in from the yard and she embraced them, promising to take care of them. 'No, you an't wanted here!' Theophilus interjected. 'We get along better without you!'[58]

Unemployed, Theophilus had been home with the children for over a year, and had appealed to the public for help. There were boxes of clothes lying around from the Missionary Society, making it all less orderly than she'd left it. But she was glad to see her familiar furniture: the china closet that she'd painted pea green herself; the sofa with the black throw.

When she instructed the children to help her clean the filthy house, Theophilus forbade them, locking doors everywhere – even the linen closet was locked, and he only gave her the key when he decreed that the sheets needed changing. It was tedious, but she'd suffered worse in the Eighth Ward. She got on with her spring clean.

And then he locked her up again.

She'd stolen a set of his keys and unlocked all the doors. In response he began confining her in the nursery overnight, nailing the windows shut as he had over three years earlier. She wasn't allowed to eat with the family, but during the days, he let her educate her children. Determined to find happiness and fulfilment in the pockets of freedom that remained, she spent organised mornings teaching grammar, algebra, reading, writing and elocution to Samuel, Libby, George and Arthur. Then she discovered a certificate McFarland had sent Theophilus, declaring her to be 'hopelessly' insane – and correspondence with a Massachusetts asylum about her forthcoming admittance there.

She managed to get word to her Manteno neighbours. This time they acted swiftly. They ascertained that, according to Illinois law, though husbands were fully permitted to incarcerate wives in asylums, they weren't permitted to incarcerate them at home.

A race began. Elizabeth's neighbours had to take Theophilus to court before he could gather all the documentation needed to put her in the new asylum. He was making good progress on this front:

one doctor after another came to the house, talked to Elizabeth, and obligingly declared her insane.

On 12 January, Theophilus was issued by Elizabeth's friends with a writ of habeas corpus. He was commanded to bring Elizabeth before Judge Charles Starr at Kankakee City courthouse that day at 1 p.m.

They left the children with Theophilus's sister, and together, husband and wife rode by trap twelve miles through the snow to a makeshift courtroom with a bare floor, and a collection of ill-assorted seats that proved insufficient for the awaiting crowds.

Theophilus was represented by Thomas Bonfield, one of Kankakee's earliest settlers, and Elizabeth by 31-year-old Steve Moore, a Methodist with an extravagantly long beard who loved practical jokes and underdogs. He had no time for Calvinism and had agreed to defend Elizabeth pro bono.

Judge Charles Starr read through the documentation that Theophilus had assembled for admitting Elizabeth in the asylum. Theophilus denied the charge of imprisonment but admitted 'the exercise of a slight necessary restraint over her on account of her insanity'. Starr was perplexed; the woman currently talking to her lawyers showed no apparent signs of madness.[59]

'Prove it,' he said.

What followed was unprecedented. As a wife whose husband had declared her insane, Elizabeth didn't have the right to a trial of her sanity. Judge Starr was displaying just the independence lauded by Tocqueville. Lawyers and judges were taking over from pastors as the guardians of family life – a change that was disastrous for Theophilus and ideal for Elizabeth, who, in another world, might have been an excellent lawyer.

A jury was assembled (five of whom were Presbyterians, but weren't members of Theophilus's church) and both sides presented their cases. When it turned out that the doctors had pronounced her insane on the grounds of her theology, Stephen Moore easily dismantled the doctors' own theological views.

Halfway through the testimony, Theophilus's sister Sybil Dole walked into the courtroom, accompanied by Libby, who escaped her aunt straight away. Libby ran up to her mother and threw her arms around her, clinging to her, in Stephen Moore's account, 'with all child-like fervor'.[60]

It's so horribly painful: the fourteen-year-old girl, seeking comfort in her mother's embrace, presumably aware that she was in the presence of the judge who would decide whether Elizabeth was able to stay home and mother her.

She was pulled away, and the crowd broke out in cries of distress. 'Not a mother's heart there but was touched,' wrote Moore. This was the moment that brought home to the jury the maternal severance that a declaration of insanity would entail.[61]

Libby was taken home and Sybil returned alone to testify. Hers was the most richly ambivalent testimony of the trial. She described how she once visited and found that her sister-in-law was out of bread, and had to offer biscuits (crackers) instead of bread to the family at dinner time. A man in the crowd turned to his wife and said: 'Wife, were you ever out of bread, and had to make biscuit for dinner? I must put you into an Insane Asylum! No mistake!'[62]

This was absurd, but this woman, who Elizabeth had vilified so cartoonishly in her asylum book, also gave the only convincing testimony about Elizabeth's madness. She said that though Elizabeth's 'natural disposition' was 'very kind and sweet', after she moved to Manteno she changed. 'I had a conversation with her, when she talked without interruption; she talked in a wild, excited manner; the subject was partly religion. She spoke of her own attainments; she said she had advanced in spiritual affairs.'[63]

What was described here seems to be at least close to mania. These may have been figments of Sybil's imagination, invented for the courtroom – but then wouldn't she have taken it further, making it all more flamboyant? This isn't the kind of behaviour that necessitates a mother being taken from her children. But if Sybil's recollections were accurate, then it does seem that at this point in the marriage, Elizabeth wasn't fully in control of her speech or her passions. Perhaps Elizabeth's brilliance, energy and self-creative zeal were already pushing her beyond the home and parish. But she had no larger outlet for her talents; instead, the couple was locked in an endless, insoluble battle over their children's salvation.

Elizabeth's greatest weapon at the trial was her own articulacy – though female articulacy has itself been vilified in plenty of custody cases. Stephen Moore put her on the stand and asked her to read out her own Bible class essay. These essays were where Elizabeth had put forward the offending views that she'd been incarcerated for; but this one turned out to be a carefully argued account of why we can't expect worldly gain in exchange for spiritual virtue.

The jury's verdict was unanimous. Elizabeth P. W. Packard was sane. She could go back home to her children. But she was immediately handed a letter, which informed her that Theophilus had already left, and had taken their children with him. She returned home to find an unknown lodger already in possession the house, and all her furniture gone. The shock was immense. It felt like a 'living death of hopeless bereavement'.[64]

'I want to live with my dear children, whom I have borne and nursed, reared and educated,' Elizabeth wrote soon after. 'I love them . . . and no place is home to me in this wide world without them.'[65]

There were no children, and she had to sleep at her neighbours' house. She didn't pause to linger by the sites of her lost happiness with her infant children. She filed, at last, for divorce, and departed for Chicago. She'd once told McFarland that he was destined to see her rising and applauded as the world's reformer. It was time to make this happen.

I have been sent transcriptions of Theophilus Packard's diaries by the Cornell Medical Center Archives. I expect to find self-righteousness and vindictiveness. I find these, but also aching grief and fear.

The diaries start in his twenties. He has been living, as he puts it in the accompanying, brief autobiography, 'without God, without hope, without religion, without prayer in the world', his mind 'carnal, sinful, absolutely depraved', and then, age seventeen, he's almost died with an infected leg wound and has had something of the conversion his pastor father has prayed for. This hasn't quite materialised, so he's gone to college, still 'completely wicked and directly opposed to holiness'; then aged twenty-one he's had a conversation with a Christian fellow student of philosophy that's increased his 'alarm and anguish'. He's pleaded for mercy from God, beginning to see himself 'at the disposal of a God whom I hated'. For a week, he's hardly slept or eaten, fearing his own sinful desires. 'I had in my moral nature those propensities and dispositions which unrestrained would have led into as great crimes as were ever committed by any', he writes, making me wonder what these depraved desires could have been – homosexuality, perhaps? At the end of the week he's proudly informed his mother that he loves God. In August 1826 he's preached for the first time ('without notes,' he records happily) and become a pastor in his father's parish.[66]

Now the diaries begin. 'My greatest difficulty is a cold, stupid and wicked heart,' he writes in 1829, worrying both about his worldliness and 'lethargy' and renouncing spiritous liquors. Month after month, he fears his own cold-heartedness towards God, finding the world dull and dead. 'Oh! For the joys of a new convert,' he writes, anxious that he must quit the ministry if his love for God doesn't 'quicken'.[67]

Once the children are born, his diaries became less about his own religious feelings and more about theirs. Reading his words, I see the tragic truth underlying all this: though he wants to punish his wife, his fears for his children's souls under her care are horribly genuine. 'Spirit of God! Come and give him a <u>new heart</u> – a heart to repent of sin, to love that Savior who died for him . . . How could I bear to see my dearly beloved George among the lost!' When it comes to his wife, he scorns the 'sham mobocratic trial' held to determine her sanity, but writes with more fear than vindictiveness about her religious influence on the children. 'To think that my sons are taught by her, and that any of them believe that morality is religion and Universalism is true, is an unspeakable grief to my soul.'[68]

I feel I'm witnessing the struggles of a man full of thought and feeling of a kind he never seems to have been willing or able to express to his wife. He's lost in his own thoughts and certainties, but he's also driven to do good, and shadowed by half-knowing that he's failed to do so. There's a photograph of the Packards, probably taken shortly before Elizabeth was sent to the asylum, where both stare out at the camera unsmiling, but Theophilus, in particular, has a kind of desolate bafflement in his small bespectacled eyes. There's sternness here, in the sharp lines framing his mouth, but there's amazement too, as though he doesn't quite know how he got here.

I find it startling, hearing his voice in the diaries, seeing the moments when he's capable of seeing the world's capaciousness and of making space for others. His grief is a form of madness, but it's one stoked by the most powerful forces within his family and culture. I didn't expect to feel so much sympathy for him. I feel that, alongside the indulgent self-pity, there's genuine desperation in his fear of his own depravity. He isn't curious about his wife; he doesn't ask himself how to make her happier. But all this talk of lethargy and of coldness makes me see him as helplessly narrow and depressive: incapable of rising to the challenge of so complicated and energetic a woman. This was an era when extraordinary women were thrown out into the world at an astonishing rate – and married off to husbands who had no idea what to make of them, in societies that told them that though the home was the wife's kingdom, the husband was somehow still in charge of it.

Women can be the wrong wives for their husbands precisely

because their initial appeal stems from attributes and energies that then go in unpredictable directions. Sometimes I think that I blighted my own husband's life by marrying him. Reading these diaries, I feel sure that Elizabeth Packard blighted Theophilus's. But she couldn't have known that he would turn out to be so fearful of complexity, of challenge, of the fireworks and vigour of a mind that wanted to question everything and found delight in doing so. For his part, he was totally unprepared. When he'd talked to her father when she was a child, she'd simply listened; all he asked for was a competent, obedient mother for his children; this new delight in theological argument wasn't what he signed up for. He had little he could rely on, only this: man's need to struggle his way towards God and, when there, to hold his ground and never leave. And yet it was all a game for her – the Bible class essays, the religious sparring. Because her real satisfactions were in earthly love, of a kind he'd only had with anxious guilt or fear. He wasn't inventing his terrors; he didn't simply want rid of a wife he was tired of. This was insanity for him: to know God and to risk nonetheless the hell he'd experienced for that awful week without food or sleep. She made it all seem so easy – loving God. What right did she have to assume she was loved by him in turn?

This isn't a Victorian father like George Norton, oblivious to his children until he uses them to punish his wife. This is a father who loved his children tenderly as well as fiercely – think of him with four-year-old Arthur on his lap – and who was concerned, hour after anguished hour, for his children's welfare, but who was absolutely the wrong man to have custody of them. Poor Theophilus. But poor Elizabeth. And poor children. In a decade of war when homes were increasingly sites of strife, theirs was a bitter fight to the death with the children as its casualties – or, as Theophilus saw it, the children's souls.

IV. Triumph

'The mother's battle was fought, and the victory won'

Elizabeth Packard went on the road, like a travelling preacher. Finally, she had an outlet for her energy, though she'd lost everything to acquire it. She went door to door, crowdfunding to publish her book, selling subscriptions to judges, soldiers and even the Mayor of Chicago.

Theo, who had supported her against his father for years, was horrified; he wrote to his maternal grandfather, who'd thus far failed to restrain her: 'If you have *any* regard for her, and wish to have her saved from ruining herself, temporally and spiritually, I hope you will take this matter in hand.' Her father did begin to take more of an interest in her cause – he now believed in her sanity, and wrote to Theophilus, demanding he return her clothes – but he wasn't going to stop her publishing. Besides, she was enjoying herself. 'The more freedom I have, the more I want,' she wrote.[69]

'*Mrs Packard, your Bill is safe!*' *(the Senate debating Elizabeth Packard's bill, from* Modern Persecution*)*

When Theophilus opposed her divorce suit, she simply abandoned it; she was going to change the law instead. She published her first book – not *The Great Drama*, but *The Exposure*, an angrier account of her travails in the asylum – and dedicated it to her children: 'The mother has died! But she has risen again – the mother of her country.'

The book was a massive success and was followed in 1866 by *Marital Power Exemplified*, focusing on women's lack of rights. She also began campaigning. In 1865, thanks to her efforts, the Massachusetts legislature amended the insanity laws. Now ten relatives had to be informed about those committed, and the patient allowed to correspond with them. In Illinois, a new statute granted everyone accused of insanity, including married women, a trial by jury before being committed. All the existing patients in Jacksonville were tried for sanity – and found indeed to be insane. McFarland was quietly discharging the more obviously sane women without trial. Elizabeth was angry – and got the senators of Illinois interested. In 1867 she accompanied a committee of senators on a visit to Jacksonville. A bitter battle ensued; there was a trial in which Andrew McFarland submitted as evidence the love letter Elizabeth Packard had written him in a desperate attempt to persuade him to publish her book. McFarland was eventually fired. It turned out that, in the new order, doctors were answerable to judges and senators, rather than to priests.

So far, Elizabeth Packard's attempts to change the law on married women's rights had been thwarted, but there was now a law passing through the Senate of Massachusetts – where Theophilus was living – allowing married women to become legal guardians of their children. In 1869 Elizabeth filed for custody, and gathered statements from her three oldest sons. The children 'would be better brought up under her care than under the care of anyone else', Isaac wrote, insisting that she was 'a most excellent mother, her judgement good, and her moral character without a stain'; 'I solemnly believe . . . that she is *my mother* in every sense of the term, and her councils

'Dr McFarland's Self-accusation: "Mrs Packard has ruined me"'
(from Modern Persecution)

I may rely upon, that her loving care and disregard of self to minister to our best interests, merits our most filial regard,' Theo proclaimed. Samuel, who for several years had supported his father, now got behind her too. Working as a lawyer in Chicago he'd come to see how powerless women were, and he told her that he wanted to commit himself 'to carrying on some great & noble reformation – as you do'.

The case began to make its way through the courts but almost immediately Theophilus followed his lawyers' advice and gave it up. Finally, in June 1869, Libby, George and Arthur came to live with Elizabeth in Chicago, in the 'nice little cottage' that she'd managed to purchase with earnings from her books.[70]

'The Reunited Family. Mrs Packard and all her children'
(from Modern Persecution)

'The mother's battle was fought, and the victory won,' Elizabeth Packard wrote.

The custody trial was the culmination of her life's work. She had fought, throughout, for her children. As with George Sand, it was motherhood that gave her a voice, and gave her the private authority that led her so naturally to assume public authority everywhere she went. If she had been denied motherhood in the private sphere, it had made her all determinedly a mother in the public sphere. It was as a mother that everyone – publishers, senators, judges – had related to her.

There were no winners here. She'd had nine years without her children; it was long enough to shape their lives, and hers. The main casualty was Libby. This was the eleven-year-old girl left weeping and calling for her mother in 1860, required to run the household, and to look after her siblings without her mother's strength or conviction. She was left clinging to the precepts of a woman whose touch she could no longer recall, regulating diet and awarding conduct marks on her behalf.

In his diary, Theophilus records his 'joyful hope' that in October 1863, the daughter who'd been a 'great comfort' to him in dark times, 'was born of the Holy Spirit into the kingdom of God, and gave her young heart to Christ'. This was when Elizabeth returned to Manteno after her years away. What happened to Libby? Did her father pray with her? Did she have some kind of collapse, frightened by the return of the mother she had missed with such anguish? Either way, there she was, a few months later, clasping herself to her mother with painful urgency in the Kankakee courtroom, only to be hurried off to Massachusetts by her father before the trial had finished.[71]

In April 1870 Libby was, as her father put it, 'taken deranged'. She was emaciated – perhaps anorexic – 'it seemed as though she would soon waste away and die'. In July, Theophilus took her to stay with Sybil and he recorded that 'in three months she seemed to have wholly recovered'. There's no record of why she went to him, or what Elizabeth thought. Perhaps Theophilus looked back to that moment when Libby threw herself on her mother in the courtroom. Perhaps he regretted his decision to take her away then – or perhaps he was too preoccupied by her salvation in the next life to dwell on her unhappiness in this one. She didn't in fact wholly recover. Within a couple of years, she had relapsed seriously, and Elizabeth took three years off from her reform work to care for her. For a while Libby was well enough to help her mother with her book business, and then she married an Irishman called Henry Gordon in 1880. Fifteen years later, her husband committed her to an asylum in California.[72]

It took a few months – why? – for Elizabeth to discover this, and then she rushed to California, removed Libby from the asylum and took her to live in Theo's house, with his four adolescent children (his wife had died). Libby's illness could take strange and lurid forms;

there were periods of raving, and days of huddled silence. Sometimes she appeared a danger to herself and others, so the family stretched some webbed wire across a room to enclose her, and Elizabeth slept on the other side of the wire. Theo's children were embarrassed by their raving aunt, so Elizabeth took her back to Chicago. In the train, Libby crouched in the upper berth and poured water on the heads of the passengers below. During the journey, Elizabeth became ill and died later in Chicago, in July 1897. There was now no one to look after Libby, who was incarcerated in another asylum until she died there, aged forty-five in 1901.

Libby's madness is a bleak shadow of this story. The daughter seems to have been destined to live out the tragedy, with all its madness and hopelessness, on behalf of her parents. There's something of George Sand's Solange in her; she's beloved, in this case, but unable to live up to her mother's energy. Neither of her parents protected Libby from their conflicts. In the years after 1863, her father retreated into pettiness; her mother indulged her own obsessions, albeit in the service of changing the world. Libby suffered because her father had the power to send her mother away and then because her mother, away from her children, was pushed into becoming such an extreme version of herself. And Theophilus's fears of eternal damnation must have affected Libby. It was a form of damnation you had so little control against – you could never know if your contact with the Holy Spirit was genuine.

And Britney? Laws wriggle into new forms. The conservatorship laws allowing her father to commit her are more complex than the laws that allowed Theophilus Packard to incarcerate his wife, but that makes them all the more difficult to resist.

Britney spent those four months incarcerated, pushed close to suicide. Perhaps there would have been more incarceration if the

#FreeBritney movement hadn't given her new confidence; and if Jamie Spears hadn't broken down the door of the bathroom to shake thirteen-year-old Sean Preston, after the boy locked himself away during an argument with him. Had the teenager acquired the habit of locking himself in bathrooms from his mother? He fared better, because there were more people prepared to protect him. Kevin Federline filed a police report and Jamie Spears was barred from seeing his grandchildren. Britney knew that she had to begin her own fight.

Perhaps Jamie Spears's diary is a howl of self-righteousness mingled with pain like Theophilus's. He might exhibit the same fear, both of damnation and of his own weakness. The fathers may be similar, but the judges have changed. It was Reva Goetz who made the conservatorship permanent in 2008; in 2014, when Britney was complaining that she was being forbidden from marrying and even from having her contraceptive coil removed, Goetz reportedly told Britney's court-appointed lawyer Samuel D. Ingham III: 'I don't recall that we made any orders about the right to marry, but you may not want to tell her that.' Where were those upstanding judges of the 1860s – where was Judge Charles Starr, or the Massachusetts lawyers who persuaded Theophilus to drop his claims to his children in 1869 – when it came to Spears's custody case?

The truth is that Tocqueville's age of ideally balanced democracy had failed to materialise and that the best interest of the child doctrine shifts its shape like the Holy Spirit. While in nineteenth-century America it saved many children from pain, it merely reflected the spirt of the age, and that was an age when mothers were idealised in ways that were ultimately more pernicious than helpful. Those applauding the forward-thinking courage of those judges were ignoring or abetting the decisions those same judges made to take children away from mothers who failed to live up to the ideal of the good mother.

'She is *my mother* in every sense of the term, and her councils I may rely upon, that her loving care and disregard of self to minister to our best interests, merits our most filial regard,' Theo wrote. What if she hadn't disregarded her self? Was she not then entitled to custody? It was through the best interests of the child doctrine that Kevin Federline prevented his wife from seeing their children; that he continued to claim a greater share of custody because she'd been given lithium in the mental asylum she was incarcerated in by her father. Do we create judges in the image of the age, or do they create the age in their image? Tocqueville liked to think that enlightened judges could lead the way to enlightenment; it may be instead that an age appalled by mothers creates the judges it desires to punish them.[73]

The law was flummoxed by Elizabeth Packard. So much so that new laws had to be invented, a court convened where no basis existed for it, and legislative assemblies bent to do the will of this mother, on behalf of her absent children. But equally, her children were flummoxed by the law. It wasn't only Libby who ended badly; the youngest, Arthur, took his own life – the son who'd lost his mother when still a baby, and never settled back into his mother's care, going back and forth between his parents in adolescence. They were brought into a world that endlessly affirmed the importance of motherhood, and assumed the guise of a matriarchy, but then they were told that their mother was both powerless and insane, and the foundations of their world were ripped away.

Britney Spears locked in her bathroom with her son; Elizabeth Packard in the snow, unrecognised by the boy who had run along the track, calling out for his mother; Libby throwing her arms around her mother in the courtroom and being dragged away; the patient in Louisiana cradling a doll while staring vacantly out; Jean Spears shooting herself on her infant son's grave, leaving her son Jamie at the disposal of a harsh father. These are all part of the same story, and it's also a story where George Sand rides with furious energy through the Pyrenees with the daughter she has just rescued but now drives to frenzied exhaustion. For Elizabeth Packard, as for George Sand and Britney Spears, self-actualisation came at the cost of the children's unhappiness, in a patriarchal world that couldn't tolerate the more extreme manifestations of the very energy that motherhood required.

Elizabeth Packard, with her combinations of domestic zeal and argumentative mania, her inalienable confidence in her right to freedom even when it was most threatened, may have been destined to change the world one way or another, and to cause conflict as she did so. Her marriage was unsustainable from the start; she was blazing into an age that was just coming into being, and her husband couldn't keep up. But perhaps, in a world that hadn't been run by men, her children could have been with her as she pursued her causes, fuelled as she was by Emerson's power not confident but agent. Perhaps they could have been there alongside her, completing their rigorous domestic tasks, doing their schoolwork under her diligent eye, and rising in turn to inherit her powers of self-determination and self-reliance – as, in actuality, only unruly Samuel managed to do.

As for Britney: she went out and got drunk, leaving her mother to babysit. Britney had issues with substance abuse – with Adderall, a medication often prescribed for ADHD. Eventually she broke down and was genuinely incapable of caring for her boys for a while. But can we separate all this from the difficulties in her marriage? What if she had been given a break from performing, if she could have been left, sometimes, to sing in the kitchen with her boys, to nap beside them as she longed to? What if she hadn't been hounded by a press that couldn't allow the nation's favourite pop princess to achieve a complicated identity of her own, or if she hadn't been asked openly by chat show hosts if she was a bad mother? She was in the middle of working out who she was and who she could be and then her father stepped in and took over the process.

These children could have been brought up without the ache of an absent mother who all the men around them told them was unfit to look after them. At least for Britney, and hopefully for her sons, there's still a chance. Let us see what the world does with her story as it finally comes to light; let us see if her sons can somehow emerge, as Elizabeth's rebellious Samuel did, to fight alongside their mother.

4

FRIEDA LAWRENCE,

and the Women Who Tramped Unwittingly Alongside Her

Consider this:

A woman abandons her husband and three children for her lover. 'All women in their natures are like giantesses,' the lover informs the husband. Left behind, the husband does his best to piece together a life for the children in the absence inflicted by this selfish – and, let us say it, unnatural – woman.

Or, consider this:

A young girl, unhappy in her unhappy home, marries the first man to propose. He takes her to a new country where, friendless, she's sustained only by her love for her three children. As the years pass, she feels more alone in her marriage: this husband who claims to adore her has never tried to discover who she is. She falls in love with one man, then another. 'All women in their natures are like giantesses,' her lover says. Surely she'll be a better mother if she can live a fuller life? She leaves her husband, assuming he'll give her the children he doesn't have time to look after. But he decides to punish her, and the law is on his side. She's forbidden from attempting any contact with her children.

Toss a coin. The unnatural, unwomanly mother or the cruel,

punitive father? For a woman trapped in the wrong story there's no way out. Any desperate, ill-conceived attempt she makes to see her children will be viewed as the machinations of a fallen temptress rather than the stumbling of a loving mother. And if she says otherwise – then isn't this what people say when they're trying to alienate the affections of trusting minors?

It's not easy for the father either. Does wanting to set up a stable, morally upright home make him cruel? Is it really in his children's interests for them to see their mother sporadically, only for her to depart with her itinerant lover? He is pushed into his stance by forces larger than he is, as she is into hers. And the judges? – the two wigged men lined up to judge this sad, salacious story are products of their time as well.

I. The three lives of Frieda

'Mrs Weekley must live large and abundantly'

Frieda von Richthofen. Frieda Weekley. Frieda Lawrence. She was all these and none; she was always just Frieda. There was Frieda the child, wild and sunburnt in their large garden, her knees scratched from climbing trees, her manners below par (she pulled faces at tea parties). She was proud of her aristocratic ancestry but joined her sister Else in harbouring qualms about class privilege ('if I were a poor washer-woman I couldn't stay in bed just for a cold'). Then there was Frieda the passionate young woman, with thick curling blonde hair, a haughty profile and a single dimple when she smiled, falling in love with officers who couldn't marry a girl without a dowry, passionately defending her feckless father when her mother complained about his gambling and affairs.

She needed to escape; there was no one to marry in Metz, a garrison town filled with German soldiers who had conquered it from the French; there was no one to marry in Berlin, where she holidayed with her uncle, laughing at the Kaiser when he complimented her uncle on his beautiful nieces, failing to find an appropriate suitor during a whole season of balls. It's not surprising that Frieda succumbed easily to Ernest Weekley, a responsible, handsome professor of modern languages from England on the cusp of middle age. She wasn't an intellectual, but she was enough of a reader to like the thought of surrounding herself with books and ideas. He kissed her large, ordinary feet in their clumsy boots, offering adoration, escape, and the admirable nobility of character of a man who'd grown up in poverty and made it through the rungs of English academia on his own merit.[1]

And so there was Frieda the young wife, the woman who never quite believed in herself as Mrs Weekley. There was a wedding in August 1899, and an awkward, estranging wedding night in Lake Como, where the husband who had eagerly kissed her booted feet turned out to be terrified of her naked body. After taking refuge alone in the hotel bar, he was understandably disconcerted to find his new wife hiding on top of a cupboard in her underwear, revealing herself as just the child-bride he feared she was.

And then she was transported, abruptly – to Nottingham, where Ernest had accepted a role as Professor of Modern Languages at the university, and where Frieda missed her parents and sisters. She had always been one of three, their characters defined by their differences – Else the genius, Nusch the beauty, Frieda the funny, lively, madcap one who was passionate about nature. How could she be funny, lively and madcap as a young wife in a suburban house with a small backyard with a privy in it and curtains twitching as the neighbours noticed her getting it all wrong? It was shopping in the mornings and social calls in the afternoons, and laundry on Mondays – how could she not know? – but soon she did, and found it easier to go along with it than to attempt to find a new way of being in this strange town.

All this was made easier by babies. Decades later, narrating her own life as she often did in the third person, she wrote that when Montague (Monty) her first-born, drank from her breasts, she felt she was feeding the universe. 'She adored him with a secret passion and would have liked to take him away to a hidden place and have him all to herself.' At the time she put it with endearing directness in a letter to her sister Else: 'Woman, have a child, and you are happy!' There was a nurse, a young German woman, but Frieda liked to play with Monty herself, glad finally of an appreciative audience for her peek-a-boo games. She liked popping up behind the curtains to say 'Bonjour Monsieur' and watch her son shake with laughter. Two little girls followed, Barbara (Barby) and Elsa. She embroidered their clothes; she invited them into her bed on Sunday mornings for pillow fights and German fairy stories. She was more sustained by their adoration than her husband's. 'It is touching how attached [Monty] is to me,' she wrote to Else, 'and it does one good when they think one is a kind of little god.' When Monty went to school she stood at the window of their new house, with its plush red curtains (they even had an indoor bathroom now) making faces. He laughed at first but then looked around, anxious that people might see.[2]

Montague and Elsa Weekley in Nottingham park, 1906

The routines continued: shopping in the mornings, calls in the afternoons. She played the piano; she read George Eliot and Thackeray, and wrote to her sister; she edited two little books for pupils of German – Schiller's ballads and a collection of fairy tales. When she felt constricted, she went out in the dark in an old hat and ran up the road, listening to the trams toiling up the hill, savouring the 'glorious feeling of escape', before going back to her house quietly, 'sane again'. Ernest was contented and proud – 'if the little girl grows up like her mother then I consider myself a happy man,' he wrote to his mother-in-law. But he was impatient with the children ('Why should I be cursed with an idiot for a son!' he said once, when he'd failed to help Monty understand something) and he was working hard, doing evening lectures as well as his university job, and writing about etymology. He wasn't a bad husband; he was admiring still, and forward-thinking enough about women's lives to give Frieda relative autonomy as a mother and wife – she could see her family and make her own friends. The problem was that family and friends were scarce in Nottingham. And she hardly saw Ernest and there wasn't much intimacy when she did, not least because she'd asked the doctor to advise him to avoid intercourse after the third baby. Ultimately, she was too much for him, and he couldn't meet her in her passions or excitements. As a result, crucial elements of life were missing, and her children weren't always enough. It was made bearable by annual trips back to Germany, sometimes with her children and sometimes alone. There she found a freer, almost frighteningly stimulating world.[3]

Her sister Else was living in Munich, entangled in the new intellectual ferment taking over Germany. She was diligently hard-working – she'd earned a doctorate in economics and was working as a labour inspector – but lived a bohemian life surrounded by Expressionist painters and futurist poets, by homosexuals and anarchists, all congregating at the Café Stephanie in Schwabing. Else had already had a series of lovers since finding her own university professor husband,

Edgar Jaffé, and was pregnant with the child of the psychoanalyst Otto Gross. Indeed, she'd found her way into a circle committed not so much to sexual freedom as to a kind of wilful debauchery: Gross was also sleeping with other women, including his own patients. He had convinced himself that women were the hope of the world, especially those 'unpolluted by all the things that I hate and fight against . . . free from the code of chastity, from Christianity, from democracy and all that accumulated filth.' Frieda found Else's world as strange as it was enticing. But it gave her the confidence to have love affairs of her own, first in Nottingham, with a lace manufacturer called Will Dowson who took her for walks in Sherwood Forest, and then in Germany with the gaunt anarchist Ernst Frick, and with Otto Gross himself, who had just extricated himself from Else. Gross spoke to Frieda about Freud's ideas, urging her to overcome repression, and she felt like the shutters of a dark house had been flung open.[4]

'You are not our old mother,' five-year-old Elsa complained after her weeks with Gross. 'You have got our old mother's skin on, but you are not our mother that went away.' She had been remade in the fire of his embrace and in the letters that followed. 'It is as if out of your letter streamed the warmth of your body, so sweet and powerful, like a wave of happy, liberating bliss, as you live and give, you whom I love with such joy,' Gross wrote, commending her as a woman of the future – she, who had been trapped in her husband's stubbornly backward-looking world. She took to dancing naked in her bedroom while her neighbours were at church.[5]

There were many ways of being a woman and a mother, she now saw. Else and her circle were rethinking how women could live, and motherhood was at the heart of this. It was hard to be a bohemian and a mother, not least because of unexpected pregnancies. Else was aided here by her aristocratic confidence; she expected her husband to give her lover's child his name, as German aristocratic husbands had done for centuries, and he played his part. She was also aided by the tumult of ideas about motherhood.

FRIEDA LAWRENCE

Frieda Weekley, photograph by L. Peudy, c. 1912

The nineteenth-century Kindergarten movement was still going strong, pioneering new forms of collective childcare. German feminists were divided on motherhood, as feminists everywhere have been before and since: some called for a gender-neutral approach to rights, downplaying maternal nurture in favour of a Darwinian emphasis on nature; others insisted on the rights of women as mothers, seeing women's capacity for care as the reason to amplify their voices in the public sphere, where they could offer an alternative from German militarism. 'The uniqueness of motherly experience shows the value of women's entry into legislative bodies,' Helene Simon and Adele Gerhard said in their influential 1901 book *Motherhood and Intellectual Work*. Living amid these gyrations gave Else and her friends the freedom to change their minds, and to place great importance on being good mothers while committing to being independent women whose lives weren't defined by their children.[6]

In Britain, the 'New Woman' – university student, suffragist – had bicycled in from the nineteenth century, smoking as she went, and become a mother. And she had new ideas about maternity, which from November 1911 could be found in *The Freewoman: A Weekly Feminist Review*. The magazine was founded by self-styled new woman Dora Marsden, a suffragette school teacher who was child-free by choice, and determined to free mothers from exhausting self-sacrifice. What is the purpose of a human as opposed to an animal life? Marsden asked in her February 1912 editorial. To be human you had to have a purpose – and motherhood made this hard. Women had to stop dreaming and become creative beings:

> They must create, and the activities which stand in the way of their creative powers must be arranged for or, if need be, put aside. If the activities relate to children, the woman has to answer faithfully this question: To whom is her first duty, herself or the coming generation? We hold, her first, second and third duty is to herself, and, that duty being fulfilled, she will have done her duty to the coming generation.

How to achieve this? Mothers needed to think of maternity as a set of finite responsibilities rather than a sentimental ideal. As she put it in another editorial, 'motherhood, when legitimate, has had an emphasis laid upon its sanctity which nothing in its commonplace nature in any way justifies'.[7]

Frieda was not an avid reader of *The Freewoman*. It was a belief in the sanctity of motherhood that made her domestic life survivable. But she had friends in Nottingham now as well as Germany who shared Marsden's ideas. Shortly after meeting Gross she'd got to know two Nottingham sisters, Madge and Gladys Bradley, who were self-styled 'new women' and were convinced that there was more to a woman's life than Ernest allowed for (though Gladys herself fell in love with Ernest, who complimented her 'fine figure in a bathing dress' when she accompanied them on a family holiday). Frieda told Gross proudly in 1908 that she'd enlisted not only Madge but her fiancé into '*your* way of thinking', apparently envisaging some recoupling: 'They must be grateful to you, the two of them and I hope I will experience something beautiful with him, I hold him very dear, but you, you who have the radiance of the sun for me, you *remain* to me what to me you are.'[8]

For the Bradleys, as for Marsden, and certainly for Otto Gross, it came easily to think of women as giantesses. Frieda was as ready for D. H. Lawrence as he was for her, when he came to lunch at their home in Nottingham in March 1912, wanting to consult Professor Weekley (whose evening course he'd been attending) on teaching possibilities in Germany.

A long thin figure entered the room with light, sure movements. 'He seemed so obviously simple,' she wrote later. 'Yet he arrested my attention. There was something more than met the eye. What kind of a bird was this?'[9]

D.H. Lawrence, photograph by W.G. Parker, 1913

She was thirty-two, and becoming more regal as she aged; he was twenty-seven, a coal-miner's son, the still unknown author of two novels. The two of them sat in the drawing room, waiting for Ernest while the children played on the lawn – Monty was eleven now, Elsa nine and Barby seven – the curtains fluttering in the spring breeze. They talked about Oedipus, and he told Frieda that he was through with women. He was younger than her husband and quicker; his delicate hands were constantly in motion and his eyes darted about. Mainly he looked at her. Later he described her at this point as 'full-bosomed, and full of life, gleaming with life, like a flower in the sun, and like a cat that looks round in the sunshine and finds it good'. They had lunch with Ernest, and then he walked the five hours back to Eastwood and wrote to her a single line: 'You are the most wonderful woman in England.'[10]

'You don't know many women in England, how do you know?' she responded.[11]

He visited again, on Easter Sunday, when her husband was away, and they hunted for Easter eggs with the children. Lawrence was disapproving when she offered to make tea and then revealed that she didn't know how to turn on the gas because the servants always did it. Between visits she read the manuscript that would become *Sons and Lovers*, reading it in bed and smoking. Years later, Montague would recall his 'vivid memory of my mother lying in bed and devouring a manuscript' – perhaps already uneasy about what this hungry reading meant for his family. And then she and Lawrence met at a station in Derbyshire, accompanied by her daughters in pink-and-white striped dresses, and walked through the spring woods. Lawrence made paper boats and let them float in the brook, forgetting about her as he crouched with the girls. Later she would identify this moment of rapt involvement with her children as the moment she knew she loved him. The girls were more ambivalent. 'This is the Spanish Armada and you don't know what that was,' he told them. 'Yes we do,' Elsa retorted.[12]

The Weekley's nursemaid, Ida Wilhelmy, with Barby, Montague and Elsa Weekley, c.1910

They borrowed an apartment from Gladys Bradley, and Lawrence got them invited to his publisher's house together. But he wanted more; he wanted to be alone with her for longer. He pleaded that they go to Germany together. 'In a sovereign way he took her for himself,' she later wrote; 'she was his and he would never let her go again while he lived; he would kill her rather. She liked it . . . Together they took hold of the earth, the solid earth, never to lose it again entirely, neither of them.' She wasn't always sure why he had selected her with such certainty. 'You have a genius for living,' he said, when she asked; she agreed, but she credited him with bringing this out in her.[13]

They went to Metz – back to her hometown. She said a tearful goodbye to her son, took her daughters to stay with Ernest's parents in London, and boarded a train with the lover she was still determined would be temporary – another in her list of dazzling conquests. Lawrence saw it differently: this was his marriage, which made it all the more frustrating when he found himself alone in an attic room in a 'semi-religious kind of family hotel', kept away from her parents and introduced only briefly to the free-thinking sisters who were at least told that he was a lover. This was a world on the verge of war – according to Lawrence there were four soldiers for every civilian – and Lawrence was arrested by the German police on suspicion of being an English spy. Frieda had to confess the truth to her father, who got Lawrence released, but now Lawrence wanted to tell Ernest about their love affair. 'No more dishonour, no more lies,' he wrote to Frieda from his cramped hotel room. 'Let them do their – silliest – but no more subterfuge, lying, dirt, fear. I feel as if it would strangle me.'[14]

Frieda wasn't going to tell Ernest herself, but she wasn't going to let go of Lawrence – and he would only remain in her life as a husband, not a lover. She didn't stop him from posting the letter that would be read out in the law court and published in the newspapers, informing Ernest that:

> Mrs Weekley is afraid of being stunted and not allowed to grow, and so she must live her own life. All women in their natures are like giantesses. They will break through everything and go on with their own lives. . . . Mrs Weekley must live large and abundantly. It is her nature. To me it means the future. I feel as if my effort of life was all for her.

In response, Ernest Weekley veered between desperate self-pity and wrath. 'Do you want to drive me to suicide,' he asked in May 1912, insisting that 'all compromises are unthinkable' and he wouldn't share the children. 'As long as I live Frieda will have a friend to whom she will never turn in vain,' he told Frieda's mother, but it was palpably untrue; the next day he said that seeing Frieda again would kill him: 'I would kill myself and the children too.'[15]

He conscripted his sister to look after his children, and she joined in recriminating Frieda, glad to have a chance to subdue the woman she'd always found self-important and lazy. 'What did you want more than he gave to you, for you must know that he has always been your slave in every sense of the word,' she asked. 'Ernest will not want me to write unless it is kindly and as I said I do love you still but oh! that you had chosen any other life than his to smash . . . You have somehow missed the best in life and the best in love.' The Weekleys' neighbour Lily wrote too, urging Frieda to come back rather than spoiling 'your own life and the lives of all the others – the little girls without a mother, no mother's love, and Monty, he *must* have a mother to protect him . . . the children you brought into the world can't be cast off like this'.[16]

'Don't you remember the night Monty was born,' Lily went on to ask, but Frieda remembered it all too well. They were her children, and she couldn't believe that they were Ernest's to claim, however much she had transgressed as a wife. It made it harder that Lawrence couldn't or wouldn't sympathise. He found her suffering unbearable and he was jealous of the three children whose claims were greater than his. Lawrence's failure to sympathise with Frieda as a mother during this crisis that he had almost single-handedly precipitated is the most unforgivable act of his life. Where Ernest couldn't allow her to be a liberated woman as well as a mother, Lawrence couldn't allow her to be a mother as well as a liberated woman. And they were both abetted in their rigidity by the legal system, with its punitive binary dividing women into adulterers and mothers. For his part Lawrence justified it with a plethora of theories. As far as he was concerned – and Frieda, with her reading of Freud, agreed with him here – his own mother had sacrificed too much for her children, and it had made her miserable, and given her sons the responsibility of lovers.

These were theories Lawrence worked out alongside Frieda as he redrafted *Sons and Lovers*. Increasingly, he blamed his mother for his own adolescent unhappiness; it was convenient to do so: he could convince himself he was saving Frieda's children from unhappiness rather than dooming them to a life of displacement and sadness. 'If Frieda and the children could live happily together, I should say "Go",' he would write in December to Frieda's sister Else, who had written pleading with him to send Frieda home. 'But if she would only be sacrificing her life, I would not let her go if I could keep her. Because if she brings to the children sacrifice, that is a curse to them . . . if Frieda gave up all to go and live with them, that would sap their strength because they would have to support her life as they grew up.' For years Frieda had attempted to find total fulfilment through her children. Gross had put an end to this, demanding she take seriously her own desires. Now Lawrence was insisting that this attempt to live through her children had been not merely unconvincing but actively pernicious.[17]

These were the conflicts and the anguish they took with them when they moved to Icking, to a small, olde-worlde Bavarian flat looking out over the Isar, owned by Else's lover, the sociologist Alfred Weber. They bathed naked in the river; they were entranced by the gentians by day, and by the fireflies and glow-worms at night. And day after day, night after night, they fought, enacting a battle of wills they both celebrated as an archetypal conflict between masculine and feminine. Lawrence had fallen in love with her as an old-fashioned womanly woman, while also applauding her new woman side – seeing that she could disregard convention and live a fuller life than most women. Frieda wanted to enact his ideal of femininity, but it made no sense to her that this couldn't include motherhood. In some of Lawrence's moods, it could; he talked about wanting to have a baby with her. But that made it all the more cruel that he seemed bent on excluding her existing children. 'The mother in you, fierce as a murderess,' he wrote in his poem 'She Looks Back':

At last, as you stood, your white gown falling from your breasts,
You looked into my eyes, and said: 'But this is joy!'

I acquiesced again.
But the shadow of lying was in your eyes,
The mother in you, fierce as a murderess, glaring to England,
Yearning towards England, towards your young children,
Insisting upon your motherhood, devastating.[18]

Lawrence was wiser in this powerfully penetrating poem than he could be in their quarrelsome daily life. For her part, Frieda continued to insist as fiercely as she could on her feelings as a mother, and on her own supremacy – she had no intention of doing any domestic labour for a man. Lawrence was appalled by her slatternliness: when she spilt coffee on a pillow she would turn the pillow over. He tried to teach her how to wash sheets and clean floors, but it was ineffectual, so he did the housework himself, bringing her breakfast in bed most days as he would do for decades.

Eventually, the quarrels found a kind of resolution. Lawrence would title the poetry collection written out of these months *Look! We Have Come Through!* One of the most movingly triumphant poems here is 'Fronleichnam', where he describes a man and a woman who have come together after stepping across the people they love, 'hurting them all', and meet at last, 'Here in this upper room', looking out over the 'jade-green river' to the mountains. This is a moment of sexual triumph – 'a quiver of exultation goes through me' – in which the lovers meet in a dance, 'Shining and touching', in a 'heaven of our own, sheer with repudiation'.[19]

For both this was happiness, wrested against all the odds; happiness conditional on the unhappiness of others and for Frieda contingent still on not losing her children, but happiness nonetheless. In a letter to his publisher Edward Garnett, Lawrence described 'F, in a scarlet pinafore, leaning out on the balcony, against a background of blue and snowy mountains', saying to him: 'I'm so happy I don't even want to kiss you.' Lawrence characteristically turned from reverie to didacticism: 'So there, you see, Love is a much bigger thing than passion, and a woman *much* more than sex.' Garnett's son David came to visit and fell half in love with Frieda, admiring her 'noble' head and green eyes, her habit of looking people 'dead in the eyes', fearless in her judgement, 'extraordinarily like a lioness'. She had cast off one life for another and was larger, fiercer, than she'd believed possible.[20]

The letters came in, from Ernest and from her parents. Two things were becoming clear, and they brought a tragic inevitability to her continued separation from her children. Ernest was not prepared to give up the children he now saw wholly as his. And Lawrence was not prepared to fight Ernest in court:

When you got to London, and had to face that judge, it would make you ill. We are not callous enough to stand against the public, the whole mass of the world's disapprobation, in a sort of criminal dock. It destroys us, though we deny it. We are all off the balance. We are like spring scales that have been knocked about. We had better be still awhile, let ourselves come to rest.[21]

What of the children, left behind, their lives parcelled out by their parents? They all wrote about Lawrence and Frieda in later years. They didn't dwell on these months of limbo, which remained only as shadowy, unhappy memories, but the atmosphere of this time emerges.

When his mother disappeared, Monty was left living alone with his father. His main memory of this time was of stomach cramps and nausea – he hardly ate. Barby and Elsa were contented at first with their grandparents, but then became confused about why their mother was taking so long. She'd only left them in Hampstead for a few weeks yet here they still were, overhearing hushed conversations about their poor father and their wanton mother. Then Ernest sold the Nottingham house and moved Monty in with his parents too. Abruptly, all the children were told to address their Aunt Maude as 'Mama'.

'Where is Mama?' one of the girls gathered courage to ask one morning.

'You girls mustn't ask about Mama just now,' their grandmother replied as their father left the room.

Together they cried themselves to sleep, again.[22]

Sunday after Sunday, Ernest left for work at the University of Nottingham. Monty cried desperately every Sunday night when his father packed his briefcase, convinced this departure was also going to be permanent. When you lose one parent so casually, who is to say you won't lose the other one?

There were new routines and regimes. Their mother's bohemianism had to be eradicated, so Maude took the children to church and tried to inculcate respectability and thrift. Wanting more space, Ernest moved the whole family to Chiswick in the autumn of 1912, to another home full of secrecy and grief. He brought the thick red velvet curtains from Frieda's sitting room and hung them amid dark, old-fashioned furniture from his parents' house. There were recitations of Tennyson from their grandmother and vituperative Bible readings from their father, his personality soured by grief. 'All wrongdoing is avenged on earth,' he shouted, sometimes in German. Maude told them sadistic stories and lashed out at Barby, who had inherited her mother's irreverent wit.[23]

'Poor Papa!' the children whispered, tiptoeing past his study at weekends.

Did they say this to protect themselves from self-pity? They no longer cried as much. Perhaps they worried that if they started to feel sorry for themselves it would never stop.

II. Reading about custody

'How to be happy though livanted'

The letters fired back and forth between the Weekleys. 'I have done with you,' Ernest wrote. 'I want to forget you and you must be dead to the children. You know the law is on my side.' Lawrence and Frieda crossed the Alps to Italy where they found an apartment overlooking Lake Garda and Frieda lay in bed, looking at the lake, conscious of nothing but the 'light and the pain in her limbs, her arms, that had longed to hold her children', thinking of the Sundays when the children had clambered on her raised knees in bed, and reading *Anna Karenina*. 'F had carefully studied *Anna Karenin*, in a sort of "How to be happy though livanted" spirit,' Lawrence told Edward Garnett in October 1912. 'She finds Anna very much like herself, only inferior – Vronsky is not much like me – too much my superior.'[24]

Lawrence had loved *Anna Karenina* for years. 'Read *Anna Karenina* – no matter, read it again, and if you dare to fall out with it, I'll – I'll swear aloud,' he had told a friend three years earlier. 'I daren't think of Weekley . . . I only know I love Frieda . . . I can think of nothing but of Anna Karenina,' he told his first love, Jessie Chambers, in June 1912. It may not be excessive to suggest that he was so sure about Frieda when he met her because he'd been unconsciously looking for a vivacious but unhappily married woman who would resemble his greatest literary love. Either way, he now found himself living out Tolstoy's plot, and Frieda found their difficulties in the book's pages – perhaps most of all when it came to the question of her children. Here was another punitive husband, Count Karenin, open in admitting that he has 'even lost affection for my son, because he is associated with the repulsion I feel for you', but asserting his right to custody nonetheless. And here was another possessive lover, who sees Anna's son as 'the most agonising aspect of his relationship with her' and reminds her dismissively that she has a simple choice:

'leave your son, or continue with this humiliating situation'. Did Vronsky license Lawrence's own cruelty about her children? It's odd if he did, given that Tolstoy makes clear how far the narrator diverges from Vronsky on these questions. Indeed, Tolstoy cares about Anna's son more than about almost anyone else in the book.[25]

Anna Karenina is more profound on custody than it is on love. The love between Vronsky and Anna is a kind of given, though an electrifying one. Vronsky is so much a type that it feels that any charismatic man could have won her heart, with enough love and conviction. He distinguishes himself by attaching his love to Anna, seeing that this apparently conventional wife and mother is a unique and superior being, overflowing with an 'abundance of something' that expresses itself 'independently of her will, now in the radiance of her glance now in her smile'. (This portrait of a woman who appears typical but turns out to have a singular genius for life must surely have been part of the novel's appeal for Frieda.) The love affair, consummated so early in the book, does act as an engine of transformation for Anna and Vronsky; both gain a new kind of vastness and complexity from rising to the situation in which they find themselves. But it is inevitably going to defeat them. If this is realism, it's realism set in the wheels of the awful train awaiting Anna at the end. The tragedy of Anna's son, Seryozha, is different. It has a greater openness to it. He is fated to be caught between the opposed destinies and temperaments of his parents, but he remains unformed, his vulnerability full of potential right until the end. As a result, his suffering can be more painful to witness than Anna's, because it feels less inevitable. And in a novel that famously begins with the question of unhappy families, the role of a child in an unhappy marriage preoccupies the book.[26]

Tolstoy was writing a tragedy, but he also wanted to expand the possibilities of realism to illuminate the darkest corners of Russian life. He was preoccupied with practical, everyday questions, and divorce is as important to the book as agrarian reform. Divorce had already become an accepted feature of Russian society; there were about seventy divorce cases a year by the 1870s. People weren't punished here for colluding as they were in England, so husband and wife could collaborate on a divorce. But only the innocent party could marry again, so an adulterous wife who wanted to marry her lover had to persuade her husband to take the blame. Usually, husbands asked for their children in exchange. This was possible because there were no formal custody arrangements made in divorce courts; couples made their own arrangements which were ratified by the court, so children became a bargaining tool. Tolstoy knew how inadequate this all was; he'd helped his sister negotiate her divorce, as Anna's brother Stiva attempts to help her.[27]

Questions of divorce coursed through Tolstoy's mind as he redrafted the book, but the answers kept shifting. The book kept changing as his thinking changed. At first, he had Karenin following through on his forgiveness by granting Anna a divorce, enabling her to marry Vronsky. But this wasn't tragic enough, so in the final draft, Anna rejects the offer of both divorce and custody that Karenin made in the saintly glow of forgiveness brought on by her near-death. She's too preoccupied by her own abjection and by Karenin's righteousness to take this chance to improve her life. It's only when she's alone with Vronsky and the baby daughter who bears her husband's surname that she's persuaded about the necessity of a divorce. By this point she misses her son too much to accept a divorce without custody, so negotiations stall, destroying Anna and Vronsky by ridding them of a shared future they can believe in.[28]

The most tender – the most committedly romantic – scene in the novel is the one where Anna returns to the marital home and creeps upstairs to her son as he wakes on his tenth birthday. Seryozha has been dreaming of his mother for weeks, falling asleep imagining her smile and the touch of her soft arms. Then, suddenly, she's there as he stretches awake, 'his little body arched back', yawning his morning yawn. Seeing him, Anna acclimatises to seeing this long-limbed boy rather than the four-year-old he's settled as in her mind. She whispers his name and he rouses, turning his tousled head from side to side as if looking for something, and then opening his eyes. Realising that she is there in the flesh, he smiles a blissful smile and, 'closing his sleepy, stuck-together eyes again', he tumbles forwards into her arms. She hugs him, enveloped by 'the wonderful sleepy smell and warmth that only children exude' as he rubs his face against her neck and shoulders. Then he falls asleep again and she cries, overwhelmed by the presence of his familiar yet unfamiliar body. They kiss, repeatedly; she strokes his hair and he kisses the hand she's stroking him with. Then his old nanny comes in to wish him happy birthday, and Anna is urged to hurry out because her husband is approaching. Seeing fear and shame on her face, Seryozha is confused, sure she has done nothing wrong. Anna urges him to love his father, insisting that he's better and kinder than she is. 'There's no one better than you!' he cries out, pressing himself against her with all his power, his arms trembling from the effort. Then she leaves, and he collapses on his bed, sobbing.[29]

This scene portrays a love more fully embodied than the love we see between Anna and Vronsky. We only find this kind of full sensuality in the scenes between Kitty and Levin, culminating in the birth of Kitty's son, which in turn takes us back to Seryozha, reminding us how much agony and love has gone into his existence. Seryozha comes alive in his scene with his mother in every sinew of his lengthening limbs. And afterwards, he remains as constant a presence for the reader as he is for Anna. As the negotiations over the divorce play out, he becomes 'the son', a mere pawn in a legal battle, but every mention of him now brings all the agonising tenderness of this scene. When we next see him properly, it's about a year later, when his uncle visits. Tolstoy shows him anxiously avoiding all thoughts of his mother. Seryozha is a child of divorce now and, like so many of the children in this book, he does his best to align himself with the parent who has custody in order to survive.

Before Anna's morning visit, he had felt ill at ease with his father, who addressed him like an 'imaginary boy such as one finds in books', making Seryozha play-act just that storybook child. Seeing his mother, all his yearning for love was reawakened. She claimed him confidently, awfully, as her son, and left him full of unrealisable dreams and thoughts. As delirious longing became serious illness, his father intervened; he sent him to school, which has had the desired effect of stretching him into self-conscious adolescence. He now drives all thoughts of his mother away, seeing them as shameful for 'a boy, and the friend of his classmates'. But Stiva's appearance threatens to reawaken these thoughts. Does he remember his mother, the man asks, and the boy responds with an angry 'no'. He won't, he can't remember her because he can't bear to find fault with his father, 'with whom he lived and on whom he depended', and because he can't bear to succumb to the sentimentality he now knows to be humiliating.[30]

By this point, it's not wholly clear that Karenin shouldn't have custody. His love for Annie, the illegitimate baby of Anna and Vronsky, who he has accepted as his own daughter, was surprising and genuine enough to elevate him as a father, and his rigorous commitment to his son's education is more effortful than anything we can imagine of Anna. Perhaps it's fair: one child each for the two of them. Except that it's not fair on Seryozha himself, and Tolstoy makes this painfully clear when he portrays the boy subduing his feelings to endure the pain of the new arrangement. All along, he has loved only his mother with the kind of spontaneous feeling that allows him to be himself in her presence. He has to make such an effort to be the new kind of boy his father expects him to be, and it becomes disturbingly evident where this effort is going to lead. By the end of the book, Seryozha seems destined to become a Karenin-like figure in turn, struggling to express genuine feelings.

Those months of profound identification with *Anna Karenina* changed Frieda forever. These were years when she acquired a grandeur that would see her through the rest of her life, even after she and Lawrence became farcically tawdry in their mutual rages. If she acquired this grandeur now, it wasn't because she was learning from Lawrence; it was more because he was learning from her. They edited *Sons and Lovers* together, with Frieda drafting pages at a time from the perspective of the female characters, opening up women's lives for him. They were learning together about what a realist novel could be, and her reading of *Anna Karenina* fed into this process. It was the Russians, alongside Thomas Hardy, who had shown Lawrence how he wanted to write in the first place; now Frieda was using Tolstoy to help Lawrence forge his writing anew. And this was a realist tradition that had been birthed, in some sense, by the advent of the system of family law that was now going to control their lives.

In the nineteenth century, as the desperate, riven worlds of Caroline Norton and George Sand became a familiar setting for ever more people, lives became more knowingly subject to legal structures; people's judgements of themselves were now inflected by the imagined judgments of a court – even if, whether they were more like Tolstoy's Anna or Hardy's Sue Bridehead in *Jude the Obscure*, they were uncertain what those judgments would actually be. And as the nineteenth-century novel gained in ambition, seeking panoramic, polyphonic stories that combined vast human conflict and domestic detail, custody provided the ideal engine to bring together social critique and moral ambiguity.

Wilkie Collins ended a literary career marked by epic, suspenseful mysteries with his 1885 *The Evil Genius*, a smaller-scale tale of domestic unhappiness and adultery that culminates in a custody decision so calamitous that the parents end up reuniting. Henry James's 1897 *What Maisie Knew* was inspired by the 1896 case *Re A and B (Infants)*, where the Court of Chancery arranged for a doubly adulterous mother and father to divide their children equally between them, in alternate stretches of six months. James set himself the pyrotechnic challenge of writing from the sharp-eyed but partial perspective of the child passed like a 'shuttlecock' between her parents. Although Dickens, more than anyone, showed the law courts to be the most fertile of settings for his distinctive blend of delirious invention and sedulous detail in his 1852 *Bleak House*, he avoided depicting custody as a legal issue. This is tantalising: Dickens was so preoccupied with questions of care – with how we take care of each other, or don't – that it would have been the perfect subject matter for him. But he was perhaps chastened by his own behaviour in these matters. He'd discarded his wife for his mistress, published a letter declaring theirs to be an amicable separation, and taken for himself nine of the ten children she'd exhausted herself bearing and rearing over the previous decades.

In France, Alphonse Daudet wrote his 1892 tragi-comedy, *Rose and Ninette*, about the effects of divorce on father–son relationships in particular, concluding with the observation that you can't truly end a marriage because you are destined to remain a family forever: 'when one has children, divorce does not solve the problem'. And in Germany, Theodor Fontane used the story of Baroness Elisabeth von Ardenne as the basis for his 1895 *Effi Briest*, the tragic tale of the transformation of a bright, giggly young girl into a depressed, sickly and deracinated woman, after her husband divorces her for adultery and takes custody of their daughter. Elisabeth von Ardenne didn't see her children for decades after her divorce, but Fontane gives Effi a sighting of her daughter Annie on a tram and then a brief visit, in which Annie stands timidly away from her mother, giving curt, anodyne answers to her questions. After this, Effi succumbs to the illness that kills her. Her tragedy is both that she has transgressed and that she believes in the rules she's transgressed: intense despair comes together with intense conventionality. Her encounter with her daughter confirms that she can find no value, no meaning in her life now.[31]

Thomas Hardy depicted life after life destroyed by questions of custody. These are people without recourse to the law, but whose terror of the legal implications of their acts can make the law all the more of a force in their lives. The story of his 1886 *The Mayor of Casterbridge* is motored by custody. At a fair, a drunk man decides to sell his wife to a sailor; she agrees to go as long as she can keep their daughter. Afterwards, Michael Henchard is full of guilt; he atones, gives up drink, and becomes a mayor. When Susan Henchard appears, now apparently widowed after her bigamous second marriage, he agrees to marry her again, grateful to have his daughter Elizabeth-Jane returned to him. Indeed, he proposes that they officially change the girl's name back to Henchard, though the girl hurts him by talking lovingly about her late stepfather. 'I can think of no other father as my father, except my father,' she says, and what exactly this signifies is far more complex than she can realise. Henchard then overturns her world by telling her the truth, promising: 'I'll do anything, as long as you will look upon me as your father!' The book's tragedy is set in motion by the revelation that Elizabeth-Jane is not in fact Henchard's child; that baby died and this one has another father, still alive and able to claim her.[32]

Hardy returned to these questions with a new vision, grotesque as well as tragic, in his 1895 *Jude the Obscure.* Jude – part visionary scholar, part artisan, always dreaming, usually failing – gets trapped into an ill-suited marriage with the sensual, worldly rural beauty Arabella that results in a child. He agrees to have custody of his son after divorcing Arabella and uniting with his beloved cousin Sue (though they don't actually marry, because they can't bear to involve the state in their love). 'As I was the petitioner, I am really entitled to custody, I suppose,' he says, though he also wishes that the law, with its questions of possession and blood ties, played no part in such questions, because 'all the little ones of our time are collectively the children of us adults of the time, and entitled to our general care'. His son is a small, pale and world-weary little boy they name Jude, who begins to call Sue 'Mother' and lives fairly happily among the children she bears, but is always aware he doesn't quite belong, and that Sue's many babies are a hindrance to her. 'It would be better to be out o'the world than in it, wouldn't it?' he asks Sue, when they have lost almost everything and are refused rooms at inns because of all the children. She responds, fatally: 'It would almost, dear.'[33]

Horrifically, he then hangs himself and his siblings in their inn. In her grief, Sue becomes convinced that because marriage is ultimately an indissoluble tie, 'Arabella's child killing mine was a judgement – the right slaying the wrong.'[34]

When Tolstoy and Hardy took the tragedy and set it on a domestic stage, they created stories in which the innocent victims of the unfurling tragedy were going to be the children. Though for James, Collins and Daudet, custody could be a semi-comic matter, between them Fontane, Tolstoy and Hardy ushered in a literary tradition in which custody was fundamentally tragic. It is indeed a fitting subject for tragedy, and we need Tolstoy's portrait of Seryozha and Hardy's portrait of young Jude to reveal what we do to children when we attempt to tear them in half.

The danger, however, was that this tragic world-view was self-fulfilling, making the destruction both of mothers and children seem inevitable. Indeed, it seemed all the more inevitable because these writers combined the tropes of classical tragedy with sociological analysis; the recognisable world of their readers became one where change seemed impossible. There was a risk in Frieda and Lawrence reading *Anna Karenina* during a custody case, because Tolstoy's isn't a world where children can emerge intact out of broken marriages, or where mothers can be happy as well as liberated.

And this was all the more dangerous because these were the values reinforced by the legal system that punished the transgressions of mothers with such energetic force. Should Frieda accept the tragic inevitability of her situation, or should she fight for change? If Lawrence saw his novels as creating a new, freer world for women and enabling him to 'do my work for women, better than the suffrage', then couldn't she inhabit it? Hardy's Jude laments that 'the time was not ripe for us! Our ideas were fifty years too soon to be any good to us.' The question was whether, almost twenty years later, Frieda and Lawrence's ideas could be any good to them and, most urgently, to Frieda's children.[35]

After she'd finished *Anna Karenina*, Frieda sent her copy to Ernest Weekley. She may have been warning him about what might befall her if he remained unforgiving. Or perhaps she was urging him to sympathise with an unhappy wife married to an outwardly impeccable husband. Accidentally or intentionally, she sent it with a copy of a letter from Will Dowson inside. 'If you had to run away, why did you not do it with me?' Will had asked her. Ernest sent it straight on to Lawrence.[36]

And then in June 1913 Frieda came to England, determined to see her children. 'Of course I don't think it's desirable that I should see the children in the street, but what can I do?' she'd written to Edward Garnett before leaving Italy. 'I know they will tell the children, "Your mother has left you." I want to tell them, "I left your father, not you."' She hoped that if the children asked their father themselves if they could see her, he wouldn't refuse. Lawrence didn't want her to go; he hated the thought of returning to England and didn't want her to sneak around behind Ernest's back. But she felt them 'slipping away into nothing from me and I simply can't stand it and *won't* stand it!'[37]

Frieda began by loitering outside St Paul's prep school in London to try to see Monty, with Lawrence waiting at a distance. One Monday, she saw Monty coming out for his midday break. Like Anna Karenina, Frieda was startled to find her son looking more grown up than she remembered him. He was thirteen now, and he was wearing long grey trousers and a blue blazer. Seeing her, he ran towards her, stopped, came nearer and stopped again.

He told his teachers that his aunt was visiting, and she took him out for tea. He darted sideways glances in her direction. She ordered strawberries and cream and began to weep. Monty gave her his grubby hanky to wipe her eyes.

He asked what she lived on.

'I wrote a novel,' she said, claiming *Sons and Lovers* as hers.

'You know it's a bad lookout,' she later recalled his saying. 'You don't make much money by writing.'[38]

She told him that she couldn't stand the life in Nottingham and that he would understand this later on. He promised to bring his sisters to see her the next morning on their way to school and she gave him a letter to read.

They met her as planned the following day at Turnham Green. 'Mama, you are back,' she recorded the girls saying, wishfully remembering that they 'danced around me in complete delight'. They asked when she was coming home and she said that she couldn't, but could see them when they wanted. The girls were confused, but agreed to secrecy.[39]

That evening, the children were agitated enough to make Maude question Monty, who told her what had happened. Maude then found Frieda's letter to Monty on the front steps, where he'd dropped it with a carelessness that seems half-intentional. A few weeks later Maude signed an affidavit listing her discoveries. Frieda's clandestine attempts to see her children were unlikely to go down well in court.

On 22 July, Frieda wrote to Else describing how much she had hated tearing herself away from her children: 'It is as when living pieces of flesh are torn from one.' She consoled herself thinking that the children didn't feel it quite as much as she did, and that once Ernest was divorced he would calm down. If she had come to London hoping for some kind of re-enactment of Anna's early morning scene with Seryozha, she hadn't got it. The awful vulnerability of a warm sweaty body, just woken from a nightmare or stroked into wakefulness for school; she was never to encounter that again, because her husband had convinced himself it would disturb the children too much to see her, and because a judge who had it fully in his power to grant her weeks of the school holidays was about to refuse to do so, precisely because she had been too clamorous in her maternal needs. She had found herself living out the circular, tragic inevitability of a realist novel in a world that lacked the subtlety and generosity of those novels. If realism and the law had emerged in tandem out of the fervent imaginations of the nineteenth century, it was the law that formed the basis of people's lives.[40]

III. The Divorce Court

'I thought he was killing mother'

It is all there in the papers which awaited Samuel Evans, President of the Probate, Divorce and Admiralty Division, when he arrived for an interim hearing at the Royal Courts of Justice in London on 28 July 1913, attended by Ernest Weekley and his lawyers. Maude's affidavit described the children's agitation and Frieda's injunction to her son to 'tell nobody of his meeting with her'.[41]

Frieda had sought legal advice from Edward Garnett's brother but chose not to turn up to any hearings. If she'd contested the adultery, there would have been a jury, and she didn't want twelve suited men to pontificate about her sexual transgressions; nor did she choose simply to campaign for access and to allow Sir Samuel Thomas Evans to shake his wigged head with disdain as he decided on the merits of her mother love.

Lawrence was right to envisage this as 'a sort of criminal dock'. But that didn't mean it wasn't worth fighting for custody, or at least access. The law on custody had changed several times since the days of Caroline Norton's landmark Act of 1839. The 1873 Custody of Infants Act had extended Norton's act, allowing the Court of Chancery to grant a mother access or custody to children right up to sixteen years of age. More radically, the 1886 Guardianship of Infants Act had granted mothers automatic guardianship of their children after their husbands' death and had allowed the Court of Chancery to make, 'upon the application of the mother of any infant', such order 'as it may think fit regarding the custody of such infant and the right of access thereto of either parent, having regard to the welfare of the infant, and to the conduct of the parents, and to the wishes as well of the mother as of the father'. For the first time, the child's welfare and mother's wishes were legal considerations. The 1886 Act wasn't explicit about adulterous mothers, though in theory adulterous mothers could apply for custody and access if this was beneficial for their children.

Over the next decades, a series of cases tested these possibilities, revealing how open this wording was to interpretation. The adulterous mother in *Handley v Handley* was refused access in 1891 because, though the judge admitted that there might be occasions when an adulteress should see her children, 'they must be very exceptional circumstances', and these weren't exceptional enough. This was challenged in *Re A and B (Infants)* in 1896, where the judge stipulated: 'The Court will in a proper case give a mother the custody of her infant children notwithstanding that the mother may have been guilty of matrimonial misconduct.' When the father appealed, the judges backed the original judgment, with Judge Lindley adding: 'Nobody can read the various sections in the [1886 Guardianship of Infants] Act without seeing that it is essentially a mother's Act,' and that to fall within the spirit of the law, judges had to take the mother's wishes into account.[42]

The terms of engagement were becoming clearer: even adulterous mothers could sue for custody. However, in the lead up to the Weekley case, decisions pushed hard in both directions. In *CD v AB* in 1908, the Scottish Chancery judge stated that although 'the fact that she has been divorced for adultery is not in itself a sufficient reason for refusing access', the main consideration was the welfare of the child, and he worried about the effect that a meeting with the mother would have on the son's relations with his father:

> The upbringing, education, and settlement in life of the boy is a duty which the father has to perform, and it is of the utmost importance that he should have the respect and confidence of his son. I greatly fear that the petitioner's influence would almost inevitably be in an opposite direction, because it is evident that she has very bitter, perhaps vindictive, feelings against the respondent.

This was the first of many cases in British history where the welfare of the child was used to justify the continuation of the status quo. The wishes of the mother – and even the (not consulted) wishes of the child – were seen as irrelevant; the judge took it upon himself to decide on what would best serve the child's welfare.[43]

There was a very different verdict in the case of Augustus and Annie Mozley-Stark, who had divorced in 1906 on the grounds of her adultery with Charles Hitchins (who she then married). Augustus got custody of their thirteen-year-old daughter Effie, with Annie given termly visits at school. In December 1909, Effie heard that her father was to marry again and she was to attend his wedding.

Not wanting to go, she wrote to her mother announcing that she was about to take a train to a station near her house and arrive there penniless. Alarmed, Annie rushed to the station and took her daughter home. Immediately, Augustus applied to the Divorce Court, asking for his ex-wife to be arrested for contempt of court. Sir Henry Bargrave Deane, Samuel Evans's illustrious sidekick at the Divorce Court, obliged: Annie was sent to prison for a week and Effie went to live with her father.

Next, Annie applied under the Guardianship of Infants Act to Chancery, where the judges cross-examined Annie and Effie and decided that, as there had been no premeditation, Annie was not in contempt of court simply for rescuing her daughter from the railway station. They went further, assessing the whole question of custody from the perspective of Effie's wishes and needs. They decided that, having interviewed the girl and found that 'she strongly desires to live with her mother and not with her father', they would discharge the custody order and leave them to their common law rights (without a custody order, sixteen-year-olds could decide for themselves where to live). The judges made a statement that ought to have changed the lives of many mothers and many daughters, but in fact would have no recognisable effect on Samuel Evans and Henry Bargrave Deane at the Divorce Court:

> We only desire to add that the matrimonial offence which justified the divorce ought not to be regarded for all time and under all circumstances as sufficient to disentitle the mother to access to her daughter, or even to the custody of her daughter, assuming her to be under sixteen. The Court ought not to lay down a hard and fast rule on the subject . . . And it is always to be borne in mind that the benefit and interest of the infant is the paramount consideration, and not the punishment of the guilty spouse.[44]

Frieda Lawrence could possibly have applied to Chancery under the Guardianship of Infants Act, citing the Mozley-Stark case as a precedent. But at this time, the law was – is it always? – at a peculiar moment of inflection. Two courts, two acts; it was difficult to make them speak to each other. The judges weren't always sure whether they even had the right to challenge custody decisions made by the Divorce Court. In *Beedie v Beedie* in 1889 the judge declared that it was always open to the Court of Chancery to see if any custody arrangement was 'the most beneficial in itself', and granted monthly access to the non-custodial father. But this judge was undermined by the judge in *Manders v Manders* in 1890 who said that the Divorce Court had full power to make orders as to access, and therefore parents shouldn't apply to an independent court. It was generally accepted that there should be some specific change in circumstance justifying the appeal to Chancery. In the first instance, you had to apply for custody within the terms of the divorce case itself. So for now this was Frieda's only option.[45]

Frieda's is a unique story, and she was a singular woman, but she was also one of 800 unhappy women who made it through the divorce courts in 1913, the year Ernest filed for divorce, and over 1,200 in 1914, when the Weekleys' divorce was finalised.

The original documents in Frieda's divorce file are now viewable online, complete with handwritten amendments and typing errors. Seeing her file there among crowds of other cases drew me into reading case after case from these years, until I'd gone through over a thousand, wanting to find out what happened to the women who did fight in court. What would have happened if Frieda had turned up with the best barrister she could find, and given all she had to her defence?

It is there, on the form for the decree nisi, as a casual statement of fact – the alignment of sexual rectitude and parental rights: 'And on the application of Counsel for the Petitioner it is ordered that the children, issue of the marriage between the Petitioner and the Respondent, do remain in the custody of the Petitioner until further order of the Court.' In all the cases I look at, I only find one where Petitioner is crossed out and replaced with Respondent (she's managed to prove that he's adulterous and she isn't), and no cases where adulterous women are given custody. There is a kind of equality to it: children go to the innocent party. But so many questions of innocence and guilt fall between the cracks. And how can you piece together these children's own stories?

You can catch traces of these children if you look hard enough back through history. There is Edward May, aged six. He's been taken by his mother Annie May at the age of four to live with her and her lover, then snatched back a year later by his father: 'By stratagem I obtained possession and have the custody of our child.' The father gets custody, using the new legal aid available from 1914 for anyone whose estate is worth less than £50. But I find a census entry, a decade later, written by Edward May's maternal grandfather William Spite in neat, slanty handwriting. Alongside William (a horse carman) and his wife Emma at 32 Percival Street in Finsbury Park, William records his fifteen-year-old grandson Edward May (now working as an engineer fitter) and his fourteen-year-old granddaughter Milly Spite, the daughter Annie conceived with her lover. The father has apparently given up custody, and the mother too has disappeared – there's an Annie May working as a lady's maid in Surrey. What kind of a life is this for Edward, parcelled between his parents at random, as their fights play out, and then shunted on to his paternal grandparents?[46]

You can also trace the presence of the children in the tales of violence.

Florence Marjorie Wilson alleges that on or about 14 November 1903, the said Kingston Charles Wilson attacked her. She alleges that on an occasion in the month of August 1904, in the public street at Waterford Road, Fulham, in the County of London and while she was carrying her first child in her arms, the said Kingston Charles Wilson violently abused her and struck a blow in her face with his fist, causing her much pain. She alleges that on or about 20 April 1905 the said Kingston Charles Wilson by falsely telling her that there were burglars in the house and then leaving her in the house alone with a very young child caused her much fear and distress of mind. She alleges that on or about 20 May 1905 he punched her on the head, causing an attack of delirium. She alleges that in February 1907, a fortnight after the birth of her second child, he left her at a strange house for three days and nights without food or fire or money and returned only to violently abuse her. She alleges that he struck a violent blow on the face and another on the body. She alleges that on 9 April 1911, while she was suffering the agony of childbirth, he refused to fetch a midwife, causing the said pains to be unnecessarily prolonged and the life of the Respondent and the said child to be endangered.[47]

There's no mention of whether the solicitor asked how this has played out for the children whose lives have been endangered alongside hers. This is almost thirty years after the Guardianship of Infants Act, but the welfare of the children doesn't seem to be on anyone's mind in the courtroom in which finally, in June 1916, a jury of twelve men finds the Respondent mother guilty of adultery and the Petitioner father innocent both of conduct conducing to said adultery and of cruelty. The children are to remain with the father in whose charge they have been since the interim order; their daughter Lily, whose birth her father caused to be unnecessarily long and dangerous, is only five.

It happens over and over again. Violent men drive their wives away, leaving them, in the absence of any other support, in need of a new man to maintain them. Adulterous men have some choice in the matter, but these women don't. They commit adultery – what else can they do? – and then the husbands swoop in and claim the children whose welfare has seemingly never previously concerned them. They win, as they know they will, because it's there on the form already – the registrar doesn't even have to write it out.

Jury after jury doesn't find evidence of cruelty. They fail to see cruelty when the husbands sue for divorce on grounds of adultery, and they fail to see cruelty when the wives sue for judicial separation on grounds of cruelty. There are few witnesses: the wife's testimony counts for so little, and the children can't testify. And it's hard to be exact when these acts are so often habitual. 'The acts complained of were so frequent that the Petitioner is unable to give any more definite dates than those given in the Petition,' says Violet Lillian Warren, asking for a judicial separation because, on diverse occasions, her husband struck her in the face, tried to strangle her, kicked and punched her and bruised her arms. Yet again, the jury doesn't find cruelty; the petition is dismissed, and it's up to Samuel T. Evans to decide on custody, as it will be in Frieda's case in a few months' time.[48]

It's not surprising that it's the same judge: almost all the 800 divorce cases that year were judged by Samuel Evans and Henry Bargrave-Deane between them. It's an astonishingly high workload for two men, and it gave them frightening power in determining what constituted acceptable behaviour for husbands and wives – and mothers and fathers – throughout the nation.

The only son of a Welsh grocer, Samuel Evans had qualified as a solicitor in his early twenties, and made a name for himself in Wales as a barrister and Liberal MP, while also finding time to conduct orchestras at Welsh music festivals. As an MP he'd been influential in blocking the campaign for female suffrage: he droned on during the relevant debates, to ensure they ran out of time, warning that women's votes would 'swamp' the votes of men and that 'if women were to be entitled to the privileges of citizenship, they ought to share its responsibilities, and to perform its duties. Would it be desirable that women should have to go out to battle?' He gave up his political career when he accepted the post of President of the Probate, Divorce and Admiralty Division in 1910, despite his lack of experience in these areas. Here he established himself as an ally of the women's rights movement with his 1911 decision that knowingly giving your wife venereal disease was equivalent to physical cruelty. But he also separated hundreds of mothers from their children, often permanently, and often in circumstances that it was very hard to claim benefited the child.

Henry Bargrave-Deane came from a grander world, boasting a Right Honourable father and a line of distinguished legal ancestors going back to the Middle Temple in the seventeenth century. He was known for his sharpness with witnesses, and his success in sniffing out collusion in divorce cases, more committed to rules and precedents than Evans. He was also known to disapprove of most of the people who entered his court. Divorce ran counter to his own religious convictions, and he thought that the Matrimonial Causes Act had been a mistake, but one it was his weary duty to implement.[49]

In response to Violet Warren's request for a separation on the basis of her husband's violence, Judge Samuel Evans rules that the son, six-year-old Jack, should be delivered to his father, Charles Stanley Warren, who only a few weeks earlier threatened to shoot both his wife and child. The problem here is that Violet has been on the stage: she's toured around the country; she's even been given presents by men. She isn't fit to mother her son and so she has to give him up – but she doesn't for long. Just over a year later she's back in court because her son has been crying for his mother so much at school that he has been moved from one dormitory to another. He's ill and she's taken him to her parents' house to nurse him but now his father demands he be sent back.

'It is a matter of the child's life,' Violet says in court. 'He must not leave his mother again.'

'You must hand him over,' responds the emergency vacation judge, complying with Evans's initial decision.

'Then I must go too.'

She doesn't, and he doesn't die. He stays alive long enough to divorce his own wife for adultery in 1934.[50]

Sometimes the children are absent from the original reports but return later to make their voices heard. The divorce file for Gertrude and George Perkins is accompanied by plaintively insistent letters from their daughter Nora in 1980 – punched out unevenly on a typewriter – asking for details of the mother she last saw aged six. Gertrude Perkins defended her suit but was found guilty of adultery with William Flood. Her husband had already obtained a judicial separation on the grounds of her drunkenness in 1912 (though he'd since taken her back, and only banished her finally in March 1913) and he claimed not to be the father of the baby she'd delivered in November 1913. His evidence of adultery was this: he'd hired a private detective who'd seen William Flood walking around her house with his boots in his hand. Gertrude claimed that he'd only visited her that once – he'd been bringing her coal and she'd given him supper to say thank you. The newspaper reported that Samuel Evans, 'in finding there had been misconduct, admitted that he had not found it very easy to come to a conclusion'. This didn't stop him removing four children from their mother, never to see her again, though he did insist that George paid her 10s.6d a week while she remained 'chaste and unmarried'.

'I think you will see from my questions that there is a great deal about my mother that I would like to trace, purely as her daughter, as I am so abysmally ignorant about the matter,' 72-year-old Nora wrote in her letter to the Divorce Registry. The information was not forthcoming, but the file is anyway less informative than the newspaper report she'd already found, where Gertrude is recorded as being asked for a sample of her handwriting in court and refusing to write the name Perkins: 'I hate the name of Perkins, and I am married to him.'[51]

Children can be glimpsed and heard when the custody arrangements go wrong, as custody arrangements so often do, and the mothers plead to alter them. Marie Gillespie has been granted access for one afternoon a fortnight at the house of her ex-husband's parents. But on arriving, she's taken by the maid to a room with no fire in a cold November, full of empty whisky and beer bottles, and a clothes horse with underwear failing to dry. When she complains, she's taken to a better room, only to have the door locked by the maid, who informs her that it will be unlocked when the visit is finished.

Three-year-old Albert cries to go to the toilet. Marie pleads with her mother-in-law to open the door, but she doesn't relent. Eventually Marie has to hold her son out of the window to pee. It's so seemingly trivial. But this is what custody is made of. It's impossible to explain in court how a particular arrangement is going to affect a child; impossible to explain what it means for a mother to look after her son in such makeshift surroundings when she has always simply lived alongside him at home.[52]

They take on a vivid, insistent presence, these children and these women, inside my house. This is piecemeal work; I read a case while waiting for my daughter's pasta to boil, another while she reads in bed. I go upstairs and she tells me what's happened in *Matilda* – a story of custody, as almost every story is starting to seem. I don't tell her about Jack Evans or Albert Gillespie – these other children who haunt our evening. I lie in bed beside her, calmed briefly by the smell of her hair, and then I go back down, still caught in the atmosphere of the files, terrified that I have somehow more to lose.

I read another eight case files before I go to bed myself. I read about Ethel Horrocks, aged thirty-eight, wife of a master printer, whose solicitor has told her to make up her mind to lose custody of her eight-year-old daughter Audrey. Her husband Frederick Horrocks promised her custody if she didn't contest the divorce petition where he cited adultery with a Richard Tootell, but now she's been told that he's asking for it anyway. For a month, she eats no food and fails to sleep. Until, eventually, she dies. 'Suit abated, Respondent dead,' has been handwritten on the printed front page of the divorce file. I brush my teeth in a silent house alongside all the women who performed their night-time rituals without the comfort offered by the sleeping presence of the children they have hitherto taken for granted.[53]

I trace the children through the censuses, and look for their names in the local newspapers. And there they are. There is four-year-old Philip Ashton-Jinks, kidnapped by his mother Alice Ashton-Jinks in Regent Street – snatched from his nurse. It was Alice herself who filed for judicial separation on grounds of cruelty in 1910. Her husband, Louis Thomas Ashton-Jinks, had struck her when pregnant, he'd thrown her around the room, he'd emptied water jugs over her and, when she was five months pregnant, stabbed her in the leg with a pair of compasses, cutting varicose veins and causing her to bleed profusely. For a while, she was given custody – indeed Louis was forbidden from removing the children from their convent school, near their house in Hendon, or 'from otherwise interfering with the said children'. But in April 1911 Samuel Evans ordered that the petition be withdrawn – her husband had succeeded in discrediting her.[54]

She tried again in June 1911; by this point she could add that he'd refused to purchase milk for her baby, he'd dragged her and her three-year-old son Philip out of the house into the garden, he'd struck the head of eight-year-old Mary with a serviette ring, he'd accused Alice of adultery, called doctors in to try to get her declared insane, and threatened to take away the children unless she denied his cruelty in court. In March 1912 Evans ordered the younger children to be placed in the care of nurse Mary Skinner at Louis's mother's house. The older children were to remain in their convent with limited access to both parents. Alice Ashton-Jinks had been punished for asking for too much – and she hadn't even been adulterous, hadn't attempted to do more than say she wanted a better life than the one offered by an abusive husband. It's at this point that I read about Alice taking matters into her own hands and kidnapping her son. The next day Louis offers a £5 reward for the boy, describing his fair complexion and short hair, his blue jersey suit and knitted top. Kidnapping doesn't go down well with the court; her petition is dismissed in 1913.[55]

Then what? – then, I find in the electoral registers, that they stay together and have a fourth child and a fifth, Therese and Rose. They are all still together in 1927, when Louis plays Colonel Calverley in the local production of Gilbert and Sullivan's *Patience* ('he was the valiant soldier of the peace time to a "T"'). Then in 1928 they separate (there's no recourse to the courts this time) and there's a newspaper report about Louis entering Alice's house to take her furniture. He's got a van outside and brings a man in to help him strip the house clean, as he puts it. They leave with some furniture and Alice bolts the door; the men smash the dining-room window and Louis enters it with his hand cut. He rushes at Alice, shakes her, and strikes her on her shoulder and head. Thirteen-year-old Rose races down the stairs and tries to pull her father away; when he pushes her off, she strikes him with a picture. She then runs for the police.

'I thought he was killing Mother,' Rose says when Louis is tried in court for assault. 'I was not strong enough to pull him away, so I picked up a picture and hit him with it. He looked very red and cross and we were frightened of him.'

Louis's lawyer tries to discredit Alice, asking the doctor who examined her bruises if he thinks she's a neurotic person, who might be subject to 'hysterical fits and uncontrollable outbursts of temper', as the doctors who Louis involved in the separation claimed. No,

Dr Speed says, he would not say so. Finally, Alice has been heard; finally she has the proof of cruelty that she was denied by the divorce court. How much unhappiness could have been prevented if Samuel Thomas Evans had believed her in 1910, or 1912, rather than putting her in the hands of the husband who would sire more daughters with her only to abuse them in turn: 'I thought he was killing Mother.'[56]

And then there's Philip – the boy who was dragged out of the house to the garden and then kidnapped from Regent Street. In June 1932, 25-year-old Clement Philip Ashton-Jinks, a young officer in the Royal Air Force, climbs onto a radiator and jumps out of the window of the hospital where he is being treated for pleurisy. He is found fatally injured on the ground, clad only in his pyjamas.[57]

It's becoming compulsive. If I can just trace these women and their children through the censuses, if I can just find out what happens to them – then what? – will I somehow restore what they lost in the courts – will it help them finally to be believed? It's an eerie feeling, seeing these women traverse the decades, seeing the husbands continuing just as they were before. Perhaps no one except me has pieced all this evidence together in the years since. Can you hear me, Alice Ashton-Jinks? – I know that you spoke the truth when you wrote the petition that Samuel Evans dismissed, making you stay in the marriage, when you'd just risked everything to prove that it was dangerous.

Would Samuel Evans have believed Frieda when she said – but what could she have said? At the time, Frieda's sisters were angry with Lawrence for writing openly to Ernest because they thought she could get custody if she took things slowly. Ask for a separation first, Else urged, and then introduce the lover into the new household. But there wouldn't have been much point in this. An informal separation agreement had no legal standing. So Ernest would have been able to divorce her for adultery and take the children – and he'd surely have done it: that's the kind of man he was, and the kind of man he was encouraged to be by a legal system that entwined custody and parental sexual guilt.

Frieda could have taken the children to Germany. But she would have fared even worse in the German divorce courts, as Else would have known. German feminists had campaigned against the federal civil code (the Bürgerliches Gesetzbuch), since it was passed in 1896. The code made things better for single women – who could now sign contracts, bring lawsuits and own property – but subordinated wives and mothers. Indeed, Germany was worse for mothers than some German states had been before the law was centralised. Mothers now had no rights during their husbands' lifetimes. Control of finance and education was given to fathers. Mothers were allowed only the 'personal care' of the child and lost even this if the fathers disagreed with their decisions. Where Prussian divorce law had been among the most liberal in Europe, allowing divorce on grounds of 'mutual aversion', evidence was now required of a serious misdemeanour. As in Britain, mothers condemned as guilty could be deprived of all contact with their children. And here, even innocent mothers with custody had to follow their former husbands' wishes on all decisions about education and employment.[58]

So should she have done it? Should she have turned up in court? Lawrence was right that the whole legal process threatened to degrade the good that they were arduously wresting out of a troubled, warring world. I know how horrible it is to turn your life into a set of legal documents and to face a barrister twisting everything you say. 'That was a very cruel cross-examination,' Violet Warren told her husband's solicitor; 'it insinuated so many things.' Lawrence persuaded Frieda not to go through this. But where could she turn to except the law to get the world to address the needs of her children? As it was, those children were present in the courtroom only as the inventions of their outraged aunt.[59]

Samuel Evans's judgment was unequivocal. On 28 July 1913 he ruled that, based on the affidavits and Ernest Weekley's barrister's report, the Petitioner (Ernest) should have custody of the three children 'until further order and that the said Respondent be restrained from interfering or attempting to interfere with the said children or any of them'. That October, this was formalised in the decree nisi. 'To live her own life. Lady leaves her husband and joins author,' reported the *News of the World*. They reprinted Lawrence's 'giantesses' letter in full on the front page, always glad of a good divorce story. Then in April 1914, Sir Henry Bargrave Deane dissolved the marriage.[60]

IV. Mrs Frieda Lawrence

'She's caught more than she bargained for, in her own offspring'

The divorce came through on the brink of war. Lawrence was a prophet of this new age; his vision of modernity bent on destruction came into its own, making him all the more unhappy as it did so, and his verve for progressively reforming society was lost. For Frieda, the threat of war brought the threat that she would be separated from what family remained. Her sisters and parents would be at war with her children and lover. She became more emboldened, the less there was to lose.

In June 1914, two months before Britain declared war on Germany, she went to Chiswick to look for her children. She wandered the streets until, remarkably, she came across the red velvet curtains from Nottingham hanging in the window of 49 Harvard Road. She let herself in the back door and, like Anna Karenina, walked straight upstairs to the nursery.

The children were eating supper with Maude and their grandmother. They had now been thoroughly inculcated into the Weekley views, and were convinced that their mother had brought shame and misery on their family. Barby later described how her mother, suddenly manifest in the doorway, seemed like a 'terrifying apparition'. Maude and their grandmother jumped up and shouted abuse at her, treating her as the 'embodiment of evil'. So Frieda might have expected, but there was worse to come. The children joined in. Frieda fled, shocked and humiliated. Barby was sad, looking back, that the bond with their mother had withered. 'She was an unreal woman to us by then. Something rather strange and even a little horrifying.' Frieda persisted: she managed to see her daughters leaving their school, and to speak to them briefly. When she tried the same strategy a few days later they had their aunt Kit with them and they ran away screaming.[61]

On 14 July, three weeks before war was declared, Frieda became Mrs Frieda Lawrence. They were trapped in England now, so they began a makeshift life staying in friends' damp cottages in Buckinghamshire and then Sussex. Soon Lawrence would write: 'the War finished me: it was the spear through the side of all sorrows and hopes'. This was the machine civilisation he hated, given free destructive play. He'd watched the Bavarian army doing its fighting practice and seen men firing at an enemy a mile and a half away. Frieda's first loves had been soldiers. It was unthinkably appalling that in a muddy field somewhere those eager, charming boys who couldn't quite bring themselves to propose to a girl without a dowry were trying to kill the sons of their closest friends.[62]

Frieda told their friend, the pacifist Bloomsbury hostess Ottoline Morrell, in May 1915 that the war had eased her situation as a mother, giving her a larger perspective. At least her children were alive, while all around her mothers were losing sons for ever. She remained outraged, however, at the divorce settlement, thinking 'that this is the law of man; and if I were a prostitute the children would be *mine* and a man would be obliged to pay me'. Lawrence added an addendum to her letter, saying that it was a 'funny thing' that when a woman did have her children, she didn't care about them, and cared more about getting a man, but now she had a man, she didn't care about him, and only wanted her children.

But Frieda couldn't have done much more to value her children when she lived with them. For long stretches of time she thought only of them. And Lawrence didn't see that the unconsciousness of maternal love is crucial. This is a love made of daily acts of care. He knew that in his novels. At this point he was writing *The Rainbow*, which contains some of the most moving descriptions of quiet parental love we have. Indeed, I would say that his intimacy with Frieda's motherhood increasingly helped to make him the writer he was becoming: attentive to the feelings of mothers and fathers as they move between ordinariness and extremity in their daily lives. It must have been all the more enraging for Frieda that *The Rainbow* includes such a moving portrait of a stepfather in Tom, who takes his wife Anna's daughter out to see the cows while Anna is giving birth to their new baby, and holds the girl tenderly while she falls asleep. Lawrence had taken from Tolstoy and Hardy an interest in children as specific, fully characterised subjects for fiction, with complex bodily and mental lives. Yet he couldn't bear to acknowledge that he saw Frieda's children in this way.[63]

She made a final, impetuous attempt to see them, waiting in pouring rain behind a hedge near the house in Chiswick, her hat dripping. She began to weep even before they appeared; so much so that she could hardly see them through rain and tears when they arrived and went through the door. Finally, from August 1915, Ernest granted occasional meetings, perhaps worn down by the war as well. There was half an hour in his lawyers' offices on Frieda's birthday in August. The girls were looking thin, because food was now rationed and Maude hoarded all the meat for their grandfather. Then Ernest began allowing occasional teatime visits and Frieda rented a flat in Hampstead for this purpose. She was even allowed to take them to see *The Marriage of Figaro* at Covent Garden in September 1916. Monty was sixteen now and aloof, but the girls had never seen an orchestra before and were thrilled. At tea afterwards she gave them each ten shillings. The girls went to the bathroom together, money in hand.

'We mustn't like Mama now that we've got ten shillings,' fourteen-year-old Elsa warned her younger sister.[64]

Montague, Elsa and Barby had to choose their version of the story. Eventually, they all tried out Frieda's, though Elsa was right that Barby was the most susceptible – she was the one who became closest to their mother as an adult.

Together, Frieda and Lawrence got to know her children after coming back from New Mexico in 1924. This was the first time the children had met Lawrence since he sailed boats with them all those years earlier, and Barby found that he was unlike anyone she had ever met: 'He seemed beyond being human and ordinary, and I felt at once that he was more like an element – say a rock or rushing water.'[65]

Can you become close to a rock or to rushing water? At first Lawrence kept apart from them. 'Privately, I can't stand Frieda's children,' he told a friend in November 1925. 'They have a sort of suburban bounce and *sufferance* which puts me off.' He thought Barby was engaged to 'an absolute nothingness of a fellow', and that Monty, working in the Victoria and Albert Museum, would probably soon 'sit in one of the glass cases, as a specimen of the perfect young Englishman'. But by March 1926, when Barby and Elsa were staying with them in Italy, he could write to Frieda's sister that: 'They are nice girls really, it is Frieda who, in a sense, has made a bad use of them, as far as I am concerned.'[66]

He had begun to paint seriously, and he painted now with Barby, attempting to rid her of the influence of the art school where she'd trained. At one point some local villagers mistook the girls for Lawrence's daughters and Barby felt that he liked it. He could incarnate a belated version of stepfatherhood, and this in turn necessitated the girls sharing Frieda and Lawrence's appalling openness to each other.

Barby was the first to join in with their fighting. 'She's too good for you,' she shouted at Lawrence during an argument, 'it's casting pearls before swine!' Soon Elsa was joining in too. 'Frieda's children are very fierce with her,' Lawrence wrote to a friend, 'and fall on her tooth and nail. They simply won't stand her egotism for a minute . . . Being her own family, they can go for her exactly in her own way, and pretty well silence her . . . She's caught more than she bargained for, in her own offspring.'

Her own family. Her own offspring. Frieda gratefully took what she was offered, including the haranguing. 'The new young element is good in our lives,' she could report in October 1926, adding that now even Monty and Lawrence were getting on. 'It's all come right – grazie a Dio!' Frieda went on holiday with Barby, and Lawrence found that she had changed on her return, as her children once found that she'd changed after returning from holiday with a lover. He didn't reproach her. 'Every heart has a right to its own secrets.'[67]

And then when Lawrence was dying of tuberculosis in France and was told he needed a nurse, he asked if he could have Barby instead, so she came out to the house they were staying at in Bandol, touched to be asked. 'My daughter Barbara is a godsend,' Frieda wrote in February 1930; 'she is lovely inside and out – Lawr is so sad, can't eat and doesn't gain weight.'[68]

Barby was ill after Lawrence's death, and could become delirious in the collective grief of the household. For a few months, Frieda devoted her life to making her daughter well again. She was a mother once more, even when she took Barby to meet her own mother and they found that she couldn't speak German: 'You ought to speak German, your mother is German,' Barby's grandmother told her.

'My mother left me,' she replied.[69]

Frieda could take it. She could take it all. She'd seen her choices in *Anna Karenina*: wither away in an unhappy marriage or choose life and love, but don't expect it to include your children or you'll drive yourself to madness and despair. After those first months of agony, she'd stopped asking Lawrence to share her feelings about her children and made her choice, choosing her lover and a belief in his genius that enabled them to live according to different codes. And so, over the past decades, she had been able to judge her life a success. It was precarious, and the years without her children had been long. But then they had reappeared in her life and she could piece together the fragments and find that her choices hadn't been as stark as Anna Karenina's after all. Her life was more a comedy than a tragedy, and half-measures were possible.

Lawrence had said that if she waited it out, then the love – if it was there – would prove undeniable. And here it was – undeniable. There were his judgements of her children to contend with (their suburban bounciness), and his outrageous assertion that she (she!) had treated them badly. But Frieda had long ago learnt to take what was offered by the present moment and do all she could with it. That was her famous gift for living that the men around her made necessary and then relied on. Years later, Monty would accuse her only half-affectionately of having her cake and eating it. Certainly, she'd made a life that included both adultery and motherhood at a time when the legal system was cruelly punishing transgressive women. But he seems wilfully to have forgotten the tears of the woman waiting outside his school to take him for strawberries and cream, or storming up into the nursery only to be shooed back down the stairs by her own children. This was not a world where mothers could genuinely have and eat cake. Ernest Weekley and

Lawrence were both forward-thinking men in their different ways, but they couldn't come up with an idea of motherhood that also allowed her to be a liberated woman, or an idea of a liberated woman that also allowed her to be a mother.

They didn't all make it, even as far as Frieda made it. Violet Warren, Alice Ashton-Jinks, Ethel Horrocks, Gertrude Perkins: the women who asked more from being a wife and a mother than they should, or simply tried to say that it didn't need to be this bad. They were too brutalised to come through, and they didn't have geniuses for lovers. Holidaying with her mother in her twenties, Barby was lucky not to be one of the children who were left writing desperate letters to the Divorce Registry in middle age, pleading to be given more details of the mothers they'd been kept away from. In October 1928, when Rose Ashton-Jinks was hitting her father on the head with a picture, frightened he was going to kill her mother, Barby Weekley was helping her mother prepare the way for Lawrence's exhibition of paintings in London. In June 1932, when Philip Ashton-Jinks was hurling himself from his hospital window, Barby was getting ready to visit her mother in New Mexico.

I have disturbed the dead and they won't quite let me go. I feel like Walter Benjamin's 'Angel of History', pulled back to the past, longing to awaken them and make them whole again. But the future is calling, and it's a future Frieda Lawrence played her part in creating. When she reconnected with her daughters as adults, she wanted most of all to show them that life could be lived actively and desiringly. For her that had meant asking for more as a woman than their father believed reasonable or even possible. They couldn't always live up to her ideals. Barby never became the great painter Frieda and Lawrence assumed she would become. But there was something in Frieda and Lawrence's honesty and rigour and commitment to a full life that did change them, and made them receptive to a future that would turn out to be more Lawrence's than Ernest Weekley's.

In her fifties, after Frieda's death, Barby looked back on her parents' divorce as 'a turning point, serving to bring about a change in the attitude towards women in my mother's position'. She, alone among her siblings, was convinced that her mother had been right to act as she did: 'All the boring women who have told me "I could never leave my children" have helped to convince me.'[70]

5

Edna O'Brien

They march on, the women, in and out of court, heels clicking on the stone floors. Women in skirts and dresses and jackets; women drab with worry, given hints of jauntiness by belts and handbags and little boots. They enter courtrooms full of men – though a few women are on juries now – to talk about their bodies. They talk about birthing their children and feeding them; about loving their husbands and cowering from their blows; about flesh encountering flesh, inside the home and, dangerous though it is to admit it, out of it.

One war has ended and people have finally seen that enough is enough; one child too many has been separated from a loving mother for this to continue. Women in the UK can vote, and there are moves towards equal rights to employment and property, but they have no legal right to their children. And so casually, epochally, the 1925 Guardianship of Infants Act advances the claims of the children. It's not all that feminist campaigners wanted, when they brought it in after the war. The point was to give mothers equal guardianship rights at the same time as the divorce laws became fairer. But politicians quailed at the prospect of parental equality. Permanent Secretary Claud Schuster feared that parents with equal rights would come to court over everyday domestic disputes, bewildering judges: 'There are no rights here. It is a question of discretion. To take a ridiculous instance, a dispute whether a child is to go to one school, or to another school – how on earth is the Court going to deal with that?' A century later precisely this will play out: overworked courts caught up in decisions about schooling.[1]

Schuster's view prevails. There's no equality in the 1925 Act for married parents, though, as in 1886, there is for divorcing ones. What's new is that the child's welfare trumps the wishes of either parent. The court, in deciding custody, 'shall regard the welfare of the infant as the first and paramount consideration'. 'Paramount' will be a rallying call in the law courts over the next decades, as ever more emphasis is placed on child welfare – to the point that children can be taken away from both parents if outsiders seem preferable. There are many dangers to the welfare principle; it will allow for children being deprived of countless lesbian mothers. But it does at least allow custody to go to adulterous women who can be proved best placed to offer a loving home. Frieda Lawrence's case might have gone differently with the 1925 Act behind her.

Is it truly loving, however, to leave the marriage bed? – to leave the house where the children sleep side by side in the nursery, to moan and sweat in the embrace of another man? The patriarchy asserts itself, before the ink on the Act is dry. Judges ask if an unfaithful mother can be a good mother – a mother who puts her children first.

Another war: women are mobilised, in their millions, called away from home by patriotic duty. Marriages spill and curdle and the divorce courts throng, and still the judgements come in. Everywhere – in every playground, every doctors' surgery – there are good mothers and bad mothers, and it can be impossible to distinguish between them, for the mothers themselves, for their disgruntled husbands, and for the judges who, after the Matrimonial Proceedings (Children) Act is passed in 1958, must profess themselves satisfied with the child arrangements for every divorce. Court-appointed welfare officers are called in to help. At last, someone from court sees the daily acts of care. They see the mothers – even the working, even the adulterous mothers – persuading their children to eat peas and take cod liver oil, resolving fights between tired siblings, disinfecting grazed knees. They hear about screams in the night from children who know change is afoot and have dreamt they've lost the mother who rushes to their bedroom but may not always be there. These welfare officers are a gift from a newly reasonable, child-centred state, but they take care to maintain their neutrality, and they understandably find it hard to believe much they hear. 'Of course many parents are out to impress us,' says a welfare officer called Miss Nowell, interviewed by the *Daily Mail* in 1960. 'You have to find out what their real motives are. Are they genuinely concerned for the child's welfare or are they trying to punish their husband or wife by depriving them of the child? When two parents are contesting custody I would be inclined to suspect they are not really putting the child first.'[2]

And so they march on, these mothers suspected not really to be putting their children first. They march on, stylishly now, in Mary Quant tunic dresses and shiny yellow ankle boots. Some wear lipstick and some don't; very occasionally, there is one in trousers; some have shorter skirts than these aging judges, emerging from the countryside in trains and cabs, have encountered in previous decades.

Among them, at the mid-point of the new decade, as The Beatles conclude their final UK tour and the National Coal Board closes the last deep mine, are the reddish-brown curls of an exhausted, terrified but passionately determined mother. She's the author of books banned in Ireland and South Africa: a woman only just holding it together after three years of separation in which her husband has controlled her and her two sons as determinedly as he did in the marriage. She doesn't yet know it, but she will win. At the end of the morning, she'll have custody of the two boys waiting anxiously for news as they get through hour after hour of lessons. But it won't make up – how can it? – for the suffering they've all endured.

I. Marriage

'I cannot see this life going on in this way'

Ireland, 1930. A childhood flickering between idyll and nightmare. There was an imposing house, Drewsboro, built from the sandstone of a 'Big House' that Edna's father had helped burn down during the Troubles; a thousand acres of land bartered off bit by bit to pay gambling debts; horses in the fields, relied on to win races and defer bankruptcy for just a few more weeks; cows, pigs and chickens whose necks they'd wring for Sunday lunch; primroses and cowslips and elderberries that could be turned into wine that had to be hidden from the father who had a tendency to disappear on drinking binges and to threaten his wife with a revolver when he ran out of money.

The house was full of prayer books that she would read each night in the bed she shared with her mother:

> May nothing in our minds excite
> Vain dreams and phantoms of the night;
> Keep off our enemies, that so
> Our bodies no uncleanness know.

Fearing the wrath of God and the heavy footsteps of a drunk man on his way up to bed, they clung to each other as they slept. Edna's love for her mother was the first great love of her life – a fascinated, bodily love that homed her, as the fields did. Years later, after she'd had her own children, she'd try to write about this bond, feeling her way into her mother's body as she gave birth, and then back into her own consuming love: 'Her mother's knuckles were her knuckles, her mother's veins were her veins, her mother's lap was a second heaven, her mother's forehead a copybook onto which she traced A B C D, her mother's body was a recess that she would wander inside forever and ever, a sepulchre growing deeper and deeper.'[3]

They lived in fear of uncleanness and sin and of the flames of Hell; if a sod fell out of the burning fire, Edna's mother would catch it with her bare hands to prepare herself for the flames of eternity. Edna prayed, and she went alone to chapel to say Paters and Aves and dwell on the Five Holy Wounds.

Out of all these fears and vivid imaginings, a writer was born. She read the few books she could find, and she went out into the fields to write stories set in their bog and their kitchen garden, and an elaborate tale about a motherless girl with a cruel father who is abducted by a gypsy and then rescued by her family, only to be returned to her old life of drudgery and submission.

Edna O'Brien, 1953

She couldn't stay. Their town had twenty-seven pubs but no library, and she quickly outgrew the school. She was sent to a convent, where she separated abruptly from her mother by falling in love with a nun. Aged seventeen, she moved to Dublin with her sister and began training as a pharmacist. She wanted to write, to fall in love, to see the world – but how to do this when she was still so fearful of sin and of her father's wrath, and short of cash. She needed to escape, like George Sand and Frieda von Richthofen had before her. If they'd met, Frieda could have warned Edna to doubt the earnestness of men called Ernest. But they didn't, and Edna O'Brien's Ernest was even wilier, even more dangerous than Frieda's.

Ernest Gébler was a handsome communist with dark brown eyes and an uncanny resemblance to the actor Conrad Veidt. He was Irish-born, with Czech-Armenian parents, and a published novelist who had made money writing in Hollywood and now owned a large house in Wicklow. She couldn't be sure he liked her at first, when she met him on a night out and then ran into him in a bookshop. But he succumbed immediately to her beauty and her innocence: her curly red hair and small delicate bones; the aquamarine eyes that one onlooker described as simultaneously appraising and apologetic; her obvious virginity. He bought her a grey astrakhan coat with a red velvet collar – the most sumptuous thing she'd ever owned – and invited her to Wicklow. The house turned out to be full of the clothes of his wife, who had recently abandoned him by moving back to America with their son. But it was springtime. The gorse was blooming, the trees were about to bud, and with fearful determination she tortuously lost her virginity to the man who referred to her as his 'child bride'. She was only twenty-two. They weren't in a hurry and there was no need for anything to change, until an anonymous letter informed her mother about the affair with a married man. Warned, Edna rushed from Dublin to Ernest's house, inviting him to protect her.

Her father tracked them down, accompanied by a neighbour and her brother. Ernest and Edna were with the American-Irish novelist J. P. Donleavy, who'd trained in boxing in New York, and between them Ernest and Donleavy put up a reasonably good fight. This was a fight between the old Irish morality and the new; in his banned 1950 novel *The Ginger Man*, Donleavy had portrayed a godless, seducing, thieving marauder of the kind Edna's parents feared Ernest

Gébler might be. The men's blows and blood were the blows and blood of the Church and State on one side, and a new, wilfully obscene and idealistically honest Ireland on the other, both sides fuelled by drink, with Edna as their half-willing, half-knowing sacrificial victim. This couldn't end well for her, couldn't imbue her with agency, whatever the outcome. Afterwards, nursing his wounds, outraged by his scuffed ankles, Ernest wrote a letter to her parents for her to sign, denouncing her family for their barbarity and ignorance, separating her from them for ever. 'I signed it,' she later wrote, 'and in the doing I knew that, by going from them to him, I had burnt my boats.'[4]

He had his child bride; he began proceedings to divorce his wife. He opened a subscription to the library for Edna, educated her about literature and politics, and for a while impressed her with his certainty, his sensuality, his wealth (he bought her a whole new wardrobe of clothes). He was always a little distant, tending to retreat, offended by perceived slights. But then she got pregnant and for a while they were folded together into tender, grateful happiness. 'There was something so gentle and astonished in his whole being,' she later wrote, 'all his hostile traits put to one side, a new life, the life he had been meant to have; the old, sad world put down to sleep.'[5]

Ernest Gébler, date unknown

As her stomach swelled, the dark moods returned. She wrote a long letter to her mother, desperate to reconnect, drawn to thinking about her own childhood. 'If only I could talk to you, if only I could confide in someone,' she wrote, and then tried to do just that: 'The man I am with is something of a mystery, he has his seasons and his dark moods . . . Sometimes I see such a dark, brooding look come over him, not aimed at me or not always aimed at me and I cower.'[6]

He could become angry even as a result of dreams; he was critical of her writing — why had she described a road as 'blue'? — and outraged when she defended herself:

> My thoughts get somewhat scrambled. If I think ahead, to say ten or fifteen years, I cannot see this life going on in this way. I make jam when the medlars and the damsons are in fruit. He likes it when I make jam, it establishes me as the housewife. His friends tend to think of me as beneath him and a mope. When I recall Drewsboro, there is always frost, early mornings on our way to or from Mass, the high grass plumed and you calling out to me to pick my steps, so that my good Holy Communion, kid shoes would not get stained. When the child is born, you and I might become friends again, it might draw us together. I am so, so terrified. Your labour has got mixed up with mine. God grant that I do not disgrace myself when my time comes.[7]

There was no disgrace; there was hardly any danger. They got married, a month before the baby was born, and then Ernest was so delighted by the baby he gave the same name as his first, lost son — Karl, after Karl Marx — that it seemed he'd given birth himself. Edna was entranced by this little creature with a tuft of black hair emerging from the misaligned crown of his head, though initially terrified of damaging him. They did manage a delicate truce with her parents, beginning the intermittent visits that would continue over the decades, with her mother becoming the close, albeit anxiously disapproving, grandmother Edna hoped for. Edna and Ernest moved to Dublin and found a nanny and a collie dog. Karl became Carlo, acquired asthma and a brother called Sasha, and grew naughtier, testing the father who couldn't bear to be disobeyed. Age four, Carlo threw a stone at a window, curious about its effect. Furious, Ernest made his son stand watching throughout the repair, accusing him of being a vandal and a thug and of inheriting these traits from his peasant mother.

Edna O'Brien and Carlo Gébler. The writing on the photograph is Ernest Gébler's

They moved to London, leaving Carlo's beloved dog behind. It was 1958 now; *Blue Peter* had started on the television and the Church of England had just given its backing to family planning. *My Fair Lady* and *A Taste of Honey* were in the theatres, dramatising female and working-class dissatisfaction in their different modes of swanky, clever metropolitan entertainment and brutally comic, sharply youthful polemic. The family had a little mock-Tudor house in Morden, looking onto Cannon Hill Common, and smelling of coal and of the sulphur Ernest sprayed on the grapes under the veranda. At night, Edna listened to four-year-old Carlo wheezing in the room he shared with his brother, and dreamt about her own childhood: dreams that veered between idyllic images of newborn calves butting each other to drink from the bucket of milk, and nightmarish visions of her throwing her father's severed limbs into the fire.

In London, missing the country, she was nonetheless exhilarated to escape, she found the freedom to return to her childhood and to write, at last, the book she'd been building up to. Each morning, after dropping her boys at school and nursery, she would rush back and write in their bedroom, her typewriter resting on the bay window ledge. She wrote *The Country Girls* in three frenzied weeks, crying as the words tumbled out 'like the oats on threshing day that tumble down the shaft, the hard pellets of oats funnelled into bags and the chaff flying everywhere'. Aged twenty-seven, she was discovering the shocking power of her own creativity: for the rest of her life it would be both the source of her purest pleasure and a force that could overwhelm her. This book was her farewell to Ireland and to her girlhood; the book where she memorialised the fields she still yearned for and where she excoriated her father and venerated the mother whose death she had anxiously dreaded throughout her childhood and now brought into imaginative being, drowning her and leaving her protagonist Caithleen adrift and alone.[8]

The day Edna heard she'd been offered a £50 advance for the book she picked Carlo up from school in a floral summer dress and took him to the ice cream van. Unused to this munificence, he chose a 99 with double flakes, red syrup and hundreds and thousands, and together they made sure he was clean enough afterwards that when Ernest performed his daily mouth inspection, there was no offending evidence. With her new income, she bought a pullover for Ernest and a tiny bottle of perfume for herself; toy weapons for the children that Ernest disapproved of; and, in penance, a sewing machine, so she could continue to play the role of housewife. She had a tender, amorous flirtation with her publisher, which ended after Ernest overheard them talking on the phone. And then in April 1960, she found herself launched into the world, aged twenty-nine, as a successful albeit notorious writer, in a literary world preparing for the publication of the unexpurgated edition of *Lady Chatterley's Lover* in August.

Edna O'Brien, like D. H. Lawrence before her, wrote with romantic but unsentimental, urgent sensuality about the needs of the body – and of women's bodies in particular – in an era before they could be easily acknowledged. Cait and her friend Baba buy brassieres and dream of love, their lips poised 'for the miracle of a kiss', grateful for the kisses they receive 'on the mouth, and on the eyelids, and on the neck when he lifted up the mane of hair'. Cait takes off her clothes to be fondled by the comically named Mr Gentleman, an older married man, touches the penis that she finds 'soft and incredibly tender, like the inside of a flower', and arranges to lose her virginity during a trip to Vienna that he then calls off. O'Brien was pushing the limits of what a woman could write about, in a world readying itself for new kinds of writing; that November, D. H. Lawrence finally won out against censorship in the era-defining trial of *Lady Chatterley's Lover* at the Old Bailey, where the prosecuting lawyer catalogued the thirteen episodes of sexual intercourse and liberal use of four-letter words and asked the jury if this was a book they wanted their 'young sons, young daughters – because girls can read as well as boys' to read.[9]

Ireland, however, proved less ready for Edna O'Brien's writing. The Minister of Culture called her debut novel 'a smear on Irish womanhood' and, back in Drewsboro, her mother inked out every offending word and the priest burnt copies in the church grounds. Ernest Gébler didn't prove a receptive audience either. 'You can write, and I will never forgive you,' he'd announced, on first reading a draft. He complained, day after day in the diary he seems to have half-intended his wife to read, about how puffed up she was with fame, resentful that he, the Writer, had writer's block, while she, the peasant housewife, had flung herself into notoriety overnight. He decided that in return for her freedom to write, he would gain complete power over the children. He took to watching his wife and sons with binoculars on the common. He monitored the boys' bowels as well as their mouths, and dictated what they could play with, read, and watch on television. Though it was Edna now earning the money, she had to endorse every cheque to Ernest, who issued her with a small housekeeping stipend. When Carlo's asthma became worse, his father commanded him to stop wheezing. 'You have to tell yourself you're not going to be sick any more,' he ordered, and such was his authority that this briefly had some effect. For days, Ernest would sulk, talking to no one. Only in the mornings, when Ernest slept late, was there freedom in the house, and even then they had to whisper for fear of waking him. Thankfully, Edna had acquired a hut in the garden in which to write her way to freedom.[10]

Carlo and Sasha Gébler in the back garden of Cannon Hill Lane, Morden, 1961

Month after month, her life became less bearable. In *The Lonely Girl*, the sequel to *The Country Girls* that she was writing in her hut, Cait's husband complains about the gulf between his fantasy of his wife and the reality: 'When I first met you those first few times in Dublin by accident, I thought to myself, Now there is a simple girl, gay as a bird, delighted when you pass her a second cake, busy all day and tired when she lies down at night. A simple, uncomplicated girl.' Edna had been twenty-one when she and Ernest had met. In the meantime she'd grown up and Ernest, like so many men before and after, had been disappointed by the reality of a complicated, adult woman, who was no longer devoted to pleasing him. Think of George Sand: 'I was lively, mad, frivolous, apparently dazed, deep down I was serious, sad, horribly unhappy.' Ernest, like Casimir, didn't like seriousness or sadness in his wife, and couldn't cope with her success. There were literary parties and talks; Ernest felt he was losing Edna to a more glamorous world and, fearing he couldn't compete, he shut her out of the world where he did have power.[11]

They weren't alone in these battles. If this was the era of the ideal woman in the ideal home, reading magazines affirming just that vision, it was also the era when second-wave feminism began its systematic attack on patriarchal power – which helped Edna O'Brien's fiction catch fire in the world. All around her, there were mothers asking for more from their lives than their mothers had asked; working mothers leaving their children with strangers, facing the disapproval of their husbands and of columnists like Monica Dickens, who informed readers of *Woman's Own* in 1961 that 'you can't have deep and safe happiness in marriage and the exciting independence of a career as well' because 'it isn't fair on your husbands'. Among these women was Margaret Thatcher, who'd been elected as an MP in 1958 despite being the mother of small twins. 'I say a wife can do two jobs,' she told the *Evening News* in 1960, adding that bad mothers were bad even if they were at home all day. It might have been easier if Edna had been fully committed to a feminist view of womanhood. But, like Frieda Weekley, Edna was up for idealising maternity and femininity, up for spending her days playing with her children, though there was now the compulsion to write in the mix. So she minded deeply that her husband was undermining her as a mother, questioning her judgement, limiting her authority over the children. He was becoming smaller and narrower the more she grew.[12]

Something had to change, but what? – she was terrified, as centuries of women had been before her, of losing her children. 'To say she loved them was inadequate,' she later wrote in her final fictional portrait of these years, *Time and Tide*; 'she needed them, they were her sustenance . . . they had only to look at her and between them passed such a flow, such love, a tender kind of love so that their eyes would cloud over, because of course they knew that there were things amiss, sensed how wretched she was.'[13]

Knowing things were amiss, the children became jesters at dinner time, laughing uncontrollably or telling invented tales about school. Sasha enacted his unhappiness through disobedience. He scraped off the new turquoise paint his father had applied to a toilet seat and interfered with the watch his father set each day, indicating the time he was to be brought breakfast in bed (Earl Grey tea, and two slices of slightly burnt toast sprinkled with olive oil). Edna made sponge cakes and bread, keeping going with grim determination and helplessness. She had a brief affair and her husband found out, stole her lover's letters, and wrote about it in his diary for her to see.

I find it hard to imagine what Ernest himself was feeling all this time; it's peculiarly difficult to get inside his head. He was hurt, of course, and bewildered. Unhappy marriages are confusing and disorientating and so the roles offered by the patriarchy can seem the only options. Back in Dublin in 1952, he can't have imagined himself becoming so rigid, so disapproving. Perhaps he wouldn't have been like this with a different wife – someone more compliant, or just less gifted in her own right; though it's hard to imagine it being good for any woman to mould herself indefinitely to the form Ernest demanded. What's clear is that he was as trapped as Edna was by the roles that he pushed them into. This couldn't end well.

She received a cheque of £4,000 for the film rights for *The Lonely Girl* and decided to keep it for herself – this time she wasn't going to endorse it. It's so tantalising: if only she had just taken the cheque and escaped, she could have made a new life for herself and immediately fought for custody. She didn't, though; she'd obeyed him throughout her adult life and doesn't seem to have had the strength to set her will against his. She allowed herself to get drawn into an argument and to listen to a tirade from Ernest about how she had destroyed the marriage. She had to leave, but out of some mixture of fear and panic and the disdainful pride she'd inherited from her parents, she endorsed the cheque first. Then she walked out of the house without even saying goodbye to the children, who were playing in the garden.

When he realised she'd gone, Carlo opened the front door to listen for her footsteps returning. He could always recognise the particular tap of her heels as they approached, even when she was a couple of minutes away. But tonight he heard nothing, and then his father told him she was gone. 'She's a selfish child, your mother,' Carlo later recalled him saying. 'I'm going to take you to New Zealand or Cornwall. You're never going to see her again. I'm going to have things the way I want them from now on.'[14]

It was September, at the start of the autumn of 1962 that would quickly turn into the coldest winter in years. As Edna walked away, the streets smelt of autumn – of the leaves that had started to fall and of neighbours' bonfires. She knew that she was walking away from her past, 'from the twin governance of parents and husband', but had no idea where she was going. She went to the police station, desperate to tell her story to a sympathetic listener, seeking guidance from state institutions now she had eluded her husband's commands. Did he or did he not molest you? the policeman asked, and she couldn't say that he had. What exactly was it that he had done to her, all those years? She went to the hospital outpatients' department, where she found bleeding, bawling children and a scampering stray dog. Eventually she saw a nurse, who refused her sleeping tablets and advised her to go home, have a gin and tonic and make up with her husband. She went to Waterloo station, where she spent the night surrounded by drunks, less afraid than she'd been in the house she'd finally left behind.[15]

The next day, she borrowed some money from the company filming *The Lonely Girl* and picked up the boys early from school, armed with a supply of chocolate and plastic swords. They went to stay in the country with the critic Penelope Gilliatt, and Gilliatt's soon-to-be husband John Osborne, the playwright whose bitter, so-called 'kitchen sink realism' plays had made him as notorious as a spokesperson for working-class Englishmen as Edna O'Brien was for Irish women. There they helped Osborne smash an old broken greenhouse, and Edna phoned for advice on the separation from Ted Allan, a friend she shared with Ernest. He was outraged on Ernest's behalf, but brokered a meeting at his flat. Ernest, unslept and hollow-eyed, spoke gently, offering to share the children equally if she brought them back until she could set herself up in a new flat. So she took the boys back to the matrimonial home, promising they'd be able to stay with her soon. They were happy enough to go – excited about the night's TV, reassured by the familiar smell of sulphur and Lapsang Souchong tea. But in the doorway, Ernest gave her a cold smile and thanked her for going along with the plan: 'You have just legally deserted them.'[16]

Had it all been a lie? His misery, his hollow eyes had been real when they met; perhaps he agreed to what she wanted but then changed his mind, once he felt less powerless again; or perhaps he'd never intended to honour his promise. Desperate, resourceless, she walked to the river, crying with rage. She went to see Ted Allan, and his neighbour Beth took her in and put her to bed. Looking out at the Thames from Beth's window, Edna heard her character Baba speaking from what would become her third novel. 'It's not the vote women need, we should be armed.'[17]

II. Stalemate

'But what is a child between injured parents?
Only a weapon'

Arming herself was a struggle. She didn't have enough money to consult a lawyer, or even to rent a flat where the children could comfortably stay. She rented a room on Wimbledon Common and began to see the boys after school when Ernest allowed it. There were trips to Wimpy where she'd count out her change to see what they could afford. The handovers took place at Wimbledon station, where Ernest liked to keep Edna waiting for hours, staring up at adverts for holidays and sun lotions, fearful they wouldn't come. Released from Ernest's car, the boys would run to her, as though also afraid they might not find her, and begin immediately to regale her with tales of Ernest's latest demands, complaining about hoovering their rooms and making his breakfast.

'For your information, we are about to blow ourselves to kingdom come,' Ernest told Carlo in October 1962, apparently relishing the chance to scare him. Soviet missiles had been detected in Cuba, and America had put a blockade in place, edging towards war. Ernest was sardonically critical of America, but was on for displaying comparable forms of brinkmanship in his marriage, with his sons left as vulnerable pawns.

According to Ernest, they might not wake up the next day. They did wake up, though, and winter set in, blanketing Wimbledon Common with snow. When Edna bought a double mattress, Ernest stipulated that she could have one boy overnight. They tossed a coin and Sasha won, but then, alone with his mother in her shabby room, he was miserable. There was nothing to draw with, so she told him to draw in the condensation on the window. The six-year-old boy wrote 'Help', pleading for release not just from his immediate surroundings but from the whole misery his life had become. She asked if he wanted to go home, and he did, so they called from a payphone and his triumphant father agreed to collect him in half an hour's time. They waited sadly in the porch for what seemed an endless thirty minutes – perhaps the bleakest moment in the whole custody battle.[18]

The next day, Edna returned the brand-new mattress and moved to a room on the river in Putney where the shutters didn't meet and the moonlight traced searchlights on the floor, but she had a bunk bed where the boys were occasionally allowed to sleep. Ernest delighted in the squalor of the flat he likened to a 'desolate morgue', confiscated the electric helicopter she had bought Carlo on a book tour in New York, and weaponised his asthma, deciding he couldn't stay with his mother when wheezing. Carlo, ever fearful, wheezed more than ever and began vomiting up his packed lunch.[19]

Carlo and Sasha in boy scouts cub uniform, Cannon Hill Lane, October 1964

Edna imagined hiding away in a deep snowdrift with her children. She was frightened to sleep in case Ernest fulfilled his threat to take the boys to New Zealand. In her dreams, the boys eluded her and she raced up the steps at Wimbledon station only to see them waving gloomily from a train as it pulled away. Once she dreamed that she was ironing and the cloth turned into their skins, stinking as it burnt. In February she heard about the suicide of Sylvia Plath, another unhappy estranged mother, though Plath had had her children with her as she attempted to make a new life in that freezing winter. She'd met Plath once, and in the years to come she would find that her poems, full of death and children, became 'bulletins to my soul'.[20]

> The child's cry
>
> Melts in the wall.
> And I
> Am the arrow,
>
> The dew that flies
> Suicidal, at one with the drive
> Into the red
>
> Eye, the cauldron of morning.[21]

At the end of February, it finally thawed. Snowdrops pushed through the dead earth and the vixen who had cried alone under Edna's window all winter appeared with a gaggle of romping cubs. This was motherhood as Edna could still only dream of it; the mother crouching confident in her maternal authority as her young suckled and then darted away to play.[22]

Gradually, money came in. She got £100 from *Queen* magazine for a piece about horses and took the children to a stamp shop and for lunch at the Savoy, where they were loaned ties and wrote letters to Edna's mother on hotel stationery. She sold her third novel, *Girls in Their Married Bliss*, bought a grey Cossack astrakhan hat, oddly reminiscent of that ill-fated astrakhan coat, and went to parties where she tried kissing a few men, only to find she wasn't ready yet – she was terrified about losing her children.

She bought a small yellow-brick house in Deodar Road, on the river in Putney, where the boys began to spend weekends, crying on the bus back to Morden on Monday mornings. She had spare clothes for them, so there was solace in the sight and smell of vests and socks and Fair Isle jumpers. Free of Ernest, she gave them everything they wanted – unlimited TV, sweets, toys. Ernest accused her of corrupting them, turning them into 'her creatures'. He was right, in a way – the last thing children need in custody battles is an endless assault of sweets. But he was also terribly, blindly wrong, because he was already losing their affection, with his proliferating rules and surveillance and control. His tendency to sulk silently continued even in Edna's absence; there were days when no one was allowed to speak. In the summer of 1963, he took the boys, age seven and eight, camping in Wales with a friend of Carlo's. When Sasha fiddled with the tent and the rain poured inside, Ernest, shockingly, went to stay in a hotel, checking in on the boys once a day.[23]

'It's a man's world, my masters,' declared the writer Elspeth Huxley in *Punch* in 1962, launching a series of articles on 'The Second Sex'. She complained that there were no female judges or priests, and of the four women at the BBC, one worked in the Wardrobe Department and another on women's programming. Huxley was one of hundreds of women beginning to question their roles in the patriarchy more vociferously. When it was published in 1962, Doris Lessing's *The Golden Notebook* became the book every educated woman was reading – a groundbreaking, stylistically revolutionary work about the aftermath of communism, and the divisions between women and men, that keeps coming back to the resentment and anger that is 'the disease of women in our time'. From America came Mary McCarthy's 1962 *The Group*, a novel demonstrating how little most college-educated women were doing with their educations, and Betty Friedan's 1963 *The Feminine Mystique*, a polemic insisting that 'we can no longer ignore that voice within women that says: "I want something more than my husband and my children and my home."'[24]

The changes of the 1960s happened piecemeal; few of these women yet knew they were part of a movement, or knew what change was coming. Edna O'Brien belonged to her era but also carried earlier eras within her, and this was true for the decade that formed her as a writer and as a woman. The soundtrack, even out in SW20, was the exhilarating sounds of The Beatles, The Rolling Stones and The Kinks, who made sexual freedom mainstream and seemed to put a whole society's values up for grabs – including its sense of class and how much anyone from any background could want from their lives. But the more the radical protests proliferated and the shorter the skirts became, the more fierce the backlashes were in the political debating chambers and law courts. Hence, in this era of increased sexual freedom, the establishment's reputation was dealt its death blow by extra-marital sex. In 1963, the Secretary of State for War, John Profumo, stood before the House of Commons and denied his affair with 21-year-old model Christine Keeler, only for the police to reveal that he had lied. After thirteen years of Conservative rule, a Labour victory began to look ever more likely in the 1964 election.

Edna O'Brien felt the reverberations of change, even as she felt bewildered by inertia. She'd later portray the protagonist of *Time and Tide* wring a single word, 'stasis', in her diary on her thirty-third birthday as she waits for her divorce hearing. Edna herself turned thirty-three in December 1963. The Profumo affair may have suggested that powerful men no longer had their own way, but it was also a reminder that if Edna did seek custody in this supposedly progressive era, the law courts would be full of people who disapproved of all forms of transgression.[25]

She was writing *Girls in Their Married Bliss*, the third novel in the *Country Girls* trilogy, which included a wearily accurate portrait of her marriage and its aftermath. Kate's son Cash writes 'Help' on the sooty window pane as Sasha did, and cries for his father in her embrace. 'He smelled of cool basins of cream in a pantry at night,' she wrote. 'When she had first carried him, his feet pressed against her stomach, and later on he bit her nipple with impatience, but at no time had she felt as close to him as now.' She was clear here, as she always would be, that the boy's misery – crying to return to his father in the embrace of a mother he yearned to be with every night in his own home – was inflicted by both his parents: 'They were each plotting, separately but thoroughly, both assuming total injury, both framing ugliness that would tear to shreds the last, threadbare remnant of their once "good" life. It was for Cash, they said. But what is a child between injured parents? Only a weapon.'[26]

The novel didn't so much open windows onto people's marriages as throw bricks through those windows. 'O'Brien Tosses a Molotov Cocktail through the Stained-glass Window of Marriage', ran a headline in a magazine that quoted the author demanding the marriage vows be rewritten in favour of the wife. Edna moved to a bigger house in Deodar Road, with a long narrow garden that ran down to the Thames, and the boys began to spend four nights a week with her, going to Ernest on Monday, Wednesday and Friday nights. He had a new girlfriend, Jane, who joined Ernest in bullying the boys, accusing Carlo of being 'stupid' (he failed his eleven-plus in the summer of 1965) and of resembling his mother.[27]

Edna could just have left things as they were, but she saw how unhappy the boys were, going up and down, from Morden to Putney. And she needed a more thorough break from Ernest, who was using the custody situation to continue the marriage. He assailed her with continual instructions, changed arrangements at short notice, and again threatened to emigrate with the boys to New Zealand if she allowed them near what he saw as her increasingly immoral writing. He sent a 6,000-word dossier on their marriage, complaining that where he'd sought a decent, honourable companion, he'd found a 'vain-glorious monster, divested of all human traits'. If she went to court, he'd fight her with everything he had, but in the face of this extremity – 'all human traits!' – it was beginning to look like the only option.[28]

What did she see, when she looked around at divorcing women trying to get custody – those women going in and out of the Royal Courts of Justice, some in Cossack hats like hers?

Things were changing. Psychiatrists and psychoanalysts were broadly agreed about children's need for their mothers. The bible here was John Bowlby's 1951 WHO report, *Maternal Care and Mental Health*. Bowlby had been appointed by the UN to study homeless children across Europe after the war. He himself had seen his own mother once a day, at teatime, and had been sent to prep school aged seven, but now he had no apparent qualms about applying his findings about these devastated survivors to all children, everywhere in his report. 'What is believed to be essential for mental health is that the infant and young child should experience a warm, intimate and continuous relationship with his mother (or permanent mother-substitute) in which both find satisfaction and enjoyment . . . A state of affairs in which the child does not have this relationship is termed "maternal deprivation".'[29]

His 1953 book, published in paperback as *Child Care and the Growth of Love*, sold half a million copies. 'A child is deprived if for any reason he is removed from his mother's care,' Bowlby warned. His ideas quickly caught on. Social commentator Ruth Anderson Oakley claimed in an influential book about education in 1955 that 'it is within the province and the power of good mothers to eradicate most of the prisons and the asylums'. Even Winnicott, defender of the good enough mother, thought that mothers should be there as much as was feasible; mothers, after all, laid down 'the foundations of the individual's strength of character and richness of personality'.[30]

These arguments kept women determinedly out of the workforce, but they also helped them get custody, even if they were adulterous. Indeed, for divorcing mothers who wanted their children, it was better than it ever had been, even if they weren't guaranteed much money. For Edna, it might not matter that Ernest had evidence of her affair. Although all custody arrangements had to come before the court, in 95 per cent of cases the parents agreed on these arrangements, so judges generally waved them through. Most children went to mothers.

What about the contested cases, though – the cases involving children like Carlo and Sasha, whose parents fought wearisomely about every night they were in their care, the children being passed up and down on alternate nights in buses and taxis, or locked away with one parent, as Carlo and Sasha had been in the first phase? I can't read the divorce files for these years – they've been destroyed – so all I can read is recorded judgments, which tend to be from the Court of Appeal. There's no handwriting here, as there was in 1914, no lists of wrongs recited by the mother or father; the only voices we hear are the lawyers' and judges'. The children feel further away than ever but can be glimpsed, as always, in the cracks: talking to welfare officers or running away, like the twelve-year-old boy in the case of *K – an Infant and Others* (1960) who escaped from the airport when he was forced to go back to his father in Canada, travelling twenty miles across London and evading police blocks and motor-cycle patrols. There's the five-year-old girl prescribed with phenobarbitone and sent to a clinic for psychological treatment in 1961 because she was terrified of being handed over to her father (the appeal judge said there was nothing 'very alarming' about being in the care of her father and paternal grandparents because she'd been accustomed to visit them in the past).[31]

'The prima facie rule (which is now quite clearly settled) is that other things being equal, children of this tender age should be with their mother,' declared Justice Roxburgh in the Court of Appeal in

Re S. in 1958, reversing an order awarding a five-year-old boy to the father he hadn't seen since the age of three. But in fact, it wasn't clearly settled at all, because men better equipped than their wives to fight court cases and hire lawyers took children of a tender age away from their mothers over and over again. No doubt there were some cases where the decision to award custody to the father was the right one, but there is little that can be said against the mothers in almost all of the case reports I read.[32]

A case I find particularly horrifying is Spike Milligan's, because the power imbalance is so extreme. In 1959 his wife June left the family home with their three children, while Spike was in Australia for four months. For years she'd found his obsessive work ethic and manic depression almost impossible to live with. She'd had an affair but wanted another go at marriage with her new lover. Spike returned from Australia, divorced June for adultery and in 1961 got custody of their children, who were four, six and nine. 'Of course, June was seen as the guilty party,' he later wrote with ruefulness that didn't make up for his cruelty, 'they didn't say anything about me being fucking mad, insane, unstable, suicidal.' Justice Blagden was satisfied with the arrangements for the children, so Milligan stifled his guilt at parting them from a woman he knew to be 'a very good mother' by telling himself that her lover was a 'rough, crude man' who would bring the children up to be like him. Having won his case, he did his best: he was on for any amount of game-playing with the children, and often left little letters from the fairies for them to find in the garden. But during his low periods he remained locked away in his room and he never forgot the haunted faces of the children missing the mother who they hardly saw again.[33]

Custody could now be determined in the magistrates' court and magistrates often disapproved of adulterous wives. In 1962 magistrates gave the four-year-old son in *Re B.* to his father because, in committing adultery, this mother had demonstrated she would always put her own interests first. The High Court reversed the decision, using

Re S. as a precedent, but then the Court of Appeal restored the boy to his father, with Lord Evershed insisting that there was no established rule that young children should be with their mothers. I read judgment after judgment giving custody of young children to fathers who have hitherto had little involvement in their care. This was the 1960s; women reading Lessing or Friedan or Edna O'Brien herself might have thought things had changed, but they only had to go to the law courts to see the forces of reaction reasserting themselves. Adulterous Elvira Marjorie Riddle lost custody of her son in 1962 because she worked full-time and thus only offered a 'part-time home', where the father's new wife was a stay-at-home mother. Claire Diplock lost custody of her six-year-old daughter in 1965 to her (also adulterous) husband simply because she didn't have a proper home and couldn't apply for maintenance payments without having custody first.[34]

I find two cases where the judges' decisions are hard to believe. One involves Lady Caragh, who had an affair with a racehorse trainer and was put on probation for obtaining £462 by fraud. It's not exemplary behaviour, but it's surely not sufficient grounds for barring her from having any contact with her one-, three- and five-year-old children? 'I do not feel disposed to make an order for access,' was all that the judge said in January 1961, apparently requiring no further explanation for making a one-year-old motherless overnight. Then, in 1965, there was a custody case involving 'Great Train Robber' Roger Cordrey and his adulterous wife. Cordrey was a Brighton florist who'd become a thief to fund his compulsive gambling, and who'd been arrested after the key to the car – where the £2 million made on the notorious robbery was stashed – was discovered hidden in his rectum. When his custody case was heard, he'd been in jail for two years, with twelve more to serve. Nonetheless, he was given custody of his son.[35]

If you left your children voluntarily – whatever cruelty or misery may have prompted this – you were unlikely to get them back, as Ernest knew when he gleefully informed Edna that she'd deserted them. In 1959 Gwen Tomkins left her six children with her husband (the youngest was three) to live with another man. Two years later, she heard that they were being ill-treated and took them away. When Leslie Tomkins applied to the court, he was given them back with no welfare report ordered because, according to Justice Marshall in the Divorce Court, though what she'd heard about the ill-treatment 'may well be right', 'it would be quite wrong for this court to give this lady any advantage for having so blatantly taken the law into her own hands', and after all, she'd abandoned them in the first place. The *Daily Mail* described her breaking down in tears as she kissed each child goodbye on a little green at Carshalton in Surrey, perhaps never to see them again. In 1962 the judge in *H (an Infant) and Another* gave the five-month-old baby to the father because the mother had initially deserted the husband and had a tendency to spend her evenings 'at entertainment', while the father's mother, as a trained nurse, would be well equipped to look after the child. The mother's appeal was rejected because, though the appeal judge might have made a different initial decision, the evidence hadn't changed, and he hoped that the mother would think of the child and know that 'its happiness in life and its best chance in life will come if it has from the start a father and mother close at hand' and return to the father.[36]

In the midst of this came the landmark *Re L.* in 1962, its judgment designed to make women like Edna O'Brien quiver with fear and return obediently to their husbands. It was Lord Denning, Master of the Rolls, who wrote the judgment. He'd served as a judge in the Divorce Court and chaired the postwar commission investigating divorce, arguing in the 1947 report that 'the preservation of the marriage tie is of the highest importance in the interests of society', and urging the use of welfare officers in determining custody because it should be recognised that divorcing parents had 'disabled' themselves from making decisions about their children. Now he had his say in the Court of Appeal.

The mother in question had custody of two daughters, aged four and six. She'd been their primary carer since birth and had been a model wife until she had an affair with a family friend when the two families were on holiday. Her husband forgave her, but she continued the affair and decided to leave. At first she planned to live in sin with the new man, but she changed her mind, promising to keep him away from her children and admitting in court that she hadn't realised 'everybody would want to be so very difficult about things'. On it went, with the mother and children leaving the home and then the father kidnapping the children back, aided by his own mother. The mother was awarded custody by a magistrate, so the father took out a counter summons.[37]

In the Court of Appeal, Lord Denning, who liked to think of his judgments each as 'useful lessons' offering 'a landmark in our law', awarded the girls to their father, who still hoped his wife might return to him, stating that while there was no doubt this mother was 'a good mother in one sense of the word', looking after her children well and giving them love and security, 'to be a good mother involves not only looking after the children but making a home and keeping a home for them with their father . . . in so far as she herself by her conduct broke up that home she is not a good mother'. Denning feared that if this mother kept her children, 'it would follow that every guilty mother who was otherwise a good mother would always be entitled to them', allowing women everywhere to leave their husbands in search of freedom. Denning shared the father's hopes that this course of action might induce the wife to return to her husband, using the children as hostages in a larger state-wide battle to defend the beleaguered institution of marriage.[38]

Disturbed by this judgment, I read Denning's memoirs and listen to him on old radio programmes, wanting to get a sense of what kind of man did this to these girls. What emerges is that he was in many ways a reasonable man, brilliantly incisive though also rather limited. He was a conservative of the old school, passionately

Ernest and Frieda
Weekley, 1911

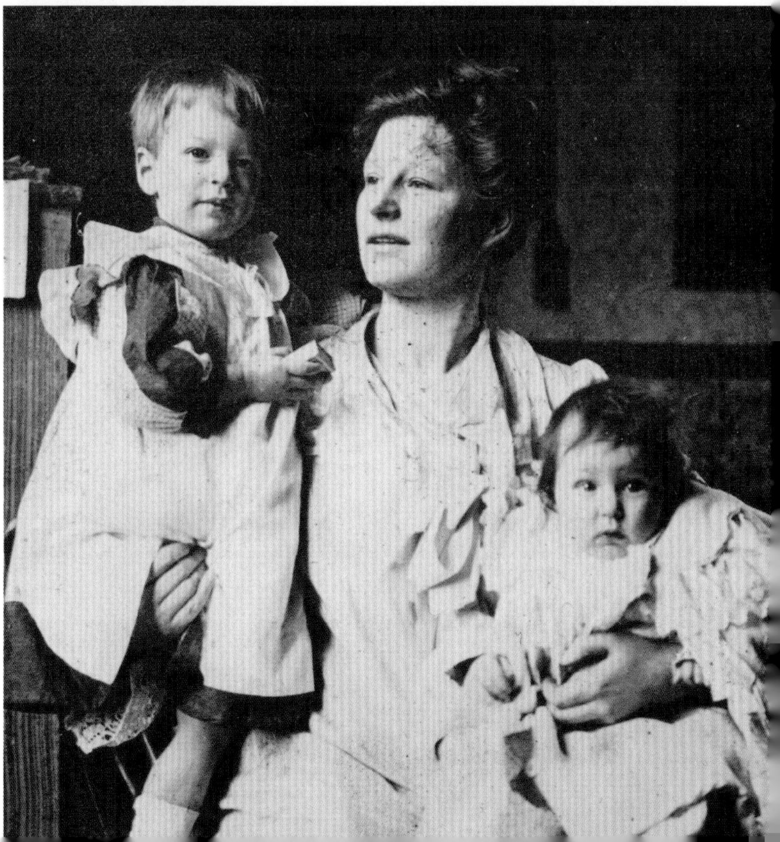

Frieda Weekley
with Montague
and Barby, 1905

Frieda Weekley with her daughter

John Middleton Murry with Frieda and D.H. Lawrence on their wedding day, 1914

Edna O'Brien with Carlo in Dublin, 1957.
The hand-written note is by Ernest Gébler

Edna O'Brien with Carlo and Sasha in Dublin, 1958

A publicity photograph of the family taken in 1961 for the publication of Edna O'Brien's *The Lonely Girl*

Edna O'Brien, photographed by the *Evening Standard*, 1966

Alice Walker, Mel Leventhal and Andrew the dog, late 1960s

Opposite: Alice Walker, Mel Leventhal and their daughter Rebecca, 1970

Alice Walker and Rebecca, 1973

Alice Walker and Rebecca

Alice Walker reading *The Color Purple*, 1982

Alice Walker and Rebecca, early 1990s

committed to upholding traditional values. This meant that he was in favour of the death penalty and wanted to keep homosexuality illegal. It also meant that he was gallantly determined to help women, albeit more as male protector than as fellow feminist. In his autobiography, as well as decrying the 'broken home' for leaving 'an indelible mark – a dark, dark mark – on the character and temperament of the child', he took credit for single-handedly improving the lives of deserted women. And it was true: he had doggedly fought, in one judgment after another even as they were repealed by the House of Lords, to give deserted wives a share of equity in their homes, using the 1882 Married Women's Property Act to argue that husbands had no right to turn wives out of the house.[39]

In his view, he didn't set out especially to penalise women when it came to divorce. He was just as outraged by adulterous husbands, and wanted to penalise everyone who casually broke the bonds of marriage. But women, he thought, did have special responsibility for keeping the home together, because 'no matter how you may dispute and argue, you cannot alter the fact that women are different from men', tasked with bearing and rearing children. He professed himself sure that a woman 'feels as keenly, thinks as clearly' as a man and that she had as much right to her freedom as him and was an equal partner in the marriage. But he also thought that she had a responsibility, in exchange for her new freedoms, to maintain a 'sound and healthy family life in the land'. Like so many judges, psychologists and politicians of his day, he managed both to load women with primary responsibility for their children, insisting on children's need of their mothers, and to rip this away when he felt there were larger questions at stake. I don't think this was active malevolence on his part – or on the part of most judges. This generation of men had been born into one world and grown up bewilderingly into another. Their educations at Britain's most prestigious single-sex boarding schools hadn't prepared them to deal with the complexities of family life at its rawest and cruellest. Many of them adored and missed the mothers they hardly saw as children; they respected the fathers whose admiration they sought; and out of this came the mixture of maternal adoration and loathing that fuelled the legal system.[40]

So many of the judgments I read use *Re L.* as a precedent – which was precisely the result Denning wanted. In 1963 Jean Nash lost custody of her seven- and nine-year-old sons because although her husband had behaved in ways that 'might amount in some cases to violence', it didn't amount to legal cruelty, so she was responsible for breaking up the home. On top of this, she was a Mormon, so was seen as exotic and perplexing. Eric Nash was awarded his sons, despite living alone and having no one to look after them while he worked full-time. In 1965, Phyllis Lowe lost custody of her four-year-old son because the judge was impressed by the father's devout Roman Catholic sister and because, though the son had been in Phyllis's care since the separation and the welfare officer described her as a 'good mother', 'any appreciation of the mother as a mother must be qualified by reference to the fact that it was she who broke up the marriage and took the child away from his father'.[41]

Outside the courts, women's magazines echoed this attitude: indeed the editors were in regular talks with the government to make sure their messages aligned. I read through a year of *Woman* magazine, the most popular of the day with a weekly circulation of 3 million. Turning the large, glossy pages, becoming stickier as they fade, I find article after article, letter after letter, upholding the institution of marriage that the government rightly feared feminists were trying to undermine:

'For twenty-three unhappy years I have been married to a man who has an appalling temper,' a wife writes to Evelyn Home, the agony aunt, in 1964. He's hurt and humiliated their oldest daughter who has left home as a result, and now he's been arrested as a thief – is it time to leave him?

'You have a very difficult partner,' Evelyn Home acknowledges, 'but let's look at his good points' – he's faithful and has stayed with you despite being 'disliked, perhaps even despised'. Perhaps, poor man, he's jealous of his eldest child. Either way it's best to stay, because 'separation can be very hard indeed for a woman used to marriage, even a faulty marriage'.

I turn the pages of one issue after another, skipping the long, serialised love stories, skimming the recipes designed to please the 'hungry husband', noting the advertisement for TCP calling out to mothers exhausted by summer's continual insect bites and bruises ('Then, as always, it's Mother who has to cope'). And in every issue, I find Evelyn Home urging women to stay with husbands who pay no attention to them ('But why did your husband lose interest like that?'), bully them ('if you were a little less unloving your husband might soften, too'), and repeatedly come home late and drunk ('be patient. Time and love should be a winning combination'). In the midst of this there are encouraging articles about how to get a job in a bank, how to work from home, even how to become an army nurse, and patterns for how you can make your own Dior suit. But in case you become too self-confident, the 'Healthy Living' column holds mothers responsible when your children are overweight, ridden with acne, or cry ('a baby's way of saying he has "caught" his mother's tension').[42]

It's hard to believe, reading the magazine, that any women could get custody if the failure of the marriage was inevitably their fault. Or perhaps it's not so much that it's their fault it ends, as their responsibility to keep it going; the men are either too grandly busy or too hapless to be tasked with the upkeep of their marriages. Nonetheless, I do find evidence in the court judgments that there were mothers – even adulterous or otherwise imperfect mothers – getting custody every month because judges decided that children should be with mothers rather than stepmothers, even if their home was less well-appointed (1960), or that the husband wasn't a good father because 'he showed indifference' when his daughter got her finger caught in the car door (1960), or because the father had stabbed his brother-in-law (1963), or because he, 'a difficult man', was deemed by the welfare officer to be 'unable to appreciate the consequences that his behaviour and actions might have upon the children' (1963), or even because he carried the child around on a bicycle, despite a diagnosis of epilepsy (1963).[43]

The danger was that even if Edna O'Brien did convince the judge that the children needed her most, Ernest Gébler would be granted custody, while she would simply be given care and control, which would defeat the point of escaping his power. This division, first adopted in the 1950s, was becoming ever more prevalent. In 1962 Judge Howard in the Divorce Court ruled that the adulterous Cynthia Giddings would have care and control of six-year-old Raymond and would have the power to decide 'the small things . . . like clothes and holidays', but that her estranged husband would have custody, making the 'long-term decisions, such as religion and education'. Judge Howard was aware that the 'harsh and cruel' Victorian principle barring adulterous mothers from having custody no longer applied, but didn't agree 'that a woman living in adultery can arrange matters entirely to her own liking'. Thus, Raymond would have the care of his mother, but Cynthia Giddings could still be punished by the husband who the *Daily Mail* described as a 'hot-blooded Irishman', adding that he hadn't seen the boy for the past year because 'he could not trust himself to keep his hands off Mr Carrington', his wife's lover. In 1963 the Appeal Court upheld the decision to give custody to the father and care and control to the wife in *Re W.* on the grounds that the father had been at a prestigious public school and, 'as I understand it, he is anxious that his son should go there, so it was obviously sound to give the father custody with that in mind'.[44]

For both Edna O'Brien and Ernest Gébler, reading the newspapers between 1962 and 1965, there would have been decidedly mixed messages about custody. The welfare of children was at the centre of every decision, and young children were broadly thought to need their mothers, but mothers could quite easily forfeit their rights to their children. And as 1965 began, Carlo and Sasha were ten and eight – were they even children of a 'tender age' any more? Yet fathers could forfeit their rights too, and wasn't Ernest a 'difficult man', unable to appreciate the consequences of his behaviour on his children? And hopefully they would be assigned a welfare officer to find out the wishes of the boys themselves. Edna O'Brien prepared to go to court.

III. The fight

'They are yours to destroy'

She found a lawyer: Bernard Main, a courteous older man with leather patches on the elbows of his tweed jacket and a desk thick with papers and dust. The case for adultery wasn't strong enough, given she'd been adulterous first, so he advised her to divorce Ernest for cruelty. Things had changed since 1914, when Alice Ashton-Jinks was denied a separation on the grounds that her violent husband wasn't quite violent enough. In the judgments I read from the 1950s and 1960s, I am reassured to find women receiving verdicts of cruelty a lot more easily. In *Baker v Baker* (1955) persistent drunkenness was counted as cruelty because it followed 'warnings that such a course of conduct is inflicting pain on the other spouse', though in this case it was accompanied by verbal abuse and forced sex (not yet categorised as rape). In *Blume v Blume* (1965) Lord Justice Russell even saw cruelty as 'consisting in undermining her authority with the children', and the Justices of Sutton Coldfield in 1964 saw the husband's application for custody in *Buxton v*

Buxton as an act of cruelty, given its effect on his wife's health. It still wasn't straightforward: in *Kaslefsky v Kaslefsky* (1951) Lord Denning had defined cruelty as behaviour that was not simply done 'for the gratification of the selfish desires of the one who does it', but was intentionally aimed 'to injure the other or to inflict misery on him or her'. And so in 1964, Judge Lee in Southampton described the behaviour listed in *Bromby v Bromby*, which included the husband bruising the wife's eye, striking his wife with a slipper ('which does not sound a very serious matter'), and kicking her repeatedly in the stomach after she refused sex, as merely part of the 'ordinary events in married life' – and not proof that the marriage had broken down – though the appeal judge in 1965 did categorise the stomach kicking as legal cruelty.[45]

Ernest's control over her money, his constant surveillance and criticism was certainly intended to inflict misery on Edna. He had not assaulted her physically, but it was worth an attempt in court. She told the children what was happening, and nine-year-old Sasha joked that the next day when his friend boasted about his mother having a fur coat he would say: 'My mummy has a divorce.' Ernest immediately compiled a dossier full of statements in his favour from the local doctor, the boys' headmaster, and their Irish nanny. Alarmed by their treachery, Edna began to search for character witnesses of her own. Meanwhile she was finishing an autobiographical novel where, powered by the destructive imaginative impulse that was always somehow a necessary counterpart to the nurturing she did in her actual life, she killed off one of her sons.[46]

Since the separation began, Edna O'Brien had thought and dreamed her way into the deaths she most dreaded. In *Girls in Their Married Bliss*, Cait has the dream that Edna herself had about ironing her son's burning skin, but it becomes more elaborate. She asks the Irish nanny to kill the child by burning him with an iron, and the boy dies quickly, without a whimper. The dream goes on, so that she lives out the months and years, running out of restaurants and hairdressers, 'sick with pain because she'd killed the only person she was capable of loving'. But in this novel the death remains a dream, however vivid. It was only, much later when she wrote the epilogue in 1987 that she added an actual death: the trilogy ends, as it began, with a dead mother. Cait gets custody and then drowns, more or less intentionally, at a health farm where she is teaching herself to swim.[47]

Why did Edna O'Brien find that reading about death in Plath's poems resonated, during these years of stasis? It wasn't that anyone had died, but that she lived in daily fear of death. She'd grown up in a culture where death was everywhere; those nightly prayers were prayers not to be spared death, but to have a good afterlife following the death that could come at any moment. Now every absence from her sons was a death, or a portent of one. She imagined it in her dreams and now she would imagine it in her fiction. She was full of guilt for murdering her children, because hadn't she brought them into being and wasn't this unhappiness – Carlo wheezing away and vomiting his packed lunch, Sasha crying as he wrote 'Help' on the window – a state she had inflicted on them? 'What is a child between injured parents? Only a weapon.'

You can feel so guilty simply about the father you have chosen for your children; about the marriage you failed to make work, which was a catastrophic mistake in the first place. I know this, as I know what it's like to wait at a station platform full of dread that when the train doors open the children you long for might not emerge. Week after week during the months of our custody case, I swallowed down tears, seeing them rush off the train, pleased to see me. I knew they were on the train, yet I still feared they wouldn't emerge from it. The stakes in a custody case feel so high that you seem to be fighting to keep your children alive. And even if you win, you have killed them a little, those children who are both a weapon and a broken body torn between their parents.

Now, in *August is a Wicked Month*, Edna O'Brien killed her son, realising her greatest fears and punishing herself for her sons' unhappiness, full of guilt and terror. This is a story about a mother whose ex-husband takes their seven-year-old son Mark camping, only for the ex-husband to behave carelessly – as Ernest himself did on his camping trip – sending the boy each morning to get the milk from the shop himself. One day the boy is run over and killed. His gruesomely mutilated body is bundled into a small coffin. Devastated, Ellen takes refuge in blame. 'You killed him,' she says on the phone. 'You did it, it was your fault', and there is a perverse pleasure in at last blaming the man who's spent years blaming her. After the phone call, she lacerates herself instead. If they were still married, she'd have been there, and she'd have gone with Mark to get the milk, holding his hand carefully to cross the road.[48]

The death takes place halfway through the book, and in the pages that follow Edna O'Brien forced herself to imagine Ellen's grief as she lives out her broken life. Her son's death is inside her 'like a lancet, like a pain, she couldn't stand it'. Ellen hears the many voices he's had since babyhood, his failed attempts to pronounce the letter 'r', his lisp when he lost a tooth, his fearful whispers to his imaginary friend in bed at night, and she frantically imagines herself reassembling his body, screwing arms back on as if he's a doll. She learns the news of his death on holiday and then has to return to his bedroom, where his fort and soldiers are laid out waiting and there's a pile of his clean clothes on the bed. She puts them away and locks the door from the outside. She is full of guilt, because of the separation, but also because even when he was alive 'she was only a mother some of the time'. She'd dote over him for months and then would have a sudden 'wild longing to go through the town and do delirious things and not bear the responsibility of being a mother, for hours, or days, or weeks'.[49]

Edna O'Brien was the great writer of custody of her century. She was George Sand in a new guise, romantic but not sentimental, fierce in her mother love, while also wholly a person apart from her children. But this was a George Sand who wrote about custody, again and again. O'Brien's vision of a world built on conflict, her combination of a very daily kind of autobiographically driven realism, and a dreamier, more lurid gothic mode, were all ideally suited to writing about the darkest effects of divorce on children. She read and reread *Anna Karenina* throughout her life, taking from Tolstoy a commitment to custody as tragedy that for thirty years would be the bedrock of her art.

Eventually the date of the hearing arrived. It was November 1965. Winston Churchill was dead and, to Lord Denning's disappointment, capital punishment had been abolished, just as Ian Brady and Myra Hindley were arrested for some of the most brutal murders of the past decades. The first female High Court Judge had been appointed, and assigned to the family courts – finally a woman was deciding on the questions of childrearing that were apparently women's responsibility. The boys were with Ernest the night before and he asked them both to write affidavits, saying where they wanted to live. 'To my Dear Dad,' eleven-year-old Carlo wrote. 'I must admit I prefer living in Putney at the moment. But in years to come I will probably have a different attitude. I just don't know. Signed your loving son Carlos xxx.' Ever telegraphic, nine-year-old Sasha wrote simply 'Putney', with the same mixture of helplessness and aggression he had traced 'Help' on the window three years earlier.[50]

Before or after exhorting these disappointing letters, Ernest went to Edna's house to leave a note, saying that he wasn't planning to contest the case. 'I am not fighting it any longer, your methods are too dirty and too devious. I will not be in court tomorrow morning, so the children are yours to destroy.' She rang her barrister with the good news, and he arranged just to send his junior to the hearing.[51]

The Royal Courts of Justice

The next morning Edna put on discreetly staid clothes and a pair of long earrings she thought of as 'giddy', with feather pendants that had the dip of catkins. She walked along the Strand, past Wren's neat stone St Clement Danes church, listening to its bells peeling, and peered distractedly into the tea shop and the pub and the bank, as so many other mothers had done before her. As she went through the main archway at the Royal Courts of Justice, the first person she saw in the courtyard was her husband, standing talking animatedly to his barristers. The letter had been a lie. Entering the extravagant gothic building, she passed the sculptures intended by the architect George Edmund Street to represent the four male pillars of the English legal tradition: Jesus, Moses, Alfred the Great and Solomon – that king who was so sure of what a good mother was that he'd threatened to kill a baby to catch out one grieving mother and reward the terrified renunciation of the other. She was then led under more archways, past pointed windows and spires, down endless corridors – the building has three and a half miles of them – footsteps reverberating on stone floors, caught in the workings of British imperial power in a way she hadn't been before.

Finally, Edna arrived in Court 23, where she was seated by an usher, across from Ernest, who had in front of him a series of white postcards with evidence written on them. Her junior barrister, next to her, looked bewildered, reading through the notes he'd been given only that morning. 'Dieu et Mon Droit' read the inscription above the judge; it remained to be seen whose God and whose Right would prevail.

Ernest's barrister called him as a witness and he informed the judge that he'd assembled evidence in three categories: his wife's character, her attitude to men, and her writing. 'The thought came to me,' Edna O'Brien later wrote, 'that Moll Flanders, were she sitting in that court, stood a better chance of getting custody.' Ernest produced a copy of her recently published *August is a Wicked Month*, reporting excitedly that it had just been banned in South Africa as 'obnoxious, indecent and obscene'. He waved around a copy of the magazine article where she'd tossed that Molotov cocktail at marriage. His principal, contradictory argument was that she didn't actually want the children. She liked the idea of them but if she was given custody she'd disappear for months on a book tour. The decision to fight the case was merely her attempt to revenge herself on men. She was both a nymphomaniac and a man-hater and she was fighting all the men in the world. The children would become 'mother-smothered, emotionally sick homosexuals' if left to her.[52]

The judge was given *August is a Wicked Month* to inspect. He looked at the passage in question, turned a few pages onwards, closed the book and said: 'It seems to me that boys of nine and eleven would not be interested in this kind of literature.' Her barrister was asked if he wanted to call her as a witness, but he declined, perhaps fearful of the nymphomania and man-hating she might evince. She indicated that she would, in fact, like to speak. Without going to the witness box, she rose and addressed the judge, shaking with fear and rage:

'I'll pose a question to you,' she said. 'Would I have fought for them so hard for the last three years – you have the evidence of how I tried and the obstacles and double-handedness I had to overcome – if I didn't love my children? Would I have fought for them so hard if I was this scallywag, running around with all these supposed men?'

Did she have anything else to say?

'I regret that my writing and my love for my children has been so misunderstood.'[53]

The judge read through his notes, his glasses slipping off his nose as he read the statements where Ernest demonstrated his own punctilious meticulousness but inadvertently revealed his obsessiveness and vindictiveness.

The judgment was ready. He gave her custody, with due consideration for the father's rights to visits and holidays. Across the aisle, Ernest stiffened in outrage. Outside the court, she went over to him and told him that she knew he was hurt, but they would share the children – 'Let us not be monsters.'

'They are yours to destroy,' he said again.

Twenty-five years later, in *Time and Tide*, she described her protagonist at this moment of triumph feeling 'not the glorious surge of victory that she had anticipated but instead a great onset of sorrow, as if in the years to come the true consequences of it all would unfold, and the heartbreak she had been party to would live like a ghost in whatever room, whatever country she happened to be in'.[54]

In the late afternoon she collected the children from their separate schools. That evening they were muted. Carlo, suddenly full of guilt at his treachery the previous evening, turned on her and said: 'Dad says you're a snob and you'll send us to a snob school and not a decent socialist school, where we would have grown up to be responsible citizens.' He cried as he said it. Silently, Sasha took their hands and piled them together on the table in a gesture of reconciliation.[55]

III. Aftermath

'I have guilt for crimes I have not committed as well as for crimes I have committed'

Edna O'Brien and Ernest Gébler's divorce came on the cusp of change. The 1969 Divorce Reform Act initiated no-fault divorce, which allowed couples to divorce after a separation of two years if they could demonstrate the 'irretrievable breakdown of the marriage'. In the Guardianship Act of 1973, married mothers finally had equal rights with fathers. Still, courts found ways to punish transgressive mothers, but the decision to desert the marital home became gradually less perilous than it had been.

At first, Carlo and Sasha continued to go to their father, once or twice a week, for an afternoon or occasionally overnight. That Christmas, he handed back the pullover and mugs they had bought him with the wrapping paper unopened, saying he knew children better and more loyal. In June 1966, six months after the court case, Ernest summoned them to his study, holding a sheaf of notes he'd prepared. Carlo later recalled how his stomach prickled and his thighs wobbled, in anticipation. Jane stood in the doorway smiling, apparently sadistically. The window was open and there were children playing cricket with their father on the common in front of the house, offering a glimpse of a more relaxed, less punitive form of fatherhood.

'Shall we look at the facts?' Ernest began, a kind of barrister in his own home. 'You were living half with your father and half with your mother. You left your father completely to live with your mother on your own choice. You abandoned your father completely although he had never been even unkind to you. You went to live entirely with your mother because you said it was "nicer" there. You had a television in your bedroom on which you could watch any rubbish you wanted, any time you wanted, and you were free to do more or less what you liked.'[56]

Carlo looked up at the profile of the man he so closely resembled, the nose large and flat like his, this family resemblance drawing attention to their lack of sympathy. Outside, a child whacked a ball with his cricket bat and began to run. Ernest continued, complaining that the boys had never written or phoned to ask how he was. Their attitude, he said, had a 'sort of calculated contempt to it'. They had forgotten that for eleven years he had tucked them in at night and cared for them with love and attention. Their visits reminded him of 'waste and desolation', depressing him for days to the extent that he couldn't write. 'Your conduct towards me has been outrageous, as your mother's conduct was outrageous. There is no reason why I should suffer it. And as you see no reason why you should see me, let me put an end to it.' They had dinner, and Ernest drove them to Wimbledon station. He meant this to terminate their relationship, although occasional afternoon visits resumed intermittently the following year.[57]

Back in Deodar Road, they remade their lives as best as they could. Edna threw them elaborate, expansive birthday parties and they sailed miniature battleships on the Thames. She met Paul McCartney at a party and brought him home to wake up the boys and play 'Those Were the Days' on Carlo's guitar in their bedroom. Carlo got a part in a film, but Ernest refused his consent, threatening legal action. 'I could kill Dad,' Carlo told Edna, and she felt that he was saying he could kill her as well, furious about his divided family.[58]

In 1968 the boys were sent to Bedales, a progressive boarding school in Hampshire. It was an odd decision to send them away, only three years after she had got them back for good. Carlo still wasn't thriving academically, and Edna felt that the boys needed the stimulation and the careful attention of a private school, without the endless rules of a big public school. They wanted to go, and they'd get to come home for weekends.

Two years later, Ernest moved to Ireland, where he refused to see the boys when they tried to visit. Edna had weekly parties now, with plentiful champagne, and the boys tending the bar on their weekends home. The actor Richard Burton came to the house to recite Shakespeare, and was mystified why Edna didn't want to go to the 'bed chamber' with him; she fell in love with the theatre designer Sean Kenny, and drank milk with Marlon Brando in her kitchen. She befriended the maverick psychoanalyst R. D. Laing and had a nightmarish LSD trip at his hands, hallucinating so badly in Paris a few days later that she had to be watched over by an itself rather hallucinatory rota of Samuel Beckett, Marguerite Duras and Peter Brook. She became involved enough in thinking about Northern Ireland to be described in an English newspaper as the 'Barbara Cartland of long-distance Republicanism' but was less interested in the women's movement.[59]

The success of her early books was partly due to the groundswell of female discontent that she became a part of, inflecting it with comedy and grief. But as the women's movement began in earnest, she distanced herself from feminism. 'I am not like any man I have ever met, ever, and that divide is what both interests me and baffles me,' she said in a 1972 interview. 'A lot of things have been said by feminists about equality, about liberation, but not all of these things are the truth.' Her scepticism seems to have been partly driven by her sense of herself as a mother – and here feminists could be ambivalent too. Simone de Beauvoir and Betty Friedan had both fought for women's rights not to mother, but Beauvoir at least had also been fascinated by the erotic bodily love of a mother for her baby – the 'carnal plenitude, not in surrender but in domination', unlike in a woman's relationships with men. And from the late 1960s, there were plenty of feminists – from Adrienne Rich in America to Juliet Mitchell in England and Hélène Cixous in France – acknowledging their bodily love for their children, alongside their claustrophobia in the forms of maternal love demanded by the patriarchy. But the relationship between feminism and motherhood would continue to be vexed and unsettled over the decades that followed, and for her part Edna O'Brien was understandably scarred by her court case, which had revealed that a woman's license to parent her children would long be contingent on conforming to standards of good motherhood and good wifehood that feminists hoped to leave behind. So she set out on her own, with a manifesto less of change than of engaging both grandly and intimately with loss and its place in our lives.[60]

All this time, the years of fighting over custody remained so painful that O'Brien would not return to it in her writing for two decades, trying out other styles and themes in the meantime. Then in 1987 she wrote the epilogue to *The Country Girls*, and in 1992 she wrote *Time and Tide*, where she describes the sorrow of victory and finally laid to rest the ghosts of the children she had lost – the happier versions of her boys she blamed herself for destroying. Here the older son looks at his mother with appalling need, pleading for attention, and the mother knows that 'everything that had happened had marked him and made him needy'. This boy too, is dogged by asthma, and when his head gets clogged up and his eyes watery, she feels that he is 'still inside her, gasping to get out'.[61]

This older boy, Paddy, disappears and is returned. Clutching his adolescent body, she feels that he clenches her with rebellion as much as love. 'He was too tall for her to carry, but he clung to her all the same, and the clinging said, "Please don't say anything, because if you say anything it will destroy what is left of us."' This is the second book where Edna O'Brien kills off one of the boys. His death is both devastating and familiar, as though imbued with the shock of his birth: 'In the first slippery unchartered moments, when the link is severed and the dark moist hush of an insideness is exchanged for the vast inhospitality of a creaking word, we know death.' If birth brings a kind of death, death brings a kind of birth, and it feels grimly appropriate that Paddy drowns – as the mothers do in the *Country Girls* trilogy – returning to the watery world he once emerged from.[62]

Every detail after this death is savagely imagined, almost as a kind of penance on O'Brien's part. She writes about the boy's burial, the rehoming of his dog, the visit to her ex-husband to tell him about the death, feeling his hate for her as a pilot light, 'waiting not for extinction but to be relit'. There is no redemption here, just a constant reckoning with the past, an attempt to provide a future for her younger son, and 'the involuntary shudder that keeps reminding us we are alive'.[63]

Eventually Carlo himself made peace with his father. Shortly before Ernest's death in 1998, Carlo was summoned to go through his papers. He read his father's diaries from the years of the custody battle: Ernest's descriptions of days spent in 1963 sitting for seven hours doing nothing except reading a film review, his chest pain resulting from 'a sort of accumulation of injustice and loneliness'; his pleas for Edna to take the TV set out of the boys' bedroom in Putney. 'Carlos is a little "backward", "retarded",' Ernest had written as his eldest son began secondary modern school in September 1964, 'but it is my wish in life he will grow through that.' Then, in February 1965, after he'd had the boys to stay during half term, Ernest wrote that when they were about to leave, he tried to prepare himself, saying that it didn't matter, and that they'd leave him anyway to live their own lives after a few years. 'But after they have been here a few days, the first night they are not here (to go in and look at their sleeping faces) I am sad and depressed, and realise what it is . . . How can you put all that you have put into your life aside for days?'[64]

Reading these diaries, Carlo began to pity the man who had clearly been depressed for all these years. 'He was ill. That was why he couldn't love us, or show us love. That was why he could only be the dour, undemonstrative, distant man I knew.'[65]

Does Ernest Gébler's apparent depression excuse him? Certainly plenty of very unhappy people manage to be loving parents. But I think back to Theophilus Packard, and Ernest Weekley. These men have deep feelings but bury them so secretively that they themselves don't often know what they are, to the point that they can seem lacking in feeling, and it can all tip helplessly into rage at the people around them. They do seem to loathe, in particular, the women who are better able than they are to enjoy life, whatever life throws at them. The women's enjoyment can seem intended to thwart the men they have blighted with disappointed love.

I write to Edna O'Brien, asking if she will meet. She's ill, so the date is postponed, and then on a bright June morning I ring the bell of her house in Chelsea and wait, long enough that I begin to wonder if she's out. Then there she is, and it's as though she's acting out the ghostliness found in her most gothic novels. She's pallid and thin, in a white nightie; her eyes, smudged with mascara, are hollow-eyed with pain after a sleepless night. She's an elder stateswoman of the literary world, her late-life reputation assured by her 2015 masterful exploration of male power and violence: *The Little Red Chairs*. She has reinvented herself at every stage and is grand even now that she lives out her own afterlife, floored by pain but brave as she offers me cold water from the fridge, determined to give me what she can of herself.

Amid the pale austerity, her literary agent suddenly sweeps in, full of verve and colour, bearing a bouquet of apricot-pink roses that Edna delights in learning are called Compassion, and peaches that she urges her to eat. Then we are left on our own to talk, struggling at first. The walls to the world around her are becoming less penetrable by the day: she cannot hear enough to listen, or see enough to read. Yet we find a way. I strip my questions down to their essentials and then the words flow, because she is lucid still, like a blade of steel cutting through the physical world she no longer needs as her body becomes ever more ethereal.

I ask her about the deaths of her sons in her books. She seems surprised by the revelation that she killed a son twice and dreamt of their deaths in other novels.

'I was raised in fear, fear and trembling,' she says. 'Some would say that the deaths were very cruel. In the state of mind that I was in it seemed reasonable and rational to me. My relationship with my sons was very umbilical, because I was young, younger than my years, and somehow because we were all three living under an arcade of tyranny.'

I ask if the writing helped her overcome her fears.

Writing and life are too intertwined for this, she says. 'Writing doesn't cancel your fears, it actually entrenches them.'

She tells me about the court case, minute by minute, and it strikes me that she doesn't seem to find it painful to be returned to that period. She lives it still, all the time; this is the shape her life has taken, and she is always in fear of judgement. At the beginning of her autobiography, she described a dream where she finds herself in a kind of prison cell within the house of her childhood: 'All the others have died. I am there to answer for my crimes. It makes no difference that my interrogators are all dead.'[66]

We talk about my book, about the other women she's fighting alongside. She is glad of the comparisons with George Sand, and outraged to hear that Sand, like Edna, had her books produced in court.

'It's one thing writing a book in private for a reader who will read it in private,' she says. 'It's a very private transaction. Bits of my book were read out in court and I was mortified. It's so easy to feel you have done something awful.'

I ask her what has been lost for her sons as adults. What have been the consequences of those years of rupture and division?

She says that her sons have been angry with her, over the years, and the upset of the past takes ever new forms.

We cry, both of us, talking about the promises we made that we could not keep; promises extracted that we believed in just about enough to make, because we persisted in believing the world to be sane. My son, night after night during our court case, used to beg me to promise that if he told the professionals that he wanted to live with me, he'd be allowed to do so. And so I promised, desperate to give him the comfort that would allow him to sleep. Was I wrong to do so, I ask Edna now, wanting some kind of absolution from her in her deathly pain.

'You make promises that you aren't sure you will be able to fulfil,' Edna says. 'That's very hard to comprehend. It comes across as treachery, which it is in a sense, not deliberate treachery but a defection of the truth.'

We should never promise anything, we agree – but what to do, when you have a little boy crying in bed, unable to sleep until you assure him that monsters don't really exist and that you will be there always to assure him of this?

Edna promised her sons they would be with her eventually, and she was right: they were. But along the way there were so many promises broken. Most horrible was that night she took them home, in the crisp-leaved September of 1962. She promised them then that they had come to an arrangement – that they would live partly with her – only for them to hear their father slamming the door like a pantomime villain and declaring this to be an act of maternal abandonment.

It's time to go.

She asks sudden, urgent questions about me, glad to hear that I have a new partner, deciding that this accounts for my unexpected cheerfulness, glad that my son isn't angry with me, right now: 'Your children love you, that's all that counts, to hell with their father.'

Then, at the last minute, she wants to return to the question of the dead children in her novels. 'I think it would have been for my own guilt,' she says.

> I have guilt for crimes I have not committed as well as for crimes I have committed. It's a very peculiar trait. It isn't wishing death on the other, it's a guilt that I have murdered. Young children think up very strange schemes, they think of little slaughters. It must be hidden sublimated guilt at having wished to murder someone as a child. Each thing kills the thing he loves. In my case, I had grief about losing my children and terror, and instead of expressing it as terror the grief is compounded by some fuck up in my own psyche – I've not only lost them, I've also killed them. Why would a mother who had lost a son then kill a son? What is the person who did that deed? It is the grief and the guilt. But I'm very glad that you're happy now.[67]

Guilt. It is everywhere, in connection with motherhood – think of those articles in *Woman* magazine. Mothers feel guilty for the children who are with them and the children who aren't; motherhood itself can seem a state of permanent guilt. What should we do with this fact? Surely it can't be inevitable, so it ought to be possible to imagine a world where mothers don't feel as guilty as Edna and I do, looking back at our court cases from our different angles.

As I leave there are offerings: gifts to each other that are also oblations to the gods who have kept us going through the nights of fearful sleeplessness, the nights of even more fearful sleep, plagued by dreams. I give her one of the sleeping aid tablets that I take when I find it hard to sleep, when I'm away from my home and children. We mark it up in an envelope. I've brought her honey from the Cotswolds. She asks me to find her a spoon, and I load it up medicinally, as I do in the night for my daughter when she has a sore throat. And then, more theatrically, Edna gives me half her bouquet of roses.

Compassion. Fifty years ago, just as married mothers acquired equal legal status with fathers, a botanist decided to cross the 'White Cockade' and the pink 'Prima Ballerina'. Pirouetting elegancy and military plumage combined and the result, in the face of all that strenuousness and striving, was Compassion. We have need of it, both of us, at either end of this peculiar process of estranged parenting that gains you no cockades and leaves no time for pirouetting. We have need of it, as Caroline Norton and George Sand and Elizabeth Packard and Frieda Lawrence had need of it before us.

Edna won her case, as George Sand did, but they can seem tragic figures, both of them, and Edna O'Brien made herself live out the pain in book after book, holding herself to account even after she had her sons back, though it is also true to say that these are wildly compassionate novels, as well as guilty ones.

I go on my way, clutching my flowers, dazed by the sunlight after her shadowy kitchen, disorientated at relinquishing the intensity of her world. It is she, not I, who is the Angel of History, I realise, thinking of Walter Benjamin's extraordinary description:

> Where we perceive a chain of events, he sees one single catastrophe which keeps piling wreckage and hurls it in front of his feet. The angel would like to stay, awaken the dead, and make whole what has been smashed. But a storm is blowing in from Paradise; it has got caught in his wings with such a violence that the angel can no longer close them. The storm irresistibly propels him into the future to which his back is

turned, while the pile of debris before him grows skyward. This storm is what we call progress.[68]

Edna O'Brien looks backwards, always, at the catastrophe; at the wreckage piling at her feet. She longs backwards, longs to make whole the smashed ravages of the past, but she's pulled by the storm towards the Paradise she once yearned for every night, saying her prayers as she lay beside her mother in bed. Her wings are caught in the storm of progress and she knows what she'll find when she makes it through; she has pronounced her own guilt, even if the courts of law found her innocent. We have to hope she finds compassion when the violence finally cedes to peace. In the meantime, there are other women caught in the storm that may or may not be progress.

6

ALICE WALKER

A novel is finished and a baby born. In the final weeks she was pregnant with her daughter, Alice Walker wrote into being one of the most appalling custody cases in twentieth-century literature. Its violence was the violence she had grown up with; she had been birthed into brutality, as her daughter would be. And in turn Rebecca Walker, whose little foetal body was infused with the bloodshed of an imagined courtroom in Georgia, would have a life shaped by some of the most distinctive custody arrangements of her generation.

Baker County, Georgia, 1963. Sixteen-year-old Ruth Copeland sits in the court's segregated 'colored chambers' beside her grandfather Grange Copeland. She's lived with him for seven years, since her father, Brownfield, murdered her mother while Ruth and her sisters watched in devastated horror. Now Brownfield has been released and wants his daughter back. Though she's almost an adult, Ruth has no voice in the court process.

The white, aging judge is a local man with a misleadingly kind face and a love of fishing. He's irritated by Grange, who extemporises on his son's shortcomings. He smiles as he gives his verdict, and then brandishes his fishing boots, ready to get on with his day. This girl, on the verge of a new life, inspired by the first signs of the civil rights movement and by her hard-won education, is about to lose everything.

'Got you this time,' Brownfield jeers.

But he doesn't get to claim his prize because, right there in the judge's chambers, Grange takes out his blue steel Colt .45 and shoots down his son. He and Ruth drive home, and then he leads the police into the woods for a shootout, protecting his granddaughter from his death.[1]

Jackson, Mississippi, 1969. It's a mild November, as Novembers always are here. Arriving at the hospital, Alice Walker finds lines of other Black women in labour in the corridors, screaming in separate pain. Her husband, Mel, is in the middle of a school desegregation court case in New Orleans, arguing on behalf of a Black community who don't have streetlights or sewage systems. There's no rush, he's told by the judge. He's planted the seed – surely he doesn't have to be there for the harvest too? But he rushes back, in time helplessly to watch the end of his wife's gruelling, 36-hour labour.

Rebecca is born with her eyes open, apparently smiling with recognition. The father fills the mother's room with red roses and the mother clutches the bundled baby sucking at her breast. A nurse comes in to check the facts. On the birth certificate, the mother's race is 'Negro' and the father's 'Caucasian'. Someone has added a questioning 'Correct?' because white men don't generally claim paternity of Black women's babies.

'Correct', they affirm.[2]

This is a baby born of the civil rights struggle, intended to heal the rift between Black and white; a baby better loved and fed than the babies in the mother's novel.

Correct? Correct. A child can indeed be the legal property of a Black mother and a white father. In that joint ownership the possibility for division is laid bare. And Alice Walker's novel, *The Third Life of Grange Copeland*, is one that knows that few marriages aren't touched by tragedy, few experiences of motherhood or fatherhood don't involve loss, and asks what lightness and grace, what renunciation of ownership, might be required to avoid this. If we own our children, then every child carries within her the seeds of a violent custody battle. And the ways in which parenthood always involves an element of ownership is especially fraught in societies where ownership itself is a virulent ideology.

So how might you set yourself and your child free? And how can you do that within a legal system that still enacts principles of ownership, decades after women like Elizabeth Packard fought to give children autonomy?

May Poole, Alice Walker's great-great-great-great grandmother

For Alice Walker, this birth brought a reckoning with the history that had made it slowly possible. A century earlier, there had been her great-great-great-great grandmother May Poole: the walker who would make Alice and Rebecca proud to be Walkers; a slave who walked from Virginia to Georgia with two children on her hips – squalling babies she managed to keep alive traversing over five hundred miles, seeking the freedom to mother without their being sold away.

In Alice Walker's own times, there had been the civil rights struggle that brought precisely this: the birth certificate of a legitimate mixed-race child, albeit one whose parents' marriage wouldn't have been allowed in Mississippi. But there were other struggles in the mix. Several generations after Elizabeth Packard, Alice Walker was part of a new wave of feminism – a struggle for women's liberation that was a struggle to the death in her case, because she knew that if she couldn't write, she couldn't live. And as one of first generations of Black women to find a voice in print, she felt she had a calling to write about her community. This meant that when she was with her baby, she'd always be somewhere else too, dreaming and strenuously willing her books into being, living among the bloodier lives of imagined mothers and children. How could she allow herself these divided loyalties and also wrest her right to mother from the violence of the South?

It was all destined to implode, and its implosion would result in the disorientating custody decision made on behalf of seven-year-old Rebecca: two years with one parent and then two years with the other; a lifetime of attempting to live two lives in parallel by living them in succession. This was a custody decision made without lawyers at a time when the law lagged behind other forms of social progress – and liberated, bisexual Black women like Alice Walker usually lost their children. It was a decision made in the face of violence; made to honour equality and freedom and to thwart the white and male brutality that combine to ruin Ruth's life in *Grange Copeland*. In the midst of seething historical change, Alice Walker and Mel Leventhal attempted to honour the gains of both the civil rights movement and feminism. But the civil rights movement was an extreme, rapid arc of hope and loss, and to place a child at the centre of the hope was also to place her at the centre of the loss, and to make her live through her nation's failures in extravagant, intense ways. And in turn their decision was a harbinger of an era of 50/50 custody decisions that can feel as though they split our children in half.

I. From daughterhood to motherhood

'I had to face up to the system that had almost done me in'

Alice Walker was the eighth baby in a family who could barely afford to feed their existing children, yet she was so adored that she smiled her way to first prize in a series of baby contests, sure of her right to love. At first she was settled under a tree while her mother planted seeds in the cotton fields. Then she was left behind with her devoted older sister and sent, ahead of time, to school. She missed her mother, the soft, loving-eyed woman who battled on behalf of the children with their white landlords when they tried to make them work; she later wrote that she 'died each day she was away'. Her mother worked as hard as the men in the community but also found time to make clothes and quilts and to grow fruit and vegetables in the ambitiously luxuriant gardens she planted outside their succession of barely liveable houses.[3]

> They were women then
> My mama's generation
> Husky of voice – Stout of
> Step

> With fists as well as
> Hands
> How they battered down
> Doors
> And ironed
> Starched white
> Shirts[4]

This was the late 1940s and they were living in Wards Chapel, a lush settlement on the banks of the Oconee River, a few miles out of the small Georgia town of Eatonton. Alice did well in the makeshift, segregated school her father and his friends had built out of an abandoned army barracks. She read everything she could find; she wrote stories with twigs and pencils on scraps of paper; and she wandered outside, less afraid than her friends of snakes and spiders, engrossed by clouds and trees. It was an idyll of a kind, darkened by the violence surrounding them, and the desperate poverty they were always only just holding back. And then when she was eight it was shattered during a game when her brother shot her in the eye with his airgun. Her father tried to hitchhike to hospital with his screaming daughter, but no one would stop for a Black man, so by the time she saw a doctor it was too late. She would never see again out of that eye and felt blighted by the 'glob of whitish scar tissue, a hideous cataract' for a decade. She felt betrayed by her brother, who made her lie about the injury, and by her parents, who didn't blame him even after the truth emerged.[5]

Her family was on the move again – twenty miles south to Milledgeville – and she was sent to a new school built in an old prison, with the imprint of the electric chair still visible in the classroom. She was miserable, so her parents sent her back to her grandparents in Wards Chapel. She would remember this banishment forever. 'My parents didn't explain why, what, when, or anything,' she would later write; 'it was decided and off I went.' When she returned, she felt a rift with her father. He was a heroic figure, in his way. Aged eleven, he'd cradled his dying mother in his arms on a dusty road after she'd been shot down by a disappointed lover. He'd risked his life to become one of the first Black men to vote in the 1940s and he was committed to educating his daughters as well as his sons. But he was narrowing, refusing to let his sons sweep a floor or wash a dish – because this was women's work.[6]

Alice Walker's determination to resist segregation came on suddenly. Under the Jim Crow laws, Black people in Georgia were forced to use separate water fountains and phone booths; the courts offered one Bible to white witnesses and another to Blacks. Alice would later write that her community didn't discuss their hatred of white people: 'It was understood that they were – generally – vicious and unfair, like floods, earthquakes, or other natural catastrophes. Your job, if you were black, was to live with that knowledge.'[7]

She realised how wearying and degrading this all was when, aged sixteen, she discovered Martin Luther King Jr. Her mother was working as a maid now and liked the white soap operas her employers watched, so she'd saved up for a small TV. In October 1960, Alice finally saw a Black person appear on the screen. Martin Luther King Jr was being thrown into a police car after leading a protest in Alabama. For the first time she heard 'We Shall Overcome' sung by protestors, and saw a Black man apparently fearless in police custody. 'He had dared to claim his right as a native son, and had been arrested. He displayed no fear, but seemed calm and serene, unaware of his own extraordinary courage. His whole body, like his conscience, was at peace.' She found out more about the civil rights movement gathering in the South: the sit-ins that had begun that February, when students occupied a department store café that refused to serve Blacks. Her older siblings had left Georgia, seeking better lives in the North, but she decided to stay and resist the forces that made it so difficult to have a good life in the South as a Black woman.[8]

She went to college at Spelman in Atlanta, Georgia's capital. Six years after Rosa Parks had helped ignite the civil rights movement by refusing to sit in the designated Black section in a bus, Alice Walker sat defiantly at the front of the bus taking her from Eatonton to Atlanta. A white woman complained and the driver ordered her to move. 'But even as I moved,' she later wrote, 'in confusion and anger and tears, I knew he had not seen the last of me.' In Atlanta she attended protests, doing her best at radicalism in a disappointingly conservative institution; the college had been founded by white missionaries to turn Black women into young ladies. She loved the landscape, with its profusions of cherry trees and the rippling hills that were so verdant that in springtime even the air seemed green. But when her most radical tutor was sacked, she decided to leave, gaining a full scholarship to Sarah Lawrence, a private women's liberal arts college in Yonkers, New York. Here there were new difficulties – Black students were a definite minority – yet a new sense of belonging. She was writing poetry and became part of a community of ambitious young writers fusing politics and literature.[9]

She had left the South, but not for long. In the summer of 1965, she joined civil rights workers registering votes in Liberty County, Georgia. Two years earlier, John F. Kennedy had declared segregation unconstitutional: 'We preach freedom around the world, and we mean it. But are we to say to the world – and much more importantly to each other – that this is the land of the free, except for Negros.' Gradually, Black students were being admitted into white schools and colleges, but for large-scale change, Black politicians and Black voters were required. Most Southern states had absurd literacy tests and property requirements that made it hard for Black voters to register, so Black and white activists were helping Black voters overcome these and face down the intimidating violence at the polls.

This dangerous aggression was too much for Alice, encountering it for the first time; she worried that the rocks and bottles thrown at the civil rights workers would destroy her one remaining eye. This was the era of the pan-African movement, with African

Americans seeking to connect to their African roots, so she left abruptly for Africa, where she helped build a school out of sisal stalks in Kenya and had a love affair with a white Peace Corps worker in Tanzania. She returned to New York disillusioned by the poverty and inequality she'd found in Africa, and pregnant.[10]

For three days she lay in bed with a razor blade under her pillow, planning to kill herself. She'd only felt able to tell three friends about her pregnancy and no one could help her; abortion was illegal and expensive. Though her family would be shocked and hurt if she died, she felt they'd be more devastated by the shame of her pregnancy. She wanted to write and to fight in an unjust world and couldn't see how she'd do this as an unmarried mother.

Then, just in time, a friend found the money for an abortion and her life began again. She finished her degree, completed her first volume of clipped, earnest, probing poems, and got a job as a case worker with the New York welfare department. Six months in, she was offered a grant by a Sarah Lawrence College donor and gave up her job in order to write. Aged thirteen, she'd seen the mutilated body of one of her classmates' mothers, who had been murdered by her husband as she walked home on Christmas Day with their groceries. There was a mass of gore where her face once had been. Alice Walker wanted to tell her story, and to find a way to witness the brutality she'd grown up with. To do this she had to return South. She booked a flight to Mississippi.

'Mississippi Goddam', Nina Simone sang in 1964, with her mixture of plainspokenness and verve dramatising the desperate rage of a generation. Bordered by the undulations of the river it takes its name from, Mississippi had the highest percentage of Blacks of any state in America (43 per cent) and the most stringent voting restrictions, though these had been made illegal by President Lyndon B. Johnson's

1965 Voting Rights Act, which nonetheless failed to establish a constitutional right to vote. Fourteen-year-old Emmett Till had been murdered here on holiday from Chicago in 1955 for talking to a white woman, with photographs of his disfigured corpse acting as a call to arms across the South; the NAACP (National Association for the Advancement of Colored People) field secretary Medgar Evers had been shot on his own doorstep in Jackson, Mississippi, in 1963. Students visiting to register voters in 1964 had found it a foreign county. One described the violence hanging overhead like 'dead air – it hangs there and maybe it'll fall and maybe it won't'. This was the place Alice Walker took on in the summer of 1966, drawn by an offer to work with the NAACP Legal Defence and Educational Fund (LDF). 'All my life Mississippi had been the epitome of evil for black people,' she later said. 'I knew that if I was to be able to live at all in America, I needed to be able to live unafraid, anywhere. I had to face up to the system that had almost done me in and so many of my people. Mississippi was the test.'[11]

500 *African American demonstrators are blocked by police in Jackson, Mississippi, in June 1963 after a memorial march for Medgar Evers*

The tests began straight away. She was sent to Greenwood with Mel Leventhal, a white law student interning with the LDF. Alice was responsible for taking depositions from Blacks evicted for trying to vote, building evidence for lawsuits. Greenwood was one of the most dangerous Mississippi cities for activists and they were terrified that the motel staff would tell the local chapter of the Ku Klux Klan that they'd checked in. So they shared a room where, too frightened to sleep, they read aloud from the only book they could find – the Bible. The Jewish law student overcame the Black writer's distrust of whites in the civil rights movement with his passionate recitation of the visionary and erotic Old Testament book the *Song of Songs*. 'Let him kiss me with the kisses of his mouth!' he read. 'For your love is better than wine.' Alice would look back on this as the moment when their 'souls touched' and she took in Mel as a 'deeply committed, passionate man'.[12]

They soon became lovers, brought together by the heady dangers of Mississippi and a shared commitment to the cause. Alice was impressed when Mel took her side after they were hauled over by the police; and when he shared her ice cream, two red tongues defying their differences of skin colour. She recreated the scene years later, in an elegiac memoir addressed to her ex-husband:

Your hair was glowing. Your brown eyes filled with warmth. You just loved chocolate, you said. Especially ice cream. I offered the cone to you, after taking a huge lick. You accepted it happily and licked rapturously, as if it were the best ice cream you'd ever had. It was a highly erotic moment, an eroticism heightened by the fact that just by licking the same ice cream cone a huge portion of the Old South that had kept my soul and my free expression of eroticism chained was forced to fall. That was it, for me. The moment we bonded, the moment we fell in love. I felt the wonder, the oddness, the lightness, the sureness of it.[13]

They continued to read aloud to each other: poetry by Yeats, Walt Whitman, E. E. Cummings. He read the beginnings of her novel, and recognised its exhilarating originality. Together they put tenderness in the way of violence, uniting in bed to outface the horrors they heard about by day. After her life as an outsider, and his struggles growing up with a single mother whose parents had immigrated to America only a couple of decades earlier, they had both found a 'miraculously compatible mate'. This wasn't going to be easy: both the whites and Blacks disapproved of interracial couples by this point. The civil rights movement was now dominated by the rhetoric of 'Black Power', with the new chairman of the SNCC (Student Nonviolent Coordinating Committee) Stokely Carmichael departing from a Jeffersonian idea of American equality in his vision of a worldwide Black struggle against colonialism.[14]

They went back to New York, where Mel completed his studies, while Alice wrote her novel. He taught her to swim, floating alongside her in the night in the university pool, and taught her to drive his little red car. Then they were ready to take on Mississippi again, but first they got married in New York, where interracial marriages were now legal. And then began perhaps the most gruelling, productive and eventually transformative decade of Alice Walker's life. They were living in Jackson, and the more of a civil rights hero Mel became, the more danger they were in. Mel kept a loaded gun at home, and they acquired a German Shepherd dog to protect them. Mel travelled incessantly, fighting lawsuits all over the South, so Alice was alone when threats of firebombs came from the Ku Klux Klan. And she was more affected than Mel when a white man in a restaurant complained: 'They're letting niggers into everything now.'[15]

By early 1968 she was pregnant. They wanted to have a baby partly to save Mel from being drafted in the war that continued, year after unwanted year, in Vietnam, so this pregnancy was desired, however frightened Alice remained that motherhood would stop her writing. But when Martin Luther King Jr was assassinated in April 1968, they joined the devastated funeral procession. Alice miscarried a week later, precipitated, she thought, by her anguish at King's loss: 'I did not even care. It seemed to me, at the time, that if "he" (it was weeks before my tongue could form his name) must die no one deserved to live, not even my own child.' During that funeral she joined other Black activists in giving up on King's doctrine of non-violence. When a man who had just led a peaceful protest on behalf of striking workers had been shot dead on his motel balcony, retaliation seemed required. Stokely Carmichael declared that 'when white America killed Dr King she declared war on black America and there could be no alternative to retribution'.[16]

Gradually, she came back to life, and another foetus settled itself in her womb. Nixon was in power, slowing the pace of school desegregation and assiduously chipping away at the liberal settlement. 'The Movement as we knew it is dead,' Alice wrote in her journal. 'The revolution of love has been betrayed. People snap at you now. Blacks and Jews are fighting each other, while the WASPS [White Anglo-Saxon Protestants] control and manipulate.' She was sick and exhausted during the first months of pregnancy, but carried on writing *The Third Life of Grange Copeland*, responding to and transforming the murder of her schoolfriend's mother. This had become a book about three generations of a Southern family mired in bloodshed. Most of all it was about the agony of being a wife and daughter in a world that disempowers women. For her frankness about the misogyny haunting the Black community, Alice Walker would be castigated for decades. 'How can a family, a community, a race, a nation, a world be healthy and strong if one half dominates the other half through threats, intimidation and actual acts of violence?' she wrote in the afterword.[17]

A man, Grange Copeland, neglects and brutalises his wife to the point that, aged ten, his son Brownfield 'thought his mother was like their dog in some ways'. Brownfield runs away, becomes the lover of his father's mistress and her daughter, and falls in love with a young schoolteacher, Mem, who he half-knows is too good for him. He spends the next decade destroying Mem, 'trying to pin the blame for his failure on her by imprinting it on her face'. She becomes haggard – a woman he 'could not want' – which makes it easier for him to abuse her. Briefly, she rises up to better her life. She signs the lease on a new house and reminds him scathingly 'how many times I done got my head beat by you just so you could feel a bit like a man'. When she becomes ill, he takes his revenge, getting into arrears on the rent and dragging them back to poverty. Their baby freezes to death, and their remaining daughters watch as he kills their mother, who doesn't even slow her steps when she returns home one day and sees her husband ready with his gun.[18]

'Why had her mother walked on after she saw the gun?' Ruth asks herself. Though Ruth can't quite bring herself to say it, her mother's death is a dual betrayal: by the father who kills, and by the mother who allows herself to be killed.[19]

One of Ruth's sisters ends up in an asylum and one as a sex worker. And Grange himself, that first abuser, steps up as a father figure to Ruth, chastened and empowered by his years in the North, where he was responsible for the death of a pregnant white woman and has somehow had his self-respect restored by his own act of murder. Able to give Ruth the generous affection he was unable to give her father, Grange helps her get the education that will take her away from poverty. The civil rights movement arrives in Georgia just in time to show her that there are other ways of being Black and a woman, and she's about to embark on a new life as a student and activist when her father claims custody.

'You want to be with your *real* daddy?' the judge asks her. But this man has no claim to father her – so Grange goes through with it, that final act of sacrificial murder: his shooting of his own son.[20]

And so, age twenty-five, while Mel laboured on behalf of the oppressed and the Ku Klux Klan planned their next assault on their home, Alice Walker completed her first novel, and her first masterpiece. *The Third Life of Grange Copeland* is a novel poised between realism and something more fabular, with a narrator who seems to carry the wisdom of centuries. She was using literary realism as a way of processing moral outrage without either scalding the world or yielding to its disasters. After the custody battle that turns out to be the most brutal kind of orphaning, depriving Ruth of two murderous parents, Ruth is left with a kind of visionary clarity. We don't see her as an adult, but it's an extraordinary achievement that this novel full of poverty and exploitation and murder, in which only one of a family of eight survives, should end with hope. It was time for Alice Walker's own baby to be born.

II. Motherhood

'She is the compact, warm, squirming bundle I love to rouse from sleep'

That baby – born to a Black mother and a white husband with his arms full of roses – was a baby conceived out of love and hope, despite the shadow of King's death and the gun by the bed. Jimi Hendrix had just revealed that a Black man could hold America to account in his clamorously plangent guitar rendition of 'Star-Spangled Banner' at Woodstock – an act of both destructive protest and dazzlingly virtuosic self-expression. A new world still seemed possible, incarnated in their wide-eyed fleshy bundle; Alice relished even the hours of pain in the labour ward, which she felt connected her to her mother, who'd done this eight times, without anaesthetic.

Alice Walker with her baby

But ahead were the hours alone with the baby while her husband worked and travelled. He told her he was making a world Rebecca could live in. 'Who would hurt you, Rebecca?' he would ask, holding his daughter nestled against his chest. Even when he was there, he spent many evenings playing poker. There was still the shared laughter and their bedroom, with its giant bed taking up most of the floor 'in frank admission that bed was important to us'. There they spent what time at home they had, 'not making love only, but making a universe' – eating and reading, writing, cuddling, playing with the baby. When Rebecca was two months old, Alice tried to count her blessings. 'She does not seem real to me yet as my daughter,' she wrote. 'But she is the compact, warm, squirming bundle I love to rouse from sleep – holding her against the warmth of my body so that waking will be pleasant, will not jar her. And her eyes, already when she smiles, a bit mischievous.'[21]

Alice was grateful for her love of Mel, and for her mother, who had stayed for four weeks, rocking Rebecca all night. But there were times when she felt locked inside herself with depression;

she'd lost her wedding ring, and she feared that she wasn't up to making a life in the South, taking the gun into bed after nightmares. 'I know that if I had not met him I would not be here now,' she admitted. 'I surprised myself today, for the first time thinking that had I married a black man we would have had sense enough to know we couldn't live in Mississippi . . . Mel wants to stay here to make his mark – am I to stay here till Mississippi makes its mark on <u>me</u>?'[22]

Alice, Mel and Rebecca

By the time Rebecca was crawling, Alice was overwhelmed. 'I can say without exaggeration that the past two years have been primarily miserable,' she recorded in July 1971, aged twenty-seven. 'I, who love dancing, danced once this year.' She worried she was unsuited for motherhood. 'Two days with Rebecca, sweet as she is, turns my hair grey.' She loved her, and missed her when away, but she couldn't disentangle the contradictory feelings. 'It is just I never really made room in myself for the presence of a child . . . But Rebecca, when she runs up to me and hugs my legs, burying her warm little head against me, is so deeply in my heart it is <u>weird</u>! Especially when, sometimes, I find it almost unbelievable that I actually have a child!'[23]

She sent Rebecca to a morning nursery, giving herself time to write, and began lecturing at Tougaloo College. There were moments of intense happiness when Mel came home and rushed to meet his daughter's 'wet and openhearted kisses, her widespread chubby arms', lifting her against his chest, 'his wide face transparent with love', before greeting Alice – 'his thin lips . . . already stuck out' as they triumphed in outwitting racism one more time and living 'to love another day'.[24]

She needed to escape, though, so she applied for a fellowship to the Radcliffe Institute in Cambridge, Massachusetts, to write another novel about the South she was desperate to leave behind. At first, she took Rebecca, but they both got sick in the unfamiliar Boston winter, so Rebecca was sent to Mel, beginning a childhood of journeying between parents and states. 'You are glad Mel is keeping Rebecca,' Alice wrote in her journal, alone in Boston in March 1972. 'It allows you to breathe, to be free in a way you have not been for five years.' Without him, she lost her self-confidence, worrying 'about small imperfections that his kisses would make lovely forever'. But *Grange Copeland* and her first poetry collection had made enough of a mark that she had established herself as a writer, and she was now deep in her new novel, *Meridian*, about a young woman who goes through with an accidental teenage pregnancy.[25]

Meridian is a young, impoverished Black girl growing up in rural Georgia to a mother who should not, we're told matter-of-factly, have had children. This mother 'was capable of thought and growth and action only if unfettered by the needs of dependents'. As a child, Meridian feels full of guilt, though she only later identifies this as guilt for stealing her mother's serenity. In the background is an enslaved great-great-grandmother, who stole back the children who were sold away and was allowed to keep them on condition she provided for them; sacrificing her own needs, she died from slow starvation. This is a book about the civil rights movement that rebirths and destroys Meridian, but it's also fundamentally a book about motherhood as endured in the face of such tragedies from the past. Finding herself accidentally a wife and mother, Meridian is so frightened by her fantasies of murdering her baby son that she conceives methods of killing herself instead. She's still only seventeen, and when her husband leaves and she meets a group of civil rights activists, she decides to give her now beloved child away, believing that she's saving her own life, and to start at the local university. Here, she's haunted by guilt about the child who visits her in nightmares, 'crying, suffering unbearable deprivations because she was not there'. She's stricken by the awful contradiction that beset and enlivened so much of Alice Walker's thinking about motherhood. If her slave ancestors died as a result of their desperate efforts to mother their children, is it a betrayal to admit to the ambivalence that 1960s and 1970s feminism fought to allow mothers: to admit to the boredom and rage as well as the love and joy of motherhood?[26]

At university, Meridian is impregnated by Truman, a Black activist who she loves but who disapproves of her abandonment of her baby and is captivated by white women. Meridian is scarred by the resulting abortion, wasting away alongside the civil rights movement, until she finds solace in the Black church. Meanwhile, the six-year-old daughter of Truman and his white wife Lynn is attacked and dies. It's as though no mother–child relationship can survive this sad book intact, and no child of this generation can sustain the hopes of the movement they were born into. Alice Walker was writing out of the near-annihilation of her first pregnancy, the grief of her miscarriage, and the contradictions of her often very happy motherhood. She couldn't yet work out how she could be an ambivalent mother and still honour the legacy of her enslaved great-grandmothers, though she knew that it was also her duty to her foremothers to take the opportunity they had lacked to live a creative life.

By December she was back in Mississippi with her husband and three-year-old daughter. She was delighted to see Rebecca, who miraculously expelled her grief about her wounded eye by announcing: 'Mommy, there's a *world* in your eye . . . Where did you *get* that world in your eye?' But she was quickly exhausted by both Mississippi and motherhood. 'Being alone all day with Rebecca drives me crazy,' she wrote. She'd started smoking a pipe, which brought out new feelings – 'sexual and strong and not always heterosexual' – that made her wonder how these fantasies might develop into an actual lesbian relationship; she was turning away from Mel.[27]

The race situation had improved in Mississippi since she'd arrived, and Mel had played his part in this. In 1973, as America finally began to withdraw from Vietnam and the Watergate conspiracies were exposed, Alice wrote an essay, comparing Jackson in 1965 – which saw angry whites jeering threateningly when a Black swimmer entered the pool in the main hotel – with Jackson now – when she and Mel could eat lunch together in that same hotel watching an oblivious Black teenager swimming lengths up and down the pool. A year later, she felt herself falling in love with Mel 'all over again, or perhaps for the first time'. However, by February 1974 she felt that 'suicide was just a matter of finding a sharp enough blade' and knew she had to leave Mississippi. She couldn't forget or forgive the harm she'd endured there, and she could no longer believe in herself as a 'Movement sort of person'. Half of her yearned to be on the barricades and felt guilty that she wasn't doing more; the other half just wanted to observe the fight. Besides, Jackson was too far away from the sea; Kentucky Fried Chicken stands were proliferating there, and neon lights were replacing trees. In April, Mel agreed to move to New York. Alice wrote optimistically about her new happiness:

Rebecca is healthy, bright, pretty and no more trouble to me the writer than Virginia Woolf's madness was to her or the worry George Eliot had that she was living unmarried with a married man. Mel shares the care of Rebecca fairly. He appreciates my work – my only worry is that he may be a poker addict. We love each other, after seven years & one near divorce.[28]

They moved to New York just as it entered a period of febrile violence. Car thefts and murders had doubled since Alice and Mel had left, and robberies had gone up tenfold. The crowded subway trains were filthy, covered in graffiti; the theatres and movie palaces of Times Square were closing or showing porn. There was still the cultural vivacity that made it an exhilarating contrast to Mississippi: Lou Reed was performing with his band; Andy Warhol was partying at his Factory. But the world waited to see whether the city was capable of regeneration or was going to collapse altogether, and the signs weren't good. In 1975, President Ford refused a bail out, saying that the bankrupt city's 'day of reckoning' had come. 'FORD TO CITY: DROP DEAD', ran the headline in the *New York Daily News*. Ensconced in a large house in Brooklyn that they set about doing up, Alice Walker took on a job as an editor at *Ms.* magazine and began a phase rooted more in feminism than the civil rights movement. She changed her name back from Leventhal to Walker, allying herself with that first walking Walker who carried her children across the South. Later she would regret marrying, because 'it is such a patriarchal construct and the vestiges of slavery are still a scar on it'. She could feel the bonds of slavery deep in her 'genetic memory' and she resented any form of ownership. Marriage was all the more complicated when it was interracial, and when the Black community was hostile towards white interlopers.[29]

Alice Walker had made it clear in *Grange Copeland* that the problems lay with all men, not just whites. That novel was written after a group of brave female civil rights workers circulated a memo about sexual inequality within the movement ('the only position for women in SNCC is prone', Stokely Carmichael had once tastelessly joked) and after the National Organization for Women (NOW), founded in 1966 by feminists including Betty Friedan, began its campaign for equality in the workplace and federally funded childcare. From the start, Black feminists criticised Friedan for seeing the combination of motherhood and a job as a hard-won privilege rather than, as in the case of Alice's own mother, a grim necessity. But Alice Walker was broadly supportive of the women's liberation movement and glad that Black feminism was finding a voice (in 1973 the National Black Feminist Organization was founded). She'd loved designing and teaching a Black women's literature course at Wellesley College during her time in Boston and she became a passionate advocate for reviving the reputation of the writer Zora Neale Hurston.[30]

Alice distressed some Black feminists with her decision to work at *Ms.*, the magazine launched in 1972 by the energetic, acute glamour-girl-turned-feminist Gloria Steinem to give feminist ideas new zip and gloss. But Alice Walker believed in writing for a mass readership rather than for already converted coteries, and Gloria Steinem quickly became a close friend. 'Gloria is wonderful!' she would write a few years later. 'And I could easily fall in love with her. I guess that's something that happens to her all the time. She's so sweet and smells so good!' Both women had come to feminism through questions of motherhood: Gloria Steinem attributed her own 'great blinding lightbulb' conversion to attending a protest where twelve women had testified about their abortions in 1969.

The civil rights movement had offered one kind of care, and enabled Alice Walker to outgrow her family of origin while also finding new ways to honour it. Now feminism offered another kind of care that gave her the courage to stake a great deal on the personal growth and love possible within a community of women, buoyed by major achievements like the 1973 landmark US Supreme Court ruling on abortion in *Roe v Wade*. The need for new forms of care became ever more urgent as the traditional family structures broke down. In her writing, Alice Walker was testing the place of care in the world, revealing how elastic and how tenacious care remained. She was aware of living in an era of change, and of the feminists around her finding fecund but also frantic ways to invent new versions of care as the old versions were eroded.[31]

She had now lost five wedding rings and wrote to a friend that she was slowly being pulled in two: 'Frankly, I think I'm unsuited for marriage . . . The problem is that Mel is magnificent and leaving him will take just about every ounce of gumption I can muster. And there is the pull of Rebecca, her happiness and so on.' She began to have her tarot cards read and embarked on a new love affair with Robert Allen, a Black writer and editor she'd known at Spelman College. He was in an open marriage that seemed to be in its final stages, though his wife expressed interest in triangulating his affair with Alice. At home, Alice moved her double bed into Rebecca's room and slept beside her six-year-old daughter, crying as she fell asleep. Recalling this time in a later memoir, Rebecca saw this as the moment when she began to look after her mother:

> Night after night Mama and I are tucked into our king-size bed on the warm side of the blood-red velvet curtains, and night after night I fall asleep with my pudgy copper arms wrapped around her neck. As we drift out of consciousness, I feel the ether of my spirit meet the ether of hers and become all tangled up. As I fall asleep I do not know where she starts and I begin. I do know that my mama is hurting and that what I have to give to stop the hurting is myself: my arms, my warmth, my little hands on the side of her face. I no longer am only for myself, but now I'm for her, too. I must be strong. I learn how to forget myself, to take my cues from her, to watch carefully so that I can know what to do.

In many ways it was a kind of mother–daughter closeness that many children long for, but it also gave the daughter responsibility for parenting her mother, and made her painfully conscious that the marriage she'd grown up inside was breaking down. Alice, too, was aware of the shift in roles. 'She is very maternal,' she wrote in her journal. 'She asks me if I would like to rest my head on her shoulder. I say yes. She puts her arm around me, her hand cupped under my chin . . . We have changed places . . . She seems a lot stronger than I was at six.'[32]

There wasn't so much a moment of rupture as a process of attrition. Both Alice and Mel knew the marriage was over, but Mel didn't agree with Alice that they should divide up the house. So in late 1976 Alice moved with Rebecca to a small apartment in Brooklyn and Mel got together with Judith Goldsmith, a white Jewish woman who wanted the affluent suburban life that his mother had wanted for him all along: swanky dinner parties and amplitude. Rebecca pretended to like being picked up from school by Judith: 'Daddy, keep choosing me because I am perfect because I don't make you feel guilty, I don't express my fear, my rage, my hurt. I say only: yes, Daddy, I like her, let's go fly kites in Central Park.'[33]

III. Divorce

'The rearing of a child requires greater stability than a roller-coaster treatment of custody'

Alice and Mel wanted to share custody of Rebecca, but Mel's work was calling him to Washington. So they agreed that Rebecca would go between them for two-year periods. The day Mel needed to get the divorce papers notarised, he was visiting Alice, so he ended up taking her lover Robert Allen with him as his witness. In a world where divorce was associated with acrimony and hatred, they wanted this to be a new model, conducted with continued respect and love. But what should Mel Leventhal write down as their proposed custody arrangements? Their frequent shifts of custody wouldn't have gone down well with the New York judges. In 1974 the Supreme Court of New York had declined a change of residence on the grounds that the court should maintain the 'aim of creating a stable environment for the child and avoiding unnecessary shifts in custody'. That same year, the Courts of Appeals refused to move children who wished to move to live with their father because 'the rearing of a child requires greater stability than a roller-coaster treatment of custody'. And in 1976, the Supreme Court gave sole custody to the mother in *Lyritzis v Lyritzis* because neither the judge nor the psychologists consulted thought the divided weeks (four days with the father, three with the mother) had been working for the child.[34]

The judges had a good point, that we're in danger of forgetting fifty years later. No one wants to live on a roller-coaster, and there's much to be said for continuity. What, though, was the alternative for Alice and Mel? Here were two loving parents, urgently in need both of time with their daughter and time to pursue their own vision of who they were and what they could make in the world. They knew that the courtroom left few people unscathed. No one could know this better than Mel: a lawyer who had fought some of the most bitter court cases of his time. And no one could know this better than Alice: a writer who had written into being one of the most brutal of custody battles; a woman who was having an affair with a married man, was openly curious about wanting to try out loving other women, and who wanted her maternal love to be part of a larger life of love.

And so 50/50 custody made sense, though it couldn't all take place in the same city. Hence their odd custody decision: a forerunner of divided weeks, divided lives, at a time when this was looked on askance by American courts. It was a decision made from within the spirit of the civil rights movement – made in a spirit of creativity and love that nonetheless painfully backfired.

Alice Walker was lucky not to find herself in a custody battle. This was ostensibly an era on the side of mothers. By the late 1930s, most American states had revised their custody laws to emphasise both the 'best interests of the child' and 'maternal preference' – children should live with their mothers where possible. As in England, the conservative idea of the primacy of mother-love enabled better custody settlements for less conventionally 'good' women as well. But by the 1970s, this situation – a distant dream when Elizabeth Packard fought for custody – was under attack from both fathers' rights groups and feminists. And the legal system continued to punish mothers who were seen to ask for too much, and certainly mothers who made time to write in their diary, as Alice Walker did on Christmas Eve, 1977, after Mel had collected Rebecca for Christmas: 'I had some wonderful thoughts about bisexuality . . . The problem with sex is that people have gotten used to thinking you have to be "ambivalent" or "committed" straight or "gay-lesbian". Either-Or. But nature is much more interesting than that.'[35]

Progress provoked reaction, and this was all the more volatile because when it came to questions of child custody, what counted as progress for most feminists had rapidly changed: few campaigning feminists saw extra time with their children as a priority. NOW's 1967 founding statement called for a 'true partnership between the sexes' with 'an equitable sharing of the responsibilities of home and children' during and after marriage. In *Watts v Watts* in 1973, the New York judge set a precedent with his statement that 'the simple fact of being a mother does not, by itself, indicate a capacity or willingness to render a quality of care different from that which the father can provide'. He quoted the seminal anthropologist Margaret Mead's 1954 article on mother–child separation, where she criticised child psychologists like Bowlby who stigmatised even brief separations from the mother, categorising their arguments as 'a new and subtle form of antifeminism in which men – under the guise of exalting the importance of maternity – are tying women more tightly to their children than has been thought necessary since the invention of bottle feeding'. And the judge asserted the equal rights of fathers, under the Fourteenth Amendment to the Constitution, seeing the 'tender years presumption' as an 'unconstitutional discrimination' against men.[36]

There was much that was desirable about these changes, which went alongside the rolling out of immediately available no-fault divorce across America, decades before it was introduced in Britain. But as the 'best interests of the child' prevailed and 'maternal preference' was laid aside, any women who transgressed a very conservative notion of good motherhood laid herself open to legal punishment again here too. As in Britain, the elevation of motherhood was accompanied by a constrictive ideology of the family that led to the scapegoating of women attempting to mother in unconventional relationships. Once maternal preference was gone, transgressive women who might have stood a chance of getting custody in previous decades no longer had a chance. And so in *Feldman v Feldman* in 1974, the mother lost custody to a father who was living in his parents' apartment, and proposed to share his bedroom with his six- and nine-year-old children, because she was having an affair with a married man and her ex-husband had found a few copies of *Screw* magazine in her house, 'indicating promiscuous and lascivious tastes on the part of the plaintiff'. (The appeal court reversed the decision, but probably wouldn't have done if it hadn't been for wholly impractical living arrangements.)[37]

And so in 1975, in Oklahoma, Mrs Brim lost custody of her three-year-old because her boyfriend stayed over a few times a week and 'when a woman starts living with a man without the benefit of marriage . . . this does not agree with the Court's concept of moral conduct'. And so, that same year, the Ohio court took custody from a mother because she hadn't promised to 'abandon the practice of lesbianism' and the court couldn't afford to 'experiment'. And so in 1975, the Texas court took nine-year-old Richard Risher, crying, from the arms of his mother, Mary Jo Risher, because her elder son, aged fifteen, had testified that he'd been embarrassed growing up around his mother's lesbianism. Her ex-husband Douglas Risher had relied on the testimony of a psychologist called Dr Robert Gordon who, though he found that Mary Jo was a 'warm and loving parent' and that Richard expressed 'warm feelings towards his mother', thought that Mary Jo had displayed 'ridiculously poor behaviour' in sending Richard to gym classes at the local YWCA and letting him borrow her lover's daughter's unisex jeans. 'Why didn't you let me tell them?' Richard asked, his body trembling, lunging against his mother when she told him the jury's decision. He went on to ask the question she couldn't answer: 'How long will I have to stay, Mamma?'[38]

And so, in 1976, in the same year and the same state as Alice Walker and Mel Leventhal made their custody decision, a mother lost custody of a ten-year-old daughter who had been in her sole care since the age of two, because, though the mother was taking care of the physical needs of her child in a satisfactory manner, 'the home environment with her homosexual partner in residence is not a proper atmosphere in which to bring up this child or in the best interest of this child'. And so, in 1977 in New Jersey, Sandra Panzino lost custody of her two daughters she'd brought up alone for the last seven years on the grounds that they might be stigmatised because of her lesbianism.[39]

The law had made more progress when it came to race than

sexuality. The 1950 judgment in *Ward v Ward* that mixed-race children would be better off with their Black parent because 'they will have a much better opportunity to take their rightful place in society if they are brought up among their own people', would have been extremely unlikely by the 1970s. In *Tucker v Tucker* in 1975, the Washington court found that 'race alone cannot outweigh all other considerations and be decisive of the question'. The Pennsylvanian judge in *Lucas v Kreischer* ruled in 1973 that though racial tension and prejudice did exist, he hoped that children raised in a 'happy and stable home' would cope with such prejudices and 'learn that people are unique individuals who should be judged as such'.[40]

But people of colour still reported experiencing racism within the court system, especially Black women who were seen as sexually transgressive. After the African-American lesbian mother Earnestine Blue lost custody in California in 1974, she said that the judge had seemed off-hand and abrupt in court. 'I think that homophobia plays into it, I think that racism plays into it. I think that the judge did not care because both of us were African-Americans. I think that they felt like I was way worse because I was a lesbian.' She didn't stay to give her children up. She fled for Utah with her lover and her children, and began again. For the children, she later said, it 'felt like a game'. Until, presumably, it didn't, and they took in the magnitude of what they'd lost.[41]

Organisations were emerging to help lesbian mothers. There was the Lesbian Mothers National Defense Fund, founded in Seattle in 1974 with the slogan 'Raising our Children is a Right. Not a Heterosexual Privilege'. And there was the Lesbian Mothers Union, founded in California by a group of activists led by Del Martin and Pat Norman in 1971. Pat Norman was herself a Black lesbian mother who had lost custody of her children to her husband Paul Norman. She'd come out as a lesbian and moved from Pennsylvania to San Francisco in 1969, planning to send for her four children once she had got herself established. In her absence, her husband filed for custody and put the children in the foster home. A year later, she went to court in Pennsylvania to retrieve her children and moved them with her to San Francisco's Haight-Ashbury district, where the drugs and hair still flowed freely three years after the 'Summer of Love', and where gay solidarity redefined family life as a community enterprise. As she tried to help her children adjust to their second rupture in two years, she tried also to prevent these ruptures in other families, becoming part of the larger movement fighting for the rights of lesbian mothers.

But should this have been about mothers' rights and fathers' rights? What about the rights of children to have agency within their own lives? In 1967, the American legal system had made a huge leap forward in the autonomy it gave children in criminal cases. In the sweltering, dry Arizona heat in June 1964, fifteen-year-old Jerry Gault allegedly made obscene phone calls to an elderly neighbour. The next day, with just an informal hearing, he was incarcerated in a correctional institution until the age of twenty-one – though an adult making lewd calls would just be locked up for a maximum of two months. His parents pointed out that he hadn't had a proper trial or been represented by a lawyer. Doggedly, his mother took the case through all the Arizona courts and then on to the Supreme Court in 1966, where the Warren Court – the court led by Chief Justice Earl Warren from 1953–69 which remains the most liberal in American history – found unanimously in favour of Jerry's right to a proper trial.

As a result, children in juvenile court criminal actions gained nearly all the same due processes as adults, including the right to lawyers. Yet no one was suggesting that they should have their own lawyers in custody cases. The whole family courts system was now predicated on the 'best interests' of the child. This assumption that the best interests of the child could be isolated and realised was flawed not because it made too much of the children, but because it too frequently ended up denying them agency. Their feelings and desires were very rarely the deciding factor; the interests were meant to be those of the child, but they were defined for them by authorities and experts. And courts were in danger of forgetting that children were part of a delicate family ecosystem, subject to court cases that too often left one parent traumatised and the other over-empowered, neither of which was in their best interests.

Rebecca Walker didn't have to ask – as Richard Risher did – 'How long will I have to stay, Mamma?' These parents were more communicative and more collaborative so she had her answers, though they may not have been what she wanted to hear. 'Our intention was for Rebecca to grow up with both of us and to have as much stability as possible, given the circumstances,' Alice later said, a little defensively. 'The decision was made out of total love.'[42]

For the first two years after they made their custody decision, Rebecca lived with Alice in Brooklyn, in their cramped rental apartment and then in a house that Alice managed to buy. At first Alice felt unmoored without Mel – she had relied on him so long, and for so much. There were nights like the one she recorded in sad detail in her diary a year in, when the kitten that Rebecca had asked to get, to keep her mother company, got lost. Alice half-knew that Rebecca shouldn't see her mother as needing a kitten, and felt all the more helpless now that she couldn't even keep it safe. She was upset that Mel was moving on faster than she was; he'd even dug up her roses in the garden of the marital home: 'In uprooting the roses they were <u>destroying my garden</u>, the metaphor and <u>fact</u> of my existence.' Tellingly, it was Mel who located the kitten, when he returned Rebecca the next day.[43]

Gradually, Alice felt less grief for her old life, and in both of their accounts, this was a period of extreme closeness between mother and daughter. Rebecca turned eight in November 1977. They would read in bed together, Alice reading Marilyn French's feminist tale of disillusioned marriage *The Women's Room* ('insight written as trash – good!') and Rebecca reading a novel about witches: 'close, warm, good'. Mel moved to Washington and Alice began to have sex with women, and to feel she could be happy on her own, 'supporting myself and Rebecca'. For her part, Rebecca tried to assert herself, showing her mother that she wasn't prepared to be taken for granted. The depression returned, though, when Alice thought of Rebecca's impending departure in July.

By April the following year, she was trembling inside, frightened by the separation. She analysed her feelings for her daughter clinically, noticing that she felt distant from her when she saw a streak of Mel's mother in her – 'self-centredness. Vanity.' By July, she was hyper-aware of each of her mood shifts with her daughter, recording their 'moments of incredible love & sweetness – as if we're missing each other already' and also their periods of estrangement – 'as when she kept wanting me to go bike riding on a hot, muggy day and I had just told her I was hot, tired and had cramps'. She admired her daughter's loving generosity and worried about her self-absorption. 'What I like is her sense of humor – if all else fails, she finds a reason to crack-up – & her laugh is loud & dumb & causes people to stare (& laugh) just like mine.'[44]

Parting: this was the first of many, and may have been the hardest. Rebecca didn't know how to say goodbye: 'Shouldn't there be something else we can do, some kind of magic trick where she can come inside my body and I can go inside hers?' She cried, and her father told her it was time to leave and go to his house. 'But where do I live? Which house is mine?' Rebecca asked herself. This is the loss children suffer in divorce: the house they can claim as home splits into 'Mummy's' and 'Daddy's' houses. Arriving at her father's house she sniffed, longing to catch a whiff of her mother's 'sweet, cherry-brown scent', longing for the bright colours of Alice's rooms in this white and beige world.[45]

And then they were apart, though they met briefly in November when Alice was in Washington, and spoke on Rebecca's ninth birthday. Mel and his wife Judy had a new baby and Alice and Rebecca mourned the loss of their family. When she saw Rebecca for the Christmas holidays, Alice assured her that her daddy would love her just the same, but she worried in her journal that she didn't really know this: 'Mel has a lot of love, but seems most comfortable keeping it in one channel.' In Washington, Rebecca gradually learnt to think of Judy as a second mother, calling her 'Mom'. She felt duplicitous, but Judy was, after all, looking after her most of the time while her father worked. This was a 'suburban fairy-tale' of white family life, complete with ballet lessons, and Rebecca felt she had to hide her difference and Blackness. The problem was that, although she felt loved in both her families, neither felt like hers: 'My little copper-coloured body that held so much promise and broke so many rules. I no longer make sense. I am a remnant, a throwaway, a painful reminder of a happier and more optimistic but ultimately unsustainable time . . . Who am I if not a Movement Child?'[46]

In August 1979, Rebecca moved to join Alice in her new flat in San Francisco. Alice had rented out the Brooklyn house and followed Robert Allen west, where she'd managed to get a flat in the St Francis Square housing cooperative – built by the unions in 1964 to provide affordable housing for people who had lost their homes in the 1950s slum clearance programme in the predominantly Black Fillmore district, described by James Baldwin as 'Negro removal'. Residents had 'Plant Days' of communal gardening and eating; they were within easy reach of Japantown and only a couple of miles away from Haight-Ashbury. It was a city of violence and riots and protest and dreams, living through the death of the 1960s in slow motion and searching frenziedly for new kinds of utopian promise. Harvey Milk had been assassinated a year earlier after being elected to the San Francisco Board of Supervisors as an openly gay man; the red-light district was proliferating but so were the feminists advocating for rights on the sex workers' behalf. At a time when the country was in the midst of financial collapse, suffering from an energy crisis and the worst inflation in decades, Alice had found a haven where she could make a hopeful life. This hope was enabled by transcendental meditation, prayer and the love of Robert – a man who was often petty and who frightened her with his love of pornography, but who gave her 'walks, the moon, pens that write smoothly, in pretty colors . . . love that is as vulnerable as my own'. But most of all this hope was enabled by writing. Sure of her literary powers, she had embarked on *The Color Purple*, the book with which she hoped to reveal the violence in the Black community that was the legacy of slavery and to find possibilities of redemption within it. Now, after two years, her life was going to include hands-on motherhood as well.[47]

Preparing for Rebecca's return, Alice wrote the poem 'My Daughter is Coming':

> I have bought her a bed
> and a chair
> a mirror, a lamp
> and a desk.
> Her room is all ready
> except that the curtains
> are torn.
> Do I have time to buy shoji panels
> for the window?
> I do not.

She listed the things she had to do first: she had to see her doctor about her tonsils, write a speech and then cross the country to 'liberate my daughter/ from her father and Washington'.[48]

'Liberate', 'my': the faultlines of joint custody emerge here in Alice's powerfully casual revelation that she sees Rebecca as freer with her. And then the examination of the bedroom continues:

> Will she like her bed,
> her chair, her mirror
> desk and lamp
>
> Or will she see only
> the torn curtains?[49]

It's a familiar image from custody: the home made strange by absence; the sense that the child who returns sees things with an objective distance. And Alice was right to be apprehensive. The easy reciprocity of Brooklyn was gone, and now they had to adjust to each other. 'Her talking exhausts me – but she tries very hard not to be too much for me, & I appreciate it,' Alice wrote in her journal. A month later, she could announce that they were becoming friends, though Alice recognised she was often distracted. Rebecca felt sad that she was living in a house her father had never been to, and that she didn't feel she could tell him about the bullying she was experiencing at school. He didn't ask much about her new life and their phone conversations began to feel false. 'I don't tell him about . . . people calling me yellow or about being hit. I keep all that inside and try to sound happy when he calls, or tough, like I am handling everything, like the world Mama lives in is perfect.'[50]

Alice had worried, in the lead up to her daughter's return, that she wouldn't be able to write *The Color Purple* alongside her. Alone, she'd been able to plunge back into the past of her community, becoming drenched in a world where daughters are raped by stepfathers, where wives are habitually beaten by husbands, and to find in it possibilities for transcendence and love. But could she do this alongside her daughter? In a playful essay, she later described her character Shug's scepticism about whether it was going to work: her own children had been raised by her mother, and the protagonist Celie didn't even know where her children were. But then, when Rebecca arrived, 'smart, sensitive, cheerful, at school most of the day, but quick with tea and sympathy on her return', her characters adored her. 'When she came home from school one day with bruises but said, you should see the other guy, Celie . . . began to reappraise her own condition. Rebecca gave her courage (which she *always* gives me) – and Celie grew to like her so much she would wait until three-thirty to visit me.'[51]

Tea and sympathy, courage given by a daughter to a mother – shouldn't it have been the other way round? Rebecca had a lot to adapt to, moving from her conventional life in the Washington suburbs to find her mother in passionate dialogue with imaginary characters. It was a huge achievement on both sides that Rebecca ended up playing a part in these conversations, and the creative symbiosis between mother and daughter was clearly intense. However, the custody situation made all this much harder. It was one thing to have a mother who was also a feminist, pursuing new goals of self-realisation, also a writer living partly inside her own head, also a lover exploring her own sexuality; but it would become apparent over the next decade that when the ruptures of custody were added to this, Rebecca was unable to feel secure.

There the mother was, nonetheless, writing her book, which begins and ends with motherhood. At the beginning of *The Color Purple*, Celie gives birth to two children conceived by rape, and then has them returned to her at the end in a final act of hard-won redemption. And though they have all been tested with extremes of suffering by this point, almost everyone around her has learnt the value of love and care – because motherhood in this book is more a way of being than a biological fact, and communities thrive here when mothering is done freely and collectively. Celie, who misses her children with a buried anguish, is relieved to find their foster mother Corrine mothering them well. Nettie, who misses Celie, becomes mothered by Corrine too, only to find herself becoming another mother to Celie's children. Unhappily married to the violent and neglectful Albert, Celie mothers his children dutifully but coldly, until she gets drawn into the love affair between her stepson Harpo and his fiery wife Sofia.

And then she meets Albert's mistress, the dazzling, defiant blues singer Shug Avery, and finds new kinds of maternal resources, persuading Shug to eat when she's close to death. Shug herself is more a petulant child than a maternal figure – she doesn't miss her own children at all – but she becomes kinder, lit by Celie's adoration, and when the two come together as lovers they learn to mother each other. Shug's mouth on Celie's breast is 'something real soft and wet . . . like one of my little lost babies mouth'. Flooded by this blend of tenderness and eros, Celie finds that 'way after while, I act like a lost baby too'. The two women become 'each other's people now', as Shug puts it, and their kinship is strong enough to transform those around them. Almost miraculously, Albert is able to find his way out of the cruelty and rage and lust he's been born to, and to become a good and gentle man.[52]

What's so notable about *The Color Purple* is its astonishing confidence. From the first page, where we hear Celie's voice in the diary she writes as letters to God, using matter-of-fact vernacular prose that becomes richly distinctive and rivetingly dramatic, the book's total commitment to its world is clear. If Alice Walker wanted to write a book for her generation to recognise and process the appalling violence still shadowing the Black community, she didn't do it with flaring, stylised sentences; she just stubbornly dwelt alongside her characters in all their confusion and wonder, remaining magnificently committed to their reality, and trusted them to carry the reader with them. And she did this in the service of a vision of care that was shaped by the bodily bonds of mother love, but moved beyond the individual mother as caregiver into an expansive sense of communal possibility.

While Alice dwelt with her imaginary interlocuters, Rebecca managed to make actual friends – just in time to leave them again. Packing to go east in 1981, she prepared to leave not just her mother, but her friends, the phone her mother had installed in her room, the bookshelves built specially for her, the bus system she was just beginning to know. She couldn't bear to say goodbye to Lisa, her best friend, though Lisa came twice and rang the bell. Rebecca looked out from her bedroom window, watching as her friend pressed the buzzer and stamped her feet in frustration. On her second visit, Lisa caught Rebecca's eye through the window: 'My stomach is churning and I break into a sweat but I do not answer the door. I never see Lisa again.'[53]

There seems to have been a kind of turning point. The move to San Francisco, when she was aged nine, would be the last time Rebecca settled easily. Her father had moved to Riverdale, a residential neighbourhood of the Bronx in New York, so aged eleven, Rebecca had a new set of friends to try to adapt to. And then they moved again, this time to Larchmont, a plush suburban village where everyone was white. Out with her siblings, Rebecca overheard a woman marvelling at their young but capable nanny. When Rebecca tried to tell her father how unhappy she was, he said she was exaggerating. He was being practical rather than cruel; he knew that there were children suffering more than this – he'd fought for many of them in courts of law – and he couldn't reasonably expect his wife to live in a suburb she disliked for the sake of a daughter he only had part-time. But by the time Rebecca returned to San Francisco, aged thirteen in 1983, she at least had decided there wasn't going to be any more moving. She was fed up with crossing from Jewish to Black, from middle class to bohemian, from planet to planet between universes that never seemed to overlap.

It's hard to know what to make of Alice Walker and Mel Leventhal allowing this situation to go on for as long as it did. Alice would write, decade after decade, about her grief at her own mother leaving her behind when she went to work in the fields; she seems to have meant it when she said she 'died each day she was away' from her. Years later, she still felt outraged at her parents' failure to 'explain why, what, when, or anything' when she was sent to her grandparents after her accident. In her seventies, on Radio 4's *Desert Island Discs*, she talked again about missing her mother, and chose John Lennon's complex, clamorous ballad 'Mother', with its fiercely poignant evocation of Lennon's own separation from his mother from the age of five. Walker recorded the programme during one of the periodic estrangements from her daughter that have characterised Rebecca's adulthood, and in speaking about her sadness in the separation, she seems to have experienced the song from Rebecca's perspective too: 'When I heard him singing "Mother" he hit just that place of pain and sorrow when the mother leaves, whether it's your mother, or whether you're the mother.' But she could never quite acknowledge the harm of her own absences, or see that Rebecca had more cause than she did to die, again and again, at the separations inflicted on her.[54]

Yet what should they have done, these two loving parents who both wanted to be involved in Rebecca's day-to-day care but had totally different needs as to where and how to live? Mel was no longer the passionate young man reading the *Song of Songs* and licking Alice's ice cream. But even as he moved his family to Larchmont, he was still the father who had rushed home to meet his daughter's kisses, the father Rebecca remembered pretending to tell her off when she got out of bed in the night to come into their room, but laughing instead, telling her she was the best daughter in the world. Mel wanted to be there for his daughter, even if being there for her meant leaving it to Judy to take her to school or explain to her how babies were conceived. Because he hasn't written anything about these years himself, Mel is a more shadowy figure than his daughter and ex-wife, seen mainly through their memories. The story of custody is a story defined and controlled for the most part by men, but it's notable how few men have written about the daily experience of custody. I wish I could read Mel's memories from these years, alongside Alice's. What's clear is that he couldn't bear the thought of abandoning Rebecca, as his own father had abandoned him, and that meant sticking to the plan of fathering her half of the time.

The alternative was for Alice to fight him in court, where she'd have probably lost. Or she could have moved to New York, where she was convinced, rightly or wrongly, she would not be able to write, and where her daughter was no happier than she was. Instead, she stuck with their imperfect compromise and in a world of Douglas Rishers and Paul Normans, Mel Leventhal managed not to fall into the narrow, punitive thinking of other ex-husbands. He gave Alice her freedom, over and over again. The result was *The Color Purple*, a Pulitzer Prize-winning novel that redefined the role of Black female writers in American literature. It was also the unhappiness of Rebecca – who felt that she'd been given too much freedom, seen too much as an independent person, while being denied genuine independence through the custody arrangements. With Alice, she was required to choose her own junior high and to look after herself during her mother's trips away on book tours, or to Boonville, the village in the Anderson Valley a couple of hours from San Francisco where Alice Walker had bought land and was building a house. During one of her mother's absences, Rebecca began to have sex with an older boy, telling him she was older than fourteen. She became pregnant, even younger than Alice had been at her first pregnancy, and Alice organised her abortion. The world had moved on: this abortion was legal, and Rebecca, unlike Alice, was escorted to the doctor by her mother. Afterwards they went to the cinema to see Prince's film *Purple Rain*.

Aged sixteen, Rebecca began to find ways to assert her own autonomy. She changed her name from Rebecca Leventhal, taking the surname Walker, wanting – like Alice – to tread the footsteps of her walking ancestor and 'determined to be on the right side of any and all equations having to do with social justice'. When Steven Spielberg made a film of *The Color Purple* in 1985, Rebecca was given a job on set. 'My daughter amazes me with her beauty and competence,' Alice wrote in her journal. 'Everyone congratulates me. It is the purest joy to hear her loud, ringing voice piercing through the set . . . I like her tallness, her directness, her characteristic cheerful & no-shit attitude. I know she would not like to get along without me, but she could. She is already herself.'

It was true: she probably could get along on her own by now. But it was also true that she wouldn't want to. Soon it would emerge just how much Rebecca still wanted the parenting she had somehow lost out on in the years dominated by custody.[55]

III. Surviving divorce

'It's gotten so that what passes for a happy ending is a no-fault divorce'

By the time Rebecca Walker was issuing instructions on the film set, it was evident how ahead of their time Alice Walker and Mel Leventhal's ideas of custody had been. Even when they made their custody decision, it was becoming more common to share legal custody, if not physical custody. In *Perotti v Perotti* in 1974, the Supreme Court of New York had given physical custody to the father but legal custody to both parents, on the grounds that the 1973 Domestic Relations Law now made a married woman joint guardian of her children, and that, though the 'traumatic upheavals' brought about by a 'broken home' were difficult for children, 'joint custody' could offer 'psychological support and uplift' to the parents and enable the child to feel their 'mutual love'. It was only a matter of time before children were splitting weeks – like Carlo and Sasha Gébler in London, or months or, less frequently, years. But arguably, this shift, driven by the fathers' rights movement on the one hand and the feminist movement on the other, was a shift towards seeing children as property once again. In the late nineteenth and early twentieth century, courts had moved away from treating children as possessions owned by fathers, and treated them instead as people with rights of their own. For most children, maternal custody meant being in the care of the parent they were most strongly bonded with and dependent on. The changes of the 1970s were driven by a sense that the parents had equal rights to their children and that men and women should be seen as equal. There was nothing wrong with these assumptions, but what followed was a kind of fantasy of fairness that risked effectively splitting the children down the middle, as Solomon threatened. And all this was justified by the doctrine of the best interests of the child.[56]

This was the era of the great divorce film. Indeed, there was so much divorce on film and TV that the columnist Ellen Goodman quipped in 1977 that in the 1970s love story, 'it's gotten so that what passes for a happy ending is a no-fault divorce'. Ingmar Bergman's *Scenes from a Marriage*, Sydney Pollack's *The Way We Were*, starring Barbra Streisand and Robert Redford – these were movies, Goodman added, 'about the people who survive romance, rather than romances that survive'. She wrote this before *Kramer vs. Kramer* inaugurated the genre of custody cinema in 1979.[57]

Kramer vs. Kramer is a film about a mother made unhappy first by the constrictions of mid-century idealised motherhood and then by the freedoms of self-realisation proffered by feminism, and a father so ensnared by the corporate advertising world that he's forgotten to love his son. When Joanna leaves, crying – frightened, like Alice Walker's Meridian, that she's no good for their son Billy and that 'one day next week maybe next year I'll go out the window' – Ted Kramer fumbles his way from comically catastrophic breakfast-making with his son to devoted fatherhood, so much so that he loses his job because he stays home when his son has a temperature and insists on attending his school play. Joanna returns and fights for custody.[58]

A bloodbath ensues. Joanna is asked to enumerate her lovers in court and blamed for the failure of the marriage, while Ted is ridiculed for losing his job and chastised for his son's fall in the playground. This is a tragedy with Billy at its heart; we've seen him grieving for his mother and now see him crying distraught at the thought that his father won't be there to kiss him goodnight. Given its all-too-convincing portrayal of the encounter with the law courts, the film leaves us with the happiest ending possible. Joanna wins but, seeing at the last minute that she can't take her son home because 'he already is home', she sacrifices him to his father. The mother who has abandoned her son becomes a good mother again through an act of self sacrifice. Arguably, she is succumbing to just the values of traditional motherhood that she rebelled against in the first place. But, for the viewer who's watched Billy struggling, it's a necessary sacrifice. The film then ends with them hugging and Ted allowing her to go up to the apartment to talk to Billy. Humanity has triumphed over the law; neither parent turns out to be morally superior or better-suited to child-rearing; some kind of hard-won equality is possible.

Kramer vs. Kramer leaves us with a potential future involving joint custody, though there's a sense that the marital apartment will remain in some fundamental sense Billy's 'home'. In 1980, psychologists Judith Wallerstein and Joan Kelly led the way in making psychologically driven arguments about the benefits of joint custody. Wallerstein was at the beginning of a decades-long study of the children of divorce that would leave her rather judgementally urging couples to stay together, insisting that unhappy marriages were better for children than divorce. At this stage, though, her emphasis was on the importance of both parents in helping children to adjust to the fallout of divorce. And she was part of a larger groundswell of change. In Britain, the Matrimonial Causes Procedure Committee hoped in 1985 that joint custody would become the usual outcome. While in the US, by 1985, thirty states had adopted joint-custody legislation, with a few states already allowing courts to impose joint custody even when one or both parents didn't want it.

There were sceptical voices out there. The psychologist Susan Steinman surveyed twenty-four families in California, the earliest adopter of joint-custody legislation, between 1978 and 1980, and found that shifting between homes only worked for children whose parents were capable of collaborating. Even then, a year later, she found that a third of the children had opted to live primarily with one parent. In a prestigious lecture in 1983, she warned parents and judges that though joint custody offered 'important benefits to parents and children', it wasn't an easy arrangement: 'It is an intricate, complex structure requiring considerable commitment on the part of parents.' She advised courts against awarding joint custody when parents were acrimonious because such rulings were based on the hope that the hostility would die down and the parents would learn to cooperate. 'Joint custody at its worst is a simple legal formula that technically divides the child's life between the two parents without consideration of the child's specific needs and capacities and that tries to end a war between parents who do not want or are not able to end it between themselves.'[59]

Reading Steinman's report forty years on, I'm inclined to agree. I remember the first years of our divorce, when my son was going up and down between us two days at a time. I remember the days he'd arrive without a coat on a sunny day only for it to rain the next day, the unfinished books or homework left behind, the half-finished drawing or Lego project he had to put aside at bedtime, knowing it would be three days before he could finish it. Every transition was a struggle, every shout of 'Daddy' changed to 'Mummy', every night in a different bed, and there would usually be tears within an hour of his arrival. Until we tried it, I'd assumed that 50/50 custody was the best arrangement for children, because it's what everyone around us was doing, and what the courts apparently favoured. But it became slowly clear that this was an absurd assault on him – a schedule inflicted on a child that few adults could cope with – a brutal attempt to give him two homes that was in danger of leaving him unhomed. What was the alternative? Which of us could give him up, and would he forgive either the one who gave him up or the one who became the main carer? It took a move and a court case to make a decision – a court case which had the effect of increasing the hostility, which was precisely what Steinman had warned against. I wish there had been some other way; I wish he could have had more agency in the process that supposedly has his best interests at its heart; I wish that our family had managed an amicable sharing of children, and that our children had proved as adaptable to their frequent moves as a few hardy children I know are. But I am glad that he's no longer a shuttlecock like Henry James's Maisie, passed up and down, day by day, between two frantic, addled lives.

Rebecca's life as a shuttlecock had ceased. When she went to Yale in 1987, it was as Rebecca Walker. In 1991, she took on her mother's mantle as a forerunner of change, declaring herself the third wave of feminism in *Ms.* magazine. The Black American lawyer and academic Anita Hill had just accused US Supreme Court nominee Clarence Thomas (the second African American to serve on the court) of sexual harassment, and she had been subsequently dismissed and vilified. Rebecca Walker used this as the basis for a manifesto:

So I write this as a plea to all women, especially women of my generation: Let Thomas' confirmation serve to remind you, as it did me, that the fight is far from over. Let this dismissal of a woman's experience move you to anger. Turn that outrage into political power. Do not vote for them unless they work for us. Do not have sex with them, do not break bread with them, do not nurture them if they don't prioritize our freedom to control our bodies and our lives. I am not a post-feminism feminist. I am the Third Wave.[60]

Alice too was still writing manifestos. She'd embarked on a series of committed relationships with women and wanted to redefine both feminism and lesbianism as 'womanism', a word she took from the Black folk expression of mothers to children – 'You acting womanish' – suggesting that womanists were 'outrageous, audacious, courageous' women who loved music, dancing, the moon and, in one way or another, other women.[61]

These were two women living public lives as Black American feminists in the circles clustered around *Ms.* magazine. But somehow the physical proximity made emotional closeness between them all the more difficult, not least because Rebecca Walker was now emerging as a writer and didn't think Alice engaged enough with her daughter's work. In 1992, Alice went to a therapy session with Rebecca and listened to her complaints: 'She says she was always at Kentucky Fried Chicken! No doubt by choice, said the therapist, and R admitted that was true. I tried to get her to say what it was she wanted from me. "Three square meals a day," she said.'[62]

They cried and argued and eventually embraced and walked back through Central Park arm in arm. But then there was a period of estrangement, followed by a rapprochement in 1996. 'This feels so good,' Alice wrote in her journal after a morning cuddling her daughter:

It is when our bond is ruptured that I feel profoundly out of sync with my world. She & I are still, at some very deep level, one, & will always be. When she falls asleep on my chest I feel her just as I did when she was an infant. Her movements in sleep are the same. Only she is larger.[63]

And on they went, with rifts followed by reconciliations – the fallout of Rebecca's peculiar childhood. She held her father to account too: there was a therapy session with both her parents where Mel cried at the suggestion that he'd cut them off as his father had cut him off. And then Rebecca wrote about her childhood and custody situation in her 2000 memoir, *Black, White and Jewish*, a passionate outpouring of honesty, self-examination, and generous but also acute reappraisal of the past. When she became pregnant herself, she was understandably determined to create a very different kind of life for her child. During her pregnancy she became estranged from her mother, and in 2008, when her son was three, she gave an interview to the *Daily Mail* that the newspaper turned into a rather lurid repudiation not just of Alice but of feminism, publishing it as an article supposedly written by her. She has been angry since then with the newspaper – and with herself for allowing this to happen. The article has her describing her joy at feeling her son's head nestling in the crook of her neck and hearing his little voice calling 'Mommy, Mommy' and declaring that she had almost missed out on becoming a mother thanks to being brought up by a 'rabid feminist' who thought motherhood was one of the worst things that could happen to women.[64]

It's upsetting to read the lucid, flexible prose of her memoir *Baby Love: Choosing Motherhood After a Lifetime of Ambivalence* turned into this diatribe – I can't hear Rebecca Walker herself writing the phrase 'rabid feminist'. But the sentiments were hers, at this time, and it was true: ambivalent 1970s motherhood combined with the ruptures of custody had been too much for this six-year-old girl to cope with, even if the divorce itself couldn't be blamed on Alice Walker. Rebecca Walker was caught in the same turn-of-the-century wave of panicky conformity that saw Britney Spears reviled as a bad mother. Alice Walker leaving Rebecca to eat KFC and lose her virginity while she retreated to the countryside to write; Britney Spears holding her baby on her lap in the car because she wanted to make a quick getaway – they were both of them imperfect, so they had to be unquestioningly condemned.

The revelation here is that motherhood is a permanent challenge to our political settlements, and sometimes even to our most progressive urges. Motherhood was a disruptive element within nineteenth-century patriarchal culture, revealing the absurdity of the whole notion of the absolute rights of male ownership. But then it had challenged and unsettled 1960s progressive culture too. Rebecca's upbringing and custody situation wasn't just affected by the curdling of the dreams of 1960s liberal progress; her trajectory revealed the tensions that had been haunting those ideas of liberal progress all along. As feminists have found for centuries, it is so difficult to reconcile the needs for emancipation and care. Stories like *Kramer vs. Kramer* resound and provoke because this is their central dilemma. And so, steadily, over the half-century since Rebecca Walker's birth, the forces of reaction have emerged, with motherhood at their centre. What is revealed is that the liberal, transgressive imagination has to keep reinventing ways of taking care of the world, creating secure places for children to grow up in, and has to come up with versions of the family that are nourishing as well as fluid. Rebecca Walker would in turn commit to this project. But in the meantime, she needed it acknowledged that she had experienced too much emancipation and not enough care.

Still, at least she was alive. Because there were children dying in the fallout of the custody cases of this generation, as there have been in every generation. I look in vain for the children of Earnestine Blue and Mary Jo Risher, but find the remaining children of Pat Norman to try to piece together her story.

What emerges, talking to Pat Norman's friends, former lovers and children, is horribly sad. Pat went on to become an influential member of the San Francisco Health Department, serving as coordinator of lesbian/gay health services during the AIDS epidemic. In 1984 she became the first out lesbian to run for San Francisco city supervisor, and Alice Walker led a fundraiser on her behalf. But along the way, her children fell between the cracks in a city running on the souring energy of riots and protests and chemicals.

By the time they were teenagers, all the children were taking drugs. And in 1984, just when Pat Norman was running for supervisor, her oldest son, Paul, died: he'd reached into the car of a man who was refusing to give him drugs and the man took off, throwing him back to bash his head and bleed to death on the street. Looking back, her youngest son James blames his mother for his brother's death, saying she was too busy campaigning to look after her children; she delegated the task of fathering them to a series of gay men, some of whom sexually abused her sons. When he told his mother about the abuse when he was eighteen, she told him it was his problem and she didn't want to hear about it. And so, according to James, his brother died, and one of his sisters spent eighteen years in rehab. James Norman will be voting for Donald Trump, he tells me, and he knows as well as I do how much this would have horrified the mother who neglected her children to fight for the rights of the oppressed. He looks back on his year in the foster home at the age of four, brought up by a Christian mother and father, as the happiest in his life. There were apple trees in the garden and rolling hills around them, and then his mother transplanted him overnight to their Haight-Ashbury apartment, full of a rotating cast of leather-clad dykes and spaced-out hippies in a community centred not around church but around Maud's bar, with its jukebox and pinball machine, illuminated by neon beer ads and by the lights of the police cars loitering threateningly outside. He was so shocked he didn't speak for several weeks. We need stable, conventional families, he tells me: 'a stable mother father environment is definitely necessary to raise a solid human being'.[65]

Perhaps history and custody are always going to be somehow at odds with each other. Children's lives lag behind the more progressive custody decisions, so you get children like James Norman complaining about their radical parents being allowed to bring them up. And the more conservative custody decisions lag behind actual lives: so you get children like Richard Risher wailing as they're taken away from radical parents by judges who fear they're going to be stigmatised by disapproving classmates. Children are at the sharp end of these disjunctions because they're so full of need and their lives are changing so fast. It's not so surprising that James Norman has joined the radical right, any more than that Rebecca Walker gave that interview to the *Daily Mail*. Politically, the right has taken hold of the narrative of the family, as it has claimed possession of the narrative of freedom. It's been a powerful imaginative achievement in its way: to reimagine what the claims of freedom might sound like if you don't want to give up on patriarchy and privilege; to claim care as a value of the right wing because of its commitment to traditional family life, conveniently forgetting that healthcare and social security are crucial elements of care.

I try to put it to James that it's not because she was radical or transgressive that Pat Norman failed him as a mother, but because she was oppressed. What if they hadn't been in the foster home that he now looks on as a refuge, offering Christian values he then lost in the abrupt move to San Francisco? What if she could have been openly gay in the first place, and could have made a life that could have fully included them, without the struggle that left her devoting every scrap of energy she had to the campaign? I think of Rebecca Walker, standing upstairs while her best friend walked away in tears. It's a natural reaction to loss: to reject the people you can't bear losing. What if this loss hadn't been inflicted on Pat Norman in the first place? But James's values are too desperately necessary to his survival to be open to question. He's done what he can: he was a dutiful son at the end, forgiving his mother and then housing and supporting her when she ran out of money and developed Alzheimer's; he's a devoted father. According to Pat Norman's niece, he holds his children close, and they have a turtle pond in their dining room in Hawaii, with turtles leaping alongside them as they eat their meals.

And Rebecca Walker? She's only four years younger than James Norman. It's a rather extraordinary coincidence that she grew up only blocks away from him in San Francisco, unknowingly crossing paths with him in bars and boulevards, and then, for over a decade, when her son was young, lived on a neighbouring Hawaiian island, surrounded by the same luxuriant scenery, picking mangos from trees. Despite all her suffering, she's fortunate that her custody situation wasn't blighted by death and collapse as his was. She's fortunate that she's had the space, the grace and the hard-won ambivalence made possible by her strength of character and by her humanist background and education, both to pull away from her parents and to return to them without disastrous consequences.

When I speak to her, her son is off to university and she's about to publish a new book; she's packing to move to Alice's childhood state of Georgia with her wife, albeit to a 'little utopic, intentional community'; her life doesn't look all that different from Alice Walker's. 'I strongly feel children need two parents and the thought of raising Tenzin without my partner Glen, fifty-two, would be terrifying,' the *Daily Mail* has her saying. But, like her mother, she's open to changing her mind; the flexibility and ambivalence of both women are among their great strengths – especially because these are combined with vital grit and tenacity. Seven years later Rebecca and Glen separated and, unlike Alice and Mel, they didn't manage to avoid the courts.

I say that sometimes, angry with the parents like Rebecca Walker's who collaborated, and the parents like James Norman's who didn't, I wonder if I'm just against divorce.

'I agree with you,' Rebecca says, sharing my despairing laughter at ending up with this view. 'I really feel like divorce should be avoided at all costs. But we do have to make tough choices, we have to figure out how to be true to ourselves and safe and happy and take care of our kids as best we can along the way.'

I ask if going through a divorce herself has changed her attitude towards her parents. She says that though she's happy now to have had the experience of living in so many places, she mourns the energy wasted in her years of adapting to loss and change, and the depression that resulted. She doesn't know how they could have done it better though. She can see that her parents were right to avoid the court system – to avoid the state 'monitoring the intimacy of our lives'. And she's glad she didn't have the split weeks and months she sees her step-children having to make their lives in now. Her main wish is that they could have kept in touch more, to try to smooth the seams between her two lives. 'I felt like my parents were in different movies – I had to jump from movie to movie.' They were the grown-ups writing the script: why couldn't they find a way to write the same film?[66]

'Be nobody's darling,' Alice Walker wrote around the time Rebecca was born:

> Be an outcast.
> Take the contradictions

> Of your life
> And wrap around
> You like a shawl,
> To parry stones
> To keep you warm.
> [. . .]
>
> Be nobody's darling;
> Be an outcast.
> Qualified to live
> Among your dead.[67]

Perhaps she was writing here for her daughter as well as herself. Both of them learnt to live within contradictions, both learnt to be the kind of outcasts who might be qualified to live alongside that first great Walker, the slave who walked across the South with two babies on her hips – even though their versions of motherhood have been more ambivalent, more beset by competing desires, than their ancestor's.

'Be an outcast': Alice Walker did this by marrying a white man and having a child with him; she did it again by divorcing that man and mothering her child half the time. And in the meantime, the era of liberal advance, of Black power and feminism, gave way to reaction and disillusionment, and Rebecca Walker lived through that frantic arc of hope and loss. She lived through it while trying to keep up with a custody situation that threw her between two homes that were also two separate worlds. In doing so, she revealed the madness that 50/50 custody can be: two-year transitions are absurd, but are they ultimately that much more absurd than two days or two weeks?

It's not surprising that Rebecca Walker lurched between declaring herself the third wave of feminism and castigating her feminist mother. She was buffeted by history as she was buffeted between her homes – and there was a third world on the horizon, a Trumpian world that she would hate as much as her mother, even as James Norman was succumbing to it. Thus, Rebecca Walker's custody situation acts as a kind of lens onto the 1970s and the legacy of these processes of historical collapse and contraction. It reveals how motherhood and care can become a block to any sense that the future will be determined by progressive liberal hope. But it reminds us how urgent it remains to make care central to politics, and to piece together complex forms of political thinking and empathy.

'Qualified to live/ Among your dead.' Alice Walker's dead included her father's mother, murdered as she walked beside her son, and her classmate's mother, murdered by her father. They were the dead memorialised in *Grange Copeland* where, only a few days before birthing her daughter, she had written that scene in a courtroom where a grandfather murders his son to save his sixteen-year-old granddaughter from a custody decision. Perhaps Alice Walker and Mel Leventhal's greatest achievement in handling their divorce was to make their custody decisions outside the court system in an era when family courts were rarely good places for children. The custody cases of this time acted, as custody cases always have, both as lagging indicators of the values of the previous era (as when it came to lesbian mothers) and as prophesies of the possibilities or disasters coming in on the horizon. Alice and Mel found ways of sidestepping the onslaught of these forces and tried to make their decisions more collaboratively. They had plenty of difficulties. But if that fundamental tension between freedom and care is present in any life, then perhaps what we see most of all in the Walkers' lives is a rich and finely grained version of this problem. They've had their difficulties, but it's their achievement that these have been subtle, equivocal difficulties rather than the crude, broken-down difficulties shipwrecking many of the lives around them. And out of all this came *The Color Purple*, one of the most profound visions of care we have. With energy, perseverance, patience and grace, Alice Walker tried out forms of love that might also leave people free, challenging and transforming her own legacy of possession and violence.

EPILOGUE

I go into court. I go between London, Oxford, Bromley, Brighton. Once again I am sitting at municipal wooden benches in cluttered, carpeted rooms. The only sign of a grander legal tradition is that 'Dieu et Mon Droit' on the wall: the festive, red-tongued lion and the sprightly unicorn have to represent the reigning monarch and through him the whole, misshapen edifice of justice. I become used to the bucket seats in the corridors; to barristers looking for clients, and clerks looking for litigants, and to the dehydrating faces of men and women who haven't slept for days, waiting hour after hour for their hearing until suddenly the judge is ready, but the solicitor is still on the phone, trying to get her laptop mended because otherwise her team won't have the court documents.

Here, day after day, the sad details of custody amass. A school-uniform pinafore zip is cut — accidentally, malevolently? Homework is left undone; a pet rabbit found strangled; tired children arrive home and cry. There are videos filmed by a father of children having clamorously insistent fun; videos filmed by a mother of a child screaming as she's handed over to the father in a pushchair. (Should she have comforted her, instead of callously filming? she's asked in court. Quite possibly, but court drives people to extremes, as it always has.)

Children run away in the street, lock themselves in bathrooms, hide under tables. Fathers kick children off beds, or just throw balls at them in swimming pools, hurting their faces – were they having fun, or did he mean to hurt her? Mothers tell children more than they should about the difficulties of the marriage.

Confident, jovial, exhausted, the judges make their pronouncements. 'They are supposed to be at boarding school,' one judge says in an apparently 'child-friendly' judgment to two girls who have begged not to board; 'and in truth I think they enjoy boarding.' The court finds new, twenty-first century ways to punish mothers and children. 'She has ended up with severe restrictions on her involvement with her son, but has only herself to blame.'

For a few decades now, the science of 'parental alienation' has gained traction in courtrooms internationally. The American child psychiatrist Richard A. Gardner introduced the notion of 'parental alienation syndrome' in 1985, characterising it as a 'disorder' wrought by the (possibly unconscious) 'indoctrinations' of the alienating parent and resulting in 'the child's campaign of denigration against the parent, a campaign that has no justification'. Gardner's alienators were generally mothers, and he invoked William Congreve's seventeenth-century phrase 'hell hath no fury like a woman scorned' to explain why a mother might invent claims about her ex-husband as a sexual abuser. The solution he proposed in cases of 'severe' alienation was a transfer to the father, or to a 'transitional site' where the children could be therapeutically prepared for the move. Gardner's own writing is no longer given much credence, and few jurisdictions now encourage the use of 'parental alienation syndrome' as an identifiable disorder. But his ideas slip in through expert reports by unregulated psychologists committed to identifying alienation and withdrawing the child from the favoured parent. Here, children are enmeshed, or unconsciously aligned with their mothers. They have no minds of their own. Their wishes and feelings aren't their wishes and feelings because it's their grasp of reality that their ever-powerful mothers have taken away.[1]

EPILOGUE

The barristers enjoy all this – of course they do, it's the life they've chosen, unlike the parents. Sometimes I enjoy the banter. A KC buys me a cup of tea in the makeshift court café with the £10 he allocates himself for daily expenses, and we chat about *Anna Karenina* and our children's nits. But the sparring, the flattery, the intellectual playfulness of the courtroom – it would be fine in commercial law but feels out of place here, where children linger offstage, suffering patiently or impatiently, waiting for news of where they are going to live.

Custody. It can seem, in court, that there is no care involved, only control. We are far now from the collaborative, if misguided, spirit of Alice Walker and Mel Leventhal, but back in the embattled, dangerous world of Caroline Norton and George Sand. It can seem that the bewildered child is the last person whose welfare anyone in these windowless rooms is truly able to consider. Not the fathers, who insist that their strained relationships with their children are the fault of the ex-wives. Not the mothers, who think they can protect their children by keeping them away from the visits the children say they don't want to go on, only to find that this results in the removal of their children. 'We must do better for children,' writes the activist barrister Charlotte Proudman in her vital and moving recent book about the family courts, saying that many of the children in cases she's been involved in have 'become like hostages traded between two households when a court orders a forced transfer of residence because it accepts a parent's, often father's, allegations that the mother has 'alienated' them from him'. According to Proudman, although there are ultimately no winners in the family courts, there are losers, and the losers are too often women and children.[2]

Many of the cases I witness are difficult to navigate, morally. There are abusive mothers in the mix. There's even a mother who sends anonymous threatening voicemails and letters to her ex-husband, claiming that their son is in danger. She's hired a private detective to stalk the father, and she's sent messages racially harassing his new girlfriend. But does she deserve to see her son only twice a year, as the judge decrees? And more importantly, does he deserve to see his mother so rarely? The son's voice is curiously absent from the judgment; indeed, custody cases can seem designed to exclude the very voices they are meant to promote. In this case, the judge decides that the mother's campaign of harassment against the father has been so severe that the court proceedings themselves are in effect an extension of the abuse. It's true that she's been found to have perverted the course of justice during the police investigation, and the judge finds that she has forged evidence relating to the current proceedings. The father is so traumatised that the judge thinks that he can't be expected to cope with any liaising over contact. These are two people whose relationship has deteriorated so much that the judge can only protect the son's interests by excluding the mother more and more from the boy's life. The problem here is partly that there's no other structure than the hostile arena of a court case to try to figure out how to make this fragmented and traumatised family more functional.

This is a boy who liked to change into his pyjamas during the supervised contact he used to have at his mother's flat, so that he could feel as though he was staying the night. He's stopped asking to stay with her since he was told that his mother has hurt his father, and she's been in trouble with the police. But asked what he'd like to happen by the social worker, he's said he'd like to see her more often than he has in the lead up to the hearing, when he's been seeing her once a month. The mother is prepared to continue paying for supervised contact, which would minimise risk, and there's never been any suggestion that she would physically harm her child. But the problem is that she hasn't repented, or hasn't repented in the right way. 'I do not consider the mother has moved on and now understands the enormous harm she has caused to the father,' the judge writes. Courts make so much hinge on these acts of repentance, while making repentance – or even self-reflection – extraordinarily hard to achieve. In this case, monthly contact is changed to biannual encounters.

And as I go from court to court, I hear it again and again: the demand for an apology; the insistence that an apology isn't merely perfunctory. The mothers accused of alienation often find this hard to do. Why should they lie and say that they don't believe the father to be a threat to their children, or say that they don't think he's brought this rejection on himself with his brusqueness or with moments of casual cruelty?

Sometimes I find myself thinking that this is a world in which feminism doesn't exist, except as the movement that has allowed women to become judges and barristers. Or perhaps it's more that feminism itself has precipitated these backlashes and perverse consequences. Outside the courtroom, women insist on their right to be ambivalent mothers, as Alice Walker did; to be merely good enough – indeed, to be bad enough; but in here we must be perfect, not only in our mothering but in our lack of hostility towards the man attempting to destroy us. Sitting in court, I want to pass on the script: say you're sorry, say that all your differences are in the past, that you think he's a wonderful father, that you will no longer allow your unconscious hostility to this man who has been found to have hit and demeaned you to influence your children.

I come to think that this is a world where children have as little agency as they did in the nineteenth century, especially when I read the newspapers and hear about cases more appalling than the ones I've witnessed: the ones where rapists and paedophiles are given custody, or where children are killed by fathers who have been awarded primary custody, despite teachers reporting injuries to social services. Most recently, there is Sara Sharif, a ten-year-old girl whose mother escaped with her to a refuge only for the father to get full custody, and who was beaten, burned with an iron, bitten, hooded, and left to lie in her own faeces before she eventually died of neglect.

CUSTODY

I try not to let my fury at Sara Sharif's father inflect my feelings about the men I see in court. These men are not psychopathic, and many aren't abusers; they are merely baffled, angry husbands, some of whose punitive urges are stoked by the court process. And these women are imperfect – some are no better than the husbands. But repeatedly I see children who are clear in their desire to be with their mothers taken away because they love their mothers too much, which can only be the mothers' fault.

London. This court has been hollowed out of two upper floors in an anonymous office building. It's a world of sleek riverside bars and stately Victorian colonnades and hustling financiers, like the one who has come to court today to fight for his daughter – who I'll call Lana. The mother is hostile, the father says; she acts unilaterally, and their 50/50 arrangement isn't working. He wants to have his daughter most of the time and to have full decision-making power. The so-called expert is on his side: a parenting coach-cum-therapist who's attempted to improve the family dynamics while monitoring their interactions. In the court process, surveillance and nurturing are often meant to be miraculously embodied in the same person.

The imbalance of power is palpable. This father is a highly paid European businessman at ease with the workings of the state. The mother was an immigrant sex worker who got together with him – her client – long enough to get married and produce a daughter and a lot of confused resentment on both sides. He took sex toys in a suitcase on business trips while she was left alone with the baby.

He's white, she's Black. He's mellifluously represented by his barrister – a large, smiley woman who puts everyone at ease except the mother she calmly eviscerates. He's also paying, indirectly, for his ex-wife's much cheaper barrister, who doesn't specialise in family

EPILOGUE

law and has to have things explained by his lawyer when she gets confused.

Already the father has won a case for 50/50 custody, costs (though the mother's only income is the maintenance money he pays) and a change of nursery. As the day unfolds, it's easy to see why. The father, giving evidence, is eloquent about his love for Lana. He demonstrates his capacity for self-reflection, describing himself imagining the questions Lana will ask him later about why he took her away from her mother. And he plays games with the mother's barrister: 'Do you want to do the answer as well as the question?' He gets away with accusing the mother of 'alienation' frequently, though his barrister takes care not to use the term herself.

The mother, giving her evidence, is extravagantly evasive. She claims not to remember the year she moved house or the year she was in prison, a decade ago, for passport fraud. Asked if there's anything good about this man, she can think of nothing. She can't comment on the good times he has with Lana because she isn't there. She can't even reassure the court that she'll support the arrangements if the father wins.

'I don't know. How can I answer that? I will be heartbroken.'

She's made mistakes and they all come out. In the last hearing, she produced photographs of him having sex to show his disregard for his own physical safety, and exposed his 'cross-dressing'. The previous judge found all this 'an exercise in humiliation on her part' – evidence of her agenda to 'severely limit the father's role' in their daughter's life. She's enrolled Lana in a nursery without his consent, and unilaterally gone along with her GP's suggestion that they should refer the girl for an autism assessment because of her delayed speech.

Yet when she says, in despair, that she did try to prepare Lana for the handovers, only for her to scream as she left the house and pee on the way to nursery, I believe her. The coach and the father claim that Lana only cries because she hasn't been properly prepared – hasn't been shown that her mother is happy for her to go. But I believe that the mother did her best: she sent her with her favourite book and toy, wanting her to be at home with him.

'I don't dispute that Lana has a strong emotional bond with her mother,' the father acknowledges. But why aren't his books and toys good enough? 'I have a library at home with about fifty books.' This is 'a complete undermining of my parenting'.

The mother's mistakes seem to me the mistakes a parent makes who is ill at ease with the system and community she's found herself in. She may have gone along with the GP's autism suggestion because she didn't think there was any parental choice involved. The first nursery she enrolled Lana in was a minute's walk from their flat; it was a merely good enough nursery, but it was embedded in her community. Now Lana has to squash in with commuting City workers on the train to her 'outstanding' nursery. The mother gives vague excuses for not attending nursery stay and plays. But as a former sex worker, she may not feel at home with the City worker parents, and she may worry that the father will attend. Shouldn't we accept that she feels intimidated by this man she remains financially dependent on – a man she alleges saw strangulation as part of good sex? Yet somehow there's no place in court to acknowledge these imbalances. Indeed, the mother's suggestion that she'd been controlled by her husband had been dismissed by a previous judge on the grounds that sexually 'she was, in fact, the dominatrix'. Findings from previous judgments are not open to challenge.

A couple of days later, the judgment comes. The father, the judge says, has been 'very much focused' on his daughter and displayed 'no underlying resentment of the mother', while the mother's evidence gave 'little reason for optimism'. The videos she filmed of Lana's distress at the handovers are evidence of 'serious harm' which will be 'ongoing' in the mother's home, where Lana is exposed to her mother's 'negative beliefs about her father'. In the witness box, the mother displayed a 'lack of warmth'. And so the father gets everything he asks for. The mother's parental responsibility has been

EPILOGUE

restricted, and Lana will now see her mother for only four nights a fortnight, even in the school holidays.

The mother's crime has been to hate the father. I try to imagine George Sand or Caroline Norton, told that in order to retain custody they are required not to hate their husbands. Isn't hatred a common feature of divorce? And isn't the legal system designed to stoke it? I remember desperately, one night during my own court case, googling: 'Why do I hate my ex-husband', feeling I was somehow entitled to get through life without hatred. The court fears that Lana will be corrupted, polluted by the hatred flowing through her mother's home.

This is the new orthodoxy: to be a good parent you must have no hatred. And this mother has lost custody because she couldn't or wouldn't say that she valued her daughter's love for her father. It may well be that this painful failure to see what's required by the system does indeed make her ill-fitted to help her daughter navigate the world. But to say that she lacks warmth as well? Wasn't it warmth that I saw, in the fierceness of her protectiveness?

The night after the judgment I wake at 5 a.m. and think of the mother, perhaps awake, listening to the sleeping breathing of the daughter she's soon to lose. A summer storm has started. Does she hear the rain and wonder, as I do, if it's a biblical torrent, punishing the world for its sins? I think of a little girl, on a Monday morning, being taken to school by her mother, knowing it's going to be a fortnight until their next weekend, and of the mother, unable to explain what has happened because she doesn't understand it herself. The mother may become less appealing to her daughter once she's forced to move after her maintenance payments have been reduced. Perhaps she'll be less missed as the years pass. It's hard to say whose fault this all is, but we can be sure it isn't Lana's. As I try to get back to sleep, I hope that Lana's sleeping through the rain, and that she'll somehow emerge from all this intact, and able to fight for herself.

My own children are with their father – I'm coming to the end of a week without them. I try to imagine them sleeping, but find there's a truth in what this mother said. That she isn't there to see the good times Lana has with her father. Children are inaccessible to you in the other home. My daughter on Facetime is subdued, monosyllabic. We have to trust that the days will pass and that our children don't miss us as much as we miss them.

The mother's barrister kept saying, plaintively, 'This would be unfair on the mother', and it's true, though it has no weight in law. The judge is not required to consider whether it would be in the child's interest to have a mother capable of thriving.

'The mother.' We lose our names and acquire this title in the process that takes our children away.

At least this child is alive, unlike Caroline Norton's son, or George Sand's granddaughter. But surely we can ask for more than that. We can ask for a world that could support this mother lovingly, that could see hatred as part of the tragedy of marriage, that could stop blaming mothers.

Oxford. Four years after my own court case, I walk again across the foggy meadows, up the stairs lined cheerlessly with children's pictures, to the coffee bar with its lacklustre sausage rolls that serve as fitting symbols of the children left unattended while their parents frantically demonstrate their love for them in court.

The case I'm witnessing today has dragged on for five years and the original issues are no longer contended, but the father now seeks a change in residence. These children are adolescents. Let's call them Esther and Ada, after Dickens's tale of a court case that goes on for so long that the disputed inheritance has all been spent on lawyers, and justice has long been forgotten.

There's an expert involved, of course. Trish Barry-Relph is best

EPILOGUE

known for a 2022 case where thirteen- and eleven-year-old sisters accused their father of sexual and physical abuse. The older girl called her psychologist from the father's bedroom while staying with him, threatening to hang herself if she couldn't go home to her mother. Barry-Relph diagnosed a case of 'severe alienation' and recommended a 'Therapeutic Residential Reunification Plan'. The children – together with their therapeutic godmother, Barry-Relph herself – were to move to the father's house for ninety days, not seeing their mother at all. The children didn't comply. They smashed up the house and broke a window to escape. Still the court didn't give up. The girls were put into separate foster care placements. The older girl ran away to her mother; the younger girl finally obeyed, moved in with her father and was rewarded with two-hour supervised weekly visits to her mother. Thankfully, the case went to the High Court in 2023. Mrs Justice Lieven did find evidence of alienation, but thought it had been an unhelpful allegation, 'embedding conflict and a sense that one parent is right and justified, and the other parent is wrong'. She found that the criticism of the mother by Barry-Relph and others 'bordered on the inhumane'. And she worried that 'somewhere in the history of this case we have lost our humanity'. She returned the older girl to her mother, though the younger one remained in limbo.[3]

I'm curious to see Barry-Relph, and she doesn't disappoint. She's grandmotherly looking in a black cardigan, and seems brisk and kind in manner, but her recommendations are far from kind. Barry-Relph no longer uses the term 'alienation' directly, saying instead that the girls have been left 'unwittingly serving their mother's unconscious needs' – viewing their father as unsafe for her benefit. For years, the girls have repeated the same allegations against the father, with Esther, the older girl, accusing him of being abusive. The things he's done have been found to have been accidents: he threw a bottle of water at her to catch that hurt her wrist; he threw a ball at her face playing in the pool; he demonstrated a 'slap', clapping his hands by her face. Both girls bring up these incidents to justify their unease, which may indeed be inflected by their sense of both parents' hostility. In the courtroom I pick up on a turbulent mixture of emotions: there are moments of rage and hatred in the mix alongside weariness and sadness and a heartfelt desire to make the best of things.

For a while, Barry-Relph was recommending that Esther should be moved to foster care while she rebuilt her relationship with her father. Now she's recommending a six-month transfer of residence to the father, but as he lives far from their schools, they're to board full-time and just see him for weekends and holidays. Esther has said she doesn't want to see him; Ada has been happy spending weekends and holidays with him and wants to continue. Both have said they don't want to board full-time: they tried it for a few months while their mother was away for work and didn't like it, so their mother came home early and they became mainly day students again. Cross-questioned, Barry-Relph is clear. If her solution isn't adopted, Esther will have poor relationships with her sister and with future peers and partners, and her own children and grandchildren will be affected too. Barry-Relph's views are shared by the social worker 'guardian' appointed to represent the children's interests.

The questioning of the parents begins. This is a packed court, because Esther is old enough to hire her own barrister (though she's not in court herself), and Ada has the barrister appointed to represent the guardian. The mother has a KC, and up to now the father has had one too, but this time he's decided to represent himself, despite his wealth. This is usually disadvantageous, but it gives him a voice in the courtroom, allowing him to cross-question the mother, asking her about a time when the police were called because the girls had phoned her, sounding frightened.

'Do you accept responsibility for calling the police?' the father asks.

It was her husband who called the police, she tells the court.

'Do you accept responsibility for coming down to my house?'

EPILOGUE

She's getting fed up, having to answer to him like this.

'I want to ask him to take responsibility for calling my husband a fucking bastard,' she replies, addressing the judge, who intervenes, insisting on the original question.

'Other judges have been critical,' the judge continues, referring to the judge at the fact-finding hearing who found that the mother was responsible for the conflict. 'When a judge says these things it's an opportunity for self-reflection.'

She follows the script. She regrets calling the police, she says.

When the guardian's barrister begins her questioning, it becomes clear why the father felt able to represent himself. This barrister is entirely on his side, effectively providing him with free legal representation – all the more powerful because she's supposedly representing the children. Repeatedly, she asks the mother if she accepts the fact-finding judgment and accepts that the children are happy with their father.

'I believe the children, is all I'm saying,' the mother says, fatally. The fact-finding judgment criticised her for taking at face value what the children say: seeing the slap and the ball accident as abuse. The barrister swiftly points out that she's doing this now.

The trap tightens as one day gives way to another and the mother returns to court in a black velvet jacket that seems to defy the muted neutrality of the courtroom. Does she see herself as a victim, the barrister asks.

No, the mother insists. But surely there is something off here, she suggests, more hesitantly – something perhaps a little chauvinistic? 'Not one person can say something nice about me.'

She's right. Here is a mother who no one is criticising as a mother, except in her failure to co-parent with the equally uncooperative father. Yet nothing is asked about her parenting. Its exemplary nature is simply taken as a given, so neither Trish Barry-Relph nor the guardian has felt the need to see the mother with the children. The father gets to show that he's a fun parent, and a thoughtful one. He buys tickets for his children to attend the VIP section at a concert (only Ada attended). He engages with commitment and self-reflection in the therapeutic process with Trish Barry-Relph – though this has hardly been difficult, given that her views have generally aligned with his. What the mother does that's fun is irrelevant, because only her crimes are relevant here. And it's true that she has doubted this man's fathering in the past and doesn't quite trust him now. But why does this mean that her daughters are better off without her?

Esther's lawyer cross-questions the father about a crucial turning point, in the spring, when Esther had been making an effort to rebuild her relationship with her father, missing the young children he'd had with his second wife. In their therapy sessions with Barry-Relph, Esther had said that she loved him and wanted to go back to how things were. The two girls were to go to him for half term, and a couple of days beforehand he and Esther discussed how often she would speak to her mother. Initially, she wanted to phone her three times a day, while he wanted twice a week. He was worried that his ex-wife would become a constant witness to their days. Esther immediately tried to compromise by offering twice a day, but this still alarmed him, so she promised that she'd think about talking to her twice a week.

But she hadn't been given the chance to think about it. The next day, the father panicked. Without consulting Esther, he'd booked a flight to dispatch her to her mother abroad instead, sending her across the world on her own.

Listening, I find it unsurprising that they've ended up where they have. The suggestion of moving to foster care, combined with this painful assertion of power: this father may not be abusive, but surely there's cruelty here, even if it's cruelty provoked and engineered by the court process and by the pseudo-therapy it gave rise to. It's not surprising that Esther took refuge in anger; that she revived old allegations, because it was easier to say that he'd thrown the ball at her face on purpose than that she was a vulnerable girl who couldn't trust in his love. Perhaps we were better off in the days when legal wrongs in the family courts were measured in terms of cruelty, rather than abuse. This man who's allegedly sworn at the mother in front of the girls, who's often been angry in their presence, who's sent Esther across the world for wanting to speak to her mother on the phone: might we not see this behaviour as cruel? If the court process didn't make so much hinge on binary accusations of abuse, Esther might have been able to give a stronger account of the actual wrongs he's done.

The final submissions come in. The charge, according to the guardian's barrister, is that the children 'have lost a meaningful grasp of reality', and this is the mother's fault. The judgment is not a surprise. 'The mother has not controlled the animosity which she feels towards the father.' 'The mother now needs immediately and irrevocably simply to change her approach.' 'I find in this case a particularly hard edge to the mother's behaviour.' For six months, the girls will board and spend weekends and holidays with their father. They'll have brief, monthly supervised contact with their mother and then she'll be hauled in again, to see if she's sufficiently repentant, and capable of releasing her daughters from their 'false narrative'.

It can go the other way. I tune in online to the Brighton court, where I witness a kind of spectacle of exemplary justice. Two girls, on the cusp of adolescence, have been saying for years that they don't want to see their father. One girl has told her teacher that he hurt her feelings and made her cry in bed; apparently he'd kicked her off the bed, and she was frightened that he'd do it again and that if she complained he'd stop her from contacting her mother, as he's done before.

For ten years, this mother has rigorously obeyed every court order. She's been told the script and she's stuck to it rigidly, insisting that she wants the girls to have a good relationship with their father and that she no longer has any animosity towards him, though he's admitted to having hit his ex-wife in the face, and having pinned down her arms during arguments. The father has secured the services of Hessel Willemsen, an expert notorious for finding evidence of maternal alienation. Because the mother has followed the script, his report has been entirely in favour of the mother. Willemsen worries that these girls feel 'their voices have not been heard very clearly' over the past decade, and that they will soon lose trust in the mother who forces them to see their father. He criticises the father for bullying the mother in his communications.

Cross-questioned, Willemsen insists on his own authority: 'It's for me, your honour, to determine as much as I can what the dynamics are. I actually don't think she did [alienate the children], in the end.'

The 'Nurture Practitioner' from school gives evidence about the girls' distress at seeing their father, and there are reports from an ex-girlfriend about the father pushing her to the ground and kicking her. The judge finds that, on the balance of probabilities, the girls' allegations are true, though it's likely that this was a 'momentary and short-lived loss of temper by the father'. It's clear that the girls fear that 'he may lose his temper at any time'. The judge is convinced that the father has 'a deep and strong love for the girls' and that they have had good times together, but he has decided that contact with their father is distressing them too much to continue.

The girls have been heard in their distress. But this is after ten years in court. It took the allegations from the school, the evidence from the other girlfriend, and Willemsen's evidence, for the children's voices to be heard. And when I speak to the mother, six months later, she tells me that the children remain overwhelmed and are reluctant to engage in therapy because they no longer trust the professionals who ask them how they feel.

Around the world, the cases proliferate. As I go to sleep, they can seem to be spinning around me: these children who haven't been believed. In America, between 2015 and 2023, there were reports from thirty-six professionals in Colorado that a father, Bruce, was harming his son, who I'll call Leo. He came back from visiting his father with a 'black and blue mark on his forehead' and 'irritated' genitals. Aged four, Leo told a psychologist that his father hit him with a stick and 'touches his junk while he touches my penis'.[4]

Bruce had confessed to sexually assaulting a four-year-old girl aged sixteen and was convicted of domestic violence towards Christine, the mother. At first, Christine was awarded primary custody and Bruce just had visitations, but as the reports of his abuse multiplied, he began to allege 'parental alienation', and the more allegations Christine made, the more powerful Bruce's own allegations became. They were living in a small town in Colorado where Bruce was popular with local parents because he designed the sets for the school plays. Even the child welfare official was a school mother, and the police officer investigating him for child abuse had acted with him in a local theatre production. This police officer told a journalist that he thought Bruce would offer a 'great home' for Leo, while Christine's 'anxiety' was harmful. The court allowed Bruce to appoint clinical psychologist Edward C. Budd as their expert, and in 2021 Budd filed his report, describing Christine as 'destructive', 'irrational' and 'pathological'; and Leo as so 'pathologically aligned' with his mother that he'd lost the ability to distinguish between 'what's real and what isn't real'. The report was so devastating that Christine was dropped by her lawyer, and had to represent herself. The judge ordered an immediate relocation and the next day, at 8 p.m., in the deserted parking lot of a bagel shop, eight-year-old Leo kissed his mother goodbye and dragged his robot duffel bag into his father's car.

Leo's case isn't unusual. In 2019 the American legal academic Joan Meier led a team comparing the results of 15,000 court cases, and found that mothers alleging physical and sexual abuse of a child lost custody in 50 per cent of cases. When fathers cross-claimed parental alienation, the courts were almost four times more likely to disbelieve mothers' claims of child abuse than when fathers didn't make this claim. Every mother who had alleged physical and sexual abuse and was found to have alienated her child lost custody. Across the world, 'parental alienation' makes its way into court proceedings: Meier has found similar outcomes in the UK, Canada, Italy, Spain and New Zealand.[5]

The law lags behind society, now as ever. As late as 2017, the family courts in Manchester excluded a transgender father from having any contact with his children because, in their orthodox Jewish community, 'the likelihood of the children and their mother being marginalised' is too great. In France, two hundred years after George Sand fought for her right to be a mother as well as a promiscuous woman and a writer, Constance Debré lost her son in the courts for just those reasons.[6]

Debré's novel *Love Me Tender* is an auto-fictional account of her decimation in the family courts after leaving her husband and giving up her job as a lawyer to attempt a makeshift life consisting of swimming, sex with young women, and writing. Her ex-husband tries to get her back and then keeps her son away from her in a punitive spirit. After months of waiting for a court date, they have a fifteen-minute hearing, in which the father's lawyer reads out pages from a novel found on her bookshelves narrated by a man delineating his obsessive love for a boy. The judge asks her why she's writing a book, and what it's about, and also why she exposes her son to her homosexuality. A psychiatrist is appointed to assess the parents and

EPILOGUE

she's meanwhile offered supervised visits in a contact centre that turns out to be too booked up to facilitate many of these, even on the rare occasions when the father responds to her messages. The problem is not that she's a lesbian, she realises, but that she's living a transgressive life, driven by a desire for freedom.

At night she dreams of her son, 'complicated dreams, dreams where I'm trying to see him but I don't know if I'm allowed to, where he's there but he doesn't speak to me'. She avoids parks, schools and bakeries because she can't bear to see children, and when she does hear the voices of boys her son's age, they leave her distraught: 'I might as well have hit myself across the face, I might as well have stabbed myself in the thigh.'[7]

Debré gambled on it still being possible to be free as a woman and also a mother, as it had been for Sand when she chucked it all in and attempted a new kind of freer life. It wasn't. Instead, she felt that the judge was telling a boy, her son, who would one day be a man, that 'his mother is guilty, just because his almighty father decided she was. Telling him that she isn't really a mother because she isn't really a woman because she doesn't really love men. Telling him that the law is always on the side of the most powerful and that freedom is nothing but a farce.'[8]

Month by month, the court cases become more consuming; they are where I want to be and where I dread being. I dream about the guardian's barrister in Esther and Ada's case. 'I cannot get over it,' I am telling her. 'I could understand it if you were the father's barrister, but you're asking questions on behalf of Ada. How can it be in the interest of a child that you should ask these questions of a mother she loves?' In my dream she tells me that she needs the money to look after her own children; the logic of motherhood is the only logic my sleeping self can comprehend.

Loitering in the court lobby, I meet a solicitor who specialises in representing children in custody disputes, who tells me blithely that the judges always get it right. She's only ever been involved in one case where the wrong decision was made. I am shocked: I can think of case after case where I disagree with the decision, or I feel that the decision wouldn't have been necessary if the whole court process had been handled differently. I talk to the retired Senior Designated Family Judge for London, John Altman, about how bewildering I have found the court process.

Altman and I talk on a Zoom call it takes him a while to make work. He's wearing an aertex T-shirt that makes it hard to imagine him in judicial pomp, but his voice is authoritative, despite some hoarseness, and I can hear him on the judge's bench, delivering his thoughts in full, elegant but practical sentences. He retired in 2015. As a judge he was aware that the combative nature of family law was bad for children and was trying to change it. Just before he retired, he'd used his authority as the lead judge in Britain's largest family court to pioneer a new way of working. He'd got the go-ahead for a 'Family Solutions Court' – a system which would have housed mediators and contact centres within the court building, allowing for more collaborative forms of justice. If he'd been able to implement these plans, which were shelved after his retirement, things might look quite different now. It's initiatives like these, disrupting the winner–loser binary and thinking about children's lives holistically, that we most need.

When he was judging, Altman thought that contact with both parents should be encouraged wherever possible, and found creative ways of achieving this. At one point he sent a father off to lunch with his angry teenage son in the middle of the court hearing, and found that they came back somewhat reconciled. It was a hands-on approach, in which the judge played the role of a sort of forbidding uncle. He acknowledges that he may not have given as much credence as he should have done to allegations of domestic abuse, and this became clear when he had to consider another judge's case where a father killed his children during a contact session. 'It made me realise that these things are for real sometimes.'

When contact didn't work, even after these makeshift but insistent attempts, Altman was prepared to give up on it. I tell him that the trend now is to order a transfer of residence rather than to give up, and at first he doesn't quite believe what he's hearing. There's a lengthy pause, before he delivers his own judicial verdict, and it's not the one I've been hearing in recent weeks.

'Having contact with the father is one thing that contributes to the welfare of the child,' he says. 'But a lot more things contribute to the welfare of the child. And the residential parent may be a very good parent in all other respects. So it's highly questionable whether it would be right to transfer the child to another parent for the one reason that there isn't contact.'[9]

I tell him about Esther, who's going to be at boarding school, instead of spending her nights at home.

'She's being punished by being sent to boarding school away from both parents? I can't understand. That's dreadful.'

He asks how much she'll see her mother and I explain that she'll only have supervised contact.

'Well, I don't think that's progress,' he says, still astonished. 'I'm absolutely appalled. As I think you were.'

After the unreality of my weeks in court, I feel I'm finally hearing a sane response to what I've been witnessing. I feel startled, but also strangely vindicated, by finding this outrage coming from someone right within the system: one of the most eminent judges in the family courts in recent years. But it's sad that he is now as powerless to do anything about these judgments as I am, looking on from the back of the courtroom.

I tell him that sometimes courts now move so-called 'alienated' children away from both parents into foster care for lengthy transition periods.

'You've taken my breath away,' he says. 'I'm sorry. That's punishing the child. It's not the child's fault that the parents have separated. The parents as grown-ups have imposed a harmful situation on a child by their own conduct and the child has now to carry the can for it. I can't begin to imagine how these children will end up.'[10]

Around us, there are campaigns for change. In 2020, the government commissioned the Harm Panel Report, where a group of academics and judicial stakeholders were categorical in condemning how the courts handled cases involving domestic abuse. The report found that the insistence on contact with both parents resulted in 'systemic minimisations of allegations of domestic abuse', that the adversarial system placed parents 'in opposition on what is often not a level playing field', and that 'too often the voices of children go unheard or are muted'. The UK government has also appointed its first ever Domestic Abuse Commissioner, who has recommended that parental alienation is made ineligible in cases involving domestic abuse; and Cafcass (the Children and Family Court Advisory and Support Service) have been slowly changing their guidelines, so that now 'alienating behaviour' is used instead of 'parental alienation'. Most radical has been the new Pathfinder courts initiative, introduced in pilot programmes in Dorset and North Wales (2022) and since expanded to South-East Wales, Birmingham, and Mid and West Wales, and West Yorkshire, as of June 2025. These are 'problem-solving' courts that try to interview the children and any social workers or police who have been involved very early in the process, and then support families to engage in out-of-court dispute resolution, reducing the winner/loser aspect of the court process. Already, I've heard about a mother who has lost a child to an abusive father in a Pathfinder court, but the main author of the Harm Panel Report, Rosemary Hunter, tells me that she thinks these new courts are working well. She thinks that because any domestic abuse allegations can be investigated early on, before lawyers are involved, counter-allegations of alienation don't seem to come up so often. And she's hopeful that

EPILOGUE

the children's voices are indeed heard more easily in these courts.

In America in 2018, seven-year-old Kayden Mancuso was beaten to death by her father after the courts had awarded him unsupervised contact, despite evidence that he'd threatened to kill family members, bitten a man's ear off and been violent towards his wife and child. Kayden's death sparked a campaign led by figures including Joan Meier to change the laws around child custody. The result was the hard-won, monumental Keeping Children Safe from Family Violence Act – also known as Kayden's Law – which was added to the federal Violence Against Women Act, signed by Joe Biden in 2022. Lawmakers in Arizona, California, Colorado, Pennsylvania and Utah have now passed legislation based on Kayden's Law. At its best this new legislation bans sending children to the reunification camps that have been set up across America to put Gardner's alienation theories into practice, locking children away with the parent they fear for intensive therapy.

Elsewhere, parental alienation is being slowly discredited. Spain outlawed parental alienation syndrome being cited in court proceedings in 2021, and Italian high courts have since moved to discredit it, though in 2023 the UN's Special Rapporteur on violence against women and girls, Reem Alsalem, found a 'highly gendered' concept of parental alienation still prevalent in courts worldwide (including Spain), with mothers depicted as 'vengeful and delusional' by judges and experts. Alsalem recommended the outlawing of parental alienation and of reunification camps in court proceedings, a revision of the Hague Convention on the Civil Aspects of Child Abduction to protect abused women and children, and independent representation for all children in legal proceedings.[11]

It remains to be seen whether the new courts, recommendations and laws effect real change. In the meantime, there are all the children living out their lives in the aftermaths of decisions made in secret by judges who are all too often unaccountable.

I see Esther, the night before she's removed from her mother's care. It's a freezing night and the snow still covering their car is a sign that they've been holed up here since yesterday morning. The mother and daughter move sadly around the big, chilly house that the mother will soon be alone in.

Esther is carrying the dog, who then sits on my lap, snorting occasionally while we talk, presenting her ears for fondling. Esther tells me how unheard she's felt in the legal process that has dominated her 'entire life', wasting her childhood:

'I feel like I have to put a lot of emphasis on how I feel because otherwise they don't listen to us,' she says. She feels that it's the legal process itself that has destroyed her relationship with her father. If he hadn't suggested foster care, she thinks she'd have a better relationship with him. She's determined now to do what she's told and get on with her father as well as she can. She hopes that if she does, she'll be allowed to come back to her mother. I tell her that she's doing the right thing.

The sadness she feels, and that I feel with her, is not about the weekends and holidays she'll spend with her father. It's about her isolation. After spending every night at home with her mother and her dog for months, she's about to be locked in a boarding school where she says that she has no friends.

'It feels like I always get punished for standing up to my dad,' she says. And in essence this is true, though it's as much the mother's punishment as hers.

I see mainly her fragility. She's a pale, pretty girl, with braces, in a school uniform, trying her best, not crying, though she says that when she first got the email with the judgment, she had to hide away and cry at school. (A child, told that they're going to leave their mother for six months, sent an email with this news that they have to read and process on their own: I cannot quite believe it.)

I see that she's gambled and lost. She's tried to have power in a world where she has none. The judge made a judgment that seems

EPILOGUE

designed to show her how little power she has, even over her own wishes – her grasp of reality: 'And in truth I think they enjoy boarding.' She may well go back to her mother in six months' time, but she'll know then that she can't assert herself, can't insist on her own wishes, can't hold her father to account. She still feels angry that he threw the water bottle. Personally, I can move on from the water bottle, as the judge can. But I think she's right to be angry that her father went along with the foster care suggestion, angry that he flew her off to her mother as soon as she showed things weren't going to be straightforward when she came to his house. It will take so much now – unimaginably much – to allow her to admit to the vulnerability of loving him and being hurt. So she insists on hating him; insists that she's merely going through the motions of being in his care.

The man I hear about from Esther is not an abusive father; he's a casually neglectful, casually cruel father, who tells his daughters that they don't have talent, who loses his temper and blusters, who sends them to summer camp when he's meant to be spending time with them, and sends his younger daughter on a sleepover for the first night that he can see her after a court judgment that will have devastated her. He's no worse than many fathers who have just about decent relationships with their children, but he's a father an adolescent girl might turn against.

At the door the mother, her face puffy with tears, tells me that she survived a month imprisoned when she got caught up in a foreign war, but she cannot survive the Oxford court. We hug and I drive back through the dark roads to my own sleeping child, who calls out to me. She hugs me, warm from sleep, and climbs on top of me, saying that she wants to go back to being a baby and sleeping next to me. She tries lying on her back, imagining that she's a baby who can't roll over, and then she clambers onto me again, saying that she wants to stay with me forever. I imagine Esther climbing onto her mother like this, and Ada. My daughter is about the age that they were when they were first interviewed by experts and got caught up in the court case that has used up their childhoods. I think of Esther and her mother hugging each other goodnight for the last time in months.

I interview an eighteen-year-old girl I'll call Sophie, who has come through a period of being separated from her mother as a teenager. She was moved to her father at the age of ten; by the time she was fifteen she'd managed to use legal aid to hire her own lawyers and to convince a judge to return her to her mother's care.

Her voice, fragile but determined, comes into my study. It's the usual story: a marriage that legally hovered somewhere between abuse and hostility; a father who shouted at, humiliated and once hit his wife, and who once held his daughter down on the bed and shouted at her. This was a mother debilitated by illness; a father who used his physical and financial strength to assert power over her. But Sophie's extreme fear of him was seen as entirely the mother's fault. They were entrapped in the past, caught in a narrative that only the mother could release them from. It's like a fairy tale: say the magic words and the spell you've cast will be undone.

They fell into some of the usual traps in a system that can seem designed to trap the vulnerable. Sophie fought and kicked when she was told to go to him. When asked why she didn't want to go, she could only say that she missed her mother too much and that she was afraid he would hurt her – though everyone around her told her she shouldn't make so much of the time she'd been held down on the bed. By this point they were caught in the court process that whipped ambivalence into fear and hatred. She was told that she was going to be isolated with her father for ten days. She felt that everyone was asking her what she wanted but no one was listening. And so she tried to run away, and when her father caught her and secured her in his house, he seemed to be enacting the violence she'd

EPILOGUE

feared. She locked herself in the bathroom and he threatened to unlock the door with a screwdriver; she called her mother in terror and her mother called the police, as mothers often do, sealing their own fate – because isn't this evidence of the underlying maternal hostility? – shouldn't she just have left them to it, or gone round and had a chat?

Hence the transfer of residence. Sophie was at home with a friend's nanny while her mother went to court; she was expecting her mother home for dinner. But it was a social worker who came home to her. She was going, straight away, to live with her father's parents, while her father was on bail. She went to her room, cried briefly, and packed her favourite outfit, some shoes, a photograph of her mother and her pink bunny. She left her white bunny on her mother's bed for her to find.

With her grandparents, Sophie had to grow up fast. She was the one who had to tell them what time she went to bed, what clubs she attended. Nothing about this move had been planned. There were brief supervised encounters with her mother in parks, with the social worker taking notes throughout. Her mother brought suitcases of things that had to be censored for fear that her alienating influence could adhere to the T-shirt of hers that she sent.

Meanwhile, there was the reunification therapy that was a kind of witch trial for Sophie's mother, Katherine. Confess, and you'll be allowed to see your daughter! Even the bunny, left on the bed, was a sign of abuse: why should the child want to comfort the mother? I've read the transcripts that the mother recorded of the so-called therapy sessions at a respected national children's mental health centre. Sophie had accused her father of being 'controlling' and of bribing her with presents. 'Sophie is literally repeating, word for word, things you say and that's not right for a child.' It didn't matter that she hadn't been with her mother for a year. 'She was very much, I'd like to say brainwashed by you before that . . . A child who hates her father has been emotionally abused and alienated.' He may have held her down on a bed, but this was a mother who made 'mountains out of little things' and it was her doing as well: 'You calling the police.' The reprimands became ever more strident. 'Her situation is down to you, Katherine, and I'm sorry. It's not down to me. It's not down to the judge. It's not down to the social worker. It's not down to [your ex-husband]. It's down to how you presented the father to her.'[12]

The message was clear. Katherine had to apologise for everything, and Sophie had to get on with her father, otherwise they wouldn't be able to see each other. 'When you were saying I don't want to see you, I don't like you, that was really painful for him,' Sophie was told. 'He's actually a lovely dad.'[13]

Sophie complied. Eventually, she was able to go to her mother's house unsupervised, every other weekend. But every parting remained a kind of death. 'I just want to go home and be with my mama, nobody understands,' she wrote in her diary aged eleven. 'I feel like somebody has just died when I am having to say goodbye to my mum. My life is about to get completely ruined in a few days and I can hardly do anything to stop it. When I am in the shower, I see my shadow and think that I see my dad on the other side of the curtain. It is probably just me, but I feel like he is following me.' At her father's house, she developed a set of forty rituals she had to carry out before she could get to sleep. She was referred to CAMHS, the Child and Adolescent Mental Health Services, for therapy but her father went to court to choose his own therapist instead.

Aged thirteen she began trying to take her father to court. She phoned and emailed solicitors, though her father blocked their numbers on her phone and read her emails. At first the judge refused to allow her independent legal representation, but she was granted permission to appeal this, aged fourteen. Finally, she was granted permission to take him to court. By the time it took place she was fifteen; at sixteen, most children are able to choose where to live. She saw that her best chance of winning was to take a 'reasonable' approach, insisting that she loved both her parents but would prefer to be predominantly with her mother, as she could talk about her feelings more easily with her. At last, she was allowed to move.

What was her father doing, fighting his young daughter in court? These years must have been bewildering for him too. He'd kept his aggression in check - he didn't shout at her, and he had a new partner. To anyone looking on, they were a happy family, laughing, chatting, going to the cinema. He may have thought he was doing his best. He loved his daughter, and the court process stoked his fears that Katherine got in the way of Sophie's love for him. Appallingly, he may really have believed that fighting Sophie in court was the best way to assert his love. But it's hard not to see him as punishing her, and punishing the mother through the daughter. Either way, it's not surprising that it estranged them further.

Sophie's story has had a happier outcome than many of the others in this book. This isn't Nini Clésinger, trapped in a convent, dying. It's a girl who moved back in with her mother at fifteen; who eventually managed to navigate an obfuscatory system and use it to escape the life she'd been forced into. But none of this should have been required of her. And the compliance came at such a cost. 'I couldn't even tell the truth,' she tells me. 'I hate not telling the truth.' Over the years the girl who fought and screamed had learnt to be quiet and to say what she was required to say. 'I miss believing that [protesting] would work. I realised from such a young age that all the things that should protect me didn't really.'

She hasn't seen her father since she turned sixteen and packed a suitcase, leaving his house never to return. This girl who once loved her father is now sure she no longer loves him. It's a sad conclusion, and one that seems to have been driven by the courts. This man staked everything on winning and insisted on his own victory. What could she do but stake everything on winning a court case of her own? And what room could there be in any of this for love?

She still dreams about him, even now she's crossed the country to go to university. A couple of nights before we speak, she dreamt that she and her mother were walking along with her father and his partner behind them. Suddenly she realised that her father was running, though no one else could see it; some sort of chase began, and she woke up to find herself shouting at him in her student room.

I think of Solange Dudevant, kidnapped by her father and then riding heroically through the Pyrenees in the snow. I think of Rose Ashton-Jinks in 1928, hurling a picture down at her father while he hit her mother. These children, whose love and hate become subject to the law – we ask too much of them. And so the centuries roll on and still there are children dying of the injuries inflicted on them by a parent, or just left sobbing into their pink bunnies, while their mothers sob into the white bunnies the children have left behind.

And yet. There is Frieda Lawrence. 'It's all come right – grazie a Dio!' There is Edna O'Brien, with her offering of the compassionate roses that seem all the more potent now that she's been waylaid by the death she always dreaded and was compelled by. 'Your children love you, that's all that counts, to hell with their father.' I hear their voices still, promising that life can be full, rich, comically various, even in the face of tragedy. Perhaps these are enough to go on. There are the children and the mother in Brighton, whose fears have been heard and acted on in court.

It's because situations of custody are so inherently tragic that we need to do all we can to avoid exacerbating conflict through the courts system, splitting parents into traumatised losers and over-empowered winners. Perhaps we can imagine a version of modernity that isn't flummoxed by motherhood, where emancipation and care can coexist; perhaps we can imagine a version of the legal system that gives children genuine agency, and has a more holistic sense of the family than patriarchal culture traditionally allows for. Here

EPILOGUE

mothers would be neither idealised nor vilified, and fathers wouldn't find themselves trapped in forms of manliness that entail cruelty and bullying. Here custody would be more about care than control, and the law would be just and humane.

ACKNOWLEDGEMENTS

Writing this book has taken me into entirely new territory. I have found myself needing to become an expert not only on two hundred centuries of legal history, but on the history of churches, asylums and civil rights, and this would not have been possible without the support of more established experts in all these fields.

I am especially grateful for the support of Rebecca Walker, who has engaged with my interest in these difficult periods of her life with extraordinary generosity and subtlety. I have gained hugely from the friendship of Antonia Fraser, who has lived alongside Caroline Norton for longer than I have. Andrew Counter has answered my questions about French literary history with patience and wit, and has proved a valuable ally in thinking about George Sand. He has also performed the noble office of introducing me to Anne Verju, and through her to Margot Giacinti, who has offered ingenious and extremely thoughtful research assistance in France. In England, Helen Sunderland has helped enormously with her meticulous surveys of cases and literatures and her deep understanding both of nineteenth-century history and the history of childhood, and Ross Belton has kindly shared his extensive knowledge of Caroline Norton. I'm grateful to Sarah Braybrooke for telling me about Elizabeth Packard.

I have been very grateful for conversations with Jennifer Aston, Katherine Gieve, Claire Fenton-Glynn, Stephen Gilmore, Ben Griffin, Henry Kha, Saskia Lettmaier, Mavis MacLean, Vanessa May, Rachel Pimm-Smith, Rebecca Probert, Pat Thane and Danaya Wright. Julia Brophy supported this project from its early stages, and was instrumental in putting me in touch with John Altman, for whose time and wisdom I am extremely grateful.

The contemporary courts have been a complex world of their own, and I thank all the judges, clerks, ushers and barristers who have made me welcome. Louise Tickle and Hannah Summers have both done so much to help me navigate the not-always-wholly-transparent transparency pilot and to demystify the world of judges and lawyers. I wouldn't have had the confidence to begin court reporting without their help, and the workshop Louise ran for the Transparency Project was instrumental in getting me started. Joe Whalen has generously helped connect me to some of the people trying to change things. Laura Rosefield has been a much-needed ally, and I have learnt a lot from her combination of clear-headed rigour and passion. Charlotte Proudman has affirmed me in my endeavours, inspired me with her own work, and given me a place to write about the courts at the Right to Equality blog. I am grateful to Lucy Hayton and Allison Quinlan for all the meticulous and thoughtful work they have done with me there. Adrienne Barnet and Rosemary Ashton have both shared their extensive knowledge of courts past and present extremely helpfully. I am especially grateful to the parents and children who have opened up to me about their stories, and hope I have found a way to represent your experiences truthfully.

These years of living and writing this book have been intense and long; that they have been far more often joyful than gruelling has been in large part thanks to my friends. Merve Emre provided early encouragement in telling me what this book could be. Kate Kilalea has been with me throughout, a loyal and stimulating friend who's been as fascinated and unnerved by everything I was discovering as

ACKNOWLEDGEMENTS

I was. Deborah Levy, and with her Sadie and Leila Levy-Gale, has been a much-needed champion, reminding me to keep up style and pleasure in this epic middle phase of life. It's been wonderful having Peter Boxall on hand closer to home, and he's provided crucial encouragement, reading drafts of many chapters in early stages and understanding exactly what it is I'm trying to do. I've been grateful for complicated conversations with Lyndsey Stonebridge and with Katherine Angel, whose loyalty and support have been invaluable, and for convivial and energising local companionship with Liese Spencer, Aida Edemariam and with Joanna Kavenna – who also made my final, not quite necessary but therefore all the more nourishing research trip to Paris into a high point of this year.

At King's College London, I have been grateful for the periods of research leave that continue to make writing possible, for the conversations with my students that help make feminism, literature and motherhood ever more stimulating and complicated topics for me, and for the friendship of colleagues including Clare Carlisle, Hannah Crawforth, Jon Day, Clare Pettitt and Neil Vickers. Edmund Gordon is a much-valued colleague and friend, whose thoughtful reading of my manuscript has helped bring balance and precision. Alexandra Harris read the manuscript in the midst of complex factors of her own; that I let her do this shows how much I continue to rely on her judiciousness and flair, seven books and almost twenty years into a friendship that continues to do so much to sustain me as a writer and reader. Lisa Appignanesi has also been reading my work for more years than I can easily count, and her expertise, insight, challenge and sparkle have once again been invaluable. Tessa Hadley shared my enthusiasm for Norman Stone's wonderful legal histories and for the nineteenth-century novel; I loved reading *Anna Karenina* at the same time as her and relied perhaps excessively and always gratefully on her ticks and underlines as I revised the manuscript.

Tracy Bohan has been a fierce supporter from the book's early stages, immediately seeing the need for it in the world. Arabella

Pike has had absolute confidence in it from our first conversation, and has proved an insightful and astute editor. I've been immensely grateful for how committed everyone at William Collins has been to the book. Sam Harding and Catriona Niven have made the process of gathering pictures easy and enjoyable. Alex Gingell has navigated the process from manuscript to book with deftness and precision. Kate Johnson proved the ideal copy editor, subtle and thoughtful in her engagement with the text. Laura Meyer is already proving a perceptive and dynamic champion of the book as it begins to make its way into the world.

My children have been with me throughout; this book has been woven into our days together, and my happiness with them has helped me to weather the sadder stories I was writing about, and to take responsibility for bringing them to light. Care is, as this book has shown, a communal enterprise at its best, and I'm so grateful for all the help with children (and pets!) offered with such generosity and enthusiasm by my parents, Ilse and Marcel, and also by Shrimp and Jay and Helen, who have all also enhanced the texture of our daily lives. Patrick Mackie has lived, month by month, inside these stories as I have; he has read them over and over again as they emerged, so that I can't now imagine not writing for an immediate, lovingly demanding reader. Writing this book has clarified for me that I am ill-suited for marriage, but that makes me all the more grateful to have our versions of commitment, care and coupledom.

LIST OF ILLUSTRATIONS

PLATES

Caroline Norton, portrait by George Hayter, 1835 (© Alamy/The Picture Art Collection).

Lord Melbourne, portrait by George Hayter, 1838 (© Getty Images/Hulton Archive).

Fletcher Norton, b. 1829 (courtesy of Lady Deirdre and Ian Curteis).

Brinsley Norton, b. 1831 (courtesy of Lady Deirdre and Ian Curteis).

Willie Norton, b. 1833 (courtesy of Lady Deirdre and Ian Curteis).

George Sand, portrait by Auguste Charpentier, 1838 (courtesy of Paris Musées/Musée de la Vie romantique).

Maurice Dudevant in national guard uniform, drawing by George Sand (courtesy of Paris Musées/Musée de la Vie romantique).

Maurice and Solange Dudevant, drawing by Nancy Mérienne (courtesy of Paris Musées/Musée de la Vie romantique).

Solange Clésinger by her husband Auguste Clésinger (courtesy of Paris Musées/Musée de la Vie romantique).

Drawing of Jeanne ('Nini') Clésinger by George Sand, 1854 (courtesy of Paris Musées/Musée de la Vie romantique).

Elizabeth and Theophilus Packard (courtesy of Bancroft Library, University of California at Berkeley).

Elizabeth Packard (courtesy of the Abraham Lincoln Presidential Library and Museum, Springfield, Illinois).

Britney Spears and her son at *The Late Show*, 2006 (© Getty Images/Brian ZAK).

Britney Spears and her sons visit the Dodgers Stadium, 2013 (© Getty Images/Handout).

Ernest and Frieda Weekley, 1911 (courtesy of University of Nottingham Manuscripts and Special Collections).

Frieda Weekley with Montague and Barby, 1905 (courtesy of University of Nottingham Manuscripts and Special Collections).

Frieda Weekley with her daughter (courtesy of University of Nottingham Manuscripts and Special Collections).

John Middleton Murry with Frieda and D. H. Lawrence on their wedding day, 1914 (courtesy of University of Nottingham Manuscripts and Special Collections).

Edna O'Brien with Carlo Gébler in Dublin, 1957. The hand-written note is by Ernest Gébler.

Edna O'Brien with Carlo and Sasha Gébler in Dublin, 1958.

A publicity photograph of the family taken in 1961.

Edna O'Brien, 1966 (© Getty Images/Evening Standard).

Alice Walker, Mel Leventhal and the dog, late 1960s (courtesy of Emory University Special Collections).

Alice Walker, Mel Leventhal and Rebecca, 1970 (courtesy of Emory University Special Collections).

Alice Walker and Rebecca outdoors, 1973 (courtesy of Emory University Special Collections).

Alice Walker and Rebecca, sitting (courtesy of Emory University Special Collections).

Alice Walker reading *The Color Purple*, 1982 (courtesy of Emory University Special Collections).

Alice Walker and Rebecca, early 1990s (courtesy of Emory University Special Collections).

LIST OF ILLUSTRATIONS

INTEGRATED IMAGES

Chapter 1

Extraordinary Trial! Norton v. Viscount Melbourne (© Bridgeman Art Library/British Library).

Chapter 2

Chateau de Nohant (© Lancosme Multimédia – Claude Darré/Musée George Sand et de la Vallée noire, La Châtre).
George Sand, portrait by Luigi Calamatta, 1837 (© Lancosme Multimédia – Claude Darré/Musée George Sand et de la Vallée noire, La Châtre).
Casimir Dudevant, drawing by unknown artist (courtesy of Paris Musées /Musée de la Vie romantique).
Bourges law court in 1836.

Chapter 3

'Kidnapping Mrs Packard' (from *Modern Persecution* by Mrs E. P. W. Packard, 1873).
'George, we have no mother!' (from *Modern Persecution* by Mrs E. P. W. Packard, 1873).
'The home from which Mrs Packard was kidnapped' (from *Modern Persecution* by Mrs E. P. W. Packard, 1873).
'How can I live without my children?' (from *Modern Persecution* by Mrs E. P. W. Packard, 1873).
Elizabeth Packard being carried to the bus (from *Modern Persecution* by Mrs E. P. W. Packard, 1873).
The Senate debating Elizabeth Packard's bill, (from *Modern Persecution* by Mrs E. P. W. Packard, 1873).
'Dr McFarland's self-accusation: "Mrs Packard has ruined me"' (from *Modern Persecution* by Mrs E. P. W. Packard, 1873).

The reunited family (from *Modern Persecution* by Mrs E. P. W. Packard, 1873).

Chapter 4

Montague and Elsa Weekley in Nottingham park, 1906 (courtesy of University of Nottingham Manuscripts and Special Collections).
Frieda Weekley by L. Peudy, c. 1912 (courtesy of University of Nottingham Manuscripts and Special Collections).
D. H. Lawrence by W. G. Parker, 1913 (courtesy of University of Nottingham Manuscripts and Special Collections).
The Weekley's nursemaid with the children, c. 1910 (courtesy of University of Nottingham Manuscripts and Special Collections).

Chapter 5

Edna O'Brien, 1953.
Ernest Gébler, 1949.
Edna O'Brien and Carlo Gébler. The writing on the photograph is Ernest Gébler's.
Carlo and Sasha Gébler in the back garden of Cannon Hill Lane, Morden, 1961.
Carlo and Sasha in boy scouts cub uniform, Cannon Hill Lane, October 1964.
The Royal Courts of Justice (© Alamy/Allan Cash Picture Library).

Chapter 6

May Poole, Alice Walker's great-great-great-great grandmother (courtesy of Emory University Special Collections).
500 African American demonstrators are blocked by police in Jackson, Mississippi, in June 1963 after a memorial march for Medgar Evers (© Getty Images/Bettmann).
Alice Walker with her baby (courtesy of Emory University Special Collections).
Alice, Mel and Rebecca (courtesy of Emory University Special Collections)

NOTES

Abbreviations used in the Notes:

CN, *SL* – Caroline Norton, *Selected Letters*, edited by Ross Nelson and Marie Mulvey-Roberts (Routledge, 2019); 2 volumes
DHL – D. H. Lawrence
FL – Frieda Lawrence
GS – George Sand
GS, *Correspondance* – George Sand, *Correspondance*, edited by Georges Lubin (Editions Garnier Frères, 1964–85); 25 volumes (translations my own)
GS, *LGS* – George Sand, *Letters of George Sand*, trans. Raphaël Ledos de Beaufort (Cosimo Books, 2009); 3 volumes
LDHL – *The Letters of D. H. Lawrence*, edited by James T. Boulton (Cambridge University Press, 1979–2000); 8 volumes
NA – The National Archives, Kew, London

Prologue

1 Maurice Dudevant to GS, 15 May 1836, in GS, *Correspondance*, III, p. 358.
2 CN to Melbourne, 2 Apr. 1836, in CN, *SL*, I, p. 168.

3 *Re L. (Infants)* (1962) EWCA Civ J0606-3.
4 Pax Thien Jolie-Pitt quoted in Seren Hughes and Kirean Southern, 'Brad Pitt made our lives hell', *The Times*, 21 Nov. 2023 (accessed 29 July 2025); Kanye West (@ye), Instagram post, 4 Feb. 2022 (deleted on 6 Feb. 2022).
5 Jacqueline Rose, *Mothers: An Essay on Love and Cruelty* (Faber, 2019), p. 7.
6 CN to Catherine Gore, 26 Oct. 1836, CN, *SL*, I, p. 250; CN to Melbourne, 9 May 1836, in CN, *SL*, I, p. 186.
7 Nora Fanshaw monologue, *Marriage Story*, dir. Noah Baumbach, Heyday Films/Netflix, 2019.

Chapter 1: Caroline Norton

1 CN to Melbourne, 2 Apr. 1836, in CN, *SL*, I, p. 168.
2 Diane Atkinson, *The Criminal Conversation of Mrs Norton* (Arrow Books, 2013), p. 49.
3 *The Times*, 26 Dec. 1828, p. 3.
4 CN to Mrs Moore, 17 June 1831, in CN, *SL*, I, p. 38; CN to Augusta Cowell, 5 Jan. 1832, in CN, *SL*, I, p. 68.
5 CN to Melbourne, 9 Aug. 1831, in CN, *SL*, I, p. 49.
6 CN to Melbourne, 1 Aug. 1831, in CN, *SL*, I, p. 43.
7 CN to Georgiana Seymour, 7 Nov. 1831, in CN, *SL*, I, p. 63.
8 CN to Mary Campbell, 10 Oct. 1843, in CN, *SL*, II, p. 122.
9 Paul O'Keeffe, *A Genius for Failure: The Life of Benjamin Robert Haydon* (Bodley Head, 2009), p. 160.
10 CN to George Norton, Dec. 1834, in CN, *SL*, I, p. 126.
11 Thomas Carlyle, *Past and Present* (Charles C. Little & James Brown, 1843), p. 160; *Evans v Evans* (1790) 161 E.R. 466.
12 CN to William Cowper, 3 Jan. 1837, 161 E.R. 466.
13 Caroline Norton, *Woman's Reward* (Saunders & Otley, 1835), vol. 3, p. 38.
14 *The Times*, 2 June 1835, p. 7

15 *Woman's Reward*, vol. 1, p. 194; vol. 2, p. 4; vol. 3, p. 41; vol. 1, p. 153.
16 Antonia Fraser, *The Case of the Married Woman* (Weidenfeld & Nicolson, 2021), p. 54; CN to Caroline Sheridan, 16 Oct. 1835, in CN, *SL*, I, p. 141.
17 CN to Edward Ellice, 6 Jan. 1836, in CN, *SL*, I, p. 162; CN to Edward Trelawny, 29 Dec. 1836, in CN, *SL*, I, p. 153.
18 CN to Edward Ellice, 20 Apr. 1836, in CN, *SL*, I, p. 178.
19 CN to Melbourne, 9 May 1836, in CN, *SL*, I, p. 186.
20 *The Magazine of Domestic Economy*, Sept. 1835, p. 65.
21 *De Manneville v De Manneville* (1804) 32 E.R. 762.
22 *De Manneville v De Manneville* (1804).
23 Lawrence Stone, *Broken Lives, Separation and Divorce in England, 1660–1857* (OUP, 1993), pp. 312, 314; *The Earl of Westmeath v The Countess of Westmeath* (1821) 37 E.R. 797.
24 *Ex parte Skinner* (1824) 9 Moore CP 278; *Ball v Ball* (1827) 57 ER 703; *R v Greenhill* (1836) 111 ER 922.
25 Michael Kohler, 'Shelley in Chancery: The Reimagination of the Paternalist State in "The Cenci"', *Studies in Romanticism* (37:4, Winter 1998), pp. 554, 556; *Shelley v Westbrooke* (1817) 37 ER 850.
26 Charles Dickens, *The Pickwick Papers* (Walter J. Black, 1900, vol. 2), p. 80.
27 Cited in Atkinson, *Criminal Conversation*, p. 172.
28 CN to Melbourne, 31 Aug. 1837, in CN, *SL*, I, p. 330.
29 CN to Melbourne, 2 June 1836, in CN, *SL*, I, p. 196.
30 *TRIAL, Norton v Viscount Melbourne, Extraordinary Trial!* (Fifth edition, 1836, price sixpence); Dickens, *Pickwick Papers*, vol. 2, p. 91.
31 *TRIAL, Norton v Viscount Melbourne*.
32 CN to Mary Shelley, 25 June 1836, in CN, *SL*, I, p. 206.
33 John Edward Trelawny, *Letters of Edward John Trelawny*, ed. H. Buxton Forman (OUP, 1910), p. 192, note 1; Mary Wollstonecraft, *A Vindication of the Rights of Woman* (A. T. Matsell, 1833), pp. 3–4; CN to Mary Shelley, 25 June 1836, in CN, *SL*, I, p. 206.

34 CN to George Norton, 26 June 1836, in CN, *SL*, I, p. 207.
35 George Norton to CN, 15 July 1836, in Atkinson, *Criminal Conversation*, p. 191.
36 CN to Edward Ellice, 5 Sept. 1836, in Atkinson, *Criminal Conversation*, p. 197.
37 CN to Melbourne, 25 Aug. 1831, in CN, *SL*, I, p. 56.
38 CN to Melbourne, 8 July 1836, in CN, *SL*, I, p. 215.
39 CN to Mary Shelley, 21 Apr. 1836, and CN to Catherine Gore, 26 Oct. 1836, in CN, *SL*, I, pp. 181, 250.
40 William Thompson and Anna Wheeler, *Appeal of One Half of the Human Race, Women, Against the Pretentions of the Other Half, Men* (Burt Franklin, 1970), p. 55.
41 Caroline Norton, *Observations on the Natural Claim of the Mother to the Custody of her Infant Children* (James Ridgway, 1837), pp. 49, 50, 55.
42 Norton, *Observations*, p. 58.
43 CN to John Murray, 24 Dec. 1836, in CN, *SL*, I, p. 262.
44 CN to George Norton, 11 July 1831, in CN, *SL*, I, p. 41; Norton, *Observations*, pp. 15, 4.
45 CN to Mary Shelley, 1 Feb. 1837, in CN, *SL*, I, p. 282.
46 CN to George Norton, 3 June 1837, in CN, *SL*, I, p. 313.
47 CN to Melbourne, 15 Mar. 1837, in CN, *SL*, I, p. 296.
48 CN to Melbourne, 15 June 1837, in CN, *SL*, I, p. 320.
49 CN to Edward Ellice, 28 Aug. 1837, in CN, *SL*, I, p. 327.
50 House of Commons, 21 Dec. 1837, cited in Fraser, *The Case*, p. 116.
51 CN to Henry Brougham, 31 July 1838, in CN, *SL*, II, p. 22.
52 Pearce Stevenson, *A Plain Letter to the Lord Chancellor on the Infant Custody Bill* (James Ridgway, 1839), p. 91.
53 CN to Thomas Talfourd, 5 Mar. 1839, in CN, *SL*, II, p. 53.
54 CN, *The Dream and Other Poems* (Carey & Hart, 1841), p. 18.
55 CN to George Norton, 12 Feb. 1840, in CN, *SL*, II, p. 65.
56 CN to Mary Shelley, 2 June 1840, in CN, *SL*, II, p. 78.
57 CN to George Norton, 11 Oct. 1840, in CN, *SL*, II, p. 78.
58 CN to George Norton, 11 Oct. 1840, in CN, *SL*, II, p. 83.

59 Fraser, *The Case*, p. 138.
60 CN to Georgiana Seymour, 20 Sept. 1842, in CN, *SL*, II, p. 111.
61 CN to Caroline Sheridan, 19 Sept. 1842, in CN, *SL*, II, p. 109.
62 CN to Georgiana Seymour, 20 Sept. 1842, in CN, *SL*, II, p. 111.

Chapter 2: George Sand

1 GS to the Countess d'Agoult, 10 July 1836, in GS, *LGS*, I, p. 261.
2 George Sand, *Story of My Life*, group translation edited by Thelma Jurgrau (State University of New York Press, 1999), p. 465.
3 Sand, *Story of My Life*, p. 465.
4 Sand, *Story of My Life*, p. 468.
5 Sand, *Story of My Life*, p. 468.
6 Sand, *Story of My Life*, pp. 490, 501, 502.
7 Sand, *Story of My Life*, p. 561.
8 Sand, *Story of My Life*, p. 169.
9 Sand, *Story of My Life*, pp. 803, 799.
10 GS to Hippolyte Châtiron, May 1822, in GS, *Correspondance*, I, p. 92; Sand, *Story of My Life*, p. 831.
11 GS to Emilie de Wismes, 30 Jan. 1823, in GS, *Correspondance*, I, p. 103 (trans. in Belinda Jack, *George Sand*, Chatto & Windus, 1999, p. 115).
12 Jean Jacques Rousseau, *Emile* (J. M. Dent and Sons, 1943), p. 322; Olympe de Gouges, *The Declaration of the Rights of Woman*, in Claire Goldberg Moses, *French Feminism in the 19th Century* (State University of New York Press, 1984), p. 10; *La feuille du salut public*, in Joan Wallach Scott, *Only Paradoxes to Offer: French Feminists and the Rights of Man* (Harvard University Press, 1996), p. 52.
13 Charles Chabot, *Conjugal Grammar*, in Patricia Mainardi, *Husbands, Wives and Lovers: Marriage and its Discontents in Nineteenth-century France* (Yale University Press, 2003), p. 68.
14 Jules Michelet, *Le Peuple* (Flammarion, 1974), p. 166; for Hugo and Balzac, see Claudie Bernard, *Penser la famille au dix neuvième siècle*,

1789–1870 (Publications de l'Université de Saint Etienne, 2007), p. 125–8; for Bouchot see Mainardi, *Husbands, Wives and Lovers*, pp. 100–02.

15 GS to Emilie de Wismes, 28 Nov. 1823, in GS, *Correspondance*, I, p. 118 (trans. in Jack, *George Sand*, p. 117); GS to Casimir Dudevant, 1 Aug. 1823 and 19 Aug. 1824, in GS, *Correspondance*, I, pp. 113, 145.

16 Sand, *Story of My Life*, pp. 854–5, 857.

17 GS to Casimir Dudevant, 15 Sept. 1825, in GS, *Correspondance*, I, p. 266.

18 GS to Dudevant, 15 Sept. 1825, in GS, *Correspondance*, I, pp. 268–9, 291.

19 GS to Sophie-Victorie Dupin, 1 Feb. 1830, in GS, *LGS*, I, p 61; GS to Casimir Dudevant, 19 or 20 Dec. 1829, in GS, *Correspondance*, I, p. 583.

20 GS to Jules Boucoiran, 3 Dec. 1830, in GS, *LGS*, I, p. 82–3.

21 GS to Boucoiran, 3 Dec. 1830, in GS, *LGS*, I, p. 82–3.

22 See Philip Mansel, *Paris between Empires 1814–1852* (Phoenix, 2003), p. 307.

23 Jules Sandeau, *Marianna*, in Jack, *George Sand*, p. 157.

24 GS to Maurice Dudevant, 16 Feb. 1831, in GS, *LGS*, I, p. 109; GS to Jules Boucoiran, 4 Mar. 1831, 13 Jan. 1831, in GS, *LGS*, I, pp. 110, 94, 118.

25 GS to Jules Boucoiran, 9 Mar. 1831, in GS, *LGS*, I, p. 110.

26 See Mansel, *Paris between Empires*, pp. 308, 319.

27 Sand, *Story of My Life*, pp. 893, 905.

28 GS to Charles Meure, 14 Apr. 1831, and to Emile Regnault, 2 May 1831, in GS, *Correspondance*, I, pp. 844, 854.

29 GS to Emile Regnault, 10 May 1831, in GS, *Correspondance*, I, p. 861; GS to Sophie-Victorie Dudevant, 31 May 1831, in GS, *Correspondance*, I, p. 886 (trans. in Jack, *George Sand*, p. 181); GS to Emile Regnault, 28 June 1831, in GS, *Correspondance*, I, p. 906; GS to Sophie-Victorie Dudevant, 31 May 1831, in GS, *LGS*, I, p.124.

30 GS to Emile Regnault, 28 June 1831, and GS to Charles Duvernet, 9

July 1831, in GS, *Correspondance*, I, pp. 906, 913.
31 GS to Emile Regnault, 23 Jan 1832, in GS, *Correspondance*, II, p. 11.
32 GS to Emile Regnault, 18 Feb 1832, in GS, *Correspondance*, II, p. 39.
33 GS to Casimir and Maurice Dudevant, 22 Apr. 1832, in GS, *Correspondance*, II, p. 72; GS to Maurice Dudevant, 4 Apr. 1832, in GS, *LGS*, I, p. 146.
34 See Jack, *George Sand*, pp. 199, 206; GS to Laure Decerfz, 2, 6, 7 July 1832, in GS, *Correspondance*, II, p. 120.
35 George Sand, *Indiana*, trans. Sylvia Raphael (Oxford World's Classics, 2008), p. 89.
36 For Balzac see Jack, *George Sand*, p. 143; Sand, *Indiana*, pp. 176, 51.
37 George Sand, *Lélia*, trans. Maria Espinosa (Indiana University Press, 1978), pp. 98–100.
38 GS to Marie Dorval, 22 June 1833, in GS, *Correspondance*, II, p. 339.
39 GS to Casimir Dudevant, 6 Apr. 1834, in GS, *Correspondance*, II, p. 559.
40 GS to Alfred de Musset, 12 May 1834, and GS to Maurice Dudevant, 8 May 1834, in GS, *Correspondance*, II, pp. 590, 577.
41 For a discussion of incest in nineteenth-century France, see Andrew Counter, *The Amorous Restoration: Love, Sex and Politics in Early Nineteenth-Century France* (Oxford University Press, 2016).
42 Sand, *Story of My Life*, p. 1058.
43 GS to Michel de Bourges, 22 Oct. 1835, in GS, *Correspondance*, III, pp. 88–90.
44 See Jack, *George Sand*, p. 250.
45 GS to Sophie-Victorie Dudevant, 25 Oct. 1835, in GS, *LGS*, I, p. 213.
46 Alfred de Musset, *The Confession of a Child of the Century*, trans. David Coward (Penguin, 2013), p. 6.
47 GS to the Countess d'Agoult, 25 May 1836, in GS, *Correspondance*, III, p. 399.
48 Jack, *George Sand*, p. 254.
49 Casimir Dudevant, 'Griefs Contre AD', in GS, *Correspondance*, III, pp. 848–9.
50 *Le Droit*, 18 May 1836, pp. 584–5.

51 GS to Charles Didier, 13 June 1836, in GS, *Correspondance*, II, p. 433; GS to the Countess d'Agoult, 10 July 1836, in GS, *LGS*, I, p. 260.
52 Maurice Dudevant to GS, 15 May 1836, in GS, *Correspondance*, III, p. 359–60.
53 GS to Solange Dudevant, 1 June 1836, in GS, *Correspondance*, III, p. 412.
54 Sand, *Story of My Life*, pp. 1065–6.
55 Dominique Desanti, *A Woman in Revolt: A Biography of Flora Tristan*, trans. Elizabeth Zelvin (Crown, 1972), pp. 163, 166.
56 For this, and the quotations from the court hearing that follow, see *Le Droit*, 30 July 1836, pp. 377–8.
57 George Sand, 'Lettres à Marcie' (Lettre VI), in *Les Sept Cordes de la lyre* (Michel Lévy frères, 1869), p. 230.
58 GS to L'Abbé de Lamennais, 28 Feb. 1837, in GS, *LGS*, I, p. 278; Sand, 'Lettres à Marcie' (Lettre III), p. 197.
59 Sand, 'Lettres à Marcie' (Letter III), p. 199; GS to the Countess d'Agoult, 25 Aug. 1837, in GS, *Correspondance*, IV, p. 283.
60 Sand, *Story of My Life*, p. 1081; GS to Louis Joseph Vincent, 8 Oct. 1837, in GS, *Correspondance*, IV, p. 199.
61 GS to Alexis Duteil, 8 Oct. 1837, in GS, *Correspondance*, IV, p. 219.
62 George Sand, *Voyage aux Pyrénées* (Librairie Hachette, 1904), p. 79 (Toulouse, 1); GS to Alexis Duteil, 8 Oct. 1837, in GS, *Correspondance*, IV, p. 220.
63 Sand, *Story of My Life*, p. 1066; GS to David Richard, May 1838, in GS, *Correspondance*, p. 424.
64 GS to Charlotte Marliani, 14 Sept 1838 and 14 Oct. 1838, in GS, *Correspondance*, IV, pp. 521, 534.
65 GS to René Vallet de Villeneuve, 7 Oct. 1847, in GS, *Correspondance*, VIII, p. 97.
66 GS to David Richard, May 1838, and Hippolyte Chatiron, 13 Apr. 1841, and Ferdinand Bascans, 3 May 1841, in GS, *Correspondance*, V, pp. 424, 274, 295.
67 Elizabeth Harlan, *George Sand* (Yale University Press, 2004), p. 197;

GS to Solange Dudevant-Sand, 13 Aug. 1841 and spring 1843, in GS, *Correspondance*, V, p. 398 and VI, p. 94.

68 GS to Charlotte Marliani, 11 Feb. 1847, and Maurice Dudevant-Sand, 16 Apr. 1847, in GS, *Correspondance*, VII, pp. 614, 660.

69 GS to Eugène Delacroix, 6 May 1847, and Emmanuel Arago, 18 July 1847, and Charles Poncy, 27 Aug. 1847, in GS, *Correspondance*, VII, p. 677 and VIII, pp. 21, 77.

70 Frédéric Chopin to Ludwika Jedrzejewicz, Christmas 1847, in *Chopin's Letters*, trans. E. L. Voynich (New York, 1931), p. 337.

71 Musset, *The Confession*, p. 78; Harlan, *George Sand*, p. 308.

72 Sand, *Story of My Life*, p. 974.

73 GS to Maurice Dudevant-Sand, 2 Jan. 1851, in GS, *Correspondance*, X, p. 16.

74 GS to Augustine de Bertholdi, 19 July 1851, in GS, *Correspondance*, X, p. 367.

75 GS to Solange Clésinger, 23 July 1851, and Pierre-Jules Hetzel, 27 May 1852 and 9 June 1852, and Pauline Viardot, 25 July 1852, in GS, *Correspondance*, X, p. 378 and XI, pp. 193, 205–206, 266.

76 GS to Prince Louis Napoléon Bonaparte, 20 Jan. 1852, in GS, *LGS*, II, p. 146.

77 GS to Emile Aucante, 10 Oct. 1852, in GS, *Correspondance*, XI, p. 410.

78 GS to Solange Clésinger, 10 July 1853, 7 Dec. 1853, and 9 Feb. 1854, in GS, *Correspondance*, XII, pp. 25, 181, 284.

79 Sand, *Story of My Life*, p. 421; George Sand, *The Bagpipers*, trans. Katharine Prescott Wormeley (Roberts Brothers, 1893), p. 214.

80 Solange Clésinger to GS, 23 Apr. 1852 and GS to Solange Clésinger, 25 Apr. 1852, in GS, *Correspondance*, XII, pp. 58–9, 64–5.

81 GS to Charles Poncy, 16 July 1854 and to Alphonse et Laure Fleury, 10 Oct. 1854, in GS, *Correspondance*, XII, pp. 512, 589.

82 GS to Louis Viardot, 21 Dec. 1854, and Solange Clésinger, 17 Dec. 1854, in GS, *Correspondance*, XII, pp. 704, 697.

83 GS to Eugène Bethmont, 23 Dec. 1854, in GS, *Correspondance*, XII, p. 705.

84 GS to Eugène Bethmont, 31 Dec. 1854, in GS, *Correspondance*, XII, p. 723.
85 GS to Eugène Bethmont, 17 Jan. 1855, in GS, *Correspondance*, XIII, p. 26.
86 GS to Solange Clésinger, 1 Jan. 1855, in GS, *Correspondance*, XIII, p. 14.
87 GS to Edouard Charton, 14 Feb. 1855, in GS, *LGS*, II, pp. 230–31.
88 Sand, *Story of My Life*, pp. 1112, 1111.
89 GS to Pierre-Jules Hetzel, 1 Feb. 1848, in GS, *Correspondance*, VIII, p. 264.
90 GS to Alfred de Musset, 12 May 1834, in GS, *Correspondance*, II, p. 590; GS to Gustave Flaubert, 31 Aug. 1872, in *The George Sand-Gustave Flaubert Letters*, trans. A. L. McKenzie (Billing & Sons, 1922), p. 260.

Chapter 3: Elizabeth Packard

1 Kate Moore, *The Woman They Could Not Silence* (Scribe, 2021), p. 17.
2 Elizabeth Packard, *The Prisoners' Hidden Life, or Insane Asylums Unveiled* (J. N. Clarke, 1871), p. 43.
3 Packard, *The Prisoners'*, p. 50.
4 'Britney Fails to Regain Custody', 31 Oct. 2007, www.news24.com (accessed 3 July 2025).
5 Britney Spears, *The Woman in Me* (Simon & Schuster, 2023), p. 148.
6 Elizabeth Packard, *The Great Drama or, The Millennial Harbinger* (The Case, Lockwood & Brainard Company, 1878), II, p. 248.
7 James Davis, *Frontier Illinois* (Indiana University Press, 1998), p. 181.
8 Packard, *Great Drama*, II, pp. 192, 268–9.
9 Packard, *Great Drama*, II, p. 307.
10 Alexis de Tocqueville, *Democracy in America*, trans. Henry Reeve, ed. Phillis Bradley (Alfred A. Knopf,1956), II, p. 192.
11 The average number of children born to white women fell from 7.04 to 3.56 between 1800 to 1900, Paula Fass, *The End of American*

Childhood: A History of Parenting from Life on the Frontier to the Managed Child (Princeton University Press, 2016), p. 14.

12 Maxine Margolis, *Mothers and Such: Views of American Women and Why They Changed* (University of California Press, 1984), p. 35; Steven Mintz, *Huck's Raft: A History of American Childhood* (Harvard University Press, 2006), p. 81.

13 Packard, *Great Drama*, IV, p. 151.

14 Packard, *Great Drama*, IV, p. 121.

15 Barbara Sapinsley, *The Private War of Elizabeth Packard* (Kodansha International, 1995), p. 61.

16 Sapinsley, *Private War*, p. 49.

17 Philip J. Greven, *Child-Rearing Concepts, 1628–1861* (F. E. Peacock Publishers, 1973), p. 145.

18 Robert Lowell, 'July in Washington', *Collected Poems* (Faber, 2003), p. 366.

19 Ann Douglas, *The Feminization of American Culture* (Papermac, 1977), p. 20; Ralph Waldo Emerson, 'Self-Reliance', in *Essays* (James Munroe & Co, 1841), pp. 41, 57.

20 Linda Carlisle, *Elizabeth Packard, A Noble Fight* (University of Illinois Press, 2018), p. 56.

21 Carlisle, *Elizabeth Packard*, p. 18

22 Carlisle, *Elizabeth Packard*, p. 73.

23 Fass, *End of American Childhood*, p. 37.

24 Richard Gundry, 'Observations upon Puerperal Insanity', *American Journal of Insanity*, 16 (1860), pp. 295, 303.

25 Moore, *The Woman*, p. 83; Carlisle, *Elizabeth Packard*, p. 88.

26 Packard, *Great Drama*, IV, p. 28.

27 Packard, *The Prisoners'*, p. 80.

28 Elizabeth Packard, *The Exposure on Board the Atlantic & Pacific Car of Emancipation for the Slaves of Old Columbia, Engineered by the Lightning Express, or Christianity & Calvinism Compared. With an Appeal to the Government to Emancipate the Slaves of the Marriage Union* (1864), pp. 95, 107; Moore, *The Woman* p. 107.

29 Packard, *The Exposure*, pp. 120, 123, 125, 130.
30 Packard, *The Prisoners'*, pp. 90–1.
31 Packard, *The Prisoners'*, p. 95.
32 Packard, *Great Drama*, I, p. 154.
33 Packard, *The Prisoners'*, pp. 60, 115.
34 Packard, *The Prisoners'*, p. 53.
35 Packard, *The Prisoners'*, p. 116.
36 For a lengthy discussion of the parallels between psychiatry and Transcendentalism, and for a discussion of Emerson's role in the incarceration of his brothers and Jones Very, see Benjamin Reiss, *Theaters of Madness: Insane Asylums and Nineteenth-Century American Culture* (University of Chicago Press, 2004), chapter 4. There was the shared nostalgia for a pre-industrialist world, the shared emphasis on the need to separate yourself from society and commune with nature; Brook Farm and the farm-containing Kirkbridian asylums may be two sides of the same impulse, at once profoundly progressive and profoundly backward-looking.
37 Packard, *Great Drama*, I, pp. 355, 358.
38 Packard, *Great Drama*, IV, p. 39.
39 Moore, *The Woman*, p. 173.
40 Packard, *Great Drama*, I, p. 344.
41 Packard, *Great Drama*, II, p. 208; see Reiss, *Theaters of Madness*, p. 16.
42 Moore, *The Woman*, p. 254; Packard, *Great Drama*, II, p. 228.
43 Packard, *Great Drama*, II, p. 56; Carlisle, *Elizabeth Packard*, p. 94.
44 Spears, *The Woman*, p. 183.
45 Eileen Reslen, 'Kevin Federline didn't use kids as "pawns" for Britney Spears' conservatorship', 30 June 2021, www.pagesix.com (accessed 3 July 2025).
46 Spears, *The Woman*, p. 5; Jem Aswad, 'Read Britney Spears' Full Statement Against Conservatorship; "I am Traumatized"', *Variety*, 23 June 2021, www.variety.com (accessed 3 July 2025).
47 Britney Spears, 15 July 2022, www.instagram.com (accessed 15 July 2022).

48 Elizabeth Packard, *Marital Power Exemplified in Mrs Packard's Trial, and Self-Defence from the Charge of Insanity* (Clarke, 1870), p. 63.
49 Statistic cited in Lawrence Stone, *Road to Divorce: England 1530–1987* (Oxford University Press, 1997), p. 387.
50 William Nelson, *The Americanization of the Common Law: The Impact of Legal Change on Massachusetts Society, 1760–1830* (Harvard University Press, 1975), p. 172; Tocqueville, *Democracy in America*, I, p. 103.
51 Grossberg, *Governing the Hearth: Law and the Family in Nineteenth-Century America* (University of North Carolina Press, 1988), p. 2.
52 David Peterson del Mar, *The American Family: From Obligation to Freedom* (Palgrave Macmillan, 2012), p. 52; Harriet Beecher Stowe, *Uncle Tom's Cabin* (Grapevine India, 2022), p. 569.
53 *Mercein v People* ex rel. Barry, 25 Wend. 64, 101 (NY) 1840; *State v Paine*, 23 Tenn 523 (1843); *Ex parte Hewitt*, 11 Rich. Law 330 (SC 1858); *Wand v Wand*, 14 Cal 512 (1860); Grossberg, *Governing the Hearth*, p. 248.
54 James Schoulder, *A Treatise on the Law of the Domestic Relations* (Little Brown, 1895), p. 393.
55 *Cowls v Cowls*, 8 Ill 436 (1846); *Miner v Miner*, 11 Ill 43 (1849).
56 *Lindsay v Lindsay*, 14 Ga 657 (1854).
57 Phyllis Chesler, *Mothers on Trial: The Battle for Children and Custody* (Lawrence Hill Book, 2011), p. 8.
58 Elizabeth Packard, *Modern Persecution, or Married Woman's Liabilities* (Hartford, 1874), I, pp. 11–13.
59 Moore, *The Woman*, p. 305.
60 Moore, *The Woman*, p. 318.
61 Moore, *The Woman*, p. 319.
62 Packard, *Marital Power*, p. 26.
63 Packard, *Marital Power*, p. 25.
64 Packard, *The Exposure*, p. 6.
65 Packard, *Marital Power*, p. 62.
66 'Theophilus Packard Diary', Barbara Sapinsley Papers (Oskar Diethelm Library, New York Hospital, Cornell Medical Center, New York), pp. 8, 21, 33.

67 'Theophilus Packard Diary', pp. 47, 54.
68 'Theophilus Packard Diary', pp. 37, 41.
69 Moore, *The Woman*, p. 355; Packard, *Great Drama*, IV, p. 12.
70 Moore, *The Woman*, pp. 428–9.
71 'Theophilus Packard Diary', p. 37.
72 'Theophilus Packard Diary', p. 42.
73 Mia Mercado, 'How Much is Britney's Lawyer to Blame?', *The Cut*, 25 June 2021 (accessed 3 July 2025).

Chapter 4: Frieda Lawrence

1 'And the Fullness Thereof . . .', in Frieda Lawrence, *The Memoirs and Correspondence* (Alfred A. Knopf, 1964), p. 74.
2 Lawrence, 'And the Fullness', p. 87; FL to Else von Richthofen, undated, in Lawrence, *Memoirs*, pp. 146, 153.
3 Lawrence, 'And the Fullness', p. 75; Ernest Weekley to Anna von Richthofen, 13 Sept 1902 and FL to Montague Weekley, 12 May 1954, in Lawrence, *Memoirs*, pp. 157, 375.
4 Janet Byrne, *A Genius for Living: A Biography of Frieda Lawrence* (Bloomsbury, 1996), p. 73.
5 Lawrence, 'And the Fullness', p. 95; Robert Lucas, *Frieda Lawrence, The Story of Frieda von Richthofen and D.H. Lawrence* (Martin Secker & Warburg, 1973), p. 37.
6 Ann Taylor Allen, *Feminism and Motherhood in Germany 1800–1914* (Rutgers University Press, 1991), p. 238.
7 Dora Marsden, 'To What End in Life?', *The Freewoman*, I, 14, 22 Feb 1912, p. 262; Dora Marsden, 'The New Morality: IV', *The Freewoman*, I, 8, 11 Jan. 1912, p. 142.
8 Byrne, *A Genius*, p. 63; Frieda Weekley to Otto Gross, Letter T, in John Turner et al., 'The Otto Gross-Frieda Weekley Correspondence: Transcribed, Translated and Annotated)', *D. H. Lawrence Review*, vol 22, No 22 (1990) p. 197.
9 Frieda Lawrence, *Not I, But the Wind . . .* (The Viking Press, 1934), p. 4.

10 D. H. Lawrence, *Mr Noon* (Granada Publishing, 1985), p. 156; DHL to Frieda Weekley, 20 Mar. 1912, in *LDHL*, I, p. 376.
11 Frieda Lawrence, *Not I*, p. 4.
12 Edward Nehls, *D.H. Lawrence, A Composite Biography* (University of Wisconsin Press, 1977), I, p. 162, III, p. 341.
13 Lawrence, 'And the Fullness', p. 104; Lawrence, *Not I*, p. 36.
14 Lawrence, *Mr Noon*, p. 185; DHL to Frieda Weekley, 7 May 1912, in *LDHL*, I, p. 393.
15 DHL to Ernest Weekley, 7 May 1912, in *LDHL*, I, p. 392; Ernest Weekley to Frieda Weekley, 10 May 1912, and to Anna von Richthofen, 12 May 1912 and 13 May 1912, in Lawrence, *Memoirs*, pp. 162, 164, 165.
16 Maude Weekley to Frieda Weekley, 14 May 1912, and Lily Kipping to Frieda Weekley, in Lawrence, *Memoirs*, pp. 166, 167.
17 DHL to Else Jaffe, 14 Dec. 1912, in *LDHL*, I, p. 486.
18 D. H. Lawrence, 'She Looks Back', *The Complete Poems* (Penguin, 1993), p. 205.
19 D. H. Lawrence, 'Fronleichnam', *Collected Poems*, p. 209.
20 DHL to Edward Garnett, 2 June 1912, in *LDHL*, I, p. 415; Nehls, *Composite*, p. 174.
21 DHL to Frieda Weekley, 14 May 1912, in *LDHL*, I, p. 401.
22 Byrne, *A Genius*, p. 117.
23 Byrne, *A Genius*, p. 119.
24 Lawrence, 'And the Fulness', pp.108–09; DHL to Edward Garnett 24 Oct. 1912, in *LDHL*, I, p. 463.
25 DHL to Blanche Jennings, 8 May 1909, in *LDHL*, I, p. 127; DHL to Jessie Chambers, June 1912, in *LDHL*, I, p. 412; Leo Tolstoy, *Anna Karenina*, trans. Rosamund Bartlett (Oxford World's Classics, 2014), pp. 368, 188, 320.
26 Tolstoy, *Anna Karenina*, p. 63.
27 See C. J. G. Turner, 'Divorce and *Anna Karenina*', *Forum for Modern Language Studies*, XXIII, 2, Apr. 1987, pp. 97–116.
28 See Turner, 'Divorce'.

29 Tolstoy, *Anna Karenina*, pp. 536–40.
30 Tolstoy, *Anna Karenina*, pp. 527, 729, 730.
31 Alphonse Daudet *Rose and Ninette*, in *The Novels, Romances and Memoirs of Alphonse Daudet* (Little, Brown and Company, 1900), IV, p. 534.
32 Thomas Hardy, *The Mayor of Casterbridge* (Macmillan, 1906), pp. 155, 157.
33 Thomas Hardy, *Jude the Obscure* (Harper and Brothers, 1923), pp. 331, 330, 402.
34 Hardy, *Jude the Obscure*, p. 420.
35 DHL to Sallie Hopkin, 23 Dec. 1912, in *LDHL*, I, p. 490; Hardy, *Jude*, p. 482.
36 Lucas, *Frieda Lawrence*, p. 90.
37 Frieda Weekley to Edward Garnett, Mar. 1913, in Lawrence, *Memoirs*, p. 178.
38 Lawrence, 'And the Fullness', p. 112.
39 Lawrence, *Not I*, p. 67.
40 Frieda Weekley to Else Jaffe, 22 July 1913, in *LDHL*, II, p. 50.
41 Ernest Weekley, 'Husband's Petition for Divorce', 1913, File 3528 (NA).
42 *Handley v Handley*, 7 TLR 74 – 1891; *Re A and B (Infants)* [1897], 1 Ch 786.
43 *CD v AB* (1908) SC 737.
44 *Mozley Stark v Mozley Stark and Hitchins* [1908–10] All ER Rep 643.
45 *Beedie v Beedie* (1889) 16 R 648; *Manders v Manders* (1890) 63 LT 627.
46 Edward May, 'Husband's Petition for Divorce', 1914, File 3263, (NA).
47 Kingston Charles Wilson, 'Husband's Petition for Divorce', 1914, File 4714 (NA).
48 Violet Lillian Warren, 'Wife's Petition for Judicial Separation', 1911, File 1799 (NA).
49 Parliamentary Debates (Hansard) 4th Series, Vol.155, 30 Mar. to 25 Apr. 1906, cols 1582–87.

NOTES

50 'Mother's Appeal for her Boy', *Daily Mail*, 18 Sept. 1913.
51 George William Hemsley Perkins, 'Husband's Petition for Divorce', 1914, File 4979 (NA).
52 Gerald James Gillespie, 'Husband's Petition for Divorce', 1914, File 5534 (NA).
53 Frederick Charles Horrocks, 'Husband's Petition for Divorce', 1914, File 4814 (NA).
54 Alice Jane Ashton-Jinks, 'Wife's Petition for Judicial Separation', 1910, File 869 (NA).
55 Alice Jane Ashton-Jinks, 'Wife's Petition for Judicial Separation', 1911, File 1703 (NA); 'Child Seized in Regent St', *Daily Mail*, 22 Mar. 1912.
56 'Hendon Woman's Story of Attack in her House', *Hendon and Finchley Times*, 9 Nov. 1928.
57 'Flight Lieutenant Throws himself from a Window', *Bucks Herald*, 24 June 1932.
58 Taylor Allen, *Feminism and Motherhood*, p. 141.
59 'Actresses' Suit Dismissed', *The Standard*, 2 Apr. 1912.
60 Byrne, *A Genius*, p. 151.
61 Lucas, *Frieda*, p. 100.
62 DHL to Cynthia Asquith, 30 Jan. 1915, in *LDHL*, II, p. 268.
63 FL and DHL to Ottoline Morrell, 19 May 1915, in *LDHL*, II, pp. 344–5.
64 Byrne, *A Genius*, p. 208.
65 Barbara Barr, 'Memoir of D.H. Lawrence', in Stephen Spender (ed.), *D.H. Lawrence: Novelist, Prophet, Poet* (Harper & Row, 1973), p. 294.
66 DHL to Dorothy Brett, 4 Nov. 1925, and DHL to Else Jaffe, 7 March 1926, in *LDHL*, V, pp. 332–3, 416.
67 Lucas, *Frieda*, p. 220; DHL to Dorothy Brett, 11 Apr. 1926, and FL to Mabel Dodge Luhan, 30 Oct. 1926, in *LDHL*, V, pp. 420, 568; Nehls, *A Composite*, III, p. 189.
68 FL to Edward W. Titus, 12 Feb. 1930, Harry T. Moore and Dale B. Montague (eds), *Frieda Lawrence and her Circle: Letters from, to and about Frieda Lawrence* (Macmillan, 1981), p. 3.

69 Nehls, *A Composite*, II, p. 466.
70 Cited in Byrne, *A Genius*, p. 393.

Chapter 5: Edna O'Brien

1 Stephen Cretney, *Law, Law Reform and the Family* (Oxford University Press, 2012), pp. 163–4.
2 'When a Home Breaks Up . . .', *Daily Mail*, 25 Oct. 1960.
3 'A Rose in the Heart of New York', Edna O'Brien, *A Rose in the Heart*, New York: Doubleday, 1979, p. 147.
4 Edna O'Brien, *Country Girl, A Memoir* (Faber, 2012), p. 117.
5 O'Brien, *Country Girl*, p. 122.
6 O'Brien, *Country Girl*, p. 125.
7 O'Brien, *Country Girl*, pp. 125–6.
8 O'Brien, *Country Girl*, p. 128.
9 Edna O'Brien, *The Country Girls, The Country Girls Trilogy* (Faber, 2019), p. 176; C. H. Rolph (ed.), *The Trial of Lady Chatterley* (Penguin, 1990); p. 17.
10 Alice Hughes Kersnowski (ed.), *Conversations with Edna O'Brien* (University of Mississippi Press, 2014), p. 84; O'Brien, *Country Girl*, p. 135; Carlo Gébler, *My Father and I: A Memoir* (Abacus, 2013), p. 67.
11 Edna O'Brien, *The Lonely Girl, The Country Girls Trilogy*, p. 431.
12 David Kynaston, *Modernity Britain 1957–62* (Bloomsbury, 2015), pp. 226, 214.
13 Edna O'Brien, *Time and Tide* (Penguin, 1993), p. 22.
14 Carlo Gébler, *Father and I: A Memoir* (Little, Brown, 2000), p. 100.
15 O'Brien, *Country Girl*, p. 151.
16 O'Brien, *Country Girl*, p. 153.
17 O'Brien, *Country Girl*, p. 156.
18 Gébler, *Father and I*, p. 111.
19 Gébler, *Father and I*, p. 120.
20 O'Brien, *Country Girl*, p. 301.

21 Sylvia Plath, 'Ariel', *Collected Poems* (Faber, 1981), p. 239.
22 O'Brien, *Country Girl*, p. 301.
23 Gébler, *Father and I*, p. 137.
24 Kynaston, *Modernity Britain*, p. 199; Doris Lessing, *The Golden Notebook* (Fourth Estate, 1993), p. 298; Betty Friedan, *The Feminine Mystique* (Thread, 2021), p. 39.
25 O'Brien, *Time and Tide*, p. 58.
26 Edna O'Brien, *Girls in their Married Bliss*, *Country Girls Trilogy*, pp. 617, 621.
27 O'Brien, *Country Girl*, p. 165; Gébler, *Father and I*, p. 192.
28 O'Brien, *Country Girl*, p. 161.
29 Bowlby cited in Ann Dally, *Inventing Motherhood: The Consequences of an Ideal* (Burnett Books Ltd, 1982), p. 88.
30 Bowlby cited in Angela Davis, *Modern Motherhood: Women and Family in England, 1945–2000* (Manchester University Press, 2012), p. 122; Ruth Anderson Oakley, *Challenge to Heritage* (Saint Catherine Press Ltd, 1955), pp. 26–7; Winnicott cited in Davis, *Modern Motherhood*, p. 120.
31 *K – an Infant and Others* [1960], EWCA Civ J1011-2; 'Court Boy Runs away from Plane', *Daily Mail*, 14 Oct. 1960; 'Child to go to Father', *Williams v Williams*, *The Times*, 7 April 1961, p. 17.
32 *Re S. (an Infant)* [1958] 1 All ER 783.
33 Humphrey Carpenter, *Spike Milligan: The Biography* (Hodder & Stoughton, 2004), p. 216.
34 *Re B.* (1962) 1 All ER 872; *Riddle v Riddle* [1962] EWCA Civ J1025-3; *Diplock v Diplock* [1965] EWCA Civ J0622-1.
35 'Children must not see Lady Caragh', *Daily Mail*, 14 Jan. 1961; 'Train robber wins custody of son', *Daily Mail*, 6 Apr. 1965, and 'Dorset's hidden link to the Great Train Robbery', 12 June 2022, www.dorstlive.com (accessed 3 July 2025).
36 'Mrs Tomkins' six goodbyes', *Daily Mail*, 6 June 1961; *H . . . (an Infant) and Another*, EWCA Civ J0327-5.
37 *Re L. (Infants)* (1962) 3 All ER 1.

38 *Re L. (Infants)* (1962).
39 Alfred Denning, *The Family Story* (Butterworths, 1981), p. 31.
40 Denning, *The Family*, pp. 194, 201.
41 *Nash v Nash* [1963] EWCA Civ J0111-1; *Lowe v Lowe* [1965] EWCA Civ J1006-1.
42 Evelyn Home, *Woman*, 25 Jan. 1964, p. 61; TCP advertisement, *Woman*, 5 Sept 1964, p. 56; Evelyn Home, *Woman*, 7 Mar. 1964, p. 77, and 30 May 1964, p. 48, and 12 Sept 1964, p. 77; Joan Williams, 'Healthy Living', *Woman*, 9 May 1964, p. 39.
43 *Shore v Shore* [1960] EWCA Civ J0429-3; *Baynham v Baynham* [1963] EWCA Civ J1023-4; *Thomson v Thomson* [1963] EWCA Civ J1216-1; *R- (an Infant) and Another* [1963] EWCA Civ J1007-4.
44 'Father knows best says judge', *Daily Mail*, 2 Mar. 1962; *Re W. (an Infant)* [1963] EWCA Civ J0723-1.
45 *Baker v Baker* [1955] 3 All ER 193; *Blume v Blume* [1965] EWCA Civ J1019-1; *Buxton v Buxton* [1965] 3 All ER 150; *Kaslefsky v Kaslefsky* [1951] P. 38 [1950] 2 All ER 398; *Bromby v Bromby* [1965] EWCA Civ J0232-2.
46 Author interview with Edna O'Brien, 24 June 2023.
47 O'Brien, *Girls in their Married Bliss*, p. 526.
48 Edna O'Brien, *August is a Wicked Month* (Faber, 2016), pp. 138, 142, 157.
49 O'Brien, *August*, pp. 138, 142, 157.
50 Gébler, *Father and I*, p. 210.
51 O'Brien, *Country Girl*, p. 163.
52 O'Brien, *Country Girl*, p. 165.
53 Author interview with O'Brien.
54 O'Brien, *Time and Tide*, p. 62.
55 O'Brien, *Country Girl*, p. 167.
56 Gébler, *Father and I*, p. 214.
57 Gébler, *Father and I*, p. 216.
58 O'Brien, *Country Girl*, p. 171.
59 Kersnowski (ed.), *Conversations*, p. 60.
60 Kersnowski (ed.), *Conversations*, p. 27; Simone de Beauvoir, *The Second*

NOTES

Sex, trans. Constance Borde and Sheila Malovany-Chevalier (Vintage, 2011), p. 568.
61 O'Brien, *Time and Tide*, p. 68.
62 O'Brien, *Time and Tide*, pp. 87, 265.
63 O'Brien, *Time and Tide*, pp. 297, 326.
64 Gébler, *Father and I*, pp. 388, 390, 391.
65 Gébler, *Father and I*, p. 402.
66 O'Brien, *Country Girl*, p. 3.
67 Author interview with O'Brien.
68 Walter Benjamin, *Illuminations*, trans. Harry Zohn (Schoken Books, 1969), p. 12.

Chapter 6: Alice Walker

1 Alice Walker, *The Third Life of Grange Copeland* (Weidenfeld & Nicolson, 2004), p. 309.
2 Rebecca Walker, *Black White and Jewish: Autobiography of a Shifting Self* (Riverhead Books, 2001), p. 181.
3 Alice Walker, *The Way Forward is with a Broken Heart* (Weidenfeld & Nicolson, 2000), p. 28.
4 Alice Walker, 'In these Dissenting Times: Women', *Collected Poems* (Weidenfeld & Nicolson, 2005), p. 159.
5 Alice Walker, *In Search of our Mothers' Gardens, Womanist Prose* (Weidenfeld & Nicolson, 2005), p. 387.
6 Evelyn C. White, *Alice Walker: A Life* (W. W. Norton & Company, 2006), p. 39.
7 Walker, *In Search*, p. 162.
8 Walker, *In Search*, p. 144.
9 Walker, *In Search*, p. 163.
10 White, *Alice Walker*, p. 78.
11 'Dead air' cited in Andrew B. Lewis, *The Shadow of Youth: The Remarkable Journey of the Civil Rights Generation* (Hill and Wang, 2010) p. 159; White, *Alice Walker*, p. 134.

12 White, *Alice Walker*, p. 140.
13 Walker, *Way Forward*, p. 20.
14 Walker, *Way Forward*, p. 28.
15 White, *Alice Walker*, p. 184.
16 Walker, *In Search*, p. 148; Bruce Schulman, *The Seventies: The Great Shift in American Culture, Society and Politics* (Da Capo Press, 2002), p. 4.
17 Alice Walker, *Gathering Blossoms Under Fire: The Journals of Alice Walker* (Weidenfeld and Nicolson, 2022), p. 31; Walker, *Third Life*, p. 316.
18 Walker, *Third Life*, pp. 5, 74, 76, 126.
19 Walker, *Third Life*, p. 161.
20 Walker, *Third Life*, p. 307.
21 White, *Alice Walker*, p. 205; Walker, *Way Forward*, p. 7; Walker, *Gathering Blossoms*, pp. 37.
22 Walker, *Gathering Blossoms*, p. 33.
23 Walker, *Gathering Blossoms*, pp. 40–2.
24 Walker, *Way Forward*, p. 30; Walker, *Gathering Blossoms*, p. 43.
25 Walker, *Way Forward*, p. 30; Walker, *Gathering Blossoms*, p. 43.
26 Alice Walker, *Meridian* (Weidenfeld & Nicolson, 2021), pp. 40, 90.
27 Walker, *In Search*, p. 393; Walker, *Gathering Blossoms*, p. 52.
28 Walker, *Gathering Blossom*, pp. 56, 58, 65, 60.
29 Rudolph P. Byrd (ed.), *The World Has Changed: Conversations with Alice Walker* (New Press, 2010), p. 169.
30 Ruth Rosen, *The World Split Open: How the Modern Women's Movement Changed America* (Viking, 1994), p 108.
31 Walker, *Gathering Blossoms*, p. 188.
32 White, *Alice Walker*, p. 278; Rebecca Walker, *Black White*, p. 56; Walker, *Gathering Blossoms*, p. 66.
33 Rebecca Walker, *Black White*, p. 57.
34 *People ex rel. BBB v CCC*, 44 A.D.2d 617; *Dintruff v McGreevy*, 34 N.Y.2d 887; *Lyritzis v Lyritzis*, 391 N.Y.S.2d 133.
35 Walker, *Gathering Blossoms*, p. 94.

NOTES

36 Walker, *Gathering Blossoms*, p. 93; Mary Ann Mason, *The Custody Wars: Why Children are Losing the Legal Battle and What We Can Do About It* (Basic Books, 1999), pp. 16–17.
37 *Feldman v Feldman*, 45 A.D.2d 320.
38 *Brim v Brim*, 1975 OK CIV APP 4; Daniel Rivers, '"In the best interests of the child": Lesbian and Gay Custody Cases, 1967–1985', *Journal of Social History* (43:4), 2010, p. 928; Gifford Guy Gibson with Mary Jo Risher, *By Her Own Admission: A Lesbian Mother's Fight to Keep Her Son* (Doubleday and Company, 1977), pp. 158–9, 241.
39 *In Re B.*, 85 Misc. 2d 515; Rivers, 'In the best', p. 922.
40 Nel Myricks and Donna L. Ferullo, 'Race and Child Custody Disputes', *Family Relations*, 35:2, 1986, p. 326–7.
41 Rivers, 'In the best', p. 923.
42 White, *Alice Walker*, p. 296.
43 Walker, *Gathering Blossoms*, p. 84.
44 Walker, *Gathering Blossoms*, pp. 92, 97, 109, 121.
45 Rebecca Walker, *Black White*, pp. 86–8.
46 Walker, *Gathering Blossoms*, p. 139; Rebecca Walker, *Black White*, p. 60.
47 Peter Cole, 'St Francis Square: How a Union Built Integrated, Affordable Housing in San Francisco', 2 Jan. 2016, *Jstor Daily*, daily.jstor.org (accessed 3 July 2025); Walker, *Gathering Blossoms*, p. 139.
48 Walker, 'My Daughter is Coming', *Collected Poems*, pp. 360–61.
49 Walker, 'My Daughter is Coming', *Collected Poems*, pp. 360–61.
50 Walker, *Gathering Blossoms*, p. 155; Rebecca Walker, *Black White*, p. 109.
51 Walker, *In Search*, p. 359.
52 Alice Walker, *The Color Purple* (Orion, 2011), pp. 113, 183.
53 Rebecca Walker, *Black White*, p. 165.
54 Walker, *Way Forward*, p. 28; Alice Walker, *Desert Island Discs*, Radio 4, 20 May 2013.
55 Rebecca Walker, *Black White*, p. 312; Walker, *Gathering Blossoms*, p. 278.
56 *Perotti v Perotti*, 78 Misc. 2d 131.
57 Ellen Goodman cited in Rosen, *The World*, p. 323.
58 *Kramer vs. Kramer*, dir. R. Benton, Columbia Pictures, 1979.

59 Julia Brophy, *Law, State and the Family: The Politics of Child Custody*, PhD submitted to the University of Sheffield, 1985, p. 237; Susan Steinman, 'Joint Custody: What We Know, What We Have Yet To Learn, and the Judicial and Legislative Implications', *UC Davis Law Review*, 16, Spring 1983, pp. 748, 761.
60 Rebecca Walker, 'Becoming the Third Wave', *Ms.*, Jan 1992.
61 Walker, *In Search*, p. xi.
62 Walker, *Gathering Blossoms*, p. 398.
63 Walker, *Gathering Blossoms*, p. 412.
64 Rebecca Walker, 'How my Mother's Fanatical Feminist Views Tore us Apart', *Daily Mail*, 23 May 2008.
65 Author interview with James Norman, 15 June, 2024.
66 Author interview with Rebecca Walker, 26 Aug, 2024.
67 Alice Walker, 'Be Nobody's Darling', *Collected Poems*, pp. 193–4.

Epilogue

1 Richard A. Gardner cited in Joan S. Meier, 'A Historical Perspective on Parental Alienation Syndrome and Parental Alienation', *Journal of Child Custody*, 6:3–4, 2009, pp. 235, 238.
2 Charlotte Proudman, *He Said, She Said: Truth, Trauma and the Struggle for Justice in the Family Court* (Weidenfeld & Nicolson, 2025), p. xxiii.
3 *Warwickshire County Council v The Mother & Ors* [2023] EWHC 399 (Fam).
4 Hannah Dreyfus, 'In the Child's Best Interest', 19 Aug. 2023, www.propublica.org (accessed 9 July 2025).
5 Joan Meier et al., 'United States Child Custody Outcomes in Cases Involving Parental Alienation and Abuse Allegations: What do the Data Show?', *Journal of Social Welfare and Family Law*, 42:1, 2020, pp. 92–105; Joan Meier, 'Questioning the Scientific Validity of Parental Alienation Labels in Abuse Cases', in Jean Mercer and Margaret Drew (eds), *Challenging Parental Alienation* (Routledge, 2021), p. 220.
6 *J v B* (Ultra-Orthodox Judaism: Transgender) [2017] 4 WLR 201.

NOTES

7 Constance Debré, *Love Me Tender*, trans. Holly James (Tuskar Rock Press, 2023), pp. 44, 47.
8 Debré, *Love Me Tender*, pp. 54–5.
9 Altman later elucidated this further with: 'Has there been any analysis of the parents' respective capacity to provide parenting for the child, would the absent parent be easy about providing contact to the residential parent after change, and, particularly, what would be the effect on a child to be wrenched from a settled and beneficial environment and away from the residential parent, if that is the effect? Is this putting the welfare of the child first? All cases depend on their own factors. I would deprecate using 'transfer of residence' as some sort of strategy or standard response. Contact cases must be judged on weighing all the facts, not by singling out one particular standard solution.'
10 Author interview with John Altman, 26 Nov. 2024.
11 Ministry of Justice, 'Assessing Risk of Harm to Children and Parents in Private Law Children Cases, Final Report', 2020; Reem Alsalem, 'Custody, Violence against Women and Violence against Children', Human Rights Council, Fifty-third session, 19 June–14 July 2023, Agenda item 3.
12 Adrienne Barnett, Arianna Riley and 'Katherine', 'Experiences of Alienation Interventions', in Mercer and Drew, *Challenging Parental Alienation*, pp. 78, 82.
13 Barnett, Riley and 'Katherine', 'Experiences of Alienation Interventions', p. 82.

INDEX

Page references in *italics* indicate images.

abortion 299, 309, 312, 313, 330
adultery: Alice Ashton-Jinks and 226–7; Caroline Norton and 4, 26, 33–40, 47, 93, 101, 162; *CD v AB* (1908) and 217; Civil Code, French (Napoleonic Code) (1804) and 69, 91; cruelty and 221–2; Cynthia Giddings and 270; Denning and 6, 267; Edna O'Brien and 261, 271; *Effi Briest* and 220; Elvira Marjorie Riddle and 264; Ethel Horrocks and 226; Frieda Lawrence and 6, 199, 216, 229, 235, 240; George IV's accuses Queen Caroline of 36–7; George Sand and 94, 96, 101, 118; Gertrude Perkins and 224; Guardianship of Infants Act (1886) 216–19, 221, 240; *Handley v Handley* (1891) 216; Henrietta Greenhill and 31, 48–9; *Lindsay v Lindsay* (1854) 167; Matrimonial Causes Act (1857) 162, 223; *Mozley Stark v Mozley Stark and Hitchins* (1908–10) and 217–19; *Re A and B (Infants)* (1896) and 210, 216–17; *Re B.* (1962) and 263–4; Roger Cordrey and 264; Russia and 206; Spike Milligan and 263; *The Evil Genius* and 209–10; USA and 163, 167

Allan, Ted 254
Allen, Robert 313, 315, 323, 324
Alsalem, Reem 370
Altman, John 366–7, 411*n*
Amherst Female Seminary 139
'Angel of History' (Walter Benjamin concept) 236, 288–9
Anthony, Susan B. 168
Ashton-Jinks, Alice 226–8, 236, 271, 376–7
Ashton-Jinks, Louis Thomas 226–8, 271, 376–7
Ashton-Jinks, Philip 226, 228, 236
Ashton-Jinks, Rose 227, 236, 376–7
Ashton-Jinks, Therese 227
Avedon, Richard: *Nothing Personal* 156–7

Baker, Abner 140–41
Baker v Baker (1955) 271
Baldwin, James 323; *Nothing Personal* 156–7
Baldwin, Joseph 165

Balzac, Honoré de 81, 84; *La Grenadière* 70–71
Bargrave Deane, Sir Henry 218, 222, 223, 230
Barry-Relph, Trish 357–8, 360
Baumbach, Noah 11
Beauvoir, Simone de 281–2
Beecher Stowe, Harriet: *Uncle Tom's Cabin* 155, 164
Beedie v Beedie (1889) 219
Benjamin, Walter 236, 288–9
Bethmont, Eugène 118–19
Beverly Hills psychiatric treatment centre, Los Angeles 157–8
Bishop, George: *Every Woman Her Own Lawyer* 165–6
Blackstone, William: *Commentaries on the Laws of England* 164
Blue, Earnestine 319, 339
Blume v Blume (1965) 271
Bonaparte, Napoleon 60, 61, 69, 70, 89, 90, 111, 113, 114, 124
Bonfield, Thomas 171
Bouchot, Frédéric 71
Boucourain, Jules 74, 77
Bowlby, John 317; *Child Care and the Growth of Love* 261; *Maternal Care and Mental Health* (WHO report, 1951) 261
Bradley, Gladys 194–5, 197
Bradley, Madge 194–5
Brando, Marlon 281
Brault, Augustine 106
Brougham, Lord 52
Buckland's, Laleham 57
Budd, Edward C. 364
Bulletin de la République 111
Burton, Richard 281
Bushnell, Horace: *Christian Nurture* 142
Buxton v Buxton (1964) 271–2
Byron, George Gordon, Lord 16, 18, 20, 32, 65

Cafcass (Children and Family Court Advisory and Support Service) 368–9
Calvin, John 145, 152
Calvinism 135, 140, 143, 145, 152, 171
CAMHS (Child and Adolescent Mental Health Services) 375
Campbell, Fitzroy 25–6
Campbell, Sir John 37
Carlile, Richard 44
Carlyle, Thomas 22
Carmichael, Stokely 302, 303, 312
Caroline, Queen 36–7
Caton, John 166–7
CD v AB (1908) 217
Chabot, Charles: *Conjugal Grammar* 70
Chamber of Deputies (French Parliament) 75, 89
Chamber of Peers (Chambre des Pairs) (French Upper House) 89
Chambers, Jessie 204
Charles X, King of France 75
Charton, Édouard 120–21
Chateaubriand, François-René, Vicomte de 65, 121; *René* 87
Chazal, Aline 97–8, 123–4
Chazal, Andre 97–8, 103, 123–4
Chazal, Ernest 97
Child, Lydia Maria: *Mother's Book* 140, 146
children: 'best interests of the child' 166, 184, 217, 316–21, 332; bodily love of mother for 76, 242, 281–2; Bowlby on 261, 317; corporal punishment for 42; divorce court records, traces of within 219–26; feminism and 316–17; foster care and 357, 358, 361, 368, 370, 371; idealized 70–71, 76, 139–42; illegitimate 27–8, 45, 61–3, 97, 208; innocence/goodness of 140–42; lesbian mothers and 319–20; Locke's idea of as tabula rasa/blank slate 140; longing for 110, 122, 147, 151; mother's capacity to hate her own 10; need of mothers/rights to maternal care 52, 54, 102–3, 133, 261–4, 267, 316–17, 338; ownership of/as property 8–9,

11, 27–33, 71, 90, 97, 163, 293, 332; parental alienation syndrome and 348–9, 351, 353, 357, 362, 364, 368–70; rights of, campaigns for 139–42, 163–6, 239–40, 270–71, 318–21; slavery and 155, 164–5; suffering of 3, 5, 12, 58, 59, 80, 95, 96, 176, 185, 220–29, 271, 322–3, 328, 331, 334, 335, 339, 341–5, 348–9, 351–2, 355–70, 377. *See also individual mother and child name*
Chopin, Frédéric 106–7, 109, 110
civil rights movement 6, 7, 292–304, 309, 311, 312, 316
Clésinger, Auguste 108–10, 113, 114, 117–19, 122, 376
Clésinger, Nini 112–23, 376
Collins, Wilkie: *The Evil Genius* 209–10, 212
common law, English 5, 45, 56, *161*, 163, 165, 167, 218
Congregationalist Church 134, 135, 140, 142
Congreve, William 348
conservatorship laws 158–9, 182, 183
control, custody and 9, 17, 22, 70, 84, 92, 127, 138, 270, 349
Cordrey, Roger 264
Court of Appeal 262, 264, 265, 266, 270
Court of Chancery 28, 29, 56, 210, 216–19
Court of Common Pleas 31, 36
Court of King's Bench 29
Courts of Appeals, US 315
Cowls, Ann 166
cruelty: Alice Ashton-Jinks and 226, 228; Auguste Clésinger and 117–18; Caroline Norton/George Norton and 22, 23, 40, 45, 49; Casimir Dudevant and 94, 99–100; court process/pseudo-therapy and 361; divorce on grounds of 226, 228, 271–2; Edna O'Brien and 271–2; fathers as forfeiting rights through extreme 28; jury not finding evidence of 222; knowingly giving wife venereal disease as 223; Matrimonial Causes Act (1857) and 162; mothers and 9; Spike Milligan and 263
custody: cinema and 332–4; control, as battle for 9, 17, 22, 70, 84, 92, 127, 138, 270, 349;
courts and *see individual type of court and court name*; definition/etymology 9, 27; 50/50 3, 6–7, 295, 315–16, 335, 343, 352, 353; history and 340; home and *see* home; joint custody 8, 166, 312–14, 325, 331–4; made without lawyers 294; madness and *see* madness; men writing about daily experience of 330; as ownership 8–9, 11, 31–2, 293; prerogative of care and 27; reading about/literary tradition and 204–13; tragic nature of 2, 11, 12, 59, 104, 110, 202, 212, 213, 275, 377; welfare officers and *see* welfare officers; winners and losers of 92
Custody of Infants Act (1839) 5, 48–54, 216
Custody of Infants Act (1873) 216

d'Agoult, Marie 59, 92, 94
Daily Mail 241, 265, 270, 337, 340, 341
Dallas, Lord Chief Justice 31
Daudet, Alphonse: *Rose and Ninette* 210, 212
De Manneville v De Manneville (1804) 28–31
Debré, Constance: *Love Me Tender* 365–6
Delaborde, Caroline 63, 64, 106
Denning, Lord 6, 265–8, 272, 275
Derby, George 37
Deschartes 65, 66
Dickens, Charles 34, 357; *Bleak House* 210, 357; *The Pickwick Papers* 37
Dickens, Monica 251

Diderot, Denis 68, 100
Diplock, Claire 264
Disciples of Christ 142
Disraeli, Benjamin 21
divorce: adultery and *see* adultery; Alice Walker and *see* Walker, Alice; *Anna Karenina* and 204–9, 212, 213; Caroline Norton and *see* Norton, Caroline; Civil Code, French (Napoleonic Code) (1804) and 69, 89–90; custody cinema and 332–4; cruelty and 222; decree nisi 219–20, 230; Divorce Court 162, 215–30, 265, 270; Divorce Reform Act (1969) 279; Divorce Registry 224, 236; Edna O'Brien and *see* O'Brien, Edna; *Effi Briest* and 210–11; Elizabeth Packard and *see* Packard, Elizabeth; fault-based 90; Frieda Lawrence and *see* Lawrence, Frieda; George Sand and *see* Sand, George; German divorce courts 229; hatred and 355; *Jude the Obscure* and 211; Matrimonial Causes Act (1857) and 162; Matrimonial Proceedings (Children) Act (1958) and 240–41; no-fault 279, 317, 331, 332; *Rose and Ninette* and 210; surviving 331–4, 342–4; USA and 162–3, 314–16
Dix, Dorothea 145, 156
Dole, Sybil 135, 151, 153–4, 172–3, 181
Domestic Abuse Commissioner 368
Donleavy, J. P. 244; *The Ginger Man* 244–5
Dorval, Marie 85–6
Dowson, Will 192, 213
Dudevant, Casimir 68, 70–75, 77, 82, 85–8, 91–5, 93, 99, 103–5, 118, 124, 251
Dudevant, Maurice 2, 59, 73, 76, 80–83, 88, 91, 97, 112, 115; birth 70; custody court cases and 100–106; fantasizes about reconciling parents 97–8; health 71, 101–2, 105–6; mayor of La Châtre 111; schooldays 85, 86–7, 95; tutor 74, 77
Dudevant, Solange 2, 59, 76, 80–81, 91, 97, 103–25, 157, 182, 376–7; birth of 73; at Bourges 98; Casimir kidnaps 103–4, 376–7; Clésinger and 108–10, 113–21; convent, goes to 116; custody case over children of 117–21; in Mallorca 106; mother, relations with deteriorate 106–10; Nini and 112–21; parentage of 73; Paris, mother takes to 82–3; poem written to by mother 120; Pyrenees, mother takes on pilgrimage to 104–5, 185, 376; schooldays 87–8, 95; separation proceedings against husband 113
Dupin, Hippolyte 61, 65, 67, 74
Dupin, Marie-Aurore 60–61, 63–7, 70, 75–6, 81, 87, 92, 103, 106, 111, 112, 116, 119, 120
Dupin, Maurice 60–63, 66, 75, 87, 91, 119, 120, 122
Dupin (née Delaborde), Sophie-Victoire 60–61, 63, 65–8, 75, 76, 91
Duteil, Alexis 88, 89, 96, 104

Eldon, Lord 29–33
Ellice, Edward 25–6
Emerson, Ralph Waldo 143, 152, 155, 185; Transcendentalist movement and 143, 398*n*
Enfantin, Prosper 79
Enlightenment 4, 22, 60, 75
Evans v Evans (1790) 23
Evans, Sir Samuel Thomas 215, 216, 218, 222–4, 226–7, 228–30
Evers, Medgar 300, *300*
Evershed, Lord 264
Ex parte Hewitt (1858) 165

fairy tales 60, 66, 191
Family Solutions Court 367
fathers: equal rights of 316–17; fathers' rights groups 10, 316, 332; forfeiting rights through extreme

INDEX

negligence or cruelty 28; good father, invention of idea 12; Guardianship Act (1973) and/ married mothers gain equal rights with 279; harmed by roles they can feel compelled to adopt in court 11–12; imbalance of power in court between mother and 352–5; ownership of children/ children as property of 8–9, 11, 27–33, 46, 71, 90, 97, 163, 293, 332; sexual and physical abuse, accused of 357–64; transgender 364–5
Federline, Kevin 131, 158, 159, 183, 184
Feldman v Feldman (1974) 317
feminism: Alice Walker/Rebecca Walker and 294–5, 309, 311–13, 316, 324, 326, 332, 335–8, 343–4; ambivalence allowed to mothers, 1960s and 1970s fight for 309; Caroline Norton and 39, 44, 47, 48, 53, 54; Civil Code, French (Napoleonic Code) (1804) and 69; court system and 352; Custody of Infants Act and 54; Edna O'Brien and 251, 267, 281–2; Elizabeth Packard and 133, 146, 163; failure of feminism to account for the demands of motherhood 7, 10; George Sand and 69, 79, 84, 96, 100, 102, 111; German 193, 229; Guardianship of Infants Act (1925) and 239; idealisation of the good feminist 10; *Kramer vs. Kramer* and 332; motherhood, ambivalent relationship between feminism and 10, 281–2, 309; 'New Woman' 194; right not to mother and 281–2; Saint-Simonians and 79, 84, 102; second-wave 10, 251; third wave 335–6, 343–4; Women's Rights Movement and 44–5
Figaro 78
First World War (1914–18) 198, 230–33, 239
50/50 custody 3, 6–7, 295, 315–16, 321–30, 335, 343, 352, 353

Flaubert, Gustave 124
Flood, William 224
Fluke, John 37
Follett, Sir William 37
Fontane, Theodor: *Effi Briest* 210–11, 212
foster care 357, 358, 361, 368, 370, 371
France 4, 5, 21, 28, 29, 59–125, 138, 139, 189, 210, 234, 282, 322, 365; Civil Code/Napoleonic Code (1804) 60, 69, 70, 89–90; Civil Tribunal of the Seine 97; Constitution (1793) 69; July Ordinances 75; Napoleon Bonaparte and 60, 61, 69, 70, 89, 90, 111, 113, 114, 124; Napoleon III and 113–14; revolution (1789) 19, 60, 61–2, 68–9, 70, 79, 89, 90, 111, 139; revolution (1830) 75–6, 89; revolution (1848) 110–12, 119; women's rights in/George Sand and 59–125 *see also* Sand, George
#FreeBritney movement 159, 183
Freewoman. A Weekly Feminist Review, The 194
French, Marilyn: *The Women's Room* 322
Frick, Ernst 192
Friedan, Betty 264, 281–2, 312: *The Feminine Mystique* 258–9

G, Vicomtesse de: *The Art of Being Loved by One's Husband* 69–70
Gardner, Richard A. 348, 369
Garnett, David 202
Garnett, Edward 201–2, 204, 213, 215–16
Gault, Jerry 320
Gébler, Ernest 244–58, *245*, *247*, 260, 262, 264–5, 270–81, 283–4
Gébler, Karl (Carlo) 2, 246–8, *247*, 250, *250*, 253, 255–8, *256*, 260, 262, 271, 273, 275, 278–81, 283–4, 332
Gébler, Sasha 2, 247, 250, *250*, 252, 255, *256*, 258, 260, 262, 271, 272, 273, 275, 279, 332

general elections: (1830) 19; (1835) 20–21; (1837) 51; (1964) 259
George IV, King 36–7
Gerhard, Adele: *Motherhood and Intellectual Work* 193
Germany 92, 189, 190–95, 197, 198, 203, 210, 229, 235; federal civil code (Bürgerliches Gesetzbuch) (1896) 229; First World War (1914–18) and 198, 230–33, 239
Gibson, Eliza 37, 38
Giddings, Cynthia 270
Giddings, Raymond 270
Gillespie, Albert 225
Gillespie, Marie 225
Gilliatt, Penelope 254
Godey's Lady's Book 139–40
Godwin, William: *Caleb Williams* 19, 39
Goetz, Reva 183
Goldsmith, Judith 314, 323, 329
Goodman, Ellen 332
Gordon, Henry 161
Gordon, Robert 318
Gore, Catherine 44
Gouges, Olympe de: in *Declaration of the Rights of Woman and of the Female Citizen* 69
Grandsagne, Stéphane de 73
Greenhill, Henrietta 31–2, 48–9
Grey, Charles Grey, Earl 19–20, 52
Gross, Otto 192, 194, 195, 200
Guardianship Act (1973) 279
Guardianship of Infants Act (1886) 216–19, 221, 240
Guardianship of Infants Act (1925) 239–40

H (an Infant) and Another (1962) 265
Hacker, Lisa 131
Hague Convention on the Civil Aspects of Child Abduction 370
Hampton Court 21, 34
Handley v Handley (1891) 216
Hardy, Thomas 209, 232; *Jude the Obscure* 209, 211–12, 213; *The Mayor of Casterbridge* 211

Harm Panel Report 368, 369
Haydon, Benjamin 21
Hegel, Georg Wilhelm Friedrich 11
Hendrix, Jimi: 'Star-Spangled Banner' 305
High Court 263–4, 275, 357
Hill, Anita 335
Hitchins, Charles 217
home: 'broken' 267, 331; children shifting between 7, 334–5, 357; homelessness, custody and 7–8; ideal 251; made strange by absence 325, 334–5; 'part-time' 264
Home, Evelyn 268–9
Horrocks, Audrey 226
Horrocks, Ethel 225–6, 236
Horrocks, Frederick 226
House of Lords 20, 52, 54, 267
Hugo, Victor 66, 70, 83, 111
Hurston, Zora Neale 312
Huxley, Elspeth: 'The Second Sex' 258

immigration 8, 352
Ingham III, Samuel D. 183

Jackson, Andrew 139, 152–3
Jackson, Mississippi 292, 300, *300*, 302, 310
Jacksonville, Florida 145, 153, 156, 169, 178
Jaffé, Edgar 192
James, Henry: *What Maisie Knew* 210, 335
James, Jayden 2
Jefferson, Thomas 133, 302
Jim Crow laws 297
Johnson, Lyndon B. 299–300
joint custody 8, 312–14, 324–5, 331–4
Jolie, Angelina 8

K – an Infant and Others (1960) 262
Kaplan, Mark Vincent 159
Kardashian, Kim 8
Kaslefsky v Kaslefsky (1951) 272
Keeler, Christine 259
Keeping Children Safe from Family Violence Act (Kayden's Law) 369

INDEX

Kelly, Joan 323–4
Kennedy, John F. 298
Kenny, Sean 281
Kent, James: *Commentaries on American Law* 164
kidnapping: Aline Chazal 97–8; Caroline Norton attempts 50–51; Edward May 220; Elizabeth Packard 127–30, *128*, *129*, *137*, 144, 145; Philip Ashton-Jinks 226–8; Solange Dudevant 103–5, 116, 117, 376–7
Kindergarten movement 193
King Jr. Martin Luther 297, 302–3
Kinnaird, Douglas 16–17
Kirkbride plan 145
Kramer vs. Kramer (film) 332–3, 338
Ku Klux Klan 301, 302, 305

La Châtre, France 62, 63, 74, 76, 80, 89, 92–3, 94, 111–12, 123
La Revue indépendante 111
Laing, R. D. 155, 281
Lamb, Lady Caroline 18
Lammenais, L'Abbé de 102
Latter-day Saints 142
law. *See individual law and nation name*
Lawrence, D.H. *196*; *Anna Karenina*, love of 204–9, 212, 214, 215; children, interest in 231; children of Frieda/Frieda as mother, failure to sympathise with 199–200, 223–4; children of Frieda, gets to know 233–4; death 234–5; First World War and 230–33; Frieda Weekly first meets 195–8; Frieda Weekly Divorce Court proceedings and 215–19, 229–30; 'Fronleichnam' 201; Icking, moves to 200; Italy, life in 204, 233–4; *Lady Chatterley's Lover* 249; *Look! We Have Come Through!* 201; marries Frieda Weekly 231; Metz, visits with Frieda Weekly 197–8; 'She Looks Back' 200–201; *Sons and Lovers* 196, 199, 209, 214; *The Rainbow* 232

Lawrence, Frieda 2, 3, 6, 187–237, *193*; leaves her husband and children for her lover 187; *Anna Karenina* and 204, 205, 209, 212, 213, 231, 235; childhood 188; Chiswick, goes to look for her children in (1914) 230–31; D.H. Lawrence and *see* Lawrence, D.H.; death 237; Divorce Court proceedings 215–20, 228–30; divorce settlement, outraged at 232; First World War and 230–33; Guardianship of Infants Act (1925) and 240; Icking, moves to 200; in Italy 204, 213, 233; letter to Ernest Weekly read out in law court and published in newspapers 198, 228–9; marriage to Ernest Weekly dissolved 230; marries Weekly 187, 188–9; marries Lawrence 231; Metz, goes with Lawrence to 197–8; name 188; returns to England, determined to see her children (1913) 213–15; *Sons and Lovers* and 196, 199, 209, 214
Le Droit 93–4, 99
Le Monde 102
legal aid 8, 220, 372
Leibnitz, Gottfried Wilhelm 121
LeRoy, Zoé 72, 104
Lesbian Mothers National Defense Fund 319
Lesbian Mothers Union 319–20
lesbianism 240, 310, 316, 318–20, 336, 339, 344, 365
Lessing, Doris. 264; *The Golden Notebook* 258
Leventhal, Mel 6, 292, 294–5, 301–308, *307*, 310–16, 318, 321–3, 328–31, 337, 342, 344, 349
Lieven, Mrs Justice 357
Lincoln, Abraham 149, 153, 155, 164
Lindsay v Lindsay (1854) 167
Locke, John 140
Louis Philippe I, King of France 75–6
Louis XVIII, King of France 75

419

Lowe, Phyllis 268
Lowell, Robert 143
Lucas v Kreischer (1973) 319
Lyritzis v Lyritzis (1976) 315

madness 1, 5, 15, 18, 37, 43, 77, 141, 144–55, 157, 167–8, 170–78, 182, 184, 191, 226, 235, 263, 286, 311, 343
Magazine of Domestic Economy, The 27
Main, Bernard 271
Mallefille, Félicien 104
Manceau, Alexandre 113–15, 118
Mancuso, Kayden 369
Manders v Manders (1890) 219
marriage: Alice Walker and 293, 294, 299, 302, 307, 311, 313–15, 322; *Anna Karenina* and 212, 213, 235; Caroline Norton and 15–19, 22–3, 25, 27–30, 32, 34–6, 40, 44–5, 48, 51–3, 55; Civil Code, French (Napoleonic Code) (1804) and 69–70; Custody of Infants Act (1839) and 5; Denning backs preservation of 265–9; divorce and *see* divorce; Domestic Relations Law (1973) and 331–2; Edna O'Brien and 242–60, 272, 279; Elizzabeth Packard and 127, 134–44, 147, 153, 154, 161–3, 166–8, 173, 175, 178, 181, 185, 187; Frieda Lawrence and 197–8, 204, 205, 228, 230, 235; George Sand and 67–9, 71–3, 76, 79, 81–4, 86, 88, 92, 96, 99, 101–102, 106, 108–10, 115, 116; Guardianship of Infants Act (1925) and 239–40; Guardianship Act (1973) and 279; interracial 293, 294, 299, 302, 307, 311, 313–15; legal standing in, women without 34; *Marriage Story* (film) and 11–12; Married Women's Property Act (1882) 267; slavery and 168; unity and 48
Marsden, Dora 194–5
Martin, Del 319–20
Mary, Mother of Jesus 12

'maternal preference' 316–17
Matrimonial Causes Act (1857) 162, 223
Matrimonial Proceedings (Children) Act (1958) 240–41
May, Annie 220
May, Edward 220
McCarthy, Mary: *The Group* 258
McCartney, Paul 280
McFarland, Andrew 145–55, 170, 173, 178, *179*
McLean Lunatic Asylum, Belmont 168
Mead, Margaret 317
Meier, Joan 364, 369
Melbourne, Lord 14, 18–24, 26, 34–40, *35*, 42, 43, 46, 47–51
mental hospitals/asylums 2, 5, 8, 43, 99, 127–86, 304
Mercein v People (1840) 165
Methodism 135, 142, 144, 171
Michel, Louis-Chrysostome 89, 94, 96, 99–101, 111, 122
Michelet, Jules 70; *The People* 70
Milk, Harvey 323–4
Milligan, June 263
Milligan, Spike 263
Mississippi, US 292–4, 299–302, *300*, 307, 310, 311
Moore, Stephen 171–3
Morning Chronicle 34
Morrell, Ottoline 231–2
Morrison, Frances 44, 53
mothers/motherhood: adultery and *see* adultery; bisexual *see* bisexuality; children and *see* children; children's need for their 45, 261–71; custody as knot where motherhood, ideology and power get tied together 10; feminism and 3, 7, 10, 53, 193–5, 198–201, 281–2, 337–8; 'good' mother 3, 4, 6, 10, 70–71, 122–3, 183, 193, 240, 261, 263, 266, 268, 276–7, 282, 317, 333; good writer and a good mother, possibility of being a 4, 122; Guardianship Act (1973) and 279; Guardianship of Infants Act

INDEX

(1886) and 216–19, 221, 240; Guardianship of Infants Act (1925) and 239–40; guilt and 287–8; ideal of 3, 4, 6, 9, 10, 12, 27, 49–50, 53, 103, 105, 146, 164, 183, 194, 332, 377; immigrant 8; imperfect 12, 104–5, 269, 352; kidnapping of *see* kidnapping; lesbian *see* lesbianism; madness and *see* madness; Matrimonial Proceedings (Children) Act (1958) and 240–41; 'mother-smothered' 277; universal mother 147, 150, 168; woman's two distinct natures and 103. *See also individual mother name*

Mozley Stark v Mozley Stark and Hitchins (1908–10) 217–19

Ms. magazine 311, 335, 336

Murray, John 46–7

Musset, Alfred de 86–7, 94, 124; *The Confession of a Child of the Century* 91–2, 109–11

NAACP (National Association for the Advancement of Colored People) 300; Legal Defence and Educational Fund (LDF) 300, 301

Napoleon III, Emperor of the French 113–14

Nash v Nash (1963) 268

National Organization for Women (NOW) 312, 316

'New Woman' 194

Nohant, Chateau de, Berri 61–4, *62*, 68, 70, 72, 75, 80–82, 85–7, 91–2, 94, 102–104, 106, 109, 111–12, 115–17, 119, 121–4

Norman, James 339–42, 344

Norman, Pat 319–20, 339–41

Norman, Paul 319–20, 330, 339

Norton, Brinsley 13–14, 18, 21, 24, 26, 40, 42, 49

Norton, Caroline 4, 5, 8, 13–58, 59; *A Plain Letter to the Lord Chancellor on the Infant Custody Bill* 52–3; abduction of children, attempts 50–51; adultery and 4, 26, 33–40, 47, 93, 101, 162; broken by the events of 1836 43; campaigner, becomes 44–5; Custody of Infants Act (1839) and 48–55, 216; health 43, 51; *Lélia* and 85; letter asking for the chance to care for her younger boys 40–41; marries 15–17, 19, 20, 21–4; Melbourne and 14, 18–24, 26, 34–40, *35*, 42, 43, 46, 47–51; Mary Shelley and 39, 44, 48, 49, 55, 56; Matrimonial Causes Act (1857) and 162; *Observations on the Natural Claim of the Mother to the Custody of her Infant Children as Affected by the Common Law Right of the Father* 45–7; presented to queen at court (1840) 55; Reform Act (1832) and 17, 19–20; 'The Dream' 54; *The Sorrows of Rosalie* 17, 18; *The Wife* 23; Willie's death and 57–8; wit 15; *Woman's Reward* 23–4

Norton, Fletcher 13–14, 17, 18, 25, 26, 40–42, 57–8

Norton, George 11, 13–17, 19–27, 30–42, 43, 46, 47, 49–51, 53, 55–8, 176

Norton, William 13–14, 18, 35–6, 49, 50, 55, 56, 58

Nugent, Marchioness of Westmeath, Lady Emily 30–31, 49

Nugent, Marquess of Westmeath, George 30–31

Nugent, Rosa 30–31

Oakley, Ruth Anderson 261

O'Brien, Edna 2, 3, 6, 11, 239–89, 243, 377; *Anna Karenina* and 275; *August is a Wicked Month* 274, 277–8; Bedales 281; childhood 241; custody court case 271–3, 275–8, *276*, 279, 282, 285, 286, 287, 289; dead children in novels 272–4, 283, 285, 287; divorce 279; Ernest Gébler first meets 244–6; *Girls in Their Married Bliss* 257–8, 259–60, 272–3; granted

O'Brien, Edna (*cont'd*)
  custody of children 278–9;
  greatest writer of custody of her
    century 274–5; guilt, on 273,
    274, 278, 287, 288, 289; husband
    undermining her as a mother
    249–52; Lara Feigel visits 284–9;
    leaves husband 253–4; marries
    246–7, 248; *The Country Girls*
    247–8, 250, 282; *The Little Red
    Chairs* 284–5; *The Lonely Girl*
    250–54; *Time and Tide* 252–3,
    254, 259, 278, 282–3
Osborne, John 254
Owen, Robert 44, 48

Packard, Arthur 154, 169–70, 176,
  179, 184
Packard, Elizabeth 5, 127–86, 284,
  288, 293, 294, 316; campaigning on
  women's lack of rights 177–80,
  177; Chicago, children come to live
  with in 179–80, *180*; childhood
  134, 139, 145; children as innocent,
  view of 140; Congregationalist
  Church and 134, 135, 140, 142;
  daughter's madness and 180–82,
  184; education 139; Emerson and
  143, 152, 155, 185; files for custody
  of children 178–80; files for
  divorce 173, 178; husband petitions
  to have 'placed in an insane
  asylum'/conducts mock trial of
  sanity 144; Illinois husbands ability
  to declare their wives insane
  without trial and 127–8;
  Jacksonville Insane Asylum
  145–56, 170, 173, 178, *179*;
  kidnapped from home 127–30,
  128, *129*, 137, 144, 145; Manteno,
  arrives in 135; Manteno, return to
  169, 181; *Marital Power Exemplified*
  178; marries 134–5; McFarland and
  145–55, 170, 173, 178, *179*;
  motherhood on the frontier 136–8;
  neighbours take husband to court
  170–73; puritanism fuels sense of
  universal love 155; released from
  asylum 161–2, *161*; religious 141;
  sanity of 154, 173; self-published
  pamphlet on subject of Jacksonville
  169; Spiritualist 141; State Lunatic
  Hospital, Worcester, Massachusetts
  145; suicide of son and 184; *The
  Exposure* 178; *The Great Drama*
  153–4, 155, 169, 177, 178; US Civil
  War and 152–4
Packard, George 128, 129, *129*, 130,
  154, 169, 170, 175, 179
Packard, Isaac 129, 138, 153, 178
Packard, Libby 130, 151, 152, 170,
  172, 179, 180–82, 184
Packard, Samuel 137–8, 141, 170,
  179, 185, 186
Packard, Theophilus 133–5, 140–46,
  151, 153, 156, 161, 162, 167–79,
  181–3, 284
Packard, Theophilus (Toffy) 141, 142,
  153, 155–6, 177
pan-African movement 298–9
Panzino, Sandra 318–19
parental alienation syndrome 348–9,
  351, 353, 357, 362, 364, 368–70
Paris, France 1, 61–4, 70, 74–5,
  78–83, 85, 95, 97, 99, 103–4,
  106–07, 111, 113–15, 118, 122–4,
  127, 281
Parks, Rosa 298
Parliament 5, 19–20, 24, 34, 50, 51
Pathfinder courts initiative 369
Perkins, George 224
Perkins, Gertrude 224, 236
Perkins, Nora 224
Perotti v Perotti (1974) 331–2
Phelps, Phoebe 168
Pitt, Brad 8
Plath, Sylvia 257, 273
Poole, May *293*, 294
Preston, Sean 2, 183
Probate, Divorce and Admiralty
  Division 215, 223
Profumo, John 259
Proudman, Charlotte 349
Punch 258

Queen magazine 257

racism 308; civil rights and *see* civil rights, US; court system and 317–18
Re A and B (Infants) (1896) 210, 216–17
Re B. (1962) 263–4
Re L. (1962) 265–8
Re S. (1958) 262–4
Re W. (1963) 270
realism 66, 84–5, 205, 209, 215, 254, 275, 305
Reform Act (1832) 17, 19–20, 32, 52
Regnault, Emile 80–82
Reynaud, Jean: *Terre et Ciel* 121
Riddle v Riddle (1962) 264
Risher, Douglas 318, 330
Risher, Mary Jo 318, 339
Risher, Richard 318, 321, 340
Roe v Wade (1973) 313
Rollinat, François 89
Romanticism 4, 22, 39, 46, 60, 75
Rose, Jacqueline: *Mothers* 9
Rousseau, Jean-Jacques 65, 68, 70
Roxburgh, Justice 262–3
Royal Courts of Justice 215, 261, 275–6, *276*
Russell, Lord Justice 271
Russia 204–6, 209

Saint-Simon, Henri de 78–9
Saint-Simonians 78–9, 84, 102, 121
Sand, George 2, 3, 4, 5, 58, 59–125, 149, 156–7, 180, 182, 184–5, 209, 244, 251, 274–5, 285, 288, 349, 355, 356, 365; birth and family background 60–61; boys' clothes, wears 65; Brault, adopts 106; Casimir Dudevant kidnapping of Solange from Nohant and 103–4, 376–7; childhood 60–64, 76; children and *see individual child name*; Chopin and 106–7, 109, 110; Clésinger and 108–10, 113, 114, 117–19, 122, 376; *Consuelo* 67; convent, sent to 64–5, 68; custody court case, first 59, 90–92; custody court case, second 92–4; custody court case, third 94, 95, 98–103, *98*; de Grandsagne and 73; de Sèze and 72–3; Didier and 94; Dorval and 85–6; engagement 67–8; Enlightenment and 60, 75; experiences life as narrative/caught up in her own story 104–5; father's corpse, embraces 66, 67, 103; *Figaro*, writing for 78; *François le Champi* 96; gothic and 67, 84, 89; health 64, 75, 77, 101; *Histoire de ma vie* (autobiography) 63–4, 65, 78, 96, 105, 115, 121; *Indiana* 81, 83–5; Indre, attempts to drown herself in 2, 4, 59, 66, 108, 110, 121, 125; Lara Feigel visits Nohant 121–2; *Lélia* 85, 86, 94; LeRoy and 72–3, 104; 'Letters to Marcie' 102–3; Mallorca, journey to (1838) 106; Manceau and 113–14; Michel and 89; modernity, inhabits institutions of 66–7; mother sells to grandmother 59, 61; Musset and 86, 91–2; name 60–61; Napoleon III, writes to 114; Nini Clésinger and 112–23, 376; Oscar Delaborde, makes herself responsible for 106; Paris, moves to 74–83, 85, 95, 99, 103–4, 111, 114; portrait by Luigi Calamatta 74; 1848 revolution and 110–12; Roëttiers and 67; romantic capacity for self-invention and passion, without alienation or egomania 75; Saint-Simonians and 78–9, 84, 102, 121; Sandeau and 76; *The Bagpipers* 115–16; *The Master Mosaic Makers* 95; 'Trianon' children's rock garden 115, 124–5; Tristan and 96–7; tutor 65, 66; *Valentine* 73, 83; vision of freedom 75; woman, on two distinct natures of 102; writer, decides to become 77–8
Sandeau, Jules 76, 81, 85–6
Satirist, The 35
Schuster, Claud 239–40
Scott Key, Francis 132

Scottish Chancery 217
Second World War (1939–45) 240
Sèze, Aurélien de 72
Shadwell, Sir Lancelot 31, 32
Sharif, Sara 351–2
Sharples, Eliza 44, 53
Shelley, Harriet 32, 33
Shelley, Mary (née Godwin) 21, 32, 33, 39, 44, 48, 49, 55, 56; *Frankenstein* 39, 67
Shelley, Percy 21, 32–3, 39
Sheridan, Richard 15
Sheridan, Tom 16
Sigourney, Lydia: *Letters to Mothers* 140
Simon, Helene: *Motherhood and Intellectual Work* 193
Simone, Nina: 'Mississippi Goddam' 299
Skinner, Mary 227
Smith, Deacon Josephus 144
SNCC (Student Nonviolent Coordinating Committee) 302, 312
Solomon, King 3, 276, 332
Southeast Louisiana Hospital, Mandeville 156
Southern Ohio Lunatic Asylum 147
Spears, Britney 2, 8, 130–32, 156–61, 182–6, 338
Spears, Jamie 156, 157, 183, 184
Spears, Jean 156–8, 184
Spears, June 156
Spiritualism 141
Spite, Milly 220
Spite, William 220
Starr, Charles 171, 183
Steinem, Gloria 312
Steinman, Susan 334–5
Story, Joseph 163
Street, George Edmund 276
Sudeikis, Jason 8
suffrage, female 69, 111, 213, 222, 239, 300
Sugden, Edward 51–2
Supreme Court, US 166, 312–13, 315, 320, 335, 166
Supreme Court of California, US 165
Supreme Court of Illinois, US 167

Supreme Court of New York, US 315, 331
Swedenborgianism 140

Talfourd, Thomas 48–54
Thatcher, Margaret 251
Therapeutic Residential Reunification Plan 357
Thiot-Varennes, Louis-Antoine 93–4, 99
Thomas, Clarence 335
Thompson, William 44–5; *Appeal to One Half of the Human Race, Women, Against the Pretensions of the Other Half, Men* 45
Till, Emmett 300
Tindal, Sir Nicholas Conyngham 36
Tocqueville, Alexis de: *Democracy in America* 139, 142, 158, 163–4, 171, 183, 184
Tolpuddle Martyrs 20, 44
Tolstoy, Leo: *Anna Karenina* 204–9, 212–15, 231, 232, 235, 275, 349
Tomkins, Gwen 265
Tomkins, Leslie 265
Tootell, Richard 226
Transcendentalist movement 143, 398*n*
transgender parents 11, 364–5
Trelawny, Edward 21, 25, 26, 39
Tristan, Flora 96–8, 102
Tucker v Tucker (1975) 319
Turley, William B. 165

Unitarianism 132
USA 94, 96, 127–86, 244, 255, 258, 282, 291–345, 349, 351, 364, 369; American dream 132, 149, 158, 164; 'best interests of the child' and 'maternal preference', custody laws revised to emphasise 316–17, 319–20; civil rights 6, 7, 292–304, 309, 311, 312, 316; Civil War (1861–5) 152–3, 164–5; constitutional promise 132–3; Domestic Relations Law (1973) 331–2; Emancipation Proclamation 155; English common law in 5, 163–5, 167; *Ex parte Hewitt* 165; *Feldman*

INDEX

v Feldman 317; 50/50 custody and 315–16; Founding Fathers stake American identity on freedom 157; Fourteenth Amendment to Constitution 317; Keeping Children Safe from Family Violence Act 369; Lincoln elected president 149; *Lindsay v Lindsay* 167; *Lucas v Kreischer* 319; *Lyritzis v Lyritzis* 315; *Mercein v People* 165; mothers idealised in 164; *Perotti v Perotti* 331–2; racism within court system 318–20; revolution (1783) 139; *Roe v Wade* 313; sexuality and law in 317–18; slavery in 149–50, 152–5, 164–5, 168–9, 294, 308–11, 324, 343; Supreme Court 166, 312–13, 315, 320, 335, 166; Transcendentalist movement 143, 398*n*; *Tucker v Tucker* 319; *Ward v Ward* 319; *Watts v Watts* 316

Victoria, Queen of the United Kingdom 47, 50, 55
violence: civil rights and 291, 294, 296, 300, 302, 303, 324, 327, 345; domestic 21–5, 53, 96, 220–23, 268, 363, 369–70, 373
Vicissitudes of Paternity, The 71
von Richthofen, Else 188, 189, 190–93, 200, 214–15, 228–9
Voting Rights Act (1965) 300

Walker, Alice 6–7, 11, 291–345, 349, 351; abortion 299, 330; in Africa 298–9; 'Be nobody's darling' 342–3; bisexuality 6, 294, 310, 316; case worker, New York welfare department 299; childhood 295–6; *Desert Island Discs* 329; divorce 314–15; eye, loss of 296, 298; feminism and 294–5, 309, 311, 312–14, 316, 317, 322, 324, 326, 332, 335–8, 343–4, 351; 50/50 custody and 6–7, 315–16, 321–6, 328–30; Martin Luther King Jr. and 297, 302–3; Mel Leventhal, marriage to 6, 292, 294–5, 301–308, *307*, 310–16, 318, 321–3, 328–30, 331, 337, 342, 344, 349; *Meridian* 308–10, 332–3; miscarriage 303; *Ms.* magazine, editor at 311; 'My Daughter is Coming' 324–5; NAACP Legal Defence and Educational Fund (LDF) and 300, 301; name 311; poems, first volume of 299; pregnancy and childbirth 6–7, 11, 291–4; Radcliffe Institute fellowship 307; rifts followed by reconciliations with children 335–7; Robert Allen, love affair with 313, 315; San Francisco, moves to 323–4; Sarah Lawrence College donor offers grant to 299; segregation, determination to resist 297; Spelman college 297–8, 299; Steinem and 312; *The Color Purple* 7, 324, 325–8, 330, 331, 344–5; *The Third Life of Grange Copeland* 291–4, 302, 303–5, 308, 311–12, 344; Tougaloo College, lecturing at 307; Wellesley College, designs and teaches Black women's literature course at 312; 'womanism' 336; Zora Neale Hurston, passionate advocate for 312
Walker, Rebecca 291, 294, 305–7, *306*, *307*, 313, 321–4; abortion 330; *Baby Love: Choosing Motherhood After a Lifetime of Ambivalence* 337–8; birth and early mothering of 292, 305–8, *306*, *307*, 310–11, 313–14; *Black, White and Jewish* 337; custody arrangement/alternates between parents for two-year periods 6–7, 294, 314–16, 321–30, 335; divorce 342; Lara Feigel speaks to 341–2; manifesto 335–6; name change 330–31; rifts followed by reconciliations with mother 335–7; Spielberg film of *The Color Purple*, works on 331; writer, emergence of 336

425

Wallerstein, Judith 333
Ward Beecher, Henry 140
Ward v Ward (1950) 319
Ware, Lucy 134, 145, 177
Ware, Samuel 134, 145, 177
Warren, Charles Stanley 223–4
Warren, Chief Justice Earl 320
Warren, Jack 223–4
Warren, Violet Lillian 222, 223–4, 229, 236
Watts v Watts (1973) 316–17
Weber, Alfred 200
Weekley, Barbara (Barby) 2, 190, 196, *197*, 202, 203, 231, 233–7
Weekley, Elsa 2, 190, *190*, 192, 196, *197*, 202, 233–4
Weekley, Ernest 189–91, 194–8, 202–4, 213, 215, 219, 228–30, 232–3, 236–7
Weekley, Maude 203, 214, 215, 231, 233
Weekley, Montague (Monty) 2, 190, *190*, 191, 196, 199, 202–3, 214, 233–5
welfare officers 240–41, 262, 265, 268, 270, 271

Wellesley, William 32–3
Wheeler, Anna: *Appeal to One Half of the Human Race, Women, Against the Pretensions of the Other Half, Men* 44–5
Whigs 17, 19, 20, 36, 51
Willemsen, Hessel 362–3
William IV, King of the United Kingdom 20, 50
Willis, Nathaniel 139
Wilson, Florence Marjorie 220–21
Wilson, Kingston Charles 220–21
Winnicott, Donald 10, 261
Wollstonecraft, Mary: *A Vindication of the Rights of Woman* 39; *Maria, or the Wrongs of Woman* 43
Woman magazine 268–70, 287
Woman's Own 251
women's rights 28, 39, 47, 48, 69, 133, 162, 168, 178, 193, 281; Women's Rights Movement 44, 45, 223. *See also individual law and nation name*

Youth's Companion, The 139